T0334279

INDIA AND THE SILK ROADS

JAGJEET LALLY

India and the Silk Roads

The History of a Trading World

HURST & COMPANY, LONDON

First published in the United Kingdom in 2021 by
C. Hurst & Co. (Publishers) Ltd.,
41 Great Russell Street, London, WC1B 3PL
Copyright © Jagjeet Lally, 2021
All rights reserved.
Printed in Great Britain by Bell and Bain Ltd, Glasgow

The right of Jagjeet Lally to be identified as the author of
this publication is asserted by him in accordance with the
Copyright, Designs and Patents Act, 1988.

A Cataloguing-in-Publication data record for this book
is available from the British Library.

ISBN: 9781787383265

This book is printed using paper from registered sustainable
and managed sources.

www.hurstpublishers.com

CONTENTS

ACKNOWLEDGEMENTS

India and the Silk Roads is based on research for a doctoral dissertation submitted to the University of Cambridge in 2013. I am extremely grateful to the United Kingdom Economic and Social Research Council (ESRC) for a full studentship to support this research; to the Ellen MacArthur Fund of the Faculty of History, and Sidney Sussex College, University of Cambridge, for numerous travel grants; and to the Centre for History and Economics for a Prize Studentship in the first year (2010–11) of my forays into the subject of my book. Sujit Sivasundaram was a wonderful supervisor and mentor, and Polly O'Hanlon and the late Chris Bayly were excellent examiners of the thesis (which was subsequently awarded the MacArthur Prize for best dissertation in economic and social history at the University of Cambridge). Their collective close commentary has strengthened the reworked analysis within this book.

I briefly dabbled at rewriting the dissertation as a monograph over the Lent term of 2013–14 when I was a Moses and Mary Finley Research Fellow—for which I thank the electors of that fellowship and the Master and Fellows of Darwin College, Cambridge, for the extraordinary privilege of a period almost solely devoted to developing a research career. My tenure as Finley Fellow was cut short by my appointment to a lecturership at University College London where, since 2014, the opportunity to teach my own courses in Indian economic history, and in the history of empire in the Middle East and Asia, to attentive and curious students has profoundly shaped this book, including its historical and historiographical analysis and arguments.

ACKNOWLEDGEMENTS

My colleagues, especially Margot Finn, Chris Jeppesen, and Zoltàn Biedermann, have played an especially important role in my intellectual life as reflected in the following pages; Margot has additionally offered encouragement during the difficult process of seeing the book through to completion. To all of them I am most grateful.

The immediate spark for the reorganisation of my doctoral thesis into the present volume came from Jos Gommans' invitation to write a new introduction to the third edition of his seminal *Rise of the Indo-Afghan Empire* (2019). Writing that piece coincided with the start of a sabbatical and proved profoundly generative, stimulating the process of restructuring and rewriting during the autumn and winter of 2017–18. Jos' scholarship had motivated my original interest in the project. Revisiting his rich corpus breathed fresh life into my understanding of India's historic connection to Central Eurasia, and so I must express my gratitude for his most generous invitation.

The imprint of Chris Bayly's vast scholarly output can be found throughout what follows. The most significant source of inspiration for my book as a whole is Bayly's *Rulers, Townsmen and Bazaars* (1983), which examined eighteenth- and nineteenth-century India's commercial life as part of a larger ecosystem with various spatial, social, ritual, material, political, and ethnic or cultural dimensions. There is probably no chapter in what follows that does not draw some insight from one or the other of Bayly's works, while his lucid prose and powers of elegant yet expansive synthesis remain something of a role model.

India and the Silk Roads has also benefited from numerous conversations with friends and colleagues—many more than I can note here—in Cambridge, London, New Delhi, Stellenbosch, and elsewhere around the world over the years. I am especially grateful to Alexander Morrison, Andrew Arsan, Anna Winterbottom, Atiyab Sultan, Audrey Truschke, Beatrice Penati, Beverly Lemire, Bishnupriya Gupta, Christopher P. Bredholt, David Washbrook, Emma Hunter, Emma Rothschild, Faridah Zaman, James Hall, James Wilson, John Slight, Joya Chatterji, Katherine Butler Schofield, Leigh Denault, Melissa Calaresu, Prasannan Parthasarathi, Rosamund McKitterick, Shruti Kapila, Stephen Thompson, Sunil Amrith, Tim Harper, and Tirthankar Roy.

Research in Lahore and Multan would have been impossible had it not been for an invitation to present my work at the Lahore University

ACKNOWLEDGEMENTS

of Management Sciences, and my friend Atiyab's help in arranging for me to stay in the home of her friend Nazish Afraz. Nazish, her husband Salman, their energetic children, and indomitable household staff were for a few weeks my family in my home-away-from-home in Pakistan. I cannot adequately express my gratitude for their willingness to take in a total stranger in April 2013.

At the Punjab Archives and Library in Lahore my thanks go to the Assistant Director, Shamim Jafri, and the staff in the records room. The bulk of the research for this book was completed in the National Archives of India, New Delhi, whose staff I must thank for supplying me with a constant stream of documents. To the staff at the Maharashtra State Archives (Bombay), the Punjab State Archives (Chandigarh), the British Library (London), and the Asia Department of the Victoria and Albert Museum (London) I also owe a great debt.

Audrey Truschke read a very early version of what are now the first three chapters, her critical comments on the writing and content leading to tremendous improvements. Fiona Clague read all of chapter 5 and offered much encouragement, and Camille Cole scoured chapter 8 to offer useful suggestions, in addition to the gift of her own developing—and inspiring—corpus of scholarship. Rukun Advani's corrections and suggestions have greatly improved the text—although all mistakes remain my own. I am very lucky to have worked with him and must thank him and the rest of the team at Hurst.

My sister and Oscar moved by happenstance to Cambridge around the time I was a student, providing me with shelter there during my weekly trips from London for seminars, teaching, and research. They also listened to rehearsals of presentations based on this material, asking questions—as scientists—that forced me to refine and improve the expression of core ideas. My parents provided material support and unwavering encouragement from start to finish. My friends in London, particularly Fiona, Florence Sutcliffe-Braithwaite, Jane Hibell, and Marcus Jaye, provided the encouragement and environment in which to complete the process of writing this book and seeing it through to the publisher. And, of course, Annabel Chown, who has brought light and space into my life.

To all these and other friends and family I am more grateful than they can know. But my deepest thanks must go to Stephen Cummins,

ACKNOWLEDGEMENTS

who opened my eyes to the craft of history, who listened patiently to various iterations of ideas from almost the very beginning of the project, whose extraordinary and incomparable intellect was the wellspring of both incisive critique and intellectual inspiration, who advised and proofread, and who beyond all this offered friendship and laughter even in very difficult times. This book is much richer for Stephen's intellectual nourishment; while the errors in it remain mine, I hope he will accept this book as a token of my gratitude as he embarks upon a new phase of his own journey.

LIST OF ABBREVIATIONS

BCP	Bombay Commercial Proceedings
BL	British Library, London
CAS	*Central Asian Survey*
CSSAAME	*Comparative Studies of South Asia, Africa and the Middle East*
CSSH	*Comparative Studies in Society and History*
EHR	*The Economic History Review*
ETP	Reports and Notes on the (External) Land Trade of Punjab
IESHR	*The Indian Economic and Social History Review*
IOR	India Office Records, British Library
IOSM	Indian Office Select Materials, British Library
JAS	*The Journal of Asian Studies*
JESOH	*Journal of the Economic and Social History of the Orient*
JGH	*Journal of Global History*
LOC	Library of Congress
MAS	*Modern Asian Studies*
MSA	Maharashtra State Archives, Mumbai
MSA-SILB	Maharashtra State Archives, Secretariat Inward Letter Books
NAI	National Archives of India, New Delhi
NAI-F	National Archives of India, Foreign Department Proceedings
NAI-H	National Archives of India, Home Department Proceedings

LIST OF ABBREVIATIONS

NAI-M	National Archives of India, Military Department Proceedings
PAL	Punjab Archives and Library, Lahore
PAL-P	Punjab Archives and Library, Lahore, Political Department Proceedings
PAL-R	Punjab Archives and Library, Lahore, Revenue Department Proceedings
PSA-F	Punjab State Archives (Chandigarh), Punjab Foreign Department Proceedings

LIST OF ILLUSTRATIONS

LIST OF ILLUSTRATIONS

Fig. 0.1: The Indo-central Asian Trading World

INTRODUCTION

Reviving the Silk Roads

On 20 July 2013, the *New York Times* website published a photostory titled 'Hauling New Treasure Along the Silk Road'.[1] Its author, Keith Bradsher, has a reputation for exposing the dark side of American multinationals driven by the logic of global capitalism into finding and maintaining cheap labour and low production costs in emerging economies such as China. However, by focussing not on the production but the transportation of 'global goods', Bradsher's piece revealed something remarkable: the resuscitation of 'ancient' land routes for the freighting of laptops and tablets worth millions of dollars from inland China to Europe, across the wide and windswept steppes of central Asia.

Making use of old Chinese and Russian track—as well as lines laid more recently in Kazakhstan in anticipation of increases in cross-continental freighting—the half-mile long 1,800-tonne train of carriages is not dissimilar to the train of caravans that criss-crossed the Eurasian continent in centuries past. These trains are secured against attack by bandits, except the guards now tote Kalashnikovs rather than the bows, swords, and muskets used by their forebears on the caravans. The trains also complement and compete with other ways of shipping goods, shaving 40 per cent off the time taken by riverine or oceanic container transport while costing only 25 per cent more (and substantially less than airfreight). This transcontinental freighting by rail represents only a small fraction of the cargo carried by container ships and is unlikely to diminish the profits of the world's shipping conglomerates. But the

Chinese authorities anticipated the value of overland freight trade would rise to $1 billion in 2014, and Hewlett-Packard (HP), who pioneered the use of the rail route in 2011, was soon joined in this freighting method by DHL as well as other tech companies manufacturing in inland China. From the multinationals' perspective, the 'new' routes offer two advantages. First, an alternative to the industrial zones along the coast, which are now clogged on account of decades of investment and suffering labour shortages (as well as attendant high wage costs). Second, an alternative route to satiating the consumer demand in Europe and thereby protecting competitive advantages.

This book is about the overland Silk Roads but focuses on an earlier epoch and a different mass of routes. It is about north India's overland connections with Afghanistan and central Asia. These longitudinal north–south networks rose to prominence in the early modern period largely in place of the more familiar latitudinal east–west routes that have lately been revived.[2] In fact, this north–south branch of caravan trade survived into the twentieth century despite the intrusion of European colonial power into the Eurasian interior and the birth of the modern global economy. Just as the very recent growth of overland traffic east–west across Eurasia reflects a particular reconfiguration of production and consumption within the global economy—a particular moment in the historical development of capitalism and globalisation—so too did the early modern north–south reorientation of caravan trade. Many of the factors at play in precipitating the shifts, sketched in the vignette above, were also evident in the earlier epoch of Silk Road trade: the interplay of long-distance trade and global politics, the effects of shifts in the location of production and of technological innovation on cross-continental trade flows, the complementarity and competitiveness of overland and overseas exchange networks, the driving forces of cultural change in reshaping consumer demand in distant markets (and, in turn, on material life and livelihoods), and, ultimately, the profound importance of ecology and geography in shaping patterns of globalisation.

This book charts the history of the world of caravan trade, focussing particularly on the period c. 1700 to c. 1918. Since caravan trade brought goods and money—but also news, ideas, weapons, and mercenaries—into the societies it connected, it shows how important the trade was to material and cultural life and to the production and exercise of political power. At the same time, it shows that caravan trade within the Eurasian interior, across imperial margins and frontiers, offers a novel vantage point from which to re-examine the histories of globalisation and empires. The making of crossings and connections is scrutinised, as is the acceleration of globalisation and the thickening of global connections that were broadly held as characteristic of the pre-1918 period by scholars fixated on maritime transport and the seas. In bringing the world of caravan trade into the study of the eighteenth and nineteenth centuries, this book contributes to global history a study of disconnection in the making of connection, disintegration in new patterns of integration, and a critique of the teleological vision that still lingers in global economic history—of the modern supplanting the archaic.

Rethinking the Silk Roads

The Silk Roads, or Trans-Eurasian Trade?[3]

The German traveller and geographer Baron Ferdinand von Richthofen (1833–1905) travelled as part of the Eulenberg Expedition from Prussia to Asia, publishing his findings from 1877 to 1912 in five volumes. Richthofen and Sven Hedin were creatures of their time, moulded in the age of high imperialism when the competitive colonialism of the European powers raised the status of geography, cartography, and exploration.[4] Hedin and his counterparts garnered much of the fame that these expeditions brought, but it was Richthofen who first coined the term *Seidenstrassen* (Silk Roads) to describe and give meaning to the latitudinal string of sites found under the deserts of Inner Asia, thereby leaving a semantic legacy that has endured.

Richthofen's legacy has not gone unchallenged, and scholars have sought to clarify and critique the concept of 'Silk Roads'. In the first place, the Silk Road was neither a single road nor a static set of routes but an unstable and shifting bundle of connections subject to the vicissitudes of ecological change and political power. The latitudinal artery across Eurasia that is commonly taken to constitute the Silk Road proper also branched off longitudinally north and south, bringing spices, cotton cloth, and other goods from across the subcontinent and the Indian Ocean world into the circuits of Silk Road trade. Each of these branches consisted of bundles of competing routes, some shorter, safer, cheaper, or more comfortable, depending on the ruling authority, the time of year, and the terrain. This fibrous mass of overland routes existed, of course, in complementary and competitive relation with overseas routes across the China Sea, the Malacca Straits, the Indian Ocean, the Arabian Sea, and the Persian Gulf.[5]

Second, the emphasis on silk is misleading, for it prioritises a single commodity and a single direction of exchange—namely, from the Orient to the Occident. The mass of connections constituting the Silk Roads meant that a number of commodities moved in a number of directions across Eurasia. These included exotic elephant ivory and rhino horn, luxury textiles of silk and other threads, and precious illuminated manuscripts. The more mundane items of exchange, with wider spectra of 'consumption', included foodstuffs, pack animals, animal products, raw cotton, and cotton cloth; among these, horses, paper, and gunpowder exerted a much more powerful and profound impact on the course of world history than silk. Furthermore, examination of the Silk Roads has tended to foreground Asia's role as a producer or supplier of global goods but has obscured corresponding attention to its patterns of consumption. This is all the more remarkable given that Asia dominated the global economy before the rise of what Immanuel Wallerstein termed the 'modern world-system'.[6] Both trade with Europe and, more crucially, 'intra-Asian trade', brought buyers—from rural-dwelling nomads and pastoralists to urban *khans* (kings) and *padshah*s (emperors)—into contact with a range of goods.

Silk Roads, as a term, is more evocative than accurate. It does not encompass everything that was exchanged across Eurasia, but can serve as shorthand for a wide array of goods moving over a range of routes. It has become deeply embedded in academic vocabulary, having proven popular amongst scholars as well as publics. It has even crossed over from Western scholarly discourse into, for example, the language of Iranian scholars from the late 1950s and 1960s, who spoke of 'carving out the historical geography of a Greater Iran whose cultural impact was felt as far away as China'. It is, in brief, a term that will undoubtedly continue to seed the scholarly imagination.[7] Such (re-)evocations of the Silk Roads, and those highlighted throughout this book, compel an imagination of broad continuities across historical epochs against relatively short interludes of flux or stasis or decline. Rather than dismantling the Silk Roads, it is worth seeing them as shorthand for the complex and changing mass of connections and exchanges that knitted together states, societies, and economies across Eurasia. Both as heuristic and historical subject, 'Silk Roads' seems a vacuous abstraction unless the most reductive conceptualisations are discarded. But thinking *with* the Silk Roads is fruitful because it helps us focus on the fact that—for most of the previous two millennia or more—long-distance exchange and circulation across continental interiors constituted the rule and not the exception. Rather than seeing the expansion of long-distance maritime trade after *c.* 1500 as the beginning of an irreversible and insurmountable transformation in the way people and things moved, it might be better viewed as only a very recent, and perhaps temporary, aberration. In the last century, air travel became a more important vector of human mobility, and in our new eco-age the railways are enjoying a renaissance in the movement of people and things.

After the Timurids

The Silk Road was neither a vast thoroughfare that cut across central Asia, nor was central Asia merely the interchange of the branches at the central section of a latitudinal axis whose role and purpose in the global economy was inextricably linked with east–west exchange. The volume and value of trade along the latitudinal routes showed signs of a slowdown around the time of the retreat of the empire established by Tamerlane (or Timur Lang: b.1336), this purported decline continuing in the wake of the European 'discovery' of the direct sea route to Asia. This latter shift supposedly resulted in the decanting of east–west trade from the Silk Road routes to maritime routes via the Cape of Good Hope.[8] Yet historians are starting to appreciate that the European discovery of the trans-oceanic routes was both trade-creating and trade-diverting, so that the increase in Europe's maritime trade with Asia resulted for the most part from the expansion of shipping traffic—and thus the extent of underlying trade and production activities—rather than from some complete displacement of the caravan traffic.[9] In other words, overland trade suffered some absolute decline, but the more important impact was the way in which the trans-Eurasian caravan traffic was gradually dwarfed in relative terms by trans-oceanic shipping and became more marginal to global trade as a whole—a phenomenon examined more closely in this book.

If central Asia is one of the keys to understanding the history of the early modern Silk Roads, the other is south Asia. A prince of Timurid heritage, Zahir-ud-din Muhammad Babur established the Mughal Empire in India in 1526, making it contemporaneous with the Safavid Empire in Persia and Uzbek rule in central Asia. It is almost a commonplace that interconnecting this Islamicate or Indo-Persian world were the movements and migrations of armies, soldiers, and slaves, of artists, architects, and poets, of ambassadors, noblemen, and fugitive former rulers, of pilgrims, saints, and traders.[10] Whatever the role of the Mughals and their counterparts in protecting and securing trade, of particular significance was the increasing volume of bullion brought to Asia in consequence of the enlargement of trans-oceanic trade with Europe.[11] The inflow of specie stimulated increased monetisation and commercialisation of production, and possibly paid for the trade balance between India and central Asia; this liquidity lubricated the expansion of overland trade along a north–south axis, which became more important than the east–west.[12]

The Mughal Empire was bloated by improved domestic revenue administration and by swelling overland and overseas trade revenues over the seventeenth century. But it was weakened and exhausted by British territorial expansion during the eighteenth century, having earlier started shattering into a number of successor states. The rulers of some successor states—such as the Maratha, Jat, and Sikh polities—openly opposed the Mughal Empire.[13] The empire's integrity also suffered because of the rise of regional powers in the imperial borderlands. Kabul and Kandahar had fallen in and out of Mughal and Safavid control over the sixteenth and seventeenth centuries. Nadir Shah Afshar of Iran conquered Kandahar in 1738, and, together with the Pashtun Abdalis, defeated the Mughal armies in 1739 before raiding and expropriating the wealth held in the imperial cities. Following the death of Nadir Shah in 1747, his former commander, Ahmad Shah (r.1747–72), was chosen as leader of the Abdalis. Adopting the sobriquet *Durr-i-Durran* (Pearl of Pearls), Ahmad Shah united the Abdalis into the Durrani tribal confederation, established the Durrani Empire in Afghanistan, and extended it into north-west India in the second half of the eighteenth century.[14]

Meanwhile, regime replacement also rippled through the Uzbek successor states in central Asia. In the Khanate of Bukhara, the Mangits (1785–1920) replaced the Janids (1598–1785), who were related to the Shaybanids through marriage, and who had transformed the city and the khanate into a culturally and scholastically thriving Muslim polity. In the Khanate of Khiva, to the east of Bukhara, the rule of the Yadigarid Shaybanids effectively ended in 1728, whereafter the Inakids or prime minister-rulers placed a sequence of khans on the throne. In Fergana after 1709, under Shah Rukh Biy and his descendants, the Khanate of Khokand emerged as a new and growing power in the region west of Bukhara. This khanate was enmeshed in diplomatic relations with the neighbouring Qing (China), Romanov (Russia), and Durrani empires, experiencing a cultural renaissance, an increase in agricultural production, and unprecedented urbanisation.[15] Whether we look from a south Asian or central Asian standpoint, therefore, the eighteenth century was a crucial moment of change in political and material circumstances.

What did this mean for Indo-central Asian caravan trade? If there is an emerging consensus about the positive significance for life and livelihoods of the immediate post-Timurid east–west to north–south reorientation of caravan trade in the continental interior of Eurasia, there is more ambivalence about the impact—in nature and significance—of the post-1700 political transition. The point of departure for this book is the work of three historians who have each focussed on north Indian commercial firms operating in central Asia: Stephen F. Dale (1994), Claude Markovits (2000), and Scott C. Levi (2002).[16] Their monographs have brought together business and economic history to elaborate how these networks were organised.[17] In different ways, however, each has glossed over the impact of the eighteenth-century 'decline' of the Asian empires, either seeing the process as sounding the death knell of caravan trade or ignoring some other significance of this process. Overall, therefore, the world of caravan trade has been sucked into the abyss of the 'colonial transition'—the shift from the final flowering of

Islamic empire to European colonial rule—in south and central Asia. This book makes a direct intervention into what is still a rather blurred understanding of the long eighteenth century. It not only argues that the political changes were transformative while being broadly positive for trade and the societies connected through long-distance exchange, but that caravan trade is integral to understanding some of the reconfigurations of power that took place in this period.

If overland trade not only survived through the eighteenth century but was purposively transformed (in ways examined in detail in what follows), how did it fare following the integration of even the more remote parts of Eurasia into European regimes of power in the nineteenth century? Of particular importance to the world of caravan trade is the expansion of the British and Russian empires. The East India Company, already administering and governing small coastal settlements as a sovereign state in the seventeenth century, gained sovereign rights to territorial revenues after victory at Plassey in Bengal in 1757.[18] As the British mulcted and steadily enlarged their territories, India's role as a global sink for bullion was reversed. The Company's policies created a cash crisis in its territories in the late 1820s, worsened by the international depression of the 1830s and 1840s. This shrinking flow of bullion through the north Indian economy possibly occasioned the increased production of trade goods to pay for the deficit in the interior parts of south Asia further from British influence. It quite possibly also facilitated their deeper integration into central Asian markets, as much as it perhaps precipitated the decline of India's overland trade.[19] Ultimately, caravan trade weathered these difficulties, for the British—following their Mughal, Afghan, and Sikh forebears in Punjab—recognised its importance to societies and economies connected through these exchange networks. Insofar as British policies in the second half of the century undermined Indo-central Asian trade through the transformation of economy or society, the motives were never to intentionally destroy or divert trade. In fact, trade showed signs of an upturn before *c.* 1880.

Meanwhile, Russia initiated imperial expansion into the Kazakh Hordes, north of the three khanates. Between 1730 and 1822, expansion was slow and steady, first taking the form of the acceptance of Kazakh vassaldom and the erection of fortifications until the reign of

Catherine the Great (r. 1762–96), when Russian peasants were allowed to undertake a creeping colonisation of the region. With the conquest of the three Kazakh Hordes, 1822–48, expansion became more direct and decisive. In the 1860s and 1870s, the final thrust of Russian expansion in central Asia brought Khiva and Khokand under the tsar's control, and the subordination and shrinkage of the territories of the Bukharan amir. Russian protectionist policies first restricted the flow of trade from India to colonial Samarkand and the suzerain state of Bukhara, until the latter was brought under the Russian customs system in 1895. India's licit trade then stopped short of central Asia, with the remainder of traffic destined primarily for Kabul and the towns of southern Afghanistan. By 1918, the decline was evident from the departure from Bukhara of the greater proportion of the Indian trading community which had formerly played a large part in commerce.

Writing the Silk Roads: Arguments and Approaches

Bradsher's invocation of the ancient Silk Roads and their rebirth after 'falling into disuse six centuries ago' is exciting journalism. But it is based on simplifications. It reduces the Silk Roads to the trade from China to Europe rather than seeing this traffic as a constituent of trans-Eurasian trade at large. And it confuses the long lull in the latitudinal traffic with the reorientation of the main routes, as well as with the growth of central Asia's trade south to India and northward to Russia. At the same time, scholarly investigation of Indo-central Asian trade after *c.* 1500 has been too narrow in scope to reveal many of the complexities of these commercial flows and their embeddedness in the material life of the local societies they connected. How, then, to write the larger history of caravan trade in the period before 1918?

Whereas the major monographs on Indian communities in central Asia have focussed on the backgrounds and business practices, the social lives and commercial activities of the north Indian merchants who controlled most of the caravans' cargoes, the approach in this book is more holistic. These mercantile communities possessed high numerical and scribal literacy, and yet none of their records have come to light. Their networks and activities have not therefore been traced through their own words. The sources used have been those left by their contemporaries—not least European travellers, traders, and political officials—and these have been supplemented by a handful of surviving (or accessible) petitions lodged in the course of commercial disputes by Indians in the law courts of their central Eurasian host societies. In the first place, therefore, using such sources to focus narrowly on north Indian magnate houses misses much valuable detail. This approach obscures a range of other agents whose participation was vital to trade, including livestock herders and peddlers. Some of these successfully eked out and enlarged a role for themselves over the long-distance exchange within the flux of the eighteenth century, thereby challenging the commercial hegemony of the very groups studied by Dale, Levi, and Markovits.

Indeed, it is difficult to separate trade from commercial life more broadly because of the imbrication of economic activity with the social, cultural, spiritual, and political concerns of participants. It is necessary to scrutinise the communities of cultivators, labourers, and artisans that produced or prepared the stuff of trade, the state officials who taxed production and trade, the rulers who patronised and protected commerce, and the consumers—in urban centres and in the country-side, mountains, and deserts—whose demand for goods stimulated trade. Moreover, the cycles of commercial life and caravan trade were interwoven with the rhythms of other movements along the Silk Roads, such as the passages of pilgrims or the seasonal migrations of merce-naries for the campaign season. In casting a wider-angled gaze over the mobilities and activities associated with caravan trade, this book high-lights the trade's importance. It looks both more broadly and in greater depth at the states, societies, and economies of south and central Asia. It therefore shows how profoundly the decline of caravan trade towards the end of the nineteenth century was related to the history of colo-nialism in Asia.

Silk Road trade involved not only the movements of merchants, nor only the intermediaries upon whom they relied, but also rather funda-mentally the things they exchanged. Focussing on these things or goods throws light on the relationships, actors, and connections constituting the world of exchange, which helps piece together a fuller picture of Indo-central Asian trade and its transformation over time. In so doing, this study unites two types of commodity-centred histories. The first originated in the late 1970s, when cultural anthropologists 'began to rethink the status of goods and commodities as bearers of meaning and artifacts of exchange', while social historians turned to the 'material culture of everyday life'. These strands came together in Arjun Appadurai's edited collection calling for the 'social life of things'.[20] The second sort of commodity-centred histories are the work of economic and business historians providing macro-narratives about networks, institutions, and integration, the unevenness of economic development across the globe, and the changing relationship between resources, ecology, and economy.[21] By bringing art and cultural histories on objects and things into economic and social histories on patterns of production and consumption, this book offers a more rounded history of the world of caravan trade.[22]

In the main, the focus on commodities has hitherto tended to buttress the study of global exchanges or connections *qua* links between the maritime rimlands of Afro-Eurasia and America, rather than the continental interiors. Alternatively, it has engaged mainly with things of concern to European societies, past or contemporary, not least because of the reliance on objects conserved in Western museum collections (a point elaborated later). This skewness need not be so. In writing his world history of turquoise, Arash Khazeni came to terms with the stone not fitting 'the patterns of existing narratives of commodity chains' and not being a 'globalised commodity'. Iranian turquoise circulated through imperial tribute and exchange networks across early modern Islamicate Eurasia, largely outside European or Euro–Asian trade circuits. For this reason, '[t]he Eurasian turquoise trade was not less documented; it was differently documented.'[23] Focussing on the movement of things is valuable precisely because it can help balance the hegemonies encountered in certain bodies of texts or collections of artefacts, and thereby reveal these alternative and overlooked geographies of interaction. Focussing on things, and moving back and forth between things and the people connected to them, also reveals a much wider world of actors connected to long-distance exchange—urban and rural, gentry and peasantry, nomadic and sedentary, male and female, for instance—and thus gives greater voice and visibility to relatively quotidian actors who, having left no testimony of their own, are frequently written out of history.

Apart from broadening the frame to accommodate mobile groups that moved between south and central Asia, this book also incorporates into the discussion a range of goods that formed the basis of long-distance exchange. Here, four 'commodities' were especially important in terms of their volume and value, their commercial, cultural, or political importance, and thus the extent of material available for the historian to study: horses, cotton cloth, indigo dye, and raw silk yarn. These four commodities belong within broader categories of the goods described here and examined more closely in the chapters that follow.

The military markets and courts that made use of central Eurasian horses were also supplied with other pack animals, alongside slaves, soldiers, mercenaries, and weapons, as well as livestock and animal products consumed more widely. In addition to Indian cotton cloth—which was vital to overland trade through to the twentieth century—silk cloth, shawls from Kashmir, and textiles from other regions were also traded, as well as other artisanal manufactures, such as ironware and brassware. Markets selling indigo were stocked with other dyestuffs, drugs, spices, and primary products such as madder, opium, asafoetida, sugar, fruits, and nuts. The cocoon of the silkworm was unwound and prepared for foreign markets, as were the skins, hides, and woollen fleece of various animals. The significance of horses, cotton cloth, indigo, and raw silk changed over time, moreover, revealing changes in the dynamics of caravan trade and its connections with other networks and exchange systems.

The Structure of India and the Silk Roads

This book shows how Indo-central Asian trade connected the states and markets of the Eurasian interior through the eighteenth and nineteenth centuries until its decline around the *fin de siècle*. It reveals how caravan trade served as a vital link between these spaces and the global economy of the maritime rimlands of Afro-Eurasia and America. In this respect, it is not the story of the Mughal, Safavid, or Uzbek, Afghan or Sikh, British Indian, Russian Turkestan, or Qajar polities. In fact, one of the implications of the material analysed over the following pages is that networks of long-distance exchange crossed and connected but were also more durable than political authorities such as states or empires. Each of the nine chapters therefore focuses on a particular aspect or theme that illuminates the history and significance of caravan trade. Reflexively, caravan trade also serves as a lens through which to look in new ways at these themes, thereby bringing inner-continental spaces into historiographies that have hitherto focussed predominately on the most densely populated and seaward-facing parts of Afro-Eurasia.

The first two chapters are relatively expansive and introduce the structure and organisation of caravan trade. Chapter 1, 'Environment', sketches the broad geography and circulatory pattern along the north–south routes. It shows that exchange was based on specialisation and interdependence between the dry zone that stretched from central Asia to the Indo-Afghan frontier on the one hand, and the wet zone of monsoon south Asia on the other. It shows that ecological change, as well as economic or political factors, could shift patterns of specialisation and thereby affect trade, illustrated through a case study of the Indo-central Asian horse trade. Chapter 2, 'Exchanges', traces the flow of goods from sites of production to consumption, thereby highlighting how caravan trade integrated the lives of urban bureaucrats and bankers and craftsmen, as well as relatively remote peasants and pastoralists, within larger economic and political structures.

Situated in western Punjab, Multan and its inhabitants occupied a central place within these local, regional, and trans-Eurasian networks. The town played a critical part in the transformation of the world of caravan trade from c. 1740 to 1840, which is the focus of chapters 3, 4, and 5. By introducing the idea of economies of violence, chapter 3, 'Power', links seasonal movements—of mercenaries, horse traders, and nomadic pastoralists with their flocks—from the dry zone to the production and exercise of hard power in south Asia. It focuses specifically on the rise of the Durrani Empire in the wake of Mughal decentralisation, showing how—alongside the eighteenth-century expansion of the Qing and Romanov empires deeper into Eurasia—the Durrani Empire brought into this space more of the liquid wealth derived from the increasingly globalised economy emerging along the continental seaboards. Chapter 4, 'Traders', traces the outcomes of this process to the empowerment of new commercial groups: former peddlers harnessed market opportunities and channelled the benefits accruing from political patronage into new business ventures, accumulating capital and widening the terrain of their operations. They thereby posed serious competition to established north Indian magnate groups, while also changing the character of commerce itself. The goods brought into urban emporia and periodic rural markets through caravan trade were not restricted to luxuries for elites (fine horses, for example), but included high-value items consumed in small and affordable quantities (such as silk as well as turquoise, and medicinal, talismanic, or apotropaic things) by a broader range of groups, as well as necessities (cloth), and raw materials or productive inputs (raw silk, indigo). Chapter 5, 'Material Culture', thus turns to examine the social, cultural, or spiritual power deriving from the possession of things, illuminating the role played by goods in processes of self-fashioning, sociability, and the expression of changing tastes in ways characteristic of early modernity in other global settings.

The final three chapters scrutinise the impact on Indo-central Asian trade of the conquest and incorporation of the Eurasian interior into the British and Russian empires. This impact was typical, inasmuch as it closely resembled the penetration of European political or commercial regimes into the continental interiors of Afro-Eurasia and America during the era of the New Imperialism. The result, as shown in chapter 6, 'Colonial Conquests', was the revitalisation of a range of routes criss-crossing and connecting inner continental spaces while also integrating these spaces into the larger world economy. Chapter 7, 'Knowledge', shows that the Indo-Afghan frontier and central Asia were of critical significance to the testing of scientific mapping and modern intelligence, ethnography and genealogy, making the spaces and networks of caravan trade fundamental to the finessing of the British Indian states' technologies of power. Yet the epistemic anxiety resulting from information asymmetry and the flow of mobile agents through this space—especially during the 'Great Game'—precipitated schemes to sedentarise populations and transform them into cultivators and soldiers, in turn integrating western Punjab's economy more deeply into that of the British Empire at the cost of connections into the Eurasian interior. Chapter 8, 'Technology', evaluates the causes of the relative and absolute decline of trade, focussing on productive and transport technologies, the rapid development and diffusion of which were the hallmarks of the era of the New Imperialism. The impact of technological change was ambivalent, with the modern nowhere supplanting more archaic motilities; instead, the existing pattern of trade was undermined where new technologies interacted with wider economic changes, particularly the institution of protectionism in Russian Central Asia.

Situating the Silk Roads: Global, Regional, Local

Today, around 40 per cent of the world's population is estimated to live within a hundred kilometres of the coast; the percentage is even higher in Asia, home to a number of the world's megacities most vulnerable to the impact of rising sea levels.[24] This spatio-demographic phenomenon is the cumulative consequence of, on the one hand, the increased thalassologically oriented connectivity of terrestrial land masses following the Age of Discovery from *c.* 1500 onwards, and on the other, a longer-term migration of human populations from the interior to the coastal littoral and river valleys and deltas of continents.[25] This process accelerated in the seventeenth century, for coastal regions fared better during the dramatic climatic changes that shocked Afro-Eurasia and America (discussed in the next chapter). In turn, this redistribution of populations has shaped historical production, not least in the wake of the global turn and the growing concern with large-scale—that is, interregional or transcontinental—connections. Amongst the new global histories, especially of the premodern world, there has been a particular focus on sites of exchange and diaspora enclaves, on cosmopolitanism and contact zones: coastlines, marine or riverine port-cities, and urban centres between waterfronts and their terrestrial hinterland.[26]

Yet the majority of the world's population still lives at a distance from the seas, so that the recent preoccupation of many global historians with the maritime rimlands of continents reflects a selective privileging of particular channels and vectors of connection—namely, seaborne networks of mobile peoples, things, and ideas. In part, this reflects the growth of global history out of world or imperial history. Integral to these older approaches was the narrative of the breakout of Europeans from the north-west Atlantic into other seas and oceans, and their shift from 'waterborne parasites' to terrestrial powers in the Americas, Africa, Asia, and the Pacific.[27] In this respect, even though the spate of recent global history writing has empowered a much wider range of actors—including women, non-whites, subalterns—and made more complex and less teleological the entangled histories of empire and globalisation, the endeavour has been uneven.[28] Focussing on trans-Eurasian networks of caravan trade is a partial corrective to the geographic unevenness of the globalist gaze.

Of the Red Sea region, which has largely been seen in macro-historical perspective or as a transitional space or as a maritime corridor between the Indian Ocean and the Mediterranean, Jonathan Miran remarks: 'deserts [...] can be imagined as seas, [...] an empty space, an ahistorical place, and an area of deprivation to be promptly traversed on the way to the more propitious areas located beyond it.'[29] This is roughly applicable to how historians have viewed—and ignored—the places examined in this book. In part, this in-betweenness of space is the result of the rigid categories of Area Studies, such as 'South Asia' or 'Central Asia', which have served to fragment knowledge production and severed formerly connected spaces. In what follows, these are rendered 'south Asia' and 'central Asia' to soften the solidity and boundedness that results from the capitalised proper noun. In part, however, this is also a product of the poverty of the historical imagination, the inability to envision thinly peopled and arid or semi-arid steppes, deserts, and mountain slopes as spaces of production and consumption, of cultural and economic exchange in their own right. Afghanistan, for example, has been described as a 'trade corridor' and a 'transit economy', while central Asia is often reduced to a transitional space in Silk Road histories.[30] Against such characterisations, the material in this book tries to foreground the agency of the places and peoples connected through caravan trade in the larger space of the Indian subcontinent and its histories. At the same time, by crossing the boundaries of Areas Studies to bridge south and central Asia, and of historical categorisations of time to connect precolonial and colonial or early modern and modern historiographies, this book embraces the challenge of the global to shift historical production out of these silos.

Bradsher's article highlights the perhaps surprising impact of successive waves of technological, political, and other changes. The change has not been the wiping out of the arcane in favour of the modern so much as the reorienting of trans-Eurasian networks and the replasticisation of terrestrial space itself. The dynamics of such processes can seem counterintuitive: just as the container consolidated the role of maritime transportation in the jet age, so, latterly, has the revival of cross-continental railway transportation arisen in competition with the haulage of cargoes by sea and air. At stake, therefore, is the relationship of different sorts of connectivity and different spaces of connection—subjects still very much in the background of the globalist approach to history. *India and the Silk Roads* is part of the slow shift within global histories of the premodern world toward the examination of 'inner spaces'. These include the Sahara, where trans-Saharan traders weathered the transformations brought by European trade with the African littoral through to the nineteenth century, as Ghislaine Lydon has so brilliantly shown.[31]

It would be wrong to continue overlooking the history of the Eurasian interior because of the boom along Eurasia's coastal fringes after *c.* 1500—around, variously, Iberia and then north-west Europe, India and China, in particular.[32] In fact, building on Stephen Dale and Scott Levi's pioneering studies, the material presented in this book shows that Indo-central Asian caravan trade survived and even expanded, not in spite of but because of the growth of intra-Asian and Euro-Asian maritime trade. Until the second quarter of the nineteenth century, the growing demand for Indian (and Chinese) goods resulted in the influx of bullion from the Atlantic world into Asia. This liquidity then increased prosperity, fuelling the purchase of goods and services that were brought into the subcontinent through the networks of caravan trade, thereby serving to integrate more tightly the Eurasian interior. *India and the Silk Roads* shows that this inner space became neither an isolated backwater in response to the global demographic shift towards the maritime rimland, nor suffered because of the intensification of connectivity—'globalisation'—brought by improvements in seafaring technologies and the unparalleled escalation of the scope and scale of exchanges after *c.* 1500.

And yet two types of globalisation were evidently in operation: one oriented around maritime exchanges, increasingly coming under the control of European regimes and constitutive of the modern world-system, the other oriented around cross-continental trade, largely remaining in the hands of indigenous agents and revolving around archaic forms of mobility.[33] As this book shows, there was a tension between these two systems; for, while money, goods, and people could move between them, they were in many respects coterminous but completely separate spheres of exchange. Globalisation and the making of new connections neither excluded the persistence and vitality of older networks, nor excluded the possibility of increasing separation and isolation, disconnection or reconnection. Globalisation was thus neither a singular(ising) process nor one with its trajectory secularly upward.[34]

What does the history of globalisation look like from the Eurasian interior? What does the history of this space reveal about long-distance trade networks, about empire and transitions of power, and in fact about global history itself? While these larger concerns of this book are global in scope, the core of the analysis is embedded in the locality and the region and is thus indebted to the early work of C. A. Bayly. In his monumental study of north India, *Rulers, Townsmen and Bazaars*, Bayly shifted focus from the upper echelons of the state and the lowest rungs of rural society to 'intermediate entities'—mercenaries, merchants, revenue farmers, gentry families—in urban centres across the Gangetic valley.[35] The merchants' commercial activities connected rural and urban, as well as local, regional, trans-regional, and global markets, and were imbricated in changing configurations of political power.[36] Bayly's study of trade and traders thus charted the transformation of economy and society in late-eighteenth-and nineteenth-century north India. In so doing, Bayly and other 'revisionists' highlighted the continued vibrancy of north Indian commercial centres and polities attendant on the eighteenth-century transition from Mughal rule to that of its successor states. At the same time, these revisionists shifted analysis of the Indian economy and society out of the narrow confines of an often mutually exclusive framework—that of an extractive, revenue-oriented, bureaucratic-agrarian state, and of the maritime economy of Indian Ocean trade.[37]

Though many of the traders and financiers studied by Bayly and others originated in Punjab, the entire region north-west of Delhi has hitherto been relatively marginal in these debates.[38] Claude Markovits'

Global World of Indian Merchants, for example, pays more attention to north-west Indian traders abroad than at home, where 'home' in the 'dry zone' is constituted of push factors (little cultivable land, small landholdings) that thrust these entrepreneurs out into markets across the globe.[39] The scant scholarship focussing on Punjab and the Indo-Afghan frontier that exists paints a picture of chaos and repeated ruin amidst the Mughal–Sikh–Afghan contest for political control from the early eighteenth to the mid nineteenth century, with wide-ranging change occurring only after the colonial conquest in the second half of the nineteenth century. This is difficult to square with the resilience of merchant communities and caravan trade, especially when the latter is understood as a wider complex of mobilities—of goods and material resources, of human and animal power. Taking a *longue durée* approach to the history of trade networks reaching out of north-west India offers the potential of reappraising this pattern of economic, social, and cultural change. Such an approach, centring on western Punjab, structures the analysis in *India and the Silk Roads*. Because, in the *longue durée*, the logic of the exchange of military services, and of warhorses and other goods, was rooted in the ecological differences between the dry and the wet zones, it is to an examination of the relationship of environment to trans-Eurasian networks that the first chapter turns.

1

ENVIRONMENT

In the middle decades of the seventeenth century, the northern hemisphere suffered massive fluctuations in temperature and weather phenomena amidst overall climatic cooling. This 'Little Ice Age' varied from place to place, but in such distant locales as Ottoman Anatolia and Ming China the oscillation from severe rainfall and flooding to deep drought destabilised agrarian production. The evidence of such widespread environmental calamity has resuscitated the notion of a 'General Crisis', famously first proposed as a European phenomenon, and most recently studied under a single geographically expansive lens by Geoffrey Parker as a *Global Crisis*.[1] The effect of climatic cooling—from Europe to east Asia and north America—and the changes in weather patterns that resulted was to stunt economic output, driving a wedge between food prices on the open market and the state's fiscal receipts. Unable to provide for the hungry masses, the legitimacy of the hereditary rulers of agrarian states was called into question as the economic crisis exacerbated. In turn, as the petty revolts that squeezed the state's increasingly slender finances proved difficult to suppress, charismatic local leaders were able to coalesce the support of peasants, roving bandit gangs, and demobilised soldiers into an assault on the centre, often resulting in regime change—as for example from the Ming to the Qing, or the Stuart monarchy to the Commonwealth and back again; or instability at the centre, as in the Ottoman Empire.[2]

The wave of late-seventeenth- to eighteenth-century regime change sketched in the introduction was part of a wider pattern of political and economic change rooted more or less deeply in environmental flux. 'Mughal decline' and its causes have been much debated, but Parker's analysis serves to draw together the detrimental effect of imperial overstretch amidst climatic change and, thus, of economic hardship on the power and prestige of the empire, on the loyalty of elites and peasants, and on their belief in the emperor's leadership.[3] The result was neither regime replacement per se nor significant instability at the centre, but a change in the balance of power between the imperial heartland and the provinces. Regional rulers slowly asserted their autonomy from the emperor, while even relative new-comers were able to carve out political niches for themselves over the long eighteenth century.[4] The harshness of Iran's environment made the Safavid economy especially fragile and much more sensitive to small changes in climatic conditions than was the case in the more fertile and agriculturally productive cores of the Mughal and Qing empires. Yet, climatic fluctuations from 1666 to 1696 combined with tectonic activity along the Iranian Plateau, the resultant scarcity and uncertainty—even if not toppling the Safavid *padshah*—perhaps weak-ened the centre's ability to deal with the early-eighteenth-century tribal assault that precipitated regime change.[5]

Alongside their neighbours in Iran, India, and China, the changing fortunes of the Uzbek khanates are also locatable within this picture. The rise of Khokand was rooted in the Bukharan crisis of the seven-teenth and eighteenth centuries, starting as a fiscal crisis connected to the contraction of the availability of silver in the Bukharan economy.[6] Scott C. Levi has contested the notion that this liquidity crunch resulted from Bukhara's growing global isolation as a result of the mar-ginalisation and decline of the Silk Roads in the era of trans-oceanic trade. But this is perhaps to miss the possibility that caravan trade might have been starved rather suddenly (and temporarily) of goods and cash in consequence of famine and scarcity in the Mughal, Safavid, and Qing domains—as well as the growing slowdown of global trade and bullion flows from the Atlantic world to India and China—during the seventeenth-century Global Crisis.[7] Ultimately, the shortage of silver compelled the rapid debasement of coinage and the dramatic loss

of its value. This made it 'increasingly difficult for an inherently decentralised regime such as the Bukharan Khanate to maintain patronage
systems', precipitating the erosion of the allegiance and loyalty of the
Uzbek elites to the khan. This meant, in turn, the erosion of the centre's military strength and political legitimacy.[8] Within this context,
rebellions became more frequent amidst incursions of mobile peoples
from beyond the khanate as well as from neighbouring powers, serving
to shatter Bukharan prestige and power. As Bukhara's control over the
Fergana valley weakened, Shah Rukh Biy established his authority in
1709 over what would become the Khokand state under the rule of the
Shahrukhid dynasty.

The environment—*qua* the physical landscape, ecology, climate—is
neither a fundamental determinant nor immutable, but a factor manip-
ulable by human agency and frequently changing or changeable.
Whether in the *longue durée* or in distinct episodes, as above, the environment is thus a powerful *explanans* of both the pattern of political
and material life and of periods of change therein, and forms an overarching framework structuring the analysis in this book. The first half
of this chapter introduces the notion of the Indo-central Asian trading
world, the space integrated by the caravan circuit, its mobilities and
exchanges. It highlights the embeddedness of the annual transhumance
within the distinctive seasonal rhythms across this space. The second
half looks at the logic of trade, rooting it within environmental differences between the dry and wet zones of Eurasia, and the opportunity
for specialisation and exchange resulting therefrom.

Hot and Cold: Geography and Climate

Fernand Braudel conceived of the 'Mediterranean world' as constituted
of the sea, the littoral, and their environs in his magisterial study published in the early twentieth century. Following his lead, in the 1960s
and 1970s Ashin Das Gupta, K. N. Chaudhuri, and Om Prakash, among
others, pioneered what has now become a rich corpus of scholarship
on the 'Indian Ocean world'.[9] According to the scholarly consensus
that has since emerged, the early modern Indian Ocean trading world
was a system of fiercely competitive and overlapping segments, each
home to particular commercial communities, and each possessing

coastal hinterlands that were sites of specialised production and distinctive consumption patterns.[10] In similar spirit, a Eurasian system can be conceived that at once also fractures 'the popular concept of the Silk Road' into its underlying trading worlds or commercial circuits and segments: trans-subcontinental, Indo-central Asian, Indo-Persian, Perso-central Asian, Russo-Persian, Russo-central Asian, Sino-central Asian, and Sino-Russian.[11] The Indo-central Asian trading world is more compact than the Indo-Persianate world that has so fruitfully framed other scholarly inquiries, but is also more expansive than Indo-Khorasan, a term recently proposed by Sajjad Nejatie to bring into focus the integrating effect of Durrani political authority from what is now eastern Iran to north India.[12] I utilise both these terms—Indo-central Asian and Indo-Persianate—to draw attention to the highly mobile holy men, litterateurs, and mercenaries who moved into and integrated the trading world, giving caravan trade a larger significance than as mere conduit for the exchange of goods. At the same time, the space that is the focus of this book had a definite and distinctive shape, even as it must be approached flexibly.

Just as knowledge of the monsoon system and sea currents were critical to Chaudhuri's understanding of the natural delineation of distinct commercial segments and seasonal patterns of circulation within them, so too is an awareness of the role played by the environment central to the definition of trans-continental circuits, including the Indo-central Asian. Writing of the Middle East and North Africa (MENA), J. R. McNeill observes that its 'settlement pattern resembles that of Polynesia more than that of China or India, with larger and smaller "islands" of habitation existing where enough water could be found.' These arid spaces were home to 'small [and often non-contiguous] zones of continual settlement, [...] together making up an archipelago', usually along or in proximity with water courses such as rivers or other sources of fresh water.[13] The land was either too dry for farming or too marginal even for pastoralism, making the availability and reliability of water a critical variable in the sort of activity possible and the density of population supported.[14]

Over time, its contours shifted in response to changes in ecologies, commercial opportunities, and political authorities, but broadly the core of the Indo-central Asian trading world covered a region represented at its southern end by the boundaries of the provincial states of Punjab and Rajasthan in present-day India, and at its northern end by the nation-states of Pakistan, Afghanistan, and Uzbekistan. Outside this region, the threads of this cobweb-like network clung to more distant outposts of continual habitation where traders took their goods for sale—on the Kazakh steppe, on the shores of the Caspian Sea, in the trade towns of Russia, China, Turkmenistan, Iran, and north India. And within this region, trade-related activities—production, procurement, packing, transportation, wholesale, retail, consumption—were spread unevenly, with some settlements or areas shifting into or out of the trade network, and others isolated from long-distance trade through-out the period covered in this book.

Punjab, as a territorial unit stretching from Delhi to the Indo-Afghan frontier (including the North-West Frontier Province carved out of Punjab in 1901), formally came into being after the British conquest of the Sikh kingdom in the 1840s. 'Mughal Punjab' did not exist as an administrative unit, except as the aggregate of the Mughal *subas* (prov-inces) of Lahore and Multan.[15] The Lahore *suba* corresponds to central Punjab and eastern Punjab (now Haryana). The Multan *suba*, which incorporated parts of present-day Sindh, is referred to as western Punjab in this book and is at the centre of much of its analysis. Within this space is the area known as Derajat and such towns as Multan, Dera Ghazi Khan, Dera Ismail Khan, and Bahawalpur, which feature promi-nently in the following pages, as well as Jhang, Muzaffargarh, Shujabad, and Ahmedpur. This was an area corresponding to what the Punjab Census of 1921 designated as the 'northwest dry area' and what today falls within the boundaries of Punjab in Pakistan.[16]

Until the reign of Abdur Rahman in the closing decades of the nine-teenth century, 'Afghanistan' was not a term used by the region's rul-ers, nor were the northern and southern borders of the Afghan state territorially fixed, both of which were of European invention.[17] Instead, a bundle of terms were employed by the Mughals, Safavids, and Durranis, and by the inhabitants of the region, including Khorasan, Balkh, Roh, Pashtunkhwa (Pakhtunkhwa), and Hazarajat. In what fol-lows, therefore, these terms are used alongside the names of specific urban centres, although the term Afghanistan is also used as shorthand for the coteries of these places and peoples. Such usage is made with appreciation of the fact that Afghanistan's borders were both bigger and smaller than the territory as it exists today, and that Afghans and Afghan polities spilled into neighbouring empires and states, and vice versa. Balkh, for example, was commercially and culturally more closely integrated into central Asia to the north than the region to the south.[18] And whereas scholars of Afghanistan have sought to support or undermine the conflation of 'Afghanistan', 'Afghan', and 'Pashtun' (today the dominant ethnic group), some sections of the following chapters aim to probe these descriptors to dispel the strict separation of Afghan and Indian, to examine the elusiveness of Afghans within central Asia, and to thereby highlight the fuzziness of individual identities.[19]

India and the Silk Roads is rooted in south Asia, both in terms of centring on western Punjab and the Indo-Afghan frontier and, in turn, on the archives and repositories left by India's rulers. The book casts its gaze from this vantage point into central Asia, broadly conceived. This category is used alongside Turan and Turkestan, which to contemporaries in the medieval and early modern periods denoted the area enclosed by the mountains to the south (Hindu Kush) and east (Tien Shan), the steppe to the north, and the (Qara Qum, 'black sands') desert to the west greened by the Amu (Oxus) and Syr (Jaxartes) rivers and their tributaries.[20] Bukhara was a critical node from whence merchants took goods for sale into the neighbouring states of Khiva and Khokand, to the steppes, and to the towns and fairs on the fringes of the Russian Empire. By the seventeenth century, Bukharan traders in Siberia were constitutive of what Erika Monahan characterises as a merchant diaspora.[21] Bukhara was the northern terminus of much of the traffic flowing around the north–south caravan circuit. It was also one of the most populous and prosperous cities of the three Uzbek polities throughout the period under investigation, and an important centre (political, commercial, cultural, spiritual) in the imaginary of European and south Asian travellers and rulers. It thus takes a central place in much of the analysis.[22] In contrast, Khiva—which was relatively inaccessible to Western merchants, travellers, and commentators—features much less prominently.[23]

Merchants and Their Mobilities

The east–west to north–south pivot of the Silk Roads' primary axis deepened the involvement of several commercial groups in south Asia, including Persian, Bukharan, and Armenian merchants. The Armenians, for example, extended their networks within the Russian Empire towards the north, and the Indian Ocean world to the south. They migrated in increasing numbers to the subcontinent in the early seventeenth century and made use of overland routes to transport Indian goods such as indigo and textiles.[24] Towards the end of the century, however, the Armenians increasingly connected their southern and northern networks via the Persian Gulf, using maritime routes.[25] Armenian Christians remained a presence in Afghan commercial centres through to the end of the nineteenth century, but the bulk of the Armenian and Persian long-distance trade shifted to the sea routes. The Bukharans meanwhile deepened their integration into networks towards Russia and China, signalling the general retreat of these groups from Indo-central Asian trade over the eighteenth century.[26]

From the rebellion at Kandahar against the Safavids in 1709, to Ahmad Shah's recurrent campaigns in north India through to the 1770s, the long eighteenth century was marked by considerable political turbulence. Trade did not decline, however. In the short term, wartime opened alternative opportunities from those in peacetime for enterprising and agile merchants: in military supplies, such as warhorses, arms, ammunition; in food supplies, such as grain; and in financial services, especially high-interest credit.[27] Indian warfare was relatively contained, seldom seriously damaging the economy, except when it was prolonged and pulled labour and land away from subsistence- and trade-related production.[28] In the medium and longer term, moreover, the impact of Durrani expansion was to invigorate the economy of western Punjab and Afghanistan, and the long-distance trade networks in which they were enmeshed. In this process (elaborated in chapter 4), Punjabi and north Indian magnates and their trade-cum-financial firms not only weathered the changes of the long eighteenth century but proved critical to the rise of the Durrani imperium. But who were these magnates?

Global Indian commercial networks are well studied and relatively well documented, despite the scarcity of historical materials authored by these actors—which precludes reaching directly into their inner worlds, this being particularly true of Indian mercantile networks in central and western Asia.[29] According to medieval Arab geographers, the first recorded Indians in central Asia were from Multan.[30] Originating as local and long-distance moneylenders, brokers, and traders, and encouraged by the Delhi Sultans and the Mughals to extend their trade across the Hindu Kush from their home base of Multan, 35,000 'Indian Multanis' had settled across central Eurasia by the later seventeenth century.[31] Levi has shown that, as rural money-lenders in north-west India, Multanis advanced raw cotton to weavers, receiving in return some of the finished fabric at below-market prices.[32] These textiles acted as capital: Multani agents took this cloth, joined the northward caravans, and reinvested the cash profit realised on the cloth sales in agricultural or short-term cash loans.[33] These investments necessitated their short-term settlement in Persia, central Asia, western China, or Russia, where they lived in designated districts or caravanserais.[34] Markovits posits that the origins of Multanis and Marwaris in the dry zone, where they held little land, was the principal 'push' factor in their entry into long-distance trade with Hindustan, Persia, central Asia, across the Indian Ocean world, and so forth. If this explains their locomotion, the nature of their mobility lay somewhere between circulation, migration, and diaspora. In contrast to Levi, who utilises the concept of 'diaspora', Markovits prefers the concept of the 'merchant network' to the 'merchant diaspora'. This is for various reasons: the magnetism or central place of cities such as Multan or Shikarpur, the formation of an active and connected network between distinct nodal points, the extent of circulation (of labour, capital, com-modities) rather than rootedness, and the internalisation of informa-tion and financial flows within the network (whereas diaspora has been associated with cosmopolitanism and cross-cultural transfers).[35]

With the rise of the Durrani Empire, initially centred in Kandahar, the centre of gravity shifted from the Khyber to the Bolan routes, the Multani financial houses thus partially relocating to Shikarpur while adapting to these changes.[36] With the ongoing changes in opportunities over the nineteenth century, and the continued diversification of the trading communities involved in overland trade, 'Indian', 'Multani', and 'Shikarpuri' were increasingly inaccurate conflations of a range of identities: Sindhi Bhatias, Punjabi Parachas and Bohras, Marwari Oswals and Gujaratis, as well as Hindus, Muslims, Jains, and Sikhs.[37] What connected some of these groups was their shared belonging to the mercantile Khatri or Bania castes.[38]

Ultimately, the mobility of the Multanis, and of other Punjabi and north Indian merchant groups, was predicated on the movements of other mobile groups. Within their commercial circuits, pastoralists combined the seasonal search for fresh pasture with transportation and carriage services for travellers and traders attracted by the idea of safety in numbers and the security provided by guardsmen.[39] Often, these pastoral groups are designated as Afghans, Pathans or Pashtuns, Powindas, and Lohanis, and sometimes as Kuchis, in sources from India and the British Empire.[40] 'Powinda' derives from Persian and Pashtu words meaning 'to graze' and 'to roam', and was the most widespread descriptor of these trading groups.[41] Most Powindas were of the Ghilzai tribal confederation, which itself was formed of various tribes and clans.[42] Lohani, for example, refers to one of the main tribes of the Ghilzai and Lodi.[43]

The Lohanis are well known because of their prominence in the early nineteenth century, when agents of the Company started to explore Punjab and Afghanistan. They were vital to the colonial state's schemes to open north-west India to trade with British India and were also tapped for strategic or commercial information.[44] But the Lohanis were only one of a number of Powinda tribes involved in long-distance trade through their seasonal migrations. Because of their geographical dispersion, various tribes and clans specialised along different routes, usually through those areas in which they were numerically dominant, thereby ensuring safe passage to the caravans.[45] On the subcontinental leg of their commercial circuits, various trading tribes sometimes specialised in a variety of commodities, which then influenced their decision to travel throughout Punjab, or as far as Bengal or Gujarat, or places within closer reach before the end of spring.[46]

As the centres of commercial and political power shifted in Afghanistan, different groups came to occupy positions at the forefront of trade. The establishment of the Durrani polity in 1747, for example, opened up opportunities for the Mahsand and Ghora Khel clans of the Babar tribe and for the Daulat Khel. The latter also served as horse traders from Persia to India via Afghanistan, returning with textiles and other goods for the Kandahar and Kabul markets.[47] The organisation of the camel caravans was competitive, with terms such as Afghans, Pathans, and Powindas belying the specific identities of the communities involved in transportation and logistics, and their flux over time. But, to anticipate arguments central to subsequent chapters, the 'Afghans' involved in trade were not merely the auxiliaries of traders proper, nor were they peddlers or petty traders. The chiefs of the trading tribes were able to amass wealth through trade and agriculture, examples being Omar Khan Lohani and Sarwar Khan Lohani, who drew themselves to the attention of British colonial agents in the early nineteenth century.[48] Within the trading tribes, the better-off traded on their own account rather than simply carrying goods for Indian and central Asian merchants, while the poorer acted as 'carriers & agents or small retail dealers' for wealthier Afghan traders.[49]

At the northern terminus of the caravan circuit, commodities were either exchanged with Bukharan traders—such as Urasko Kaibulin, who was active in Russian Siberia in the seventeenth century, or Irnazar Maksyutov, who from 1745 to *c*. 1775 took Indian goods for sale in Russian towns such as Astrakhan and Orenburg, or to the Kazakh steppe.[50] But 'Bukharan'—like 'Indian' or 'Multani', 'Afghan' or 'Powinda'—is something of a simplification. The commercial classes of Bukhara, the traders and artisans, were Persophone Tajiks (Parsivans) and Jews, and also Uzbeks and Tatars, settled in the city and elsewhere in the polity.[51] Travelling northward and eastward, these Bukharan traders encountered the nomadic Kalmyks and Kazakhs, numbering several million and scattered across the northern steppes. With them they exchanged the manufactures of sedentary societies for their animals and livestock products, taking these for onward sale in China or Russia, as well as in central Asian marts and the south Asian markets these traders serviced.[52]

Seasonal Rhythms

The Hindu Kush mountain range runs through Afghanistan, adjoining the Pamirs and the Karakoram to form a snow-capped curtain of rock and ice separating the Indian subcontinent from central Asia, the narrower passes through which were occasionally closed by deadly avalanches. The annual schedule of the *qafilas* (caravans) was thus shaped by climate into a well-worn pattern over the centuries.[53] Journeying south of the Hindu Kush, the subcontinental leg of the circuit was completed during the dry season of the autumn and winter months, when the five rivers—*panj ab* (Jhelum, Chenab, Ravi, Sutlej, Beas), the tributaries of the Indus—ran relatively dry and were more easily crossed, perhaps even sparing the cost of ferries or bridges of boats necessary when the currents ran high.[54] The dry season opened opportunities for mercenaries offering their services to warmongers, as well as camel drivers and horse dealers whose animal power was critical to the premodern military. Then, hoping to avoid the enervating summer swelter followed by monsoon torrents, merchants concluded their purchases of cotton cloth and other commodities in north India before April or May, reconvening with the caravans in Punjab.

Traffic travelling northwards took the Khyber Pass from Peshawar to Kabul. Traffic taking a more south-westerly direction flowed through Multan to the Bolan, Sanghar, or Gomal passes towards Quetta and Kandahar. Having arrived in Kabul or Kandahar around June and July, where they paused to permit the merchants to conduct their trade, the caravans continued toward central Asia in August. The Khyber–Kabul traffic proceeded to Kunduz, Khulm, Balkh, and Bukhara. The Bolan–Kandahar traffic to Bukhara branched either eastwards via Balkh and Karshi or westwards via Herat. In October, the caravans arrived in Bukhara, capital of the Khanate of Bukhara, coinciding with the caravans of Khivan, Khokandi, and Orenburg merchants with whom the traders exchanged their goods and competed in the bazaars. Indian goods reached Russian markets either via Orenburg or via Persia, for some of the merchants taking the Bolan–Kandahar route continued to the southern shores of the Caspian, their wares ferried to Astrakhan for onward trade in Russia.[55]

With the spring snowmelt the traders returned towards Afghanistan, reaching the high pastures in June and July. Until the end of the wet season on the Indian plains, when trade and warfare were impossible and cultivation was the necessary occupation of the majority of peasants, Afghan pastoralists grazed their flocks in these drier and cooler climes. With the arrival of colder weather in the Afghan highlands, they continued through the mountain passes in October or November, the Powindas and horse dealers grazing and fattening their animals on pasturage in the Derajat, before descending onto the temperate plains for the start of the autumn–winter trade and campaign season. The caravans taking the Khyber route generally continued towards Lahore and Delhi, following the Ganges and Yamuna rivers eastwards towards Bengal. Those emerging through the Bolan Pass travelled towards Multan and Bahawalpur, moving parallel to the coast of western India through Rajasthan, Kutch, and Gujarat, towards the south. The horse merchants headed for particular markets or the annual autumn fairs (*melas*), such as those held at Pushkar and Haridwar, sometimes reinvesting their profits in specialised local textiles for sale along their return trip.[56] As the sun hung lower and grew hotter, it heralded the beginning of a new circuit between India and central Asia.

If climate chiselled the physical geography and itinerary of caravan trade, changes in political and economic circumstances influenced the choice of particular routes. The Khyber route was much used in the seventeenth century following improvements ordered by Akbar and Shah Jahan, for example, and returned to prominence in the nineteenth century. Trade shifted to the routes through the Bolan, Sanghar, and Gumal passes after the mid eighteenth century. As the shortest routes between Afghanistan and India, these routes rose in strategic and commercial importance alongside the expansion of the Durrani Empire, the capital of which was located in Kandahar until Timur Shah (r. 1772–93) relocated it to Kabul. Chapter 3 examines the factors that made merchants calculate the efficiency versus safety of different routes.

Wet and Dry: Environmental and Economic Interdependence

Today, western Punjab's arable land is fed not only by rainwater but by canals from the five rivers and the Indus. When Timur crossed the Indus en route to Delhi in 1398, however, this part of north-west India had an annual rainy season.[57] The early modern period was witness to a number of ecological and climatic fluctuations, the impact of which was amplified in the drier parts of the province because of their greater sensitivity to change. 'Because', as Clive Dewey has noted, 'all the tributaries of the Indus ran into one another, a major change in the course of one river affected the others.'[58] The Sutlej was the most wayward, earlier flowing through the parched lands of Bikaner and into the sea through its own mouth in Kutch, until it joined the Beas in 1593, then shifting course again toward the desert, only 'permanently' rejoining the Beas in 1796.[59] André Wink notes similar mobility in the Ravi, as well as particularly heavy rainfall in the middle decades of the seventeenth century, roughly concurrent with the climatic changes of the Little Ice Age.[60] One impact of this was to undermine the economic centrality to Punjab and north-west India of Lahore in favour of Multan (examined more closely in chapter 2). Another was to make navigability of the Indus more difficult as the river shifted course and silted up, adversely affecting the delta port of Thatta, and to some extent severing the commercial centres of Punjab from the Arabian Sea and the Indian Ocean.[61] Some changes have been man-made, however. These include clearance of the Lakhi Jungle that once stood on the floodplain of the Beas and Sutlej rivers in central Punjab, the transformation of dry wasteland in western Punjab—formerly used for grazing—into arable over the eighteenth and especially the nineteenth century, and the reclamation of tracts from the Thar Desert in Sindh through the development of river-fed irrigation.[62]

Thus, far from being fixed, the environment was changing, each natural or man-made fluctuation exerting an active and powerful effect on the economy. Against the impact of episodic environmental change within particular regions is the longer-term influence of environmental variations between regions, the latter illuminating the logic of long-term and large-scale spatial interaction. The analysis in this section is structured by Jos Gommans' conceptualisation of the Arid Zone.[63] In the wet zone, roughly stretching from eastern Punjab to the Ganges delta, a hostile disease environment was one of the challenges that beset animal husbandry, the other being the high opportunity cost of grazing as against the substantial loss of marketable crop surplus. Across much of the Indian subcontinent, therefore, and especially the Gangetic valley, state power revolved around the promotion of settled agriculture and surplus production. This facilitated taxation of the peasantry by a sophisticated and hierarchically organised bureaucracy that penetrated to the lowest levels of agrarian activity to connect the imperial centre with the countryside. In contrast, cultivable land in the dry zone, stretching from the semi-arid tracts beyond the canal-fed land of western Punjab to the arid zone proper ranging north of the Indo-Afghan frontier into central Eurasia, was relatively less productive, so here the lower opportunity cost meant that large tracts of land were ideal pasturage for the herds of (semi-)nomadic pastoralists. The shift of the Oxus' course around 1576 and the subsequent expansion of the Qara Qum allowed eastern steppe peoples to transform 'the Black Sands Desert into a tribal frontier ground through their exceptional horse breeding and equestrian culture.'[64]

Because of these environmental differences, the dry and wet zone economies specialised in different sorts of production, the benefits of which were harnessed through exchange. Both cotton cultivation and weaving were widespread in parts of Afghanistan and central Asia, for example, resulting in a lively interregional textile trade.[65] Evidence that the fine-cloth weavers of Benares recorded their origins in twelfth-century central Asia suggests similarities in technical skill across central and south Asia.[66] Yet the Indian wet zone was more productive, so that cotton and other non-food staples could be cultivated alongside food crops. The production of surplus also sustained a larger population, so that there was an abundance of cheap labour. The combination of land and labour productivity reduced costs, making Indian cottons competitive in central Asia even after paying taxes and transport costs, not to speak of the desire there for the wide varieties of Indian cloth that were without substitute.[67] And, finally, some parts of Afghanistan and central Asia were suited only to pastoralism, with pastoralists exchanging their animals and animal products—camels, horses, sheep, goats, wool, leather, and hides—and other goods for the products of sedentary societies, including cloth, thus integrating the 'steppe and the sown'.[68]

This interdependence was the basic logic of Indo-central Asian trade, which can be elaborated via analysis of the horse trade.[69] The overland and overseas horse trades were of long standing, a major drain on the balance of payments of Indian kingdoms, and perhaps the most important in volume and value of all the commodities brought to the subcontinent from abroad in the early modern period. Military and political changes from the fifteenth century were responsible for steadily enlarging the demand for cavalry horses and, in turn, enlarging the extent of the overland horse trade. Since the reorientation of trans-Eurasian trade toward the north–south axis was closely connected to India's growing demand for warhorses, it is important to emphasise that the eventual decline of the horse trade neither sprang from the decline in Indian demand nor entailed the slowdown in caravan trade as a whole. Rather than a demand-side phenomenon arising from the replacement of cavalry with infantry under the auspices of the European powers in Asia, the decline from the mid eighteenth century onward of the overland horse trade was linked to supply-side changes in central Asia.

The Mughal 'Cavalry Revolution'

Aside from a few choice breeding grounds, India's ecology was ill-suited to the raising of horses, Indian-bred specimens generally being deemed inferior in stature and strength compared to Arabs and Persians (Farsi), as well as Afghans (Baladasti) and central Asians (Turki).[70] Gommans has traced these shortcomings to dietary differences deeply rooted in ecological differences: the high opportunity cost of giving productive land over to grassland and grazing meant that oats and hay were scarce in much of the Indian wet zone, and were often substituted by chickpeas and lentils, making the horses relatively smaller and weaker.[71] At the same time, an inhospitable disease environment reduced not only human but also equine life expectancy in the wet zone.[72]

In central Eurasia, by contrast, nomadic pastoralists dispersed across the steppe exchanged their animals and livestock products for goods brought into their orbit from sedentary societies between the Caucasus and China—what Anatoly Khazanov famously characterised as the symbiosis or mutual interdependence between steppe and sown.[73] India was a major market for central Eurasian horses brought through overland routes. These horses were markedly less expensive—perhaps by as much as a factor of four—than those brought from Persia and Arabia by ship.[74] Gommans estimates that late-Mughal India's annual needs were in the tens of thousands of horses, on the reasonable assumption that the horses required replacement every seven to ten years, given what is known of their average life expectancy.[75] In this respect, India's demand for foreign horses was part of a larger picture, also evident in such locales as equatorial west Africa, for example. In the subcontinent, ecological disadvantages in the wet zone shaped a pattern of long-distance exchange with the (semi-)arid zone, these trade connections assuming an unprecedented importance following the start of the early modern cavalry revolution.[76]

The cavalry revolution was driven by two developments. The first was related to Mughal expansion, which propelled institutional innovation in the empire's defensive and offensive capabilities, namely, the *mansabdari*. This was a hierarchical system of salaries and honours awarded on the basis of civil or military service to support specified numbers of horsemen and footmen, their salaries often tied to *jagirs* (parcels of land over which the recipient possessed rights to revenue collection).[77] The extension of this system through the late sixteenth to the seventeenth century enlarged the demand for horses and, thus, the scale of the overland horse trade.[78] The second development lay within the localities. Across the subcontinent, men entered military service to secure and extend their rights to the revenue of their *watan* (homeland), receiving in return for the services of their retinues a share of local tax receipts.[79] As the cavalry revolution continued to skew the composition of armies towards horsemen, who were the highest paid and highest esteemed, more and more horses were required each year, or else as bloodstock for local horse breeding.[80] The demonstration of martial skill as a cavalryman was a means of social mobility in the Mughal Empire, or offered the means to challenge Mughal political authority as military strongmen carved out their own territories. In so doing, these groups continued the longer-term trend of 'Rajputisation', whereby pastoral peoples from Rajasthan to Bengal secured and sometimes succeeded in bequeathing land and landed status to their heirs.[81] Over the seventeenth and eighteenth centuries, as the degree of subinfeudation intensified in the former Mughal domains, and as new regional rulers asserted their independence from the imperial centre, 'the ethos of horse service [...] reached people never before associated with it' and horse-based systems of honour and revenue assignments, akin to the *mansabdari*, emerged or were elaborated across south Asia.[82]

The Eighteenth-Century 'Infantry Revolution' Reconsidered

Between the 1740s and 1760s, as Anglo-French confrontations in south India demonstrated the advantages of European-equipped and European-trained infantry, some Indian rulers responded by adopting and honing these new military technologies.[83] Having expanded rapidly, the horse trade showed signs of decline in the eighteenth century;

one contemporary estimate placed imports at approximately 50,000 animals in the 1770s.[84] It would be wrong to link the slowdown of the horse trade to the so-called infantry revolution, however. In the first place, the epicentre of the infantry revolution was in south India—on the margins of the overland horse-trade network—with decline ante-dating the northward spread of infantry units.[85] In north India, more-over, military leaders were witness to the efficacy of new technologies and modes of warfare flowing from Persia and Afghanistan—including horse-mounted musketeers and camel artillery—which undergirded the role of cavalry and mounted warfare, and, in turn, the overland animal trade.[86] Because the cost of drilling and provisioning a European-style infantry unit was high and rising in the eighteenth and early nineteenth century, and since small infantry units were relatively ineffective against large cavalry charges, the establishment of suitably sized modern regiments was out of reach for most participants in the military market.[87] From the mercenary's perspective, moreover, a career as an infantryman offered fewer of the material and symbolic rewards of the cavalryman, thus failing to appeal to those in search of honour.[88] In this context, cavalry retained a prominent place in north Indian militaries, not least amongst the Sikhs, with Ranjit Singh's investment in European-style infantry complementing—not replacing, although at the cost of modernising—the cavalry.[89] The strength of the cavalry, and its its suitability to the flat battlegrounds of the Indian plain resulted in heavy losses to the Company during the Anglo-Sikh wars.[90]

Much as other Indian rulers, the Company faced the difficulty of securing suitable and well-priced cavalry mounts for its armies. The fraught history of the Company's procurement and breeding efforts reveals that the problem was primarily deficiency of supply, not demand.[91] The establishment of its stud farm at Pusa in 1796 had little ameliorating effect on account of inhospitable breeding conditions and an inadequacy of bloodstock. The Company's second veterinarian at the stud, William Moorcroft, spent 1811 travelling across India, lamenting the depletion of the better breeds and better breeding grounds and fairs.[92] A significant proportion of overland trade had been monopolised by the rulers of north-west India, with the stables of the Sikh ruler Ranjit Singh supplemented by an annual tribute of 'none but the best' Persian and Turki horses from the Afghan ruler

after 1818.[93] Advised that the fabled breeds of central Asia were pro-
curable in more proximate markets, Moorcroft set off in 1819 with
great optimism.[94] Yet, at each of the major marts—Peshawar, Kabul,
and Bukhara itself—he faced disappointment, each time rationalising
or believing that better horses had been bought by local magnates or
existed elsewhere.[95]

In part, his assessments of the Turki horse rested on its increasingly
unfavourable comparison with the tall and agile English Thoroughbred,
the 'creation' of careful breeding between Arab and Turkish stallions
and English mares over the seventeenth and eighteenth centuries.[96] In
part, Moorcroft was probably unaware of the complexity and dispersion of procurement networks—namely, the premiums paid in large
urban centres or upon use of brokers over direct purchase from pastoralists.[97] These issues aside, Moorcroft's disappointments could be read
as revealing the extent of the transformation of the Indo-central Asian
horse trade, which was only one of the circuits constituting the mass of
trans-Eurasian trade networks.

Moscow's animal and livestock needs were serviced in the seventeenth century by the Nogays of southern Russia and the Caucasus,
thereafter shifting eastward to the Kalmyks' lands until the devastation
of their herds in the early eighteenth century, to reach the Kazakh
steppe by the 1740s.[98] In servicing Russian demand, part of the live-
stock-for-goods exchange with the central Asian polities to the south
was displaced.[99] In turn, trade with Tsarist Russia came to surpass that
with (Mughal) India; for, as Russia's empire expanded in the eighteenth
century, its demand for horses rose steeply.[100] With the establishment
of Cossack regiments across the steppe north of the three khanates—at
Orenburg in 1748, Uralsk in 1775, Sibir in 1808, and Semireche in
1867—Russian demand and access to supply increased simultaneously,
possibly displacing part of the trade toward south Asia.[101]

The Sino-central Asian circuit was also of long standing and similarly large. With the establishment of the Qing dynasty in 1644, and
the incorporation of Xinjiang or Chinese Turkestan into the Qing
Empire in the mid eighteenth century, two changes came about. First,
much of the official tribute was transformed into trade, even as it was
conducted within the ritualised submission of the tribute system that
informed Qing relations with the frontier nomads.[102] Second, the
Qing imperial army's need for supplies of horses intensified as it

moved to consolidate control in the newly conquered territories, these horses often supplied via Andijani merchants.[103] Yet Qing expansion in the 1750s ramped up demand for horses as it changed the epidemiological environment on the eastern steppe in ways that undermined supply. One chronicler reported that the Qing were able to extinguish pastoralist power because of their inadvertent introduction of smallpox, which killed 40 per cent of the population, 20 per cent fleeing to Russian lands, and only 30 per cent killed by Qing forces in the final campaigns.[104]

Thus, as larger numbers of animals were sold through the Russo-central Asian and Sino-central Asian exchange networks, Indo-central Asian trade was possibly crowded out by the squeeze on supply. Also, in this context, Durrani expansion from the 1740s enlarged the Afghan cavalry, further restricting supply destined for the subcontinent's animal fairs and markets.[105] Until the Durrani rulers' income streams from the subcontinental domains dried up in the early nineteenth century, the Afghan state was able to pay out sizeable service grants to the Afridis, Shinwaris, and Orakzais for the maintenance of *mansabdari*-style forces.[106] Perhaps because of the supply-side crunch, Afghan traders and dealers were reliant on more proximate sources of supply by the early nineteenth century, especially around Balkh and Badakhshan (Afghan Turkestan).[107] Balkh's ecology and economy were transformed as a result of the wars fought for its control through to the mid eighteenth century, with pasturage and pastoralism replacing fields for crop production—a reminder that the interdependence of steppe or sown was never fundamental, as pastoralists could move from nomadism to a sedentary existence, and vice versa.[108] Balkh's twice-weekly horse market provided relatively plentiful supply at reasonable prices. But Balkh's economy was devastated by the cholera epidemics of the 1830s, which were rooted in the same causes—the disrepair of the irrigation channels—that had initially brought about the decline of arable land and the increase in pasturage and pastoralism.[109] And quality as well as quantity remained a problem, for the limited supplies of the tallest and largest horses were purchased by the elite, with only the middling sorts available for cavalry, much as in earlier times.[110]

The few Balkhi horses still bred in the later 1830s were undersized and unsuitable for the British Indian cavalry, therefore, and increasingly difficult to sell profitably once north-west India was annexed by the

Company.[111] From Kabul, an average of only 1,500 horses passed towards the Khyber, worth around Rs 600,000 at average prices of Rs 400.[112] From Multan towards Lahore, this slimmed down to a meagre trade worth Rs 50,000, or no more than 125 horses.[113] Profits were variable, sometimes high enough to incentivise the sale of Afghan royal cavalry horses, at other times eroding the incentive to trade altogether.[114] The Company's wars in Afghanistan (1839–42), Sindh and Gwalior (1843), and Punjab (1845–6, 1848–9) exhausted its cavalry and depleted the remaining breeding grounds in north-west India.[115] By mid century horse stocks were so short that inferior specimens brought through Kabul were offered for inflated and unreasonable prices in India.[116]

Into the Global Dry Zone

With the establishment of the Company's empire on the Indian subcontinent, and the subsequent expansion of Company and Crown power from the Persian Gulf to south-east Asia, the Indian Ocean was transformed into a British lake.[117] The result, as shown throughout this book, was the deepening integration of parts of south Asia, even those previously distant from the sea, into the economy of the Indian Ocean and, ultimately, of the British Empire. Frequently, although not always intentionally, this came at the expense of pre-existing connections and networks, not least those reaching into the Eurasian interior.

By the 1840s, the inadequacy of its stud farm as well as supply through overland networks prompted the governor general of India to ascertain alternative sources for the procurement of cavalry horses. Indian sources were deemed deficient: despite their finding some for sale in Bombay, Baluchi and Sindhi horses were regarded as inferior and not worth improving.[118] Egypt and Syria were ruled out as unsuitable sites for breeding suitable horses.[119] Some hope, however, came first from Persia and Arabia. A trade on hired 'country boats' (*dhows*), each loaded with thirty to sixty horses at Persian Gulf ports between November and March, serviced markets inland from the western coast of India.[120] Bombay was the hub of this trade, re-exporting surplus stocks further south, to Bengal, and even to China. If the governor general needed further information about Persian sources, it was because trade was falling short of demand, not because this source was untapped or unfamiliar.

Although suitably sized for British cavalry, and suitably priced—being cheaper than desert-bred Arabian horses—fewer than 400 Persian horses were annually imported into British India via Bombay in the 1830s.[121] Aside from freight costs and mortality rates, the supply was unreliable: the Ottoman authorities in the Persian Gulf prohibited the export of horses for a brief time in 1837, 1866–7, and 1874–5, when exports were limited to ten to fifteen horses, and 1883–4, when the authorities resorted to stopping steamers and confiscating Arab and Persian specimens.[122] On the Ottoman side, this practice was of long standing: because horses—and therefore the quality of bloodlines—were a military technology, the state sought to control trade when necessary to cut off rival military power, at once also amplifying the preciousness and political value of gifts of horses made to other rulers. On the Indian side, trade was jealously monopolised by Bombay horse merchants, mostly Parsis, who had agents in Bushire, Baghdad, Basra, and throughout southern Persia, and who resisted interference and competition from the Company.[123] Persian supply sources never solved the problem of military procurement, the authorities repeatedly revisiting the suitability and logistics of animal transportation from Persia and Arabia, as well as central Asia.[124]

Australia was another option drawn to the Government of India's attention. Horses first reached Australia from England alongside convicts on the First Fleet in 1788.[125] Initially, land and convict labour were abundant and cheap enough to nullify the opportunity costs of horse breeding in Australia.[126] Bred in arid areas, Australian horses were first shipped to India in 1816, with a second procurement mission sent from Madras in 1833–4.[127] British Indian procurement was routinised only after the rise in land prices (and, thus, breeding expenses) following the Australian Gold Rush of the 1830s, with the Bengal Army receiving its first shipment in 1843 from New South Wales.[128] With technological improvements, horse shipments from Australia became more reliable, and, although cost remained a problem, regular shipments were inaugurated in 1869.[129]

Conclusion

While never the raison d'être of caravan trade, the horse trade makes visible the geographic scope of the Indo-central Asian trading world in the period under study, as well as the role of the environment in the *longue durée* and in periods of flux in reshaping trade patterns. Because caravan trade comprised the exchange of a wider range of goods and services with varying geographies and 'supply chains', the basic picture presented here is made more textured and complex in chapter 2, which breaks down the different exchanges constituting the 'supply chain' or movement of different sorts of good from sites of production to consumption. Focussing on the overland horse trade also reveals how closely tied India's military economy was to long-distance exchanges between the Indian wet zone and the dry zone stretching from the Indo-Afghan frontier into central Eurasia. This is elaborated in more detail in chapter 3, which returns to the unwinding of the Little Ice Age in the Iranian and Indian contexts. There the thesis of 'tribal breakout' is interrogated as part of a wider exploration of the relationship of caravan trade and the financial, commercial, mercenary, and animal power of its participants to eighteenth-century state building, and vice versa.

Among the causes of the diversion of the horse trade away from India were also factors making for the closer integration of central Eurasia—namely, as chapter 4 shows, Qing and Russian expansion, and the liquidity and commercial opportunity they brought into Khokand and Bukhara, enlivening local, regional, and long-distance exchange networks. Ultimately, the present chapter has highlighted that from differential environmental and, hence, productive possibilities arose the interdependencies which engendered mobility and circulation: between the dry zone and the wet, the steppe and the sown, the (semi-)nomadic and the settled, the martial and the scribal. Within albums produced in cities such as Lahore and commissioned by Europeans of Indian artists working in Punjabi ateliers in the early decades of the nineteenth century, there are pictures of 'characters' to be found in Punjab, among whom are Pashtun horsemen and horse traders.[130] Once the fabled horse trade had slowed down, the Pashtun dealers that remained became part of the glamour and lore of caravan trade and were documented in such albums.[131] The mobility of these and other *passeurs culturels* integrated the Indo-central Asian trading world, giving it a larger shape and significance. The early modern 'culture of mobility', as Daniel Roche terms it in *Humeurs Vagabondes*, forms a larger canvas against which the subject of this book is framed, analysed, and understood.[132]

The formation of the Indo-Persianate world—or, as Usman Hamid and Pasha M. Khan have lately characterised it, the 'Persian cosmopolis' in south Asia—was a 'sedimentary process' in which Persian 'as a language of political expression came about because of successive waves of conquest and migration', commencing with the first of the Delhi sultans in the eleventh century, and 'continuing intermittently until the eighteenth'.[133] But it was also an iterative process, for the embedding of each layer paved the way for further flows—circulatory or migratory—between Iran, central Asia, Afghanistan, and India, to the extent that the Indo-Persianate world was an organic, evolving entity.[134] Movement forged and animated the Indo-Persianate and Islamicate worlds within which the Indo-central Asian trading world was nested, as long-distance trade also became more deeply entangled with developments in these intrinsically trans-regional religious, linguistic and literary, and cultural landscapes. Movement was integral to caravan trade and the economies which it engendered or within which it was enmeshed: the economies of pastoralism and sedentary societies, of traders and free or forced labour, of violence (chapter 3), of capital and technologies (chapter 4), for instance.

Sufi leaders (*khwajas, pirs, shaykhs*), Sufi orders (*tariqahs*), and their ideas were highly mobile—vectors of other kinds of mobility as a new 'religious economy' was embedded in Islamicate Eurasia.[135] Especially important to understanding the connection of central and south Asia is the Naqshbandi order, which dates to the twelfth century, but which was structurally renovated under the leadership of the politically active and powerful Khwaja 'Ubaydullah Ahrar (1404–90), whose descendants formed a distinct branch (the Ahrari) from those of others (the Juybari, the Dahpidi, for instance). Such leaders of Sufi orders were becoming patricians of considerable wealth and influence as they gained larger followings.[136] Reflexively, association with a Sufi order and its leader brought spiritual and political legitimacy, as well as resources and capital (financial, human, moral), to political notables and dynasts, including the Mughals and their counterparts.[137]

Naqshbandi patronage by the Mughals and the imperial nobility occasioned a steady stream of migrants from central Asia to India, but there were also revivals or repatriations of ideas and practices from south to central Asia. The Punjab-born Shaykh Ahmad Sirhindi's reorganisation and expansion of the Naqshbandi *tariqah* in the early seventeenth century was such that it became known as the Naqshbandi-Mujaddidi (from *mujaddid*, 'renewer').[138] With the retreat of Mughal power and patronage in Punjab in the wake of the growing depredations of the Sikhs and the destabilisation brought by Nadir Shah's invasions, the disciples of the distinctly Indian Naqshbandi-Mujaddidi order sought patronage elsewhere. Some travelled to other Indian centres, including Delhi and Rampur. Some travelled to central Asia, where the order was patronised by the new Mangit rulers of Bukhara (from 1785), thus 'retransmitting' the order, to use Jo-Ann Gross' characterisation.[139] Others, however, travelled to Afghanistan, where Sufism and patronage of Sufi *tariqah*s was firmly established, and where they received Durrani patronage, as Waleed Ziad has shown. The 'burgeoning Afghan imperial capitals [Kabul, Peshawar]', Ziad writes, 'attracted Sufis and *'ulama* from Hindustan, eventually becoming fulcrums of reoriented intellectual-exchange circuits.'[140] From the Durrani perspective, such patronage brought some of the most important and expert practitioners of Sharia, jurisprudence (*fiqh*), and Sufism into the life of the polity, where they could build the spiritual-political authority of the new dynasty through the religious, judicial, and bureaucratic apparatus that accompanied the foundation of their orders in local soil, a strategy mirroring that of their Uzbek counterparts and, earlier, the Mughals themselves.[141]

Such was the top-down influence and importance of Sufism in providing an integrative superstructure to the trading world through the large-scale movements of Sufis, the establishment or expansion of *tariqah*s, and the transmission of ideas in embodied or written form between important spiritual centres. But the more localised circuits of movement were as important, whether of wandering Sufi mystics (*qalandars*) who reached directly into local communities in the course of their perambulations, or of lay pilgrims—Muslim, but often also Hindu or Sikh—to the tombs and shrines of Sufi saints.[142] In studying Afghan historiographies produced within the Afghan diaspora in Mughal India, Nile Green has highlighted both the historic process of incorporation of Sufi 'blessed men' (*sayyids*) within Afghan tribal societies and its significance as a historical subject to the production of early modern Afghan identity. 'By absorbing *sayyids* into the working models of society that constituted the Afghans' clearly fluid kinship structures,' Green writes, 'the tribal communities were able to build into their social organisation persons able to mediate between the social unit of the tribe or clan and other groups counting themselves as members of the wider Islamic *umma* (worldwide community of believers).'[143] The result was the further entanglement of commerce, religion, and power within the trading world.

What can be called 'caravan trade' was made up of imbricated or inter-looped circulatory mobilities of different scales, some piggy-backing or building on other contemporaneous mobilities, others on the sedimentations of prior migrations or movements. The seasonal, circular migration—or, more aptly, transhumance—of pastoralists lay at the heart of the Indo-central Asian commercial circuit, the caravans acting as terrestrial fleets that made other forms of mobility possible. At the same time, the largest significance of the caravan circuit lay in its interlocking into other trans-Eurasian networks—into Iran, onto the steppe, toward western China, for example—permitting the safe movement of other people and things.

There were also important differences in the spatialities and visibility of the movements constitutive of caravan trade.[144] Take, for example, the perambulations of Muslim physician itinerants and purveyors of talismans between Punjab and central Asia. These men followed the seasonal rhythms of the caravans. But the wider geographies of their movements were not structured by the search for elite patronage—tied, in turn, to the changing fortunes of Indian dynasts, old and new—as much as servicing the needs of relatively quotidian patrons or 'customers'. They frequently journeyed 'off-piste', so that traces of their activities appear in the extant records on occasions when they were tapped for political information by Company servants in the early nineteenth century, for example.[145] Beyond this invisible yet voluntary movement, furthermore, was that of men, women, and children taken into captivity and bondage.[146]

If the environment gave shape or body to the trading world, and religion and language a sort of skeletal structure and musculature, then the caravan networks—and the localised exchange networks that fed them—were its circulatory system. Within this system, cities played a part like the organs of the body. In fact, the city helped contemporaries picture and understand the integrity of the constituent parts that 'built up' the human body. This was akin to the (idealised) Persianate city being conceived in anatomical terms within Sufi tradition, which drew analogies between the beauty of Man and the beauty in which Man might best live. 'The central bazaar (the backbone) began at the palace (the head), grew toward the Jami Masjid (the heart), and continued to the city gate'—as Stephen Blake has summarised this anatomy-scape on the basis of his analytical dissection of the Mughal plans for Shahjahanabad (Old Delhi). In turn, the 'smaller streets inserted themselves into the body proper as ribs and the vital organs—bathhouses, schools, sarais, bakeries, water cisterns, teahouses, and shops—developed in proximity to the skeletal centre.'[147] The focal point of the next chapter, Multan—a city famous as a Sufi pilgrimage centre from the medieval era on account of its numerous shrines—is thus a particularly apposite site to examine material life through these spatial-anatomical imaginaries.

2

EXCHANGES

Viewed from above, the bustling bazaar and teeming side streets appear as the heart and arteries of old Multan, the epicentre of circulation and exchange within the city. Despite the jumble contained in the surveys conducted in the late 1830s by Company agents into towns and trade in western Punjab and Derajat, Multan seems similar in its spatial organisation to towns throughout north India.[1] Dotted over the city were bakers and barbers, grain and grocery sellers, and food and drink vendors. Jostling alongside Multan's 109 mosques and 112 temples were 160 entertainment establishments, where nautch girls wearing scents from one of the city's twelve perfumeries served spirits from the city's 8 distilleries or drugs from the city's 65 intoxicant sellers. Other commercial and artisanal activities tended to agglomerate in Multan along patterns recognisable in urban centres across north India and Islamicate Eurasia.[2]

Along the streets through the old city were the 85 establishments of the main moneymen (*shroffs*) and 60 merchants' houses whose trade took their agents to villages beyond the city walls, sometimes as far away as Bukhara and Moscow.[3] Surrounding the central cluster of financiers and traders were separate streets for different crafts.[4] Billowing through the Multan sky were the smoke clouds and clamour of 9 glass-blowing workshops, 52 iron smithies, and the establishments of 42 ironmongers, 10 tin-metal workers, 19 metal polishers, 7 stone polishers, 6 amulet makers, 5 jewellers, 45 enamellers, and 112 gold-smiths. All were tucked away along a side street, the messiest or dirti-est at the greatest distance from the centre. Furthest away were the odorous dyeing, bleaching, and tanning tanks: 24 indigo dyers, 35 saf-flower dyers, 65 specialist silk dyers, and 150 cloth bleachers.

This chapter plays with scale to examine the spaces of exchange. The first section, on the towns and cities of cotton-textile manufacture, zooms out to take in developments across the region north-west of Delhi—namely, Punjab and Sindh—and thus examine Multan's posi-tion as the central node in networks of caravan trade south of the Hindu Kush. Towns specialising in weaving for proximate and more distant markets mushroomed along arterial routes in central and east-ern Punjab in the Mughal era, with Lahore as the regional hub of pro-duction and exchange. A number of factors, not least ecological changes in combination with conflicts associated with the retreat of Mughal power, empowered productive centres further west at the expense of Lahore and its subsidiaries. Multan was already an impor-tant entrepôt before the eighteenth century, but political change enhanced its role within the regional economy and thus within long-distance exchange from that time onward.

The second section zooms into Multan, tracing the flows that brought goods into and took them out of the city, connecting the sites and actors and itineraries that constituted the exchange relationship *in toto*. After cotton cloth, indigo and silk emerged by the later eighteenth century as the most important articles of caravan trade in terms of the volume and value of exports, trade-related revenues to the state, and cultural and social significance.[5] A focus on these commodities reveals the capillary-like networks of traders and their agents and brokers who intermediated between peasants, landlords, and local revenue officials in the countryside to move goods. Animal drivers moved them along the arterial routes to major commercial centres, from whence goods were diffused into cities, their environs, and even the most remote steppe or highland through peddler networks. In other words, caravan trade *qua* long-distance exchange actually comprised numerous moments of exchange and different sorts of exchange relationships across a space extending far beyond urban emporia.

The approach of much of this chapter, therefore, is biographical. The biography of goods or things—their economic and social lives—is a method much employed in global history to trace connections and draw comparisons. The final section of this chapter zooms out once again, bringing Punjab and Bengal into focus in a single frame. After *c.* 1750, both regions became more deeply integrated into existing webs of connections, Punjab into caravan trade toward central Eurasia, Bengal into Euro–Asian maritime trade. In both regions, this process was based on commodities, including indigo and raw silk. Yet, despite Punjabi weavers' need for silk yarn, for example, Bengali silk was increasingly difficult to procure at precisely the time that production was increased. This was the result of the East India Company's exclusionary practices and the growing disconnection of the increasingly regionalised economies of south Asia. Punjab and Bengal were parallel worlds of exchange by the early nineteenth century.

The analysis of this last section thus foregrounds a theme running through this chapter and this book. The argument is not that globalisation is a zero-sum game, whereby greater interaction in one arena sucks up people and resources from another, shifting rather than creating added connectivity. Rather, it is that global historians must confront the Other, for in the history of connection can be seen disconnection, in integration also disintegration; inclusion is oftentimes predicated on redrawing the boundaries of exclusion, and comparison does not preclude incommensurability. Oftentimes, however, historical reality might not be best or straightforwardly described by such discursive opposites. On Barak's study of time and temporality in modern Egypt proposes the notion of 'countertempos'—a panoply of alternative temporalities born of the 'discomfort' of the 'homogenous, mechanical time of modernity' associated with the clock as well as 'a disdain for dehumanising European standards of efficiency, linearity, and punctuality.'[6] Just as modern globalisation did not produce universal synchronicity and homogeneity of timekeeping practices, so, too, did it nowhere flatten and universalise space through greater connectivity; to this extent, it is fruitful to think of the multiplicity of counter- or alternative spatialities, their relation, and the agency engendered by or embedded within their articulation.

To see such spatial relations or spatialities, it is necessary to step back from more familiar spaces and exchanges. This does not mean a retreat from the maritime rim of continents to their interiors, or from overseas to overland trade, for example, but means bringing these spheres into dialogue—much as Barak has drawn the time of the clock *qua* railway time, for instance, into an exploration of its countertempos. Punjab was one of the four major centres of cotton-textile production in the subcontinent before *c.* 1850, but has been written out of the global history of Indian textiles because it does not fit into the narrative of global integration via trans-oceanic exchanges, its output having been oriented towards the needs of central Eurasian societies rather than the Atlantic or even the Indian Ocean worlds. Punjabi weavers relied on Bengali silks until they were shut out of these markets. Thereafter they turned to central Asian sources of supply, integrating more deeply into older networks of overland trade at the same time as the still relatively young oceanic connections were multiplying in volume and complexity. These cases serve as a lens for thinking about the spaces and scale of exchange, about the geographic unevenness of connection, and of global histories of disconnection.

Exchanging Places: Cotton Cities

India was responsible for 'clothing the world' and cotton cloth was the most commercially and globally significant of India's exports in the early modern era.[7] Textiles for far-flung markets were woven in workshops along arterial road or river routes, or in the vicinity of coastal ports.[8] Several of the main markets for south Asian textiles were sited around the Indian Ocean. South-east Asian consumption of Indian cloth is best known because of its connection to the spice trade and because European traders found it necessary to purchase textiles to exchange for nutmeg, mace, and cloves. Indian textiles formed the basis of exchange closer to home, as in Burma, but also beyond the Indian Ocean, in China and the Congo. Indian textiles also moved eastwards—to Persia, Egypt, and Ethiopia. The European companies interacted with this system of exchange, transforming it over time. But their trading activities also created new markets and significances for Indian textiles, including the use of cloth as currency in the Atlantic World.

The most well-documented and well-researched centres of textile weaving are those of Bengal, Coromandel, and Gujarat, therefore, for they were integrated into an oceanic system of exchange across the

Indian Ocean and with the Atlantic World.[9] Before the eighteenth century, Indo-European trade expansion scarcely affected Gujarat or Bengal's pattern of trade. The European companies' purchases represented a small proportion of total trade, and there was sufficient spare capacity in the economy to increase production to meet rising demand.[10] But these textiles, shipped to Europe in increasing quantities through the seventeenth and eighteenth centuries, eventually provoked protectionism, imitation, and industrial innovation in Europe, enabling Britain to usurp India as clothier to the world in the nineteenth century.[11] The global history of cotton cloth is thus seen as a lens through which to reinterpret British industrialisation and 'the rise of the West', now conceived in terms of the Great Divergence, with an appreciation of the role of Asian knowledge, technologies, and agency.

Obscured from view in older narratives and more recent globalist retellings is the role of India's fourth major centre of cloth production: Punjab, which was oriented toward overland markets.[12] It cannot have helped that textiles seldom survived the ravages of the subcontinental climate, and that few Punjabi textiles were destined for Europe where they might have been documented, described, imitated, or conserved in the cooler climate of London or Amsterdam, as were textiles from other regions of India.[13] Yet India's textile industry boomed in the seventeenth century, and Punjabi weavers were part of this process, their output expanding because of the boom in demand from Afghan and central Asian markets.[14] Additionally, cloth from Gujarat and Bengal, such as Dacca muslin, was taken to markets in the Eurasian interior, which were thus well integrated with inland and overland markets as well as overseas markets.[15] What, therefore, is revealed by bringing the history of Punjab's textile industry into the picture about the economy of Punjab, of India, and of the early modern world in the first age of globalisation?

The work of Indian historians of various stripes shows that urbanisation was a hallmark of the seventeenth and eighteenth centuries, resulting from the growth of gentry and other intermediate entities benefiting from the inflow of revenue associated with economic expansion.[16] Lying around halfway along the arterial routes from Afghanistan to Hindustan, and along riverine routes to Sindhi ports on the Arabian Sea, Lahore was a primate city of the Mughal Empire, its growth stimulated during its stint as an imperial capital from 1585 and continuing under imperial patronage through the seventeenth century.[17] When the East India Company's Henry Bornford journeyed from Agra to Tatta in March 1639, however, north-west India was still little traversed by Europeans, symptomatic of a myopia that persisted through the eighteenth century. Bornford took the well-worn commercial highway, the Grand Trunk Road, along which weaving and other industries had mushroomed in centres such as Panipat, Thanesar, Samana, Sirihind, Macchiwara, and Bajwara, as well as Sialkot and Multan, which lay slightly further afield, and where artisans turned out *bafta*, a sort of plain coarse cloth, chintz (printed, not painted), napkins, and handkerchiefs.[18] The specialised workshops in these towns funnelled inputs from the surrounding fields in the cotton-cultivating tracts of Punjab, where artisans received advances and worked on a putting-out system (*dadani*).[19] They were frequented by Armenian, Persian, and Multani traders procuring textiles primarily for consumers in central and west Asian markets—to whose distinctive demands weavers had specialised—rather than those of the Indian Ocean world (Fig. 2.1).

Fig. 2.1: Punjabi textile towns and commercial centres

An expansion in the number of urban centres and the size of urban populations does not preclude the experience within particular towns and cities of episodic or prolonged stagnation or decline, however. Lahore's economy was ailing in the second half of the seventeenth century according to the noted French traveller François Bernier, and the receding of the bed of the Ravi in 1663 is attributed as an initial turning point by later observers such as Victor Jacquemont, the French botanist and geologist sent to India in 1828.[20] Whereas Lahore once funnelled trade from across India during the reigns of the Great Mughals, the situation was considerably changed at the end of the eighteenth century.[21] This was part of a wider population decline in Mughal India's primate cities—Delhi, Agra, Lahore. That in turn was the result partly of the vibrancy and growth of existing cities as the capitals of new regional kingdoms that sucked in people from elsewhere, and partly of an increase in the number of smaller urban centres as new towns were established across north India by the growing number of increasingly prosperous gentry elites.[22] Although Lahore eventually served as Ranjit Singh's capital from the beginning of the nineteenth century, the earlier cross-fire between the Mughals, Afghans, and Sikhs eroded its position as the regional economic epicentre.[23] Additionally, these conflicts disturbed and dislocated textile production in towns along the Grand Trunk Road in central and eastern Punjab, though the rise of a new Sikh gentry (analysed in chapter 5) eventually contributed to the revitalisation of princely patronage around the turn of the century.[24] The result was the reduction of traffic through Lahore to 'a trifling commercial intercourse'.[25]

Multan also suffered during the eighteenth-century upheaval but showed signs of recovery towards the end of the eighteenth century, its rising prosperity in part fuelling Ranjit Singh's ambition of absorbing it into the Sikh Empire.[26] It was the home and headquarters of the Multani traders, as well as the kinsmen of Pashtun semi-nomadic pastoralists involved in caravan trade. It was commercially well situated along the roads towards the northerly and southerly passes through the Hindu Kush, and along the banks of the Indus. It was a major mint town and the heart of the Multan *suba*, the political and economic centre of Mughal (after 1526), Durrani (after 1752), and Sikh (after 1818) rule in the region.[27] And it was a spiritual and pilgrimage centre with many Sufi shrines dotted throughout the city, crystallisations of successive waves of perambulations by blessed men from central Eurasia.[28] Thus, the regional centre of gravity shifted to the south-west from Lahore to Multan, which became the central node of caravan trade in south Asia and the centre of growth in Punjab's economy proper over the later eighteenth and early nineteenth century.[29]

What, then, happened to *western* Punjab's trade in cloth to overland markets over the eighteenth century? Relatively little can be gleaned from the Persian- and Punjabi-language materials that are catalogued or otherwise accessible to scholars. And the disinclination to establish a European base or factory in Punjab means there are none of the rich commercial records to be found for Gujarat or Bengal. However, a small tranche of sources from the mid-eighteenth-century Indus delta offers a rare snapshot into the work of weavers in north-west India.[30] In 1757, the Dutch ship *het Pasgeld* docked in Sindh, its captain, Wolphert Abraham Brahe, and a merchant, Nicolaas Mahuij, authoring a report incorporating some description of Sindh's economy and trade.[31] In the following year, a group of English East India Company merchants established a factory on the delta, their correspondence revealing a limited knowledge of local commerce, scarcely incorporating insights from earlier factors and travellers.[32] Unprofitable, the factory was forced to close in 1777–8, but the factors' letters to their masters in Bombay give a good indication of the types of textile bought in the markets linked to caravan trade.[33]

There are signs of famine and scarcity around the time of Nadir Shah's campaigns into north India and then those of the Durrani rulers, the result being reduced quantities and qualities of piece-goods and a rise in prices.[34] There is also clear indication that weavers continued to produce cloth for Persian and central Asian markets, however, as noted by the head (or 'Resident') of the factory, Robert Erskine, upon his submission of musters for consideration in Bombay in 1760.[35] A second muster, sent in October 1760, was accompanied by some 'Remarks on the Scindy Jorees, Chints &c.' of local manufacture, which gives a good indication of the particular dimensions and also the heavy yet coarse weight of the fabrics as reflecting specialisation towards local markets and those in the mountains, deserts, and steppes.[36] Chintz used as coverlets for beds and for dressmaking, as well as plain coarse cloth—

including that commissioned to specific sizes—and finer *adras* and 'bearums' were destined for sale in local markets as well as in Afghanistan, Persia, and towns deeper in the Eurasian interior.[37] Sindh was a tributary province of the Durrani Empire and Afghan power stabilised the regional economy (as the next chapter elaborates). Sindh's markets were well within the orbit of Multani and Afghan merchants, furthermore, the English factors noting trade towards Kandahar and Bukhara.[38] While political upheaval had disturbed commerce between the Indus and the Oxus, it had not entirely destroyed the larger region's pattern of trade.

Once considered inferior, Multani chintz acquired repute in the late seventeenth century and eclipsed its competition; by the mid eighteenth century it was held in high esteem across Hindustan, Rajasthan, and possibly as far as Clive's Bengal.[39] Multan perhaps sucked in weavers from Lahore, for relocation was a common response to changing circumstances in the north-west, as elsewhere in India.[40] Multani textile production encompassed the finest sorts, but the bulk was probably of the type widely 'worn by the common people' of Afghanistan and central Asia, which complemented the little locally woven coarse cloth and chintz of Kabul, for example.[41] By the early nineteenth century, textile production was a major industry in the city, weaving and related occupations representing 42 per cent of establishments.[42] Other important commercial centres surrounded Multan: Dera Ghazi Khan, Dera Ismail Khan, and Bahawalpur, whose weavers were famed for their capability with complex commissions, as well as a small branch of trade in cloth manufactured by Shikarpuri weavers.[43] The area between Ludhiana and Lahore was also still home to the production of plain and unbleached cloth, the finest white cloth fetching four rupees per yard, the coarsest one rupee, some of which was bought by merchants involved in caravan trade.[44]

Punjabi cottons were not only bought by the denizens of Kabul and Kandahar, but also those in more remote areas through the efforts of peddlers, through periodic fairs and markets, or through the tribes' direct trade with weavers.[45] Pastoralists, for example, bought plain coarse cloth of varying fineness or coarseness, which was made into *chogas* (cloaks) or turbans, or else used as blankets or linings, while the apotrapaic and talismanic motifs stamped onto chintzes were worn close to the skin, not least as linings for other garments.[46] Perhaps because of their growing relative contribution to cloth consumption, the spatial organisation of weaving oriented towards overland trade was slowly shifting westward towards the Indo-Afghan frontier. Jhang and surrounding settlements astride the Chenab and Indus also manufactured unwashed white coarse cloth for foreign markets, taking it to larger marts such as Dera Ismail Khan, from whence Afghan traders took 2000 camel-loads of this textile in 1847, for example.[47] A corresponding change was the shift in central Punjab towards the production of finer cloths, a process that accelerated and culminated in the second half of the nineteenth century (to which chapter 8 returns).[48]

Places of Exchange:The Vascular Economy

As the age of global empire turned towards Asia, in 1757 the East India Company established its first territorial and revenue rights in Bengal, the bridgehead of British expansion across the Indian subcontinent but also a critical site in the history of the globalisation of commodity production.[49] After the East India Company's sovereign rights to revenue collection were significantly extended in scope in 1764, it turned to the utilisation of cheap local labour for the cultivation of cash crops— including indigo and mulberry for raw silk—to maximise the repatriation of revenue to Britain.[50] The effect was the transformation of Calcutta into the hub of increasingly global markets, and the remittance of Indian revenues to Britain in the form of commodities such as silk and indigo, produced on plantations of mulberry or indigo newly established in the hinterland.

But the resultant upsurge—what can be called 'proto-globalisation'—should be balanced with an account of what C. A. Bayly termed 'archaic globalisation'.[51] Based on older technologies and trades, ecologies and economies, archaic connections were slowly subordinated to the global capitalist division of labour and information order represented by proto-globalisation, 1750–1850. These processes unfolded unevenly, as archaic connections farthest from the forces of proto-globalisation were slowest to succumb to their impact. Whereas Bengal's economy and trade were transformed rather rapidly and fundamentally after 1757, comparable changes were experienced only a century later in north-west India. Yet the repercussions of the transformations in Company territories *were* felt in north-west India, for Punjab and Sindh's archaic connections stretched not only to central Asia and Persia but also to Gujarat and the Gangetic valley.

The history of certain commodities, not least indigo and silk, is central to analysing the subsuming of archaic to modern forms of globalisation. Yet, *the* global commodity chain traced by scholars is frequently only *a* global commodity chain, foregrounded and given prominence only by ignoring numerous (insufficiently sized?) production centres, trade networks, and markets. Punjab—by the latter half of the nineteenth century, when statistical comparison is possible—was a major site of indigo production, the third largest in the subcontinent, trade in the dye to Afghanistan and central Asia exclusively of Punjabi rather than Bengali manufacture. Punjab's role in global histories of indigo remains marginal, however, reflective of the privileging of particular sites and a reminder that the picture painted in most global history writing is inherently partial.[52] The challenge for global historians is to grapple with this partiality, to challenge the hegemony of particular agents—be they people, networks, spaces, things—in historical production. What, then, does the indigo or silk commodity chain look like in other geographic contexts? What does the coexistence of multiple commodity chains reveal about the first age of global imperialism, *c.* 1760–1850? Piecing together some rather fragmentary evidence, the remainder of this section sketches a response to the first question, the final section then comparing the experience of Punjab and Bengal to examine the second.

Indigo

If Multan's bazaar was the city's heart, then commerce was the lifeblood that circulated through the city, the locality, and beyond. This trade flowed up and down a hierarchy of local settlements, through a series of small village *mandis* (daily or weekly markets) and a few larger *qasbahs* (commercial towns), at the apex of which was Multan, reached by road or river.[53] Generally, primary products—such as grain or indigo—flowed upwards from the village *mandi* to the *qasbah* and onwards to Multan, whereas finished or manufactured goods went downwards from the city to the villages, with seasonal marts at places of pilgrimage springing up at festive times to supply goods to those for whom specialised products of Punjabi or foreign origin were otherwise difficult to obtain.[54] This trade also flowed to and from Afghanistan and central Asia, to the north, and Rajasthan, Hindustan, and Bengal, and out into the Indian Ocean world, to the south. Multan's favourable situation supported its position as the primary entrepôt or nodal point in caravan trade, located on roads towards the major passes through the Hindu Kush, certainly by the mid eighteenth century. Muzaffargarh, Dera Ghazi Khan, and Dera Ismail Khan were secondary nodal points because of their relatively smaller size and more distant location from the epicentre of trade, Multan. Bahawalpur—a semi-autonomous strip-like state in Derajat—was the locus of both buying outside supplies of indigo and despatching its own dye to markets abroad; as such, its commercial and political positions were intertwined.[55]

From Multan's city centre, brokers were dispatched to the outlying *mandis* and *qasbahs* to procure supplies of indigo, of foremost importance to the region's export trade to Afghanistan and central Asia after 1750. The dry indigo cakes bought in village markets were the finished result of a long process of peasant production. It is unclear what sort of landholdings prevailed in the indigo-growing tracts of Derajat before *c.* 1850, but peasant proprietorship and tenant farming for zamindars was not unusual.[56] In Dera Ghazi Khan, around the mid nineteenth century, cultivation was undertaken by the tenants of large landholders and by small peasant proprietors, for whom it was extremely profitable (Rs 3000 on 400 acres, according to one estimate), rather than by non-proprietary peasants, for whom the tax burden and the food risk in case of crop failure (from substituting grain with indigo) was immense.[57]

Brokers negotiated between buyers and sellers in the countryside on the basis of indigo quality, receiving around four rupees per maund (*c.* 37 kg) of indigo, with local officials also taking a tax of anything from less than a rupee to four rupees a maund.[58] They broke up and examined the dried indigo, looking for cakes unadulterated with silica or other impurities and showing a vivid violet colour throughout, either offering a lower price if unsatisfied or taking a greater quantity if desired.[59] Quality differences, however, were welcome and integral to the servicing of foreign demand. Over time, Dera Ghazi Khan and

Multan had specialised in the production of different sorts of indigo. Because the former was on the western side of the Indus, Afghan traders were spared the expense of the river crossing and additional ferry tolls, as well as the city tax or octroi (*chungi*) payable in Multan or Muzaffargarh. Dye manufacturers in Dera Ghazi Khan made the most of this advantage, producing coarser but cheaper indigo.[60] Multan and Muzaffargarh, however, were famous for their finer indigo—the greater expense of which was enough to render insignificant the additional cost of carrying the dyestuff out of the cities and across the Chenab and Indus.[61]

Across the indigo-producing tracts, indigo surpluses were sent from villages to towns to trade entrepôts.[62] With a mark-up of as much as 30 per cent in the larger towns, Afghan traders cut out some of the middlemen, purchasing indigo directly themselves or through their own agents from *mandis* in the indigo districts.[63] In the latter half of the nineteenth century, if not earlier, such 'agents' were working to procure supplies for several firms of traders. In the reign of Sher Ali Khan of Afghanistan (r. 1863–6, 1868–79), for example, Dada Sher Kabuli purchased indigo in Multan for sale in Kabul, for sale to agents of the firm of Mian Illahi Bakhsh in Tashkurghan, and for sale to firms trading towards Bukhara.[64] Upon arrival in the bazaars of Kabul, Kandahar, and Bukhara, Afghan traders deposited the indigo with brokers, who took a few rupees per maund successfully sold.[65] In Bukhara and other parts of central Asia, the use of and trade in dyestuffs and finished textiles—as well as weaving—were controlled along ethnic lines. Much as Hindus dyers (*rangrez*) eschewed both blue and dyeing with indigo in north India, which was the responsibility in Punjab of the Muslim *lilari*s (indigo dyers), so Bukharan Jews—who were discriminated against and distinguished by prescriptions upon their dress and restrictions on their movements—were responsible for handling and dyeing with indigo.[66]

Silk

Not far from the moneymen and merchants in the heart of Multan, in a series of side streets off from the main arteries through the bazaar perhaps, were the weavers' workshops, 610 in total, of which most turned cotton yarn into cloth, while 250 were specialist silk-weaving establishments. This physical proximity reflected a relationship, albeit an asymmetric one, between the fortunes of the trader-financiers, who secured supplies of silk yarn, and the weavers, who often worked to a 'putting-out' system to supply the traders with wares for overland, overseas, regional, and local markets. Underlying this relationship was the weavers' remoteness from the silk-producing peasants: without commercial-scale sericulture in the region, north-west India's weavers relied increasingly over the eighteenth and nineteenth centuries on silk supplies from central Asia.

Although sold as 'Bukharan', 'Samarkandi', and 'Khorasani', such descriptors disguised the rural origins of most yarns, for silkworm rearing—if not also the processing of cocoons into thread—was often the work of peasants in the environs of these cities or wherever there was water in the countryside of the oasis states.[67] From these dispersed sites, silk was despatched to entrepôts such as Bukhara, the principal depot of the trade, as well as Samarkand and Herat.[68] These centres also received and re-exported raw silks from more distant regions such as Kashgar, Khotan, and Yarkand in the east, and vice versa, with Yarkand silks sometimes including yarns from farther west. Khorasani silks included the output of Herat, Khulm, Meshed, Nishapur, Qarshi, and Yazd, for example.[69] Silk was also produced in Balkh around Mazar-i-Sharif, some most likely sent north to Bukhara, some south towards Kabul and Multan.[70]

From their city-centre shops, the heads of the Punjabi merchant houses instructed their agents and intermediaries to procure silk for weavers from such markets in central Asia.[71] The agents then transported this merchandise towards India, selling it to merchants who negotiated the price with the assistance of local brokers (*dalals*), often of the Hindu Khatri caste, the same caste as the Multani and Shikarpuri traders, if not their kinsmen.[72] For their market knowledge and assistance, these brokers earned a modest commission. Alternatively, central Asian peasants sold their yarn, perhaps with the payment of an advance, to Afghan or Indian agents, who transported the merchandise to Multan and other entrepôts, where it was left with the *dalals*.[73] In either case, the absence of insurance reflected the extent of risk associated with the overland routes, rather than the want of financial instruments or institutions. The persistence of overland trade in spite of such risk, in turn, suggests its great value and profitability.[74]

Undyed, and often covered in some sort of size to add weight to increase the sale price, the silk skeins were transported to India, and cleaned, dyed, and woven as needed. The brokers sold the silk to merchants, who then sent it to carders and winders (*phat-pheras*) working either for the merchants or for themselves. Winding created three reels: the fine or regular thread was twisted to form warp threads (*tani*), another less fine thread was used for weft (*vana* and *peta*), and the coarse refuse could be used for embroidery (*kachar*).[75] The silk would then go to dyers (*rangrez*) and weavers based either in these cities or in towns and villages further afield.[76] Often, raw silk was manufactured into thread in the nodal towns or entrepôts and from thence re-exported for the use of weavers: Multan was home to forty-five thread sellers, although Bahawalpuri, Sindhi, and Kutchi weavers received silk thread from Shikarpur, for example.[77]

In the complexity of minutiae, therefore, is the world of connections and exchanges constituting caravan trade, extending far beyond the nodal points of trade and consisting of numerous relationships between a diverse range of actors. The long-distance trade in indigo connected peasants and dye manufacturers with local rulers and urban merchants, Afghan and Indian traders with distributors and dyers in central Asia, and society's most marginalised with the masses and elites. The silk trade, similarly, brought the business of trade together with that of credit and finance, merchants and their intermediaries with artisans, and the power of sedentary population centres with dispersed and mobile labour. On the one hand, the logic for trade was partly cultural rather than economic, driven by the value that people placed on things of particular provenance. On the other hand, trade was also a calculus of anticipated revenue and profit, cost and risk dictating where to procure and where to sell goods. Thus, for western Punjabi artisans, for example, what were the alternatives to silk yarns from central Asia, if any?

Parallel Exchanges: Punjab and Bengal After c. 1750

From their city-centre shops, Multan's merchant-moneymen orchestrated a network of agents that stretched across Asia. Bringing goods for sale, the junior agents would plough their profits into the local market as loans, returning to their masters on the subcontinent upon receipt of payment of principals and interest.[78] For the Punjabi weaver, reliant on these agents abroad for supplies, silks from the four corners of the compass were nevertheless within reach. Punjabi traders were active in silk-producing regions within Kashmir and Persia, as well as small-scale production in Afghanistan and Sindh. And, yet, Punjabi merchants bought little of these silks, so that Punjabi weavers mostly made use of central Asian yarns.[79]

Punjabi, Multani, and Sindhi merchants were also active at the ports of Surat and Bombay, and moved goods towards the south by road as well as on country boats, with European sources revealing that the Multanis received 'large annual consignments from Bengal' while also having 'agents at Surat and Bombay'.[80] Bengal was indeed the most proximate major silk-producing centre to Punjab, where peasant producers were connected by two routes to Punjabi and Gujarati weavers, one by sea, the other cross-country.[81] The overland networks stretched from the Indus to the Ganges delta, and comprised Hindu Khatri commercial houses with whom merchants could transact or raise funds, complementing (or competing with) the networks of Gujaratis, as well as individual agents acting for traders from Lahore, Multan, and other north Indian centres involved in the cross-country silk trade from Bengal before c. 1800.[82]

Agents made their purchases in the important silk centre of Kasimbazar as well as other lesser centres further afield. Those working for the Lahore weavers bought silk worth Rs 300,000 in Kasimbazar in March 1731, for example, roughly a third of the Rs 980,000 of combined annual exports by the English and Dutch companies.[83] Between 1775 and 1777, shortly after the severe famine in Bengal, 12,568 maunds of silk were transported to Mirzapur—a redistribution centre—and therefrom to destinations further northwards and westwards. From Mirzapur, the next largest locales for imports of Bengal silk were Lahore (3,851 maunds) and Multan (1,649 maunds), the significance of Punjabi merchants attested in Dutch sources.[84] The question, therefore, is when and why the use of Bengal silk was supplanted, in absolute or relative terms, by central Asian yarn in the Punjabi workshops.

Bengali silk imports into Punjab remained noticeably large as late as the 1760s and 1770s. But this trade was to fall alongside the growth of

British power.[85] From the 1760s, the Company was able to take advantage of its territorial and revenue rights by exerting its influence upon the silk economy of Bengal, one element of which was the inducement of 'experts' to 'improve' silk manufacture.[86] The effect of the Maratha raids of the 1740s and 1750s and a famine in Bengal in 1770, however, was depopulation, which disrupted the labour-intensive process of silkworm-rearing in eastern India.[87] The effects of this problem were ameliorated through the policy of peasant inducement, whereby the Company government lowered rents and offered cash advances (*taqavi*). Yet war in Maratha territories and Punjab in the closing decades of the century disrupted and depressed the north-westward trade even as production was stabilised in Bengal.[88]

British policy also affected the cross-country trade. Amongst the merchants in Benares in 1787, were 'Sundry Merchants of Kabul, Punjaub and Multan', who wrote to the Company's Resident for fairer treatment with respect to the duties charged on their raw silk and silk-cloth trade towards the west, and on their return cargoes of shawls.[89] Their petition was put in the hands of 'Mohamed Azeem [...] our Gomustah or Agent', and survives appended to a number of trade-related returns and statements from the Company's government at Fort William in Calcutta.[90] Typical of an increasing number of petitions lodged at this time, it reflects the new regime's failure to understand the complex political economy of precolonial north India: namely, that different trading communities paid different duties and rates according to their status and antiquity at various courts.[91] Instead, the Company attempted to 'free' trade and eliminate perquisites and privileges in what Sudipta Sen has called the 'Permanent Settlement of marketplaces [...] the other prong of the Permanent Settlement of revenue' that is much better known.[92]

Other returns illustrate the size of the raw-silk trade. Bengal's most extensively exported raw silks were varieties called 'Perryah, Seh Nukhee, Kutcher' to the value of Rs 468,716 (4,253 maunds), followed by 'Lahoree' of two qualities, worth Rs 127,095 (353 maunds) and Rs 9,909 (45 maunds), respectively.[93] Even if 'Lahoree' designated the destination of the silk, rather than the sort of silk most commonly purchased for the Punjab market, the trade was still relatively small. Bengal's exports, furthermore, went westward to Sarangpur and

Bundelkand, as well as north-westward to Braj and Multan.[94] The meagre trade of over half a million rupees was probably divided amongst these commercial centres. Despite some signs of overland trade recovering and widening in the 1790s, Punjabi merchants' purchases in Kasimbazar did not expand beyond the pre-1757 peak, causing the contribution of Bengal silk to the fulfilment of north-west Indian demand to dwindle, a trend which continued into the nineteenth century.[95]

But this contraction also came as a consequence of the Company's exercise of its monopsony power over the silk market and the silk-producing peasants (*ryots*).[96] Although the Company was well aware of Bengal's silk trade with Punjab, and that it could use such markets to offload waste silk, officials chose not to enter this trade.[97] This was symptomatic of the Company's wider disinterest in developing inland trade after the acquisition of *diwani* rights in 1765, for fear of Company-sanctioned activity coming under fire as an illegal abuse of sovereign rights.[98] This is also symptomatic of the ways in which the British started to cut off or drive out Asian producers, traders, and financiers.[99] Between the 1750s and 1760s, Company servants evicted local traders and used other intrusive measures to restrict the export of silk from Bengal.[100]

From the observations in 1772 of Thomas Pattle, the Company's commercial resident in Bauleah, north of Calcutta, it appears that agents were allowed to use contracts (*machulkas*) with the peasant producers to obtain the types of silk desired by the Company. These agents were responsible for collecting the silk, enforcing contracts, and punishing defaulting peasants.[101] Additionally, they tried to thwart Punjabi and Gujarati merchants' procurement of silk, believing it detrimental to the activities of the Company.[102] A range of practices continued through to the 1830s, their effect being to mop up the sorts of silk used by local weavers in Bengal, while depriving other traders of raw silk.[103] By these means, Punjabi merchants were rarely able to purchase the peasants' silk in Bengal or the waste silk unwanted by the Company, with scarcely any yarn sent by road from Kasimbazar or Mirzapur to Multan through to the 1830s and 1840s.[104]

Controlling the supply of silk in Bengal was the means of obtaining the type of silk desired in Europe, and some of what was taken away from overland traders in Calcutta was made available through the Company's export trade to Bombay.[105] The Bombay Government's Commercial Proceedings record all registered trade each year from May to the following April through Bombay and Surat and, later, other coastal and inland customs houses throughout the Bombay Presidency. Of course, some traders evaded customs controls, but the statistics show much of what was flowing from the Bay of Bengal to western India (Fig. 2.2).[106] Of the silk trade from Bengal, Bombay's share already outstripped that of Surat at the beginning of the nineteenth century; after 1814–15, the silk trade to Surat was routed through Bombay.[107] From 1800 to 1810, the Company's silk industry in Bengal shrank at an average rate of 2 per cent per annum, associated with the disruption to Britain's export trade in Europe as a result of the Napoleonic Wars.[108] Silk was said to have been stockpiled in the Company's warehouses in London, but the Bombay trade returns show that the Company also offloaded stocks in western India, with imports into Bombay peaking at Rs 2,384,072 in 1812–13.

Fig. 2.2: Value of Bombay raw silk imports, 1801–2 to 1848–9

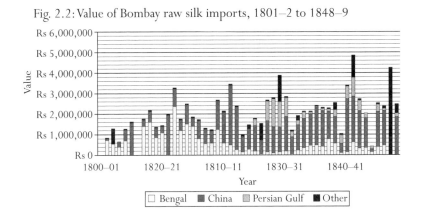

With the Company's trade monopoly to Europe opened at that time, and the worst of the wars over, Bengal's silk trade to Bombay dwindled to less than half a million rupees. Alongside the growing import of Persian silk, which was larger than the Calcutta trade from 1825, Chinese silk steadily took the place of Bengal silk and dominated the markets on the western coast. Initially much more expensive than Bengal silk—at least around *c.* 1800—Chinese raw-silk prices fell much faster than Bengal prices, so that the price differential between the yarns was negligible by mid century.[109] Although the Nanking Treaty (1842) terminated Qing imperial restrictions on the silk trade, thereby initiating the rapid increase in silk exports, China overtook Bengal in the import and re-export trade at Bombay as early as the 1820s. This dominance was driven by increasing availability and affordability, trends that culminated in the second half of the nineteenth century (as shown in chapter 8).

Fig. 2.3: Value of Bombay re-exports of raw silk

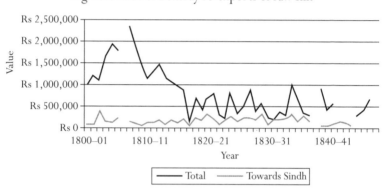

Through their agents at Bombay and Surat, the Multanis ought to have been able to procure silk for the weavers in Punjab. Notwithstanding transport costs from Bombay to Multan, which were easily spread across such a valuable cargo, Bengal silks were considerably cheaper by mid century than those from central Asia.[110] But the internal or overland trade returns show little sign of trade from the west coast towards Punjab. On the one hand, this may reflect that the destinations of such trade were not revealed or recorded accurately. On the other hand, there is scarcely any silk trade through the hinterland: only Rs 11,400 through the 'Maratha Country' in 1811–12, for example.[111] Weaving in this region was both highly urbanised and concentrated along the coast, so it is unsurprising that silk shipments were distributed before the bullock-carts reached very far into the hinterland.[112] Aside from the recorded trade with Punjab, there was a fairly sizeable trade with what was categorised as 'Cutch and Scinde' (Fig. 2.3). Most of this rather meagre trade was for Kutch rather than Sindh, however, suggesting a negligible or non-existent onward trade to Punjab.[113] To this can be added the ability of Sindhi weavers to absorb most of the imports, as well as the difficulty of navigating the Indus and the extent of tariffs en route towards Multan and Bahawalpur, discouraging onward trade from the lower reaches of the Indus toward Punjab.[114] Unsurprisingly, therefore, Bahawalpuri weavers seen working with small shipments of silk from Bombay by British Indian agents in 1837—Chinese and Bengal silk—could have coped with double the amount of yarn.[115]

Starved of Bengal silk from the Ganges entrepôts as well as Bombay, where were the traders of north-west India to turn before 1850? From central Asia came 'one of the most important branches of the import trade' by the 1830s, its silk appearing to be '[an] article [...] of a superior description', at least to the weavers and silk-cloth wearers of Punjab.[116] While the yarns of Bukhara and Herat might have supplemented those of Bengal before *c.* 1800, the scale of the import trade across the Hindu Kush by the 1830s and 1840s seems almost to match the import from Bengal to Punjab in the 1770s, before the introduction of exclusionary practices.[117] Whether or not central Asian peasant-silk exports to Punjab had expanded after 1750, it is undoubted that it was of unprecedented *relative* importance by 1850. Until the establishment of railways connecting Multan and Lahore with Karachi and Bombay, Bukharan silks would remain the pre-eminent and the preferred source of silk on looms throughout Punjab.

Conclusion

The chaos of the 'Oriental bazaar' is a hardy trope in Orientalist depictions of Asia and the Levant.[118] Yet, to return to the descriptions that opened and have been laced through this chapter, Multan and other urban centres across the Indo-Islamicate world were not disorderly, for a logic of spatial organisation was at work in the location of particular activities and communities in particular neighbourhoods in proximity to—or at a distance from—others. Another logic of spatial organisation, one conventionally summarised as the theory of central places, ordered the relation of Multan with secondary urban centres and other settlements down to the level of villages. Trade had its own supply-side logic of specialisation and demand-side logic of taste and preference. Thus, whether at the level of long-distance trade or a sale made in the bazaar, economic exchange was an intricate human opera composed of various ordered but complex relationships between a diverse body of actors.[119] At the same time, the metaphor of the body employed throughout this chapter serves to demonstrate how this complexity was ordered into a whole. To overlook the capillary-like networks of distribution from, or funnelling of goods to, cities such as Multan, for example, is to overlook the integrity of long-distance exchange within larger economic spaces.

Of course, the material presented in this chapter captures only some of the multitude of different exchanges integral to caravan trade. The journey of indigo from the village level to ever-larger urban centres for onward trade or use by dyers is probably akin to that of raw or partly processed cotton for re-export or use by weavers, as well as other primary products, such as grain. Fruit was grown both in orchards surrounding cities in the oasis towns but also deeper in the country-side. The movement of such comestible and perishable produce was comparable but also contrasted with that of non-comestible (indigo) or less perishable (grain) primary products.[120] The channelling of silk from dispersed production sites to urban centres for local use and long-distance trade is comparable to other productions of (semi-) nomadic or dispersed populations, such as animal skins, fats, and dairy products, for example. But the generalisability of these exchange relationships is limited, especially in light of a number of goods whose production, and thus trade, was strictly controlled. In south Asia, salt was so essential that it was often subject to royal monopoly or farmed out as a perquisite in the delegation of royal power, for example.[121] The salt mines of the trans-Indus tracts supplied local markets as well as those in Kashmir and Afghanistan, the salt exchanged for ghee.[122] In Iran, the turquoise mines of Nishapur were brought under crown land (*khassa*) and bureaucratic regulation—so important were the revenues from turquoise, as Arash Khazeni has revealed in a study of tributary exchange of turquoise in early modern Asia. The consequence was a lower degree of intermediation, with a closer alliance of both state officials and state-appointed merchants (most probably Armenians in the case of turquoise) on the one hand, and of merchants with buyers for whom orders were fulfilled, on the other.[123] Thus, although urban–rural marketing and distribution networks characterising the indigo or silk trade capture the nature of a wide range of exchanges of such less-specialised goods, there was a multiplicity—rather than a singularity—of forms of exchange.

Shopping, furthermore, is hardly apposite to describe how most people procured most of the things they needed or wanted, as material in this chapter has shown. In the first place, even in the bazaar, shops carried out wholesale as well as retail functions. Second, exchange frequently involved barter rather than the use of commodity money, both in towns and in the countryside. This was neither the consequence of shortages of specie nor of constraints on turning goods into liquidity: even well-capitalised merchants with access to specie exchanged cotton or shawls for silk, rather than coin or bills of exchange, or collected debts in money, grain, or pawned items.[124] Rather, this was deliberate, for peasants were paid in cash for certain goods in certain locales—such as silk cocoons in urban bazaars. This was a 'closed' and specialised market, unlike the handling by peddlers of trade in a wide range of other goods, and the transacting in kind by nomads of their livestock (rams, sheep, camels, ponies, horses) for products from sedentary areas.[125] While historians have vigorously ousted the peddler from the history of early modern Asian trade, he was in fact integral to the disbursement of goods to the lowest and remotest reaches of village or steppe society. His portfolio of goods often included the things channelled through networks of caravan trade at the behest of portfolio capitalists; these modes of exchange were overlapping. The peddler, moreover, was capable of harnessing changing circumstances to capitalise and organise his operations within an agency structure, acting as principal or agent (an instance of this historical process from *c*. 1750 to *c*. 1900 is documented in detail in chapter 4).

But the procurement of things was also a conversation, even where it was intermediated by traders who relayed information about specific sizes of cloth or patterns required, for instance. Multani printers stamped chintzes for overland markets in winter, presumably to coincide with the caravans' arrival around the trans-Indus marts, the traders then commissioning them to produce what was in fashion in

Afghanistan and central Asia—which were large flower patterns in mid-1830s Kabul, for example.[126] Once the merchants had returned to Kabul or Kandahar in the spring, Multani printers turned to designs and patterns suited to the north Indian and Rajasthani markets (yellow backgrounds being favoured in the later 1830s, according to one source).[127] The 'amplitude' of such conversations depended on whether merchants or other actors were conveying the desires of particular buyers, or of the market at large.[128] As Gagan Sood has highlighted, traders also sweetened their deals by despatching gifts to their patrons and clients as a way of bringing pleasure and longevity to these conversations.[129] In these respects, caravan trade was a conduit for various sorts of information flows (some of which are analysed in detail in chapter 7). More proximately, gentry in towns might intervene (repeatedly) as artisans undertook to realise a commission, transforming foreign materials into a unique piece (the early moderns' desire for differentiation of their individual selves from others through the goods they possessed is explored in chapter 5).[130]

The metaphor of the body employed in this chapter is also productive because it hazards against the mapping of globalisation onto the vitality of the local, regional, or global economy, for the intensification of global connection centring on such sites as Bengal was as much a healthy development as a sign of ill-health. In *Rulers, Townsmen and Bazaars*, Bayly hinted at a phenomenon analysed more closely in this chapter: 'what is striking is the rise of rich overland trade routes to compensate for the clogging of the great Mughal arteries.' This points to the increasingly bloated successor states that regionalised economic prosperity—at the expense of long-distance exchange—along the course of the Ganges–Yamuna across north India, as well as the displacement of established trading groups by 'families drawn from [local] rural commercial communities'.[131] The comparison to the recent economic boom and clogging of the coastal rimlands—the consequence of decades of China's support for trade-oriented production for world markets, reported by multinationals such as HP in the introduction to this book—is striking.

But this process was also the consequence of the deliberate severing of Bengal's reoriented economy from north India under Company rule; the deliberate if distant outcome of the exertion of colonial agency. By the close of the eighteenth century, Bengal was no longer a significant source of yarn for the looms in Multan and other centres, which were instead supplied with silk from central Asia. Both Bengal and Punjab grew but grew apart after 1750. In the century between the conquest of the Company's first territories in Bengal in 1757, and the completion of Punjab's annexation into British India in 1849, the indigo and silk economies of the two regions coexisted without competing or coalescing. With proto-globalisation and the upsurge in global connections during the first age of global imperialism came interregional disconnection and disintegration on the one hand, and an entrenchment of archaic connections on the other. The exchanges excavated in this chapter thus disturb the neat geographies of much recent work on global connections while using comparison to illuminate disconnection and disintegration.

Within this process Multan, rather than Lahore, became the central node of the economy of caravan trade at the southern end of the circuit. Multan and the networks of caravan trade played a pivotal role in the rise of the Durrani Empire, creating a new political and economic order that knitted north-west India, Afghanistan, and central Eurasia together more tightly. Although the exchanges examined in this chapter were relatively pacific, caravan trade was vitally important to the production of hard power and political authority in south Asia. The next chapter thus examines the relationship of highly mobile pastoralists and their animals to the markets for force of arms. Just as Bengal was the bridgehead of British expansion, so was Multan—home to Ahmad Shah's kinsmen and to financiers supportive of the establishment of political order—simultaneously the stepping stone of Afghan empire-building in north-west India.

3

POWER

In the desiccated and mountainous borderlands between Iran and India, the 'tribal breakout' of the Hotaki (Ghilzai) tribes in 1717 set in motion the process that led to the toppling of *de facto* Safavid rule in 1722, the rise to power of Nadir Shah of the Afshar tribe by 1738, and his campaigns into the Mughal domains with the support of the Abdali (Durrani) tribes in 1738–9. The campaign resulted in the ransacking of Mughal cities and their coffers of treasure—including the peacock throne and the Koh-i-Noor diamond—worth tens of millions of rupees, and the claiming of *de jure* sovereignty over the swathe of territory from Iran to the Mughal domains. A second tribal breakout commenced following Nadir Shah's assassination in 1747 as his former cavalry commander, Ahmad Shah Abdali, set about uniting the various Abdali tribes to launch his own campaigns into the Mughal Empire. Six successful campaigns from 1747–8 until Ahmad Shah's death in 1772 not only resulted in the transferring of north Indian treasure—taken either as plunder or as tribute—into Afghan hands, but also the ceding of the Mughal provinces (*subas*) of Lahore and Multan, so that liquidity, land, and its revenues now circulated within a growing Durrani Empire.[1]

Unsurprisingly, the Afsharid and Durrani raids have been blamed for accelerating the waning of Mughal power and, in turn, the instability associated with imperial fragmentation. In the 1880s, events of over a century earlier were still remembered in Punjabi oral tradition, two of which were recorded in *Panjab Notes and Queries*, a monthly magazine that collated contributors' pleas for information and offers of eclectic local knowledge.[2] In these rhymes, cotton and cotton cloth become metaphors for life and livelihood in Punjab, for the efflorescence and expansion during the imperial 'golden age' until Aurangzeb's death, and for the 'dark age' under the incompetent and impotent Mughal lineage whose weakness allowed Nadir to ravage the empire. Scholars have steadily interrogated the notion of eighteenth-century turbulence. The consensus that has emerged since the late 1970s has instead emphasised gradual transfers of power away from the centre, with evidence of shifting pockets of regionally centred prosperity.[3] Punjab, however, remains associated with disorder and decline.[4] Precisely because it was on the campaign route towards the capital and the battleground between first the Mughals and Sikhs and Afghans, and then the Afghans and Sikhs, as well as between various Sikh rulers, the province continues to be seen as a particularly fractious space, stability arriving only after Ranjit Singh's unification of the territories from Peshawar to Delhi and the cessation of these conflicts.[5] The vernacular rhymes of Punjabis committed to paper in the 1880s seem to give credence to these views. But with what accuracy do these ditties capture changes in the economy and the extent of trade in the eighteenth century? And were political factors—whether the weakness of the Mughal centre or the disturbances brought by the Afsharid and Durrani raids—really responsible for the transformations that took place?

At the heart of these issues is power and its relationship to warfare and violence on the one hand, and the functioning of state authority and economic management on the other. This chapter first examines power by looking at collectives and their relationship to violence.[6] Taking, as a point of departure, the fact that early modern states were unable to monopolise violence, the first part of this chapter foregrounds the commonplace nature of (un)armed conflict and the prevalence of patrons and clients in 'markets' for violence in the early modern world. By conceiving the caravans as a collection of circuits and networks as well as groups of people involved in trade and transhumance, the analysis in this chapter shows the caravans as an actor within these markets. By harnessing control over these networks of organised violence—as Ahmad Shah succeeded in doing, for example—it was possible to challenge the power of imperial states to establish an alternative authority. The second half of this chapter then turns, reflexively, to examine how new rulers supported long-distance trade and economic prosperity in the eighteenth century, patronising production and trade while pumping liquidity seized during 'tribal breakout' into the local economy to secure streams of revenue from the land in the longer term. A seemingly unlikely focal point for the examination of these issues, caravan trade was thus both integral to the exercise of (hard) power and implicated deeply within its networks, which stretched from the Indian subcontinent to central Asia and Iran. At the same time, the analysis also points towards the experience of regional economic prosperity from western Punjab towards central Asia.

The Caravan Circuit and Its Economies of Violence

Violence is a subject treated with some trepidation by historians of the premodern Islamicate world, the preference in recent decades having been to emphasise harmony, peace, and stability.[7] Violence was carefully controlled by the state and orchestrated within a strict normative framework, scholars seem to suggest. The notion of non-state or interpersonal violence is scarcely addressed at all. This picture is so at odds with how historians have more recently come to understand the state and violence in early modern Europe, that Asia looks like a sort of utopia: in replacing the fancy of decadent and despotic Oriental potentates ruling over a chaotic and conflict-ridden East, historians have produced—in its mirror image—an alternative fantasy of the powerful but benevolent state.[8]

The state's monopoly over violence, as Janice E. Thomson argues, is 'neither timeless nor natural' but of relatively recent genesis.[9] Within European states, the loci of violence were overlapping and diffuse. They ranged from state armies, private armies of regional grandees or rival claimants to royal power, to those rural or urban militias, police forces, and gangs of armed men supporting fiscal agents responsible for the maintenance of law and order, for example, but also those highwaymen, outlaws, and bandits who challenged local or larger sources of authority. In other words, there were numerous outlets for men of arms, with competing pools of demand only making more complex the tangle of conflict and its causes. But the (re)sources of organised violence were also extraterritorial and transnational in the premodern period, something exploited and thus expanded by states themselves. On the one hand, there were those whose activities were deemed legitimate (by their own sovereigns, if not others), namely merchants and mercantile companies or privateers.[10] On the other hand, were those deemed illegitimate: smugglers, pirates, and freebooters. Others, such as mercenaries, fell into either category, depending on who was employing them.

Because the state was initially incapable of controlling violence and violent men in the extraterritorial realm, a chaos of 'unintended consequences' developed, such as mercenaries dragging their home states into war with foreign powers. The process of territorialising these sources of violence was thus crucially linked to the establishment of modern forms of state power, itself hinging on the state's deployment of force beyond its borders, Thomson shows. In tandem, the state was also compelled to demarketise violence so that the use of violence fell within the political rather than the economic realm of authority. Only in the course of the nineteenth century, therefore, did the territorially bounded state rather than the (potentially) unbounded market come to control and almost monopolise violence; almost, because extraterritorial violence accompanying smuggling—as Eric Tagliacozzo argues in the case of colonial south-east Asia, for instance—served as a form of resistance to state power and demonstrated the state's inability to wholly monopolise violence.[11] More recently, the resurgence or growth of private violence in the international sphere—the activities of pirates, bandits, mercenaries—highlights the incompleteness and fragility of even the modern state's control of men of arms.[12]

The picture beginning to emerge of the Levant and Islamicate Asia from analyses of the state and power in relation to politics—rather than violence, per se—is broadly similar. Within the Mughal and Ottoman empires, and probably also their Safavid and Uzbek counterparts, the topography of power was more contested in their so-called 'golden ages' than previously believed. It became lumpier still from the late seventeenth through the eighteenth century as part of the renegotiation of obligations—fiscal and military, in particular—

between imperial centres and existing or newly emergent power holders in the provinces and localities.[13] If centralised authority was always more of an intention than a fact in the premodern period, the state's control of violence only reached at but never remotely constituted a monopoly. Its grip loosened as it ceased to be the major or most lucrative source of employment for men of arms in the more decentralised landscape of the long eighteenth century—as scholars focussing on large households within the Ottoman and Mughal empires have begun to tease out.[14]

Dirk Kolff's rich reconstruction of the north Indian market for military labour throws into relief the role of the peasantry in challenging central authority: so well armed and numerous were peasants that it was necessary either to co-opt and channel their martial services towards the needs of the state through *naukari* (paid service) on imperial campaigns, or else to extinguish their resistance altogether by razing their villages, executions, and sale into slavery.[15] In elaborating the workings of this massive commercialisation of military manpower, Jos Gommans has highlighted the centrality of economic rationality and the transactional nature of violence.[16] Upon entering service, peasants were able to exercise some degree of choice. Deciding for whom to fight was a choice about allocating embodied technologies and techniques of physical violence to the highest bidder. Deciding to switch sides during battle reflected the dynamic nature of strategic choice, this recalculation of the odds motivated not only by a concern for personal safety but for securing a share in the spoils of war, the booty divided amongst the victorious. Decentralisation surely made this calculation more complex, as the imperial centre and its allies were no longer the default best bet for servicemen. At the same time, the opportunities for *naukari* became both more numerous and more diverse in nature, much as in Europe.

In an ambitious exploration of political violence in Mughal India, Gommans has focussed on the upper echelon of imperial servicemen (*mansabdars*) to argue—following Norbert Elias' famous thesis—that the restless martial *ghazi* (raider-warrior) was inculcated into the *mirza*'s (prince's) world of courtly refinement, where bloodlust was supplanted by diplomacy and ritualised relations.[17] Yet, the *mansabdari* was but a thin slice of the imperial political elite as a whole, beneath which were a vast number of military entrepreneurs and men of arms. Such men were not civilised into the court but most likely serviced the violent instincts of courtiers, or else were in the service of other Indian elites, political or commercial. 'Civilization', as Stuart Carroll writes of early modern France in a rebuttal of Elias' work, was fundamentally 'built on violence'.[18] Courtly ritual and intrigue did not replace martial violence; rather, the two continued to exist interdependently. Blood feud and vendetta persisted through the Renaissance into the eighteenth century as the warrior class was not so much pacified as redeployed by the state, its provision of violence thus institutionalised into the polity itself.[19]

The notion of an economy of violence aims to foreground such relations. It refers to the relationship of violence to the push of material hardship or the pull of material reward, in some cases taking place on the market as the services of armed men are offered in exchange for cash or a share of plunder. More precisely, there were distinct economies of violence, each specialised in a particular sort of exchange, albeit often overlapping in terms of skills or personnel: the market for military labour that sprung up each campaign season, the market for protection services, and so forth.[20] In other contexts, historians have unearthed details of economies not discussed in this chapter: men trained in Chinese martial arts who could be hired to maim or kill, soldiers outfitted in Ming imperial uniforms brandishing imperial weapons who could take to the streets to trade violence for cash.[21] In south and central Asia, likewise, wrestlers performing in Kabul or Delhi could conceivably have offered their services for less entertaining ends, but the lack of ready evidence means this can be no more than suggestive speculation.

Whatever the impossibility (and the danger) of disarming Indian society, late-Mughal India and its neighbours were likely neither more lawless nor more violent than other areas of the early modern world, and its rulers seem to have faced comparable problems of controlling the multiple loci of violence to exercise their power.[22] In turn, the complexity and place of violence within society were more profound than historians of south Asia have lately admitted, for a wide array of persons forged a livelihood and found profit in violence (some of whom appear in what follows). In starting to flesh out this picture, the extraterritorial and transnational dimensions of violence in south Asia deserve further attention. In claiming universal sovereignty, the rulers of the terraqueous Mughal, Ottoman, and Safavid empires also projected their sovereignty into the Indian Ocean, more often in rhetorical or legal rather than effective terms.[23] The Mughals were typical of early modern rulers in devolving the use of violence in the protection and maintenance of their sovereign interests. What, then, of (organised) violence around or beyond the empire's landward borders? And, what roles did caravan trade play within these markets for violence?

Princes and Bandits

From the open plains to the narrow passes through the Hindu Kush, the caravans were conspicuous, as much a target for the state's fiscal officers as for men who turned to highway robbery and banditry. A prince's dispensation of justice in the world of trade was twofold. First, in the levying of taxes, the total burden of which was not to be so heavy as to unduly squeeze traders.[24] In practice, the actual burden of taxation depended on the actions of various authorities—not only the state's tax and customs collectors, but also those acting on behalf of local lords, for instance—each of whom might attempt to skim merchants above what they had been permitted to collect as their perquisite.[25] Over time, not least as the state renegotiated its power *vis-à-vis* a range of provincial or sub-imperial elites over the long eighteenth century, the itinerary of the caravans was increasingly cluttered by men making demands for various dues. Traders could petition rulers to eradicate especially corrupt bureaucrats and enforce scheduled rates of taxation where and when princely power was sufficiently strong for this to be effective. In other contexts they simply re-routed or evaded venal officials, as evidence presented elsewhere in this book demonstrates.[26] In this respect, taxation was also a negotiation or process in which traders possessed significant clout, particularly in relation to the state proper.

The prince's second obligation was to safeguard the activities of traders and the flow of trade through his domains. This happened both by issuing passes that also signified sovereignty within and beyond his lands, and by redistributing revenues for the architecture and maintenance of protection services.[27] The (re)construction of roads and bridges, wells, and caravanserais were as practically important as they were symbolic acts of imperial power and munificence for Mughal, Safavid, Uzbek, and Ottoman rulers.[28] Within the caravanserais, merchants were offered some degree of protection from theft, although the quality of protection probably varied according to the amount of revenue made available for—and the rectitude of—the appointed officials.[29] Whatever their investment in the provision and policing of caravanserais, the Mughal rulers and their counterparts in central Eurasia were well aware that marauders were most active in areas well beyond the imperial frontiers.[30]

In other words, there were significant gaps not only between the ideals and realities of good kingship, but also between the state's services of protection and what was actually needed by the qafilas. These gaps widened or exhibited greater complexity by the early nineteenth century. In both India and Iran, with the waning of imperial power after c. 1700, even the centre's enforcement of regional governors' safeguarding of trade steadily evaporated, let alone direct intervention from the centre. The result was the resort by private merchants to private security.[31] If corrupt bureaucrats or bandits robbed the caravans (of cash, commodities, persons, livestock), the immediate financial loss was likely supplemented by increased transportation charges and insurance premiums, eating into profits where these could not be passed on to consumers in the longer term. Beyond a point, epidemic criminality could precipitate the decline or cessation of caravan trade.[32]

The qafilas, therefore, were necessarily driven into the economy of violence via the purchase of protection services, and in order to add to their bargaining clout.[33] Escorting the train of caravans across the Indo-Afghan frontier were a few hundred heavily armed horsemen, mostly drawn from the dominant Pashtun tribe in the area through which the caravans passed.[34] Even caravans travelling along relatively secure highways employed a superintendent, bowmen, and armed Jat peasants.[35] Some of these horsemen sallied ahead of the caravan, gathering information about the condition of the routes and the activities of robbers.[36] Such men, from the dominant ethno-social groups of particular regions, also represented the most proximate political authority with which the qafila interacted in spaces that were beyond or between the physical reach of any centralised state. By hiring such men, the caravans voluntarily paid protection money in place of being harassed for cash.

Of course, protection could take a pacific or benign form. Sufism having permeated the trading world (described in chapter 1), the caravans began employing or else benefited from the presence of holy men for protection. Unsurprisingly, given their passage between marketplaces and emporia, some Sufis also participated in commercial exchanges. The caravans of Muslim merchants of Punjab could include certain 'Sayyids of Multan' whose 'holy character allows them to pass unarmed where other Pathans would infallibly be murdered.'[37] In the 1830s, a wealthy Lohani merchant, Lal Khan, annually took a relatively unsafe but shorter route across the Hindu Kush that cut through the territory of caravan-raiding Waziris by securing the religious influence of the venerable Sufi *pirs* of Multan and paying off the tribesmen to the tune of Rs 20,000.[38] Here, therefore, the similarity of life within the caravans to the armies of the emperor and other imperial grandees—which were 'provisioned' with Sufi adepts and Hindu *sadhus* (holy men) for the spiritual protection and religious guidance of soldiers—is truly striking.[39]

The weapons of the Sikh gurus and other leading figures in Sikh history have acquired the status of relics, which points to the retrospective valorisation of violent power as righteous command in the making of Sikh identity.[40] Ultimately, just as those organising the *qafila* employed armed Jats when traversing the north Indian plain, so too did they employ Sikh merchants to empower their negotiating position and passage through the Sikh kingdoms from the mid eighteenth century. If the Sikhs were discriminating against Muslim traders, then it was expedient—as some traders took to doing—to employ Sikh traders known as Nanakputras (after Nanak, the first guru) to carry merchandise.[41] The boundaries between nomad and mercenary, trader and holy man were often blurry. This is evidence of the profound integration of the world of caravan trade within a number of intersecting networks—some more localised, others regional or transregional, some more commercial, others spiritual or political, some more pacific, others violent.

Bandits and Pastoralists

Who were the bandits from whose raids the caravans were to be protected? The open country and jungle or shrub beside the roadways were probably teeming with gangs capable of attacking at least part of a caravan; there were not only outlaws and bandits but also armed peasants, as well as tigers and other beasts.[42] Because they joined the caravans as fellow itinerants and picked off individual victims—often hapless pilgrims or travellers—the threat posed by the infamous Dacoits (bandits) and Thugs or Phansigars (stranglers) was to individuals rather than to the collective, to be protected against by vigilance rather than by armed guards.[43] But the Thugs' expeditions—in common with the activities of other types of thieves and robbers—were seasonal. They coincided with the autumn–winter respite between harvests and toil on the land, indicating the intersection of various economies of violence at the time of year when men were most mobile yet concentrated in the caravans or the war camps or *melas*.[44] Ultimately, it was groups that could be termed 'social bandits' or brigands which posed a larger threat to the caravans. These were commonly identified as men with roots in the rural economy who worked not as lone rangers but in gangs capable of halting and attacking a whole caravan train or a large part of it.

Inspired by an often-critical reading of Eric Hobsbawm's seminal *Primitive Rebels* (1959) and *Bandits* (1969), scholars working on historical or more contemporary societies have engaged with the questions of *who* turns to this form of banditry and *why*. They have debated explanations revolving around push–pull factors that are often structural and economic in nature.[45] Frequently, these include hardship born of the ruggedness and remoteness of the landscape and its long-term impact on economic competition (for grazing land, for example); or else pestilence, poor harvests, and famines in the short term versus opposition to feudal aristocracy or to central authority, moneylenders, and merchants. Their crimes could be anonymous, not least theft to survive, or targeted, the pursuit of personal vengeances, for example. Occasionally, bandits formed alliances or worked for political and commercial elites. Stephen Cummins describes this as a 'relational world of "service" that spanned illicit and licit systems of clientage.' Such alliances blurred any clear-cut social distinctions within their complex of shifting and sometimes political motives.[46]

In the context of early modern south and central Asia, the phenomenon of social banditry has not been the subject of admirable social histories, perhaps because of the absence here of trial records and other sources containing the testimony or traces of bandits that have provided rich rewards for European and east Asian historians.[47] Yet, certain spaces were closely associated with the activities of bandits and can thus serve as the canvas for a broader-brush social history of brigandage and associated violence. Along the Indo-Afghan frontier, Pashtun tribesmen acquired a degree of notoriety as social bandits and brigands, this appellation shifting between tribes for reasons elaborated below.

In the nineteenth-century colonial imagination, the Pashtuns were a race of noble savages. The ethnographic gaze turned upon tribesmen to paint admiring portraits of armed and rugged highlanders, each so committed to the defence of his honour and property—which included his womenfolk—that he was readily drawn into violent blood feud.[48] Perhaps, where Pashtun vendettas spilled into inter-tribal conflict, attacks on the caravans could be read as the infliction of injury on a rival tribe or tribal grouping.[49] Yet, in several respects, Pashtuns were the archetypal social bandit of Hobsbawm's conception: the harsh landscape sharpened competition for grazing pasturage, which has been a persistent and powerful explanans in the history of Afghan migration into the Indian subcontinent throughout the early modern period.[50] Where they remained in the highlands, their predation on passing caravans complemented their livelihood from the land, or substituted for the loss of earnings in times of severe hardship. Where they joined such movements as the charismatic sixteenth-century Roshaniyya sect, with its anti-Mughal bent, they were articulating resistance to interference that sharpened the fierce competition for livelihood.[51] 'Given his 'seasonal unemployment, [...] his separation from familial ties, and his special expertise in the mountainous terrain,' John Marino writes of the shepherd in the early modern kingdom of Naples—at once also capturing the life of his counterpart in the Indo-Afghan frontier—'he was a prime candidate for the bandit armies.'[52]

What became apparent to the Mughals by the mid seventeenth century was that the most effective response to the local Yusufzai and Afridi tribes' raids on caravan traffic and other obstructions was not military pacification but the payment of subsidies and recruitment into Mughal service.[53] Such efforts to widen opportunities for the tribes reveal part of the true nature of the problem; namely, the prior narrowing of political independence and the sharpening of economic competition over static resources through the assignment of rights to imperial allies over the extraction of land revenues, which had heightened anti-Mughal as well as inter-tribal conflict.[54] With regard to the security of trade, more specifically, such strategies of tribal recruitment and co-optation were used by traders themselves when Mughal power and patronage retreated. In turn, the Durrani and, eventually, the British colonial state resumed tribal patronage to subdue those restive frontier tribes that found themselves outside the pastoralist-cum-merchant economy of the caravan trade or other economic opportunities that increased their sense of relative hardship (as chapter 7 demonstrates).[55]

In other respects, Hobsbawm's framework fits poorly or is problematic. Bandits were not necessarily 'actual champions of the poor and the weak' but often 'terrorised those from whose very ranks they managed to rise'—which, in the context of the Indo-Afghan pastoral economy, involved raids between rival Pashtun tribes.[56] Yet, while scholars have been more attentive to the diversity of bandits and banditry than admitted by Hobsbawm, Cummins discerns two still-neglected issues: the *agency* of men in turning to banditry and the *identities* these men fashioned as part of the process of becoming or being a bandit.[57] In contrast to the Dacoits or Thugs, whose life and identity was tied to their criminal activity, men of Indo-Afghan origin recruited as mercenaries across the subcontinent turned to brigandage between campaign seasons as a means of survival. They were 'itinerant warriors living off the detritus of combat', to borrow Mesrob Vartavarian's words, identifying foremost as honourable men of arms, their thievery born of necessity.[58]

Returning to the Indo-Afghan frontier, it is unlikely that the Pashtuns described as bandits desired this identity. Rather, banditry was simply instrumental, compatible both with the Pashtun honour code (*pakhtunwali*) and with the achievement of more honourable livelihoods. Aside from the competition over grazing land, some Pashtun tribes competed for the organisation of the caravans. In part, their success depended on factors outside their control, such as the extent of demand in particular markets that dictated the choice of particular routes, which might (not) pass through their areas of influence, or the patronage and favour of particular political authorities (prominent examples are discussed in more detail in the next chapter). To stand a chance in this competitive world, however, tribesmen needed sufficiently large herds of horses, ponies, camels, and other animals used in carriage and auxiliary services. Their decimation through disease or use in disastrous military campaigns could transform a tribe's fortunes or necessitate sideways moves into other occupations. This could involve a shift from pastoralism to arable farming (as discussed in chapter 1) in the context of changing ecological and epidemiological conditions in early-nineteenth-century Balkh, or from legitimate trade to raids, for example. Plunder offered a rapid route to the accumulation of animal capital necessary for caravan trade, as well as the goods and liquidity to participate profitably in long-distance exchange. But the caravan trade was even more deeply entangled within the economy of violence, in ways that also reveal further links between banditry and the necessity of accumulating large herds of livestock.

Pastoralists and Mercenaries

Between the deluge of the monsoon rains in summer and the roaring heat of spring, life on the Indian plain was relatively quiet once the land was sown with the *rabi* crop in early autumn. But the autumn–winter season could easily be filled with the march of court, for early modern rulers were peripatetic, their movement serving both to reaffirm patrimonial bonds of loyalty and reward between king and nobleman, while making visible the might and majesty of kingship down to even the lowest echelons of society.[59] Viewed from the perspective of the centre, this was not only the season for *shikar* (the hunt), but a time to enjoin seasonally underemployed men, oftentimes recalcitrant in relation to central authority, into *naukari*.[60] Where the demand for human and animal power was larger than these men could provide, Indian rulers benefited from the coincidence of the winter campaign season with the arrival of the caravans, for the supply networks and circulatory patterns of the *qafilas* were also those of mercenaries, horses and horsemen, beasts of burden, and other military technologies. This coincidence was the result of deep interdependencies of the dry and wet zones of south Asia.

Ultimately, therefore, caravan trade was integral to the dynamics of imperial power and the production of organised violence, as well as interludes of more disorganised yet violent brigandage. Unsurprisingly, given their ability to control the supply of the embodied technologies and techniques of warfare, Pashtuns had the ability to make or break centralised authority. The origins of several Indian dynasties lay in the horse trade, namely the Ghurids (879–1215) and Lodis (1451–1526), as well as the short-lived Sur dynasty during the Mughal interregnum (1540–56), making more fraught the reliance upon men of arms from the frontier.[61] Whereas emperors from Akbar onward thus sought to break the power of the extant Afghan nobility by restricting their role within the Mughal state through the seventeenth century, the trend was reversed over the eighteenth century as Afghans were recruited into imperial service and rewarded with offices and grants of revenue-yielding land.[62] The accumulation of such prebendal rights allowed a number of Afghans to forge their own 'successor states'. In doing so they sought not to overthrow the central state per se, but to secure a share in the spoils becoming available as the centre renegotiated its relations with other power holders over the eighteenth century.[63]

If India's fertile and revenue-rich economy was the ultimate prize for political aspirants, especially those from central Eurasia—Timur and Babur, Nadir Shah and Ahmad Shah, for instance—the path to its treasures could be meandering. Situated between the Safavid and Mughal polities, Pashtun tribesmen in the seventeenth and early eighteenth centuries were involved in the competitive frontier politics of these two empires in the Kandahar region. Abdali tribesmen were settled around Multan, in western Punjab, where they traded in camels, presumably as nodes in a larger network reaching further into north India and Afghanistan. This Indo-Afghan diaspora proved instrumental in the successful contest with their Ghilzai opponents in Herat in 1717, prior to Nadir Shah's and Ahmad Shah's campaigns, and it was within the community of Multani Abdalis that Ahmad Shah had either been born or else spent his early life.[64] Within this context, Nadir Shah's recruitment of Ahmad Shah is unsurprising, explicable not merely as playing off the Abdalis against their Ghilzai rivals, but also as a way of tapping the networks and resources possessed by the former. In turn, service to Nadir Shah was to bring greater rewards and resources to the Abdali tribes in the form of grants of prebends (*tiyul*, akin to the Mughal *jagir*) over more than half of the cultivated land in Kandahar in southern Afghanistan.[65] Here, then, is the larger context to the mobilisation of the networks of long-distance exchange in the emergence of a new and powerful force in the political life of the trading world—the Durrani Empire—whose existence, in turn, supported caravan trade between south and central Asia.

The State and Its Political Economy of Trade

Commerce and Princely Redistribution

The Afshari and Durrani raids rocked north India in the middle decades of the eighteenth century. The areas ransacked by Nadir Shah and Ahmad Shah along the Grand Trunk Road from Lahore towards Delhi were adversely affected by the combination of climatic change, hardship, and peasant unrest from the late seventeenth century. Then, in the early eighteenth century, eastern Punjab became the battleground for Mughal–Sikh conflict, as well as conflicts between various Sikh chieftains vying for political power. It was in this part of the province, therefore, that those sorrowful and lugubrious rhymes of Nadir Shah—metaphorically taking the form of the 'dog' who made the cotton crop shed its flowers as he ripped apart Mughal unity—were recited in the 1880s. It was in this part of the province, after all, that prosperity was already so precarious and political life so turbulent.

India, however, was still a sink for the world's bullion, its political and commercial elites rich in cash and liquid assets, the Mughal imperial treasures a prize for anyone audacious enough to lay claim to them. The sequestration and transfer of liquid wealth and mobile property—including animals of war and carts—during the Afsharid and Durrani raids ran into the tens of millions of rupees, to which must be added a similar figure as total assessed revenue (*jama*) of the territories incorporated under Durrani authority.[66] The scale of this transfer is too large to be dismissed as banditry or rapine writ large. Moreover, numerous beneficiaries had backed Ahmad Shah's campaigns and the expansion of the Durrani imperium from Afghanistan into western Punjab.[67] Aside from Ahmad Shah's Abdali kinsmen, other Pashtun trading tribes had also established roots in the countryside surrounding Multan. The Mian Khels and Musa Khels of the Lohani Powindas, for example, were settled in the area around Dera Ismail Khan on the left bank of the Indus as zamindars, and sometimes participated in the trade with central Asia.[68] Others were absentee landlords in Daman near Kandahar.[69] On their migratory circuits, therefore, these tribes summered in Afghanistan and wintered in north-west India, not on wasteland or jungle but on land settled by tribal chiefs.[70]

Bankers and merchants were deeply implicated in seventeenth- and eighteenth-century state-building across the Indian subcontinent (as also in the Ottoman world). They frequently exploited the fracturing of the political landscape by financing or else encouraging competition between political opponents where they thought the outcome would support their long-term interests, of which the collusion of Indian bankers with the East India Company in 1757 is perhaps the most infamous example.[71] With their financial and scribal skills, and extensive networks of credit and information, these merchants—mostly of Hindu and Jain Khatri castes, but also including Sikhs and Muslims— were certainly closely connected to power holders in the north-west.[72] Indicative of the overlapping of trade with finance and private enterprise with political office in Sindh and Punjab, Khatris won lucrative contracts from their host states while staffing the state's revenue machinery down to the *amil* (revenue collector) in the countryside.[73] In Afghanistan and Herat, too, Khatris were working as government officials or else purchased tax farms.[74] And, even where Durrani power was relatively weak, such as in eastern Afghanistan, Hindus worked as accountants to the local khans, or else as bankers, wholesale and retail traders, pawn-brokers, and goldsmiths, with as many as fifty families in the larger villages.[75] In Bukhara, Indian traders' activities were also appreciated by the nobility and ruling elite, ensuring their protection in return for their considerable tax income to the state and their investment in handicraft production and agriculture.[76]

Most of these men were agents within networks headquartered in Multan, but the rise of Durrani authority also empowered merchants from Shikarpur, or else caused bankers and traders to resettle in that city.[77] By providing cash advances to the peasantry (or to artisans), and buying up products at below-market prices for sale in proximate or more distant markets, Punjabi magnates were crucial to the further commercialisation of the economy and, in turn, the flow of cash into the Durrani treasury.[78] According to one early-nineteenth-century European account, the Shikarpuri bankers had financed all of Ahmad Shah's campaigns—a likely occurrence, the remembrance of which several decades later revealed the degree of interdependence between the Durrani imperium and the fortunes of Indian banking houses.[79] In other words, these trader-financier firms formed a state–market nexus—not merely a merchant diaspora or network—across the Durrani Empire, its suzerain states, and its neighbours in north-west India, Afghanistan, and central Asia.[80] These were functions that the financial community—'portfolio capitalists'—provided elsewhere in India, but, crucially, were already being rolled back by the East India Company in its expanding empire around the turn of the century.[81] In short, the expanding Durrani polity was enriched by both the sequestration and transfer of a vast amount of wealth from the Mughal heartland and the receipt of revenues from the territories formerly remitting monies (or else occasionally submitting tribute) to the Mughal centre.[82] In this process was included a range of participants with some connection to caravan trade. What, then, were the consequences of this vast sequestration and transfer of wealth from the perspective of the trading world?

Wealth transferred from north India represented an enormous injection of liquidity into the Durrani economy, trickling downwards through princely redistribution via patronage—of litterateurs and artisans, of religious institutions, of urban building projects, and of commercial activity—in the manner typical of early modern Indo-Islamicate monarchs.[83] In turn, this supported economic activity in north-west India and Afghanistan that sustained pastoralists and magnates, peasants and artisans, gentry and clergy.[84] Quickly, this bullion coursed through trade networks into central Eurasia, lubricating exchange at the Russian garrison-cum-trading post at Orenburg, for instance.[85] The influxes of cash from north Indian hoards supported long-distance, large-scale exchange rather than local transactions.[86]

Thus, Nadir Shahi rupees—some minted en route from Delhi to Iran—remained in circulation within the circuits of caravan trade for some time after Nadir's assassination in 1747, for the Abdali tribes were rewarded with booty for their military service in these campaigns and were also active in commerce.[87]

Princely duty, as much as necessity and contingency, dictated the Afghans' support of commerce. Perhaps nowhere in eighteenth-century south Asia was the importance of patronage of production and long-distance trade greater than in the Durrani polity, for it was located squarely within the Arid Zone. Upon each campaign to north India, Ahmad Shah instructed his agents to make purchases with the wealth formerly or freshly plundered from north Indian towns, or the tribute and revenue extracted from proxy rulers.[88] One such agent was 'Hussein Caun [Khan]', whom the Company's employees encountered upon 'the Pattan King having sent a Commission' for the purchase of textiles in Sindh.[89] Because these exchanges were predicated upon the transfer of wealth from north India, the Company's servants regularly received payment in a mixture of *sicca* (the standard rupee in circulation across north India, outside Company territories) and Nadir Shahi rupees.[90] Occasionally, the factors received payment in other sorts of treasure, including a diamond and string of pearls from Mirza Mendi in 1771–2, for example.[91] The goods bought by the Durrani agents were for court consumption but also as investments in caravan trade. The latter stands as further evidence against the misrepresentation of early modern Asian rulers as all-powerful potentates scoffing at merchant-princes.[92] In this same spirit, high-ranking members of the Afghan royal family—women as well as men—maintained a hand in caravan trade through to the twentieth century.[93]

Additionally, the Durranis supported private merchants for the tax receipts that trade brought the state. After the campaign of 1762, Ahmad Shah and his vizier issued the 'Pattan' merchants with 'perwunnahs' or warrants granting them freedom from tolls and duties when passing through what was now Durrani territory beyond the Hindu Kush mountains; the warrants served also as instruments of the articulation and projection of Durrani sovereignty.[94] But the Durranis also patronised production in the countryside—much like other eighteenth-century Indian rulers—as a means of augmenting their revenue streams. By incentivising the production of cash crops such as indigo for sale in proximate or more distant markets, commercialisation—and, thus, the cash-revenue nexus—could be deepened. The result was the introduction of indigo as a cash crop at a time when old supply sources were declining and interregional trade was curtailed by rising security costs on the roads.[95]

Gradually, therefore, Punjab indigo emerged as an article distinct from the indigo of other regions of India.[96] From the mid eighteenth century, Afghan and, later, Sikh rulers encouraged indigo planting and processing in the Multan *suba* through taxation and irrigation policies, and exports to overland markets assumed an unprecedented importance.[97] By the late eighteenth century, therefore, indigo was well established as a cash crop in the canal-irrigated tracts in the region straddling the Indus and Chenab rivers and along the arterial trade routes between Afghanistan and Hindustan, with production concentrated in villages around Multan, Dera Ghazi Khan, Dera Ismail Khan, and Bahawalpur. By the early nineteenth century, Multan was famous for its indigo, and European travellers and East India Company officials travelling through western Punjab towards central Asia noted not only the preponderance of, but also the preference for, Punjabi indigo in markets such as Kabul, Kandahar, Bukhara, and those further afield.[98]

Hydraulic Power

From the melting snow and ice of the Hindu Kush and the Himalaya, the Pamirs and the Karakoram, streams trickled into the rivers that ran through central Asia and north-west India. To control these water sources and supplies was crucial to economic and political power in the semi-arid expanses between the Oxus and the Indus.[99] At the same time, the organisation of labour necessary for the cleaning and careful management of irrigation channels necessitated the state's exertion of its power, either directly or through its appointed officials and feudatories. Reflexively, as Karl August Wittfogel famously postulated in his theory of 'hydraulic society' or the 'Asiatic mode of production' almost a century ago, the existence of complex or large-scale irrigation systems was evidence of the development of centralised authority.[100] Insofar as maintaining irrigation systems was a test of the state's efficacy and competency, turning to indigo and silk—both highly water intensive in their production—sheds light on the hydraulic power of the state.

The Oxus, its tributaries, and man-made canals irrigated cotton crops, orchards, vegetable gardens, and groves of mulberry bushes, their leaves the food of the silkworm.[101] These canals could not sustain water-intensive crop cultivation, the desert oases an alien and inhospitable habitat for the thirsty indigo plant and the water-intensive process of extracting the dye.[102] The principal and prime indigo-producing tracts in Derajat lay in tracts of light or sandy soil between the Indus, Chenab, and Sutlej.[103] The fields were repeatedly irrigated with canal water between preparatory ploughings in winter, inundated immediately before seed was sown in April and May, and then irrigated every two to three days until the plants reached a foot high, irrigation every eight to ten days sufficing thereafter.[104] Harvesting involved hacking the stems, which were tied into bundles and taken to the vats, where they were covered with canal water for steeping and churning until a pulp was produced, this process deemed vital to the quality of the finished dye.[105] Removed, drained, and dried on a sand heap to reduce bulk and water weight, the indigo paste was rubbed with a little oil for shine, moulded into balls, and allowed to dry out completely.[106]

In Bukhara, the state controlled the larger canals (*nahar*)—including the Shahri-i-Rud, the most important canal—that fed the smaller subsidiaries (*ariqs*) which criss-crossed and connected individual villages and towns.[107] Throughout the eighteenth and the first half of the nineteenth century, the rulers of Khokand and Bukhara ordered not only the construction of marketplaces and caravanserais, but also the cleaning, construction, and reconstruction of irrigation canals, for this permitted productive expansion, including the irrigation of more mulberry bushes to feed silkworms.[108] The state's revenue-administrative apparatus was wide-reaching and agile, allowing it to finance these expenditures according to the differential price elasticities of different sorts of suppliers. The Islamic taxes of *kheraj* and *zakat* were levied at varying rates in Bukhara and Balkh, for example, to which were added cesses such as *su-puli* (water tax), *tanob-puli* (a form of land tax for market-gardens, orchards and, presumably, also mulberry groves), and *mirabona* (a charge for payment of canal inspectors) where permissible.[109] Levi's work on Khokand highlights the role of liquidity influx especially from *c.* 1750 (examined in the next chapter) in stimulating the state's efforts to expand productive capacity, particularly through the construction of new irrigation canals (*ariqs*, *says*) to open land for cultivation.[110]

In western Punjab, similarly, successive Durrani and Sikh rulers also constructed and cleaned irrigation canals. Multan was not the larger sort of Durrani administrative unit (*wilayat*), such as Kabul, but a *hakumat-i ala*. The centre appointed its governor, who was given relative autonomy, receiving the centre's share of revenue in turn.[111] Yet, it is evident that Durrani-appointed administrators made investments in productive infrastructure, such as Ali Muhammad Khan (of the Pashtun Khugiani tribe, appointed 1752) or Muhammad Muzaffar Khan (of the Sadozai tribe, appointed 1780), many of the Sikh-era transformations simply extending earlier initiatives and continuing the improvements made in the period of Afghan rule.[112] This is not to say that the Pashtun tribes were always welcoming of such influence and interventions ordered by their overlords, whose impetus to 'development' they even recorded as precipitating moral decline in eighteenth-century ghazals (poems), as Robert Nichols has illuminated in the context of the Peshawar valley.[113] The Durrani interventions were thus seen as a continuation of earlier Mughal interference; those of the Durranis' successors came with the added injustice of being the work of infidels.[114]

Improvements were nevertheless made, increasing the area of cultivable land. An inquiry into the state of the canals in Multan's indigo tracts compiled shortly after the British conquest notes the Sikhs were able to realise five times more revenue around the Sutlej than the Durrani authorities had collected a few decades earlier, and without considerably changing the rate of revenue assessment.[115] This resulted, in part, from the extension or elaboration of earlier Afghan initiatives. But it was also because each authority focussed their efforts in different areas—the Afghans focussing on canal cleaning or construction around the Chenab, the Sikhs around the Sutlej—as each nevertheless realised the revenue potential of producing larger surpluses for export.[116]

The profits reaped by peasants fluctuated with the rise and fall of the rivers.[117] If the meltwaters from the Himalaya arrived too late or was too little, the plants withered. If the combination of the meltwaters and the monsoon was excessive, the plants were liable to blight and other diseases. Between these extremes and vulnerabilities, cultivators could reap sizeable profits.[118] Because of its high value, the indigo fields were assessed on the *zabti* system, whereby state officials measured the standing crop periodically, taking as state revenue around one-fifth to one-fourth of the output.[119] Under Sikh rule, peasant producers in Multan and nearby tracts were taxed much more leniently than in Lahore and the eastern regions of Punjab, 'owing to the distance from control [...] the insecurity of property, and the scarcity of population.'[120] Although the advantages to the cultivators were offset as a result of the payment of additional charges and cesses (*abwab*), which tended to be higher in areas where the revenue demand was lower, the peasant proprietor was still left with more than half of his output, and not taxed so heavily in years of poor harvests.[121] The surcharges included fees to government watchmen (*mohassil*) policing the indigo fields, a royalty (*moghala*) of eight rupees per maund on indigo, and 'thank offerings' (*shukrana*) paid in grain or kind rather than cash before the dyestuff was carried towards the towns.[122]

In tying rights to property to the provision of irrigation, furthermore, the Multani administration under the Sikhs incentivised the 'private sector' expansion of cultivation.[123] This expansion was supported through revenue rewards and lenient rates of revenue assessment on wastelands brought under indigo cultivation, as well as Sawan Mal's advances of seed and money for sinking wells, encouragement to moneylenders to invest in infrastructure, and the protection of cultivators from excessive exactions.[124] Because state revenue was so intertwined with output, the *kardars*—who were the general administrators of the *talluqa* or *pargana* (district)—were as responsible for the effective clearance and punctual opening of the canals as for the efficient collection of dues and taxes.[125] As in Bukhara and Khokand, local landlords also owned and operated their own canals, and payment demands were lowered accordingly.[126]

The financial burden on the community as a whole was relatively light, especially since the cleaning of the state canals was paid in the form of labour rather than in cash.[127] Throughout Derajat, the *chher* system substituted cash payments with an annual quota of labourers forwarded by local landowners for the cleaning of the state canals, with corvée labourers under the *kardar* fined a few annas for each day of non-attendance, the monies paid to those taking their place.[128] Alongside corvée, the irrigators could contribute towards the payment of additional labourers where the work was exceptionally heavy, or received assistance from the state in return for a larger share of the harvest.[129] Through these interventions, output increased considerably after 1750, much of it for foreign markets. In sum, the systems of revenue extraction and expenditures in place were relatively decentralised and flexible, with the state's power exerted through layers of intermediaries who were affected through the interlocking of their rights with certain obligations—the *kardars* with the zamindars, the zamindars with the peasants, the latter with the community as a whole.

Conclusion

From the 1740s, the growth of Sikh political power in the region north-west of Delhi was intertwined with the erosion of the last vestiges of Mughal political authority in the wake of the Afshari and Durrani raids. Although the peasant groups that converted to Sikhism, such as the Jats, had long participated as hired military servicemen (*naukar*) alongside the Pashtuns and other non-Pashtun groups from Afghanistan within the Indian military labour market, the thinking within the Sikh orthodoxy (or Khalsa) evolved to view such careers (*naukari*) as contemptible. It was thought that loyal service to a master brought the soldier into conflict with his faith (*dharam*).[130] This was especially likely when Sikhs were in the service of Muslims, such as the Mughals or Afghans ('Turks'), with whom the Sikhs were in religious war (*dharamyudh*). Such ideas hardened in textual prescripts as conflict intensified over the eighteenth century.[131] Yet the political exigencies of the eighteenth century shaped, and perhaps even necessitated, a more complex pattern of interaction between Sikh chiefs and other power holders.[132] In the first place, this was possible because *dharamyudh* was malleable as an ideology or rhetorical device, rather than a crystallisation of inter-religious conflict. A number of prominent Sikh chiefs had in fact cut their teeth in the service of non-Sikh masters, including the Marathas, Mughals, and Afghans.[133]

The formation of alliances with the Afghans is tacit evidence of the latter's emergence as the sovereign or, at least, hegemonic political power in later-eighteenth-century Punjab. In this light, the role of the destabilising political and economic effects of Nadir Shah and Ahmad Shah's incursions in north India ought to be balanced much more carefully with the longer-term stability that the extension of Durrani rule brought Punjab's economy, which happened in the context of concentrated conflict in the eastern parts of the province against the Afghans' role in bringing about peace or stability in the west. Although the rhymes recited in the 1880s did not name Ahmad Shah—but his patron, Nadir—as the progenitor of devastation, the geography of 'memory' reveals as much about the spatiality of economic growth and stagnation as it does about the real or constructive or fictive practices of remembrance, especially as related to violence.

Rather than smothering the early moderns and their interactions within the frameworks of multiculturalism or pluralism, cosmopolitanism or syncretism, this chapter has taken their experience of dissonance as a point of departure. Violence was a fact of life for the early moderns. Most of them had some interaction—either as consumers or producers, sometimes both, other times merely as victims or as instigators—within markets for the services of men of arms which did not involve brandishing weaponry in the pursuit of private feuds. Some economies of violence, such as the economy of armed protection or of military labour, were marketised in that men of arms—Pashtuns and Jats, for instance—offered their services to one or other patron. Others, such as social banditry, were non-marketised, but this did not preclude the bandit from offering himself to the highest bidder for his services when desired. In the context of the early modern caravan trade, therefore, men who were accused one year of brigandage might the next be organising long-distance exchange; men who offered their animal and human power in the campaign season might also enjoin fellow mercenaries in the pursuit of political power; men who might one day be fighting side by side on the battlefield might the next be foes. The alignments of such men changed in line with the continually renegotiated and redrawn alliances and opposition amongst Mughals, Sikhs, and Afghans.

Whereas previous chapters emphasised the role of the *qafilas* as vectors of mobility, this chapter has highlighted that the world of caravan trade was far from politically neutral or politically epiphenomenal. Rather, it has foregrounded the deep integration of caravan trade and the economy of pastoralism (outlined in chapter 1) into economies of violence. It has sought to show also the implication of transhumant armed men within the messy, oftentimes fractious and brutal, political life and exercise of power on the subcontinent. As they traversed the violent landscapes of early modern Asia, the organisers of the *qafilas* drew upon the services of men of arms for protection; at the same time, these circuits served to channel mercenaries into the military markets of the subcontinent. In this general sense, the activities of merchants were deeply implicated in the economies of violence in south Asia. Occasionally, their interaction was more direct, not least when playing political contests between actors integrated within one or more of the overlapping economies, a regional power holder and his private army, or a tribal leader in command of armed men. Thus, caravan trade was a sort of microcosm of eighteenth-century north India, a novel lens through which to examine the contours of the overlapping settings of violent action and the effects of the increasing diffusion of power.

Yet this chapter has also shown that the channelling and control of men of arms were critical to the production of new order. The erosion of Mughal power away from the capital—especially in the imperial frontiers—made more complex this marketised violence, increasing the number of patrons, in particular. On the one hand, these circumstances did not necessarily produce disorder and decline, for they also made opportune Ahmad Shah's effective harnessing of Pashtun tribesmen and their herds of horses and camels in carving out the Durrani polity. On the other hand, this is not to deny that the Afshari and Durrani raids were accompanied by brutal violence. Remembered by Sikhs as a holocaust, the 'Vaddha Ghallughara' ('great massacre') of 1762 was part of a pacification campaign in which Ahmad Shah's forces executed some 25,000 Sikhs in Punjab, according to an account left by Tahmas Khan.[134] In his oftentimes hagiographic yet still singular biography of Ahmad Shah, Ganda Singh reported the available details relating to the Vaddha Ghallughara, noting that most of those slain were women, children, and old men.[135] Singh also noted that Ahmad Shah then moved to Amritsar, the holy place of the Sikhs, before the Baisakhi festival in 1762, where he is said not only to have enjoined his men to use explosives in the destruction of the Golden Temple (or Harmandir) complex, but also ordered the desecration and pollution of the sacred tank (*sarovar*).[136] If early modern societies were brutalised by the regular incidence of various forms of violence, they were more episodically subjected to terror such as the atrocities of 1762. Surely this cannot be understood as legitimate destruction within the common normative framework of political rivalry that explains, for example, Indian rulers' destruction of their rivals' temples and idols.[137] Still, calling it communal violence produced by the hardening of communal identities requires due care.[138] Ultimately, to examine power and transitions of power, violence must be acknowledged and cannot be wilfully ignored or explained away.

Ahmad Shah was typical of the Indo-Islamicate prince in his dispensation of power, and his polity was typical of the relatively compact states in eighteenth-century south and central Asia forged by men of all confessions. The crucial characteristics of such men included revenue redistribution, the patronage of artisanal production and support for commerce and commercial elites, and investment in the commercialised sector of the agrarian economy. The last hinged on the state's management of hydraulic power, which from the Indus to the Oxus depended more on coercion than violence. Viewed from the perspective of the trading world, and appreciating its embeddedness within politics and the lives of political actors, the eighteenth century was not turbulent so much as a period of change with new winners and old losers. It was not detrimental to trade as a whole so much as productive of a new regional order that supported regional economic prosperity. The relative political stability of western Punjab, compared to the Sikh kingdoms further east, supported production and the flow of trade through Afghanistan toward central Asia in the later eighteenth century. In turn, Ranjit Singh's administration supported and enlarged this regional economy following his conquest of western Punjab in 1818. Against the backdrop of this new phase and pattern of regionalisation, the next chapters examine the implications for traders and consumers, before turning to the demarketising of violence that followed colonial conquest and efforts to pacify the frontier in the nineteenth century.

4

TRADERS

An Afghan fruit seller has travelled across north India, hawking his wares along the way to Calcutta, where a young girl named Mini calls out his arrival: 'Kabuliwallah, Kabuliwallah!' Then, terrified, she hides while her father purchases some of the man's raisins. To his surprise, some days later Rahamat the Kabuliwallah and Mini are sat together, the foreigner listening to the girl's chatter. The Kabuliwallah has given her some raisins (*kishmish*) and almonds (*badam*), later returning to her directly the eight annas her father had paid upon discovering what had been made over as a gift. This is the opening plot of the much-loved short story 'Kabuliwallah' by Rabindranath Tagore, set around the time of its publication in 1892.[1] The story and its retellings have done much to embed Afghans and caravan trade within the cultural memory of north India.[2] But who is Tagore's Kabuliwallah? And who is he *not*?

In the history of Indian Ocean trade, Muslims—whether of Indian origin or diaspora communities of Arabs and Persians, as well as Pashtuns—appear repeatedly as seafarers, pirates, and merchants.[3] In the scholarship, these Muslim communities largely recede from view by the eighteenth century, becoming merely an artefact of an earlier golden age of trade. In their place, most attention on the autochthonous trading groups of the Indo-centric Indian Ocean world focusses on Hindu mercantile communities as well as Armenians.[4] In part, this reflects a primary concern with the colonial transition, both in terms of explaining the role of 'portfolio capitalists' in paving the way to British rule, and yet also showing that Indian mercantile groups were resilient in the face of growing British hegemony on the land and in what eventually became a 'British lake' after *c.* 1750.[5] Other histories are, in this way, crowded out by the Hindu Bania. In part, however, this also reflects the bias of the sources upon which historians have relied to examine trade. Just as British Orientalists came to view the Brahmin at the apex of a hierarchical ordering of Indian society and as the locus of authentic knowledge about India, so, this chapter argues, did they see Hindu Banias as the true commercial class above all others, with the result that they are more present in much of the source material.[6]

Much of the work connected to the history of caravan trade likewise focuses primarily, if not solely, on the Multanis and other Punjabi Banias subsumed within that descriptor. Their repeated appearance in previous chapters certainly makes a strong case for their centrality to commercial life in the trading world. Their long-distance settlement-cum-circulatory networks lubricated long-distance exchange, not least by financing production in both countryside and towns across the swathe of territory between the Oxus and Indus, and beyond. Their ubiquity in large and small urban centres across central Eurasia into the closing years of the nineteenth century, through multiple changes in the ruling regime, is testament to the durability of both the demand for their specialist services and of their financial networks themselves.[7] The Multanis also lubricated and ran the revenue-bureaucratic machinery of the state in Afghanistan and precolonial north India, and possessed the power to make or break political dynasties. The Kabuliwallah of Tagore's story—a grubby peddler, not a Mahajan (moneylender)—seems to reinforce this notion. At stake, therefore, is whether the character Rahamat is a figure representative of the Afghan who participated in the actual business of long-distance trade.

What is obscured by fixing on Multanis and tracing the history of their commercial operations through the post-Mughal and colonial transitions is the extent to which they relied on other actors, not least in the disbursing of goods deep into the country through peddler networks at greatest distance from emporia such as Multan or Kabul or Bukhara (as outlined in chapter 2). Afghans did not only occupy such roles as petty traders or horse dealers, however, and their trade networks (as outlined in what follows) complemented and competed with the Multani operations. If the turnover of a political regime could hurt the fortunes of a family where they were not sufficiently distant or adaptive to this change, as Gagan Sood observes, new political authorities could also shift their patronage to groups previously outside or on the margins of trade.[8] This is precisely what happened following the establishment of Durrani power over the thoroughfares of Indo-central Asian trade; as this chapter shows, patronage provided one means through which peddlers could transform into merchants proper over the later eighteenth and nineteenth century. What is thus also revealed by focussing on groups other than Banias is how race mattered to European contemporaries'—and thus historians'—understanding of the world of merchants.

Who is Afghan?

Just as Multan and Shikarpur were the conjoined centres of an 'Indian' trading world that radiated outwards across central Eurasia and the Indian Ocean world, Kabul and Kandahar, Peshawar and also Multan, were at the centre of a similar, overlapping trading world. To the west was Persia, towards which the Durrani Empire expanded, absorbing Herat in the second half of the eighteenth century, with Afghans' business in Bandar Abbas noted by the Company's servants, for instance.[9] To the north were Bukhara and Samarkand, the termini of the caravan trade in central Asia, although some adventurous merchants even made the onward journey to Russia.[10] To the south lay Multan, the main mart of overland trade in India, the city and its surrounding countryside home to Pashtun migrants long before the rise of Ahmad Shah and its passing into and out of Durrani control until it was lost to the Sikhs in 1818.

To the east, Kashmir was briefly a suzerain of the Durrani Empire, and slightly south-east were Hindustan and Bengal, laced with Afghan trade networks along the courses of the Ganges and the Yamuna.[11] Afghan (or Rohilla) dynasts had established kingdoms throughout the Ganges–Yamuna *doab* (thereafter, Rohilkhand) by the eighteenth century, their founders' origins traceable to the horse and slave trades, and their local gentry often combining moneylending and military service to maintain an attachment to commerce.[12] After the Rohilla states lost their independence in 1774, many of their Afghan inhabitants fanned outwards across the subcontinent, building on older connections with south India, where some became traders and moneylenders, others tax collectors and heavyweights for local *taluqdars* (hereditary landlords).[13]

In other words, Afghans integrated the dry and wet zones through both circulation and settlement. The annual comings and goings of the caravans were complemented by the entrenchment of kinsmen in political life, not to mention the spiritual networks connecting Sufi blessed men, Pashtun traders and gentry, and north Indian townsmen. Afghan state-building in the eighteenth century revitalised these networks, ushering in the widening and deepening of Afghans in the life of Indian markets, whether for violence and military power or goods and commercial services. At stake, however, is whether those Afghans involved in long-distance exchange were any more than the peddler or itinerant of Tagore's 'Kabuliwallah'.

In histories of caravan trade, the relationship of Indians and Afghans has been painted as one of functional separation, the former acting as traders and financiers, the latter as intermediaries or organisers of the caravans. Stephen Dale, for instance, identifies all Muslim traders in Iran and Turan as Afghans and Powindas, in contrast to Hindu or Jain Indians. Although he attributes to some of these Muslims a role in retail trade, the picture he paints is of the petty trader. This picture contrasts with that of non-Muslim Indians who formed sophisticated, secretive, and thus closed networks of credit services, currency exchange, and trade, their impermeability safeguarding their specialist commercial skills from rivals, making them matchless throughout the trading world.[14] In his work on the Multani–Shikarpuri mercantile networks, Claude Markovits recognises the limitations of focussing too narrowly on kin networks, noting that the institution of trust could as easily be eroded by brotherly rivalry within kin networks as by agents breaking away or reneging on commitments in networks located outside kinship ties.[15] Nevertheless, Markovits focuses almost exclusively on Hindus, ignoring the role of Muslims within caravan trade, a consequence perhaps of being enticed by repute of the generations-old and well-honed financial skills of north India's merchant communities such as the Khatris.[16]

Afghans were not merely the auxiliaries of Indian merchant-money-men or just petty traders, however. In the first place, it would be wise to interrogate the categories of Afghan and Indian, and their mapping onto corresponding descriptors, namely, Pathan, Pashtun, and Powinda; Hindu, Jain, and Sikh; and Muslim, Kabuli, Multani, and Shikarpuri. 'Multani', for instance, is an inaccurate, imperfect, and partial descriptor of the identities of the Indian merchant-moneymen in these regions, more probably a signifier of the sorts of services offered to customers and a signalling mechanism for reputation to build trust. While many men abroad took the epithet Multani in the sixteenth and seventeenth centuries—such as Darya Khan Multani, Khoja Ibrahim Multani, Mangui and Ustad Gazor Multani—a few were Lahoris.[17] These names also reveal that an Indian or Multani identity was neither incompatible with being Muslim, nor was Multani exclusively the preserve of Hindu, Jain, or Sikh Khatris, for such descriptors were flexible designators rather than revealing fixed identities. The Sikh Khatris were themselves converts from Hinduism and known as Nanakpanthis (followers of Nanak), a sect that was more eclectic (and difficult to distinguish from Hinduism in Punjab) than Khalsa Sikhism, to which it was steadily subordinated over the eighteenth and nineteenth centuries.[18]

Hindus also converted to Islam. From the sixteenth century, at least, Hindu Rajputs who had converted to Islam were called 'Pathans' (a term commonly used for Afghans), highlighting how easily one identity elided into another, and how much more it meant than tribal, ethnic, or geographical origins.[19] Indian Muslim traders—that is, non-Pashtuns who spoke Punjabi or other subcontinental languages—were known as Hindkis in Afghanistan, their importance increasing after the First Anglo-Afghan War, ending abruptly around the turn of the century.[20] There was also a community of converts to Islam known as Parachas involved in caravan trade. According to Denzil Ibbetson, deputy superintendent of the 1881 Punjab Census, the Parachas were 'converted Khattris', some of whom were wealthy, others hawkers and peddlers.[21] Ibbetson offered two accounts of their origins, the first tracing their roots to 'the Bannu district' from whence they relocated 'to Mukhad in Shahjehan's time', the second suggesting that 'they were Khatris of Lahore, deported by Zaman Shah', the Durrani amir who held Lahore from 1798 to 1801.[22] According to the living descendants of the Sethis of Peshawar, interviewed by Shah Mahmoud Hanifi in the early years of this century, their origins were in Bhera, from whence they migrated first to the outskirts of Peshawar in the Sikh era, establishing a network with representatives in Kabul, Shanghai, and Vladivostok.[23] (The rising fortunes of such families are examined later in this chapter.)

With conversion, the Khatris' business secrets crossed confessional boundaries, although this does not mean they spread outside these Muslim family firms to (Muslim) rivals. Ultimately, however, such facts make the distinction of Afghan, Pashtun, or Muslim traders from Indian Hindu, or Sikh, or Jain Khatris and Banias untenable. What, then, is the reason for the drawing of these distinctions in contemporary accounts and the scholarship that has relied upon such sources? Returning to the Kabuliwallah of Tagore's short story helps expose some of the causes that produced these constructions. Tagore's writing is not entirely free from the normative racial essentialisation of the Afghans or Pathans as 'noble savages' that Thomas Metcalf has found in the work of such writers as Rudyard Kipling.[24] Tagore's Kabuliwallah is a counterpoint to the narrator, after all; the former a kindly but grubby itinerant ('[d]ressed in dirty baggy clothes, pugree on his head, bag hanging from his shoulder') of the 'martial races' whose future is sealed when he fatally stabs a man for refusing to pay for a Rampuri *chaddar* (cotton sheet) bought on credit; the latter a writer from that most effete of Bengali social classes, the *bhadralok*.[25] Tagore's writing reveals, therefore, how deep was the reach of the social categories and stereotypes current by the late colonial era: even an enlightened litterateur such as Tagore was working this imagery into his short stories, where well-worn archetypes helped paint the characters and plot in the reader's mind, at the same time caricaturing these categories.

In fact, the *bhadralok* were creatures of the colonial transition and the long process of empowerment of Brahmins by Company Orientalists who sought authentic sources of knowledge about India.[26] In tandem, the Bania—high-born merchants—were elevated in such a way that the Mahajan must be seen as the analogue of the priestly grandees. True, unlike either Armenian or Parsi merchants, Marwari and Punjabi bankers had been critical to the Company's expansion up the Gangetic valley from Calcutta or inland from Bombay: the Jagat Seths' wealth was unparalleled anywhere across the eighteenth-century world, so the importance of Khatri magnates or Banias was not a fiction of colonial rule. The consequence, however, was the creation of an alternative fiction; for, in not being able to countenance the fact that representatives of Muslim trading groups were on par with those of Hindu magnate firms, colonial officials became blind to their operation at the very time that particular networks were expanding and enriching their masters. The Company's factor at Sindh, Robert Erskine, called the Afghans 'People of small Substance and Credit' who 'generally give Goods in return, but rarely ready Money'.[27] Although this characterisation fitted well with frustrations over the poor sales performance of the operation at Sindh, Erskine's description also drew comparison with the Multanis, who were not as 'exclusively Ignorant, and entirely guided by their Brokers' as the traders from Kandahar.[28] From the mid eighteenth to the mid nineteenth century, British commentators continued to recognise the Afghans' incomparable role in the trade between India and central Asia, but certain Afghans' reliance on barter and their unease around financial intermediaries remained a source of disbelief and derision.[29]

Further into the networks of caravan trade, at greater remove from the seats of Company power and knowledge, the contradictions inherent within such categorisations became apparent. In central Asia, through restrictions on dress and through spatial segregation, Hindus and Hindu temples were noticeable and noted by contemporaries, ossifying a sense of separation between what were conceived as Hindu Indians and Muslim Afghans.[30] Outside the caravanserais, moreover, Indian and Afghan Muslims were difficult to distinguish from 'Bukharans', a term employed by Europeans to refer rather generally to Turkic Muslims.[31] But nineteenth-century sources reflect the limitations of colonial knowledge, showing what Europeans saw, or wanted to see, rather literally in the case of colonial photography. Alongside the general aim of documenting pre-conquest—that is, 'pre-civilised'—central Asia, the ethnographic volumes of the *Turkestanskii Al'bom* (Turkestan Album) reflect a desire to classify and thereby comprehend the peoples of Turkestan following the tsarist conquests of the 1860s.

The *Turkestanskii Al'bom* is evidence of the desire to order colonial society in a fashion also typical in British India, and of the emergence of the ethnographic state in the Russian Empire (subjects to which chapter 7, on colonial knowledge, returns more thoroughly). The volume is remarkable for capturing the likenesses of Afghans at all, distinguishing them from Indians as well as Turkestan Muslims—evidence of the struggle to rapidly make sense of the multiple and overlapping self-descriptors to order a society still virtually alien to its new conqueror-rulers, its people more often lumped together as 'Sarts'.[32] But the figures described as 'Afghans' are all 'Muslims' (Fig. 4.1), whereas the 'Indians' are all 'Hindus' or 'Jains' (Marwaris) (Fig. 4.2).

Fig. 4.1: Details of portraits of Afghans in Russian Turkestan

Fig. 4.2: Details of portraits of Indians in Russian Turkestan

There is seemingly no noticeable difference in dress—these Afghans and Indians alike adopting the *khilat* (robes)—but the Hindus all wear the mark or *tilak* on their foreheads and the Hindu and Jain Marwaris a distinctive sort of cloth cap, whereas the Muslim Afghans wear distinctive types of turban.[33] Even their postures sought to affirm religious differences between the Indians, cross-legged, and the Afghans, shown as if in the seated stage of the *salah*—the sequence of postures performed by Muslims in prayer. The photographers and compilers of the album at once recognised the role of Muslim traders—non-indigenous, probably from Afghanistan or Punjab—but consciously simplified their identities, mapping onto one another the categories of region and religion or ethnicity.

The conspicuousness of Hindus and Jains in central Asia, combined with knowledge of their role in the revenue-bureaucratic apparatus of the state and the markets for goods and financial services in south Asia, has helped to bring to light the networks of Punjabi or Multani or Shikarpuri trader-financier firms stretching into central Eurasia. In this way, scholars have substituted evidence *of* these firms' operations for evidence *from* the merchants themselves, such as account registers, records, or diaries. In turn, scholars of the Multani firms—like those of other Indian trading communities, such as the Marwaris or Chettiars—have been able to emphasise the financial sophistication of 'family firms' even as networks of kin or caste, evicting the idea of the peddler that has scourged the economic history of early modern and modern south Asia.[34] And, yet, in light of the foregoing discussion, distinguishing such groups as exceptional in terms of their commercial acumen and network organisation is fraught with difficulties. Even if Muslim trading groups observed injunctions against charging interest, leaving Hindus, Jains, and Sikhs to finesse this area of specialisation, this is not to say that they were poorly capitalised and working either as lone rangers or in collectives that trucked and barterered.

The authors of most of the material on the Hindu family firms in precolonial north-west India were as subject to the sorts of slippages, misidentifications, and misunderstandings as the photographers of the *Turkestanskii Al'bom*. In central Asia, the Company's agents were much more attuned to the activities of men such as Mulla Rahim Shah or Fakir Mahomed. When Naib Badrundin of Kabul took to Russia with almost Rs 50,000 of Kashmiri shawls in 1833, the trader realised a profit of 100 per cent, far from the profits of a peddler.[35] In India, however, the British remained rather ignorant of these Afghans, often only seeing them as the men who organised the caravans, unless they were conspicuous in colonial cities such as Calcutta or Bombay.[36] British Indian officials frequently conflated Afghans with Powindas and Pashtuns, although the distinction sometimes made between 'Cabul and Powindah merchants' was at least an implicit recognition of the difference between the wealthy urban-dwelling merchants and poorer migratory pastoralists who organised the caravans and dabbled in trade.[37] But the British showed such awareness only infrequently.

On the eve of the Anglo-Afghan War, when the British were in need of information regarding the routes from western Punjab to Kabul and Kandahar, they turned to a Pashtun named Lal Khan.[38] A wealthy Lohani merchant, he had paid Rs 20,000 to Waziri tribesmen in exchange for safe passage of his *qafilas* through their territory. This sum was twice what the British were able to advance a Lohani merchant named Sayyid Mohin Shah in 1835 for the purpose of procuring goods in Calcutta to open trade in British manufactures with Afghanistan and central Asia.[39] Although he was clearly no peddler or petty trader, the British continually turned to 'the most influential Hindoo Traders' before 'well informed Mussalman residents' of the trade towns of north-west India—let alone Afghan merchants, whether Powinda or Parsivan—when attempting to ascertain information about trade and finance, rather than trade routes and logistics.[40] The silences and the source material that exist on Afghan trade and trading communities must thus be read critically.

Organisationally, too, the Afghans, Pashtuns, and Muslims from the Indo-Afghan frontier shared similarities with the well-studied Multani networks, especially in operating through an agency structure.[41] On this subject, much more information is available for the later nineteenth century, when (as the last section of this chapter shows) Muslim trading firms from the Indo-Afghan frontier came to the attention of the British through their connection to the Afghan state. Barat Ali, for example, worked as an agent of the firm of 'Sayad Jan, Cabuli' in trade operations to Khokand—evidence, furthermore, of the deep penetration of Sufism into the world of trade.[42] Indeed, the organisation and operation of traders headquartered or originating in Bhera and Mukhad in Punjab, and Attock, Nowshera, and Peshawar on the Indo-Afghan frontier followed a familiar pattern common across the trading world, as evinced by a roll compiled in 1886 of British subjects trading in central Asia (Appendix I).[43] Aside from the city of Bukhara, where most were concentrated, these traders were also working in Afghanistan (Kabul), Bukhara (Katta-Kurgan, Karshi, Kulob), Khiva (Charjui, Urgench), and Chinese Turkestan (Tashkurgan, Yarkand).

This diffuse and far-flung trade necessitated the employment of agents, and their agency networks were as sophisticated as those associated with the Multan and Shikarpur firms. Muhammad Rawar in Yarkand was an agent of Mahesh Das of Peshawar (unlisted), and Muhammad Bakhsh in Kabul was an agent of Ilahi Bakhsh of Peshawar (listed), who perhaps were related. Indeed, some operations were family affairs, such as those of the Uddins of Nowshera in Bukhara, the Saids of Bhera in Karshi, and Muhammad Sadig and Muhammad Said of Nowshera in Tashkurgan. The representatives of others firms, such as the Sethis, were perhaps contracted employees if not family members.[44] These firms took over the long-distance wholesale trade, transacting with the Multani and Shikarpuri firms which were increasingly specialising in rural moneylending as well as the retail and grain trades within central Asia. There is no evidence of commenda or partnership per se, despite the Multanis' use of such institutional and contractual arrangements in the seventeenth and eighteenth centuries.[45] But Ilahi Bakhsh, for example, was a well-known Peshawari trader and banker, head of his own firm with trade operations stretching to Afghanistan, Russian and Chinese Turkestan, and short-term loan issues valued at Rs 100,000 in Kabul alone.[46] Clearly, therefore, these traders were not itinerants or peddlers wandering with their wares from town to town.

Afghans, Indigo, and Trade Networks

Although Afghans frequented north Indian marts and *melas* each autumn–winter season, offering goods and military service to commoners and kings, there is no evidence of their establishing entrenched agency networks in north India. In the eighteenth century, Kabuli moneylenders swept across the north Indian plain and down the Gangetic valley during the autumn leg of their annual commercial circuit, offering loans to peasants at extremely high interest rates, presumably because of the risk of the debtors' departure before their return the following year.[47] In the horse trade, Sayyid Mohin Shah worked with Basra merchants in Bombay to pass off his horses as Arab rather than Afghan specimens; not an agency structure so much as an impermanent partnership.[48] While Afghan communities were common throughout India, the Kandaharis and Kabulis living in port cities such as Bombay were not noted as agents of the overland traders, and the networks in the south of the subcontinent were probably structurally separated from the northern networks due to distance, the tight itinerary of the Indo-central Asian commercial circuit, and processes of historical evolution.[49] Why, then, did the richer and sufficiently capitalised Muslim traders from the Indo-Afghan frontier prefer an unrooted and mobile presence in south Asia just as they were putting down roots in central Asia?

Perhaps Afghans favoured working through branches of north Indian firms or in collaboration with the Rohilla gentry. Perhaps they did establish agency networks which simply slipped under the radar of the British and other Europeans. Coinciding with the establishment and expansion of Punjab's indigo economy was the Company's transformation of Bengal into a plantation economy where indigo was one of the primary cash crops, processed into dye for markets in the Atlantic and Indian Ocean worlds. Returning to Punjab's indigo economy, and tracing the journeys (not) taken by Punjab indigo from the fields to the markets where it found sale, it is possible to contrast the incentives for the deeper integration of Punjab with Afghanistan and central Asia with the disincentives of setting down roots in Hindustan and Bengal in the later eighteenth and early nineteenth century.

Reaching the commercial centres of western Punjab through the mountain passes around October or November, Afghan merchants had fewer than six months within which to exchange their goods in these marts, to make commissions for textiles with weavers, and to travel to markets further afield to buy and sell their goods. As for the procurement of indigo, Afghan proximity to peasant production around the Chenab, Sutlej, and Indus privileged dye from Punjab over other sources of supply, such as Bengal after *c.* 1750. Unlike silk, the bulkiness of indigo limited the extent to which transport costs could be spread across a camel-load of cargo without significantly affecting the unit price. Spreading transportation costs across a camel-load of cheap indigo (Rs 250) without passing on costs to consumers was harder than spreading it across a camel-load of cheap silk (Rs 2,400), which was worth almost ten times as much. From Kabul to Multan, the cost of camel transport was about Rs 30 to Rs 40, or between Rs 4 and Rs 7 per maund.[50] But transportation costs also encompassed charges at toll-posts or to traverse the mountain passes, for ferries, and for break-of-bulk onto bullock-carts or ponies.[51] This was only one of the routes through Kabul to Multan, and traders could also choose to take the more southerly routes via Kandahar. These charges could also vary from year to year depending on the commodity or customs officer, as bemoaned by Afghan traders and British Indian agents attempting to negotiate trade treaties with Indian rulers. Trade across the Hindu Kush remained relatively vibrant, however, Afghan and central Asian towns remaining more important markets for indigo and cotton cloth than Rajasthan and Hindustan (as noted in chapter 2).[52]

Unless transport costs between Punjab and Calcutta or Bombay could be brought below those between Punjab and Kabul or Kandahar, there was scarcely any incentive for traders dealing in indigo to extend and entrench their networks further into the subcontinent. At this time, trade towards Bombay or Calcutta from western Punjab was becoming slower and more expensive. Transiting through the successor states and nominal Mughal territories, traders were charged cesses (*abwab*) and taxes (*mahsul, rahdari*) that the Mughal emperors had earlier either eliminated or reduced.[53] Rather than taxing peasant producers, some eighteenth- or nineteenth-century Indian rulers found it more lucrative to shift more of the tax burden onto traders. Whatever the efforts of individual rulers to encourage trade, the increasing number of territories through which traders passed pushed up the total cost of transportation.[54] On the one hand, the Sikh *misldars* (rulers of Sikh states or *misls*) and their officials continued to charge a number of dues, the burden heavier on merchants from outside Punjab.[55] On the other hand, while the Company abolished *abwab* within its territories in 1793, these measures were seldom enforced, and its single *ad valorem* levy was often more burdensome than the multiple charges paid beyond its territories, so that the problem of free(ing) trade was not exclusively confined to Indian states.[56]

Following the end of the Anglo-Maratha wars and the start of the so-called Age of Reform in the 1820s, Company rule and free-trade ideology was rolled out towards Punjab.[57] After the establishment of Company administration in Ambala in 1823–4, and the abolition of existing customs and transit duties by the government's agent in Delhi, the British Residents at Ambala, Delhi, and Ludhiana received petitions from traders complaining of excessive charges levied in the independent Sikh states, as well as neighbouring states, such as Bahawalpur and Bikaner.[58] Although the Company took some comfort in the lighter levies implemented by Ranjit Singh in 1832, they became concerned that commercial traffic from the Yamuna to the Sutlej—from British India to the Sikh Empire and beyond—was suffering from 'frequent stoppages and demands from duty', and hoped that the rulers of the Sikh states to the east of Lahore might follow the maharaja's lead for the betterment of trade.[59] After Ranjit Singh's death in 1839, there was no substitute for his personal authority in the form of institutional checks on the *kardars* of Punjab, the result being that these local officials started charging ever more exorbitant *abwab*.[60]

Despite their exactions, these rulers seldom sufficiently or efficiently reinvested their receipts in infrastructure improvements or facilities for traders, such as caravanserais, which were reportedly in ruin.[61] The Calcutta government's correspondence with its agents in Delhi and Agra in 1834–5, for example, reveals that the maintenance of security along the newly reconstructed Grand Trunk Road between Ludhiana and Karnal rested with the Sikh *sardars* of Shahabad, and that the British were dissatisfied with the *sardars'* efforts.[62] In part, the problem stemmed from the depression in the north Indian economy in the early nineteenth century: falling fiscal receipts and rising or stationary expenditures forced Indian rulers to impose heavier levies and make less investment in infrastructure, for example. The disease also afflicted the Company, and only after the First Anglo-Afghan War—which demonstrated the danger of inadequate access and escape routes—was investment made in the Bahawalpur–Sirsa, Delhi–Firozpur, and Kabul–Karnal roads, together significantly improving infrastructure for commercial and military traffic to the frontier of British India.[63] Running south of the Grand Trunk Road, the Bahawalpur–Sirsa road connected western Punjab with Company territory, and was revamped and reopened in the early 1840s following the construction of *serais* and water tanks for travellers and traders.[64] Ultimately, the flow of trade traffic was rather insignificant, and the reconstruction of the road thus reveals as much about the mismatch between colonial knowledge and commercial interests on the one hand, as it does about the decline in cross-country trade and the dilapidated state of roads in the immediate precolonial period on the other.[65]

In this context, the cost of transporting one maund from Calcutta by river up the Ganges to Farrukhabad and then overland to Amritsar was Rs 6 and 2 annas, exclusive of taxes, taking 4 months and 21 days. Upriver transportation was slightly cheaper yet slower.[66] Faster was transportation from Bombay to Shikarpur via Rajasthan, taking only 1 month and 25 days, but this was so much more insecure that it cost almost ten times as much as cargo destined twice the distance from Bahwalpur to Kabul.[67] Virtually nothing, therefore, was sent between east and west—at least according to Charles Trevelyan, writing on the state of north Indian transport infrastructure in the 1830s.[68]

For the Afghan or Indian trader, therefore, trade from Punjab to Bombay or Calcutta was equally if not more expensive than trade from Punjab to Kabul or Kandahar. This is not to say that there were no cross-country connections, however: *eastern* Punjab and the *upper* Gangetic valley were connected through a steadily expanding trade in the early nineteenth century—as eastern Punjab recovered from the eighteenth-century economic dislocation and disruption of commerce—especially in small quantities of high-value goods such as shawls and salt, for example.[69] But more extensive trade between urban centres closely connected to Indo-central Asian trade, such as Multan in *western* Punjab, and those that were becoming more and more closely connected to intra-regional and Indo-European trade in the *lower* Gangetic valley, had dwindled.[70] The staple products of western Punjab, such as indigo, were not deemed worth the cost of transport to Calcutta, according to brokers in the city.[71] If the extent of transport charges raised the total costs of trade from Punjab to Bombay or Calcutta, then the widening differential in product quality between Punjabi indigo and Bengal indigo destined for European markets significantly reduced the expected revenue returns, further dis-incentivising trade.

During its sojourn in the Americas, the global indigo industry was subjected to 'improvements' in planting, processing, and production. Bengal's pioneer planters not only incorporated these improvements—alongside Indian knowledge about the peculiarities of the local ecology and geography—to produce a competitive product. They also operated within a space that shut out 'inferior' indigo from outside Bengal, the Company extending its support through legal and market mechanisms, including tariff restrictions on imports into Bengal, while demi-official naturalists disseminated information on the techniques to improve the quantity and quality of indigo.[72] Although these measures did not thwart the spread of indigo cultivation further up the Ganges, incentivised by the expansion of exports from Calcutta, they did distance Bengal and Punjabi indigo processing in terms of the finished product.[73]

With indigo processing in the Gangetic valley in the hands of Europeans, to whom the north-west was an alien land, innovations in indigo manufacture were not instituted in Punjab at this time.[74] Seeing Punjabi indigo and its manufacture for the first time in the 1830s and 1840s, even those British Indian agents utterly unqualified in the manufacture of indigo thought the Punjabi peasants' production techniques primitive or rude, with 'plenty of room for the introduction of a superior system, as employed by the European powers of Bengal.'[75] While the techniques and the production set-up in Punjab was a far cry from that in Bengal, there were those who thought that Punjab indigo 'would appear to possess equal advantages with Bengal and the Delta of the Ganges', including Bengal planters who were taken aback by the quality of some of the best Punjab indigo.[76] Such debates and disputes, however, were part and parcel of a process that Prakash Kumar's account of the Bengali indigo enterprise calls the 'creation and validation of knowledge about indigo'. This was as central to the establishment of Bengal indigo's reputation in the eighteenth and early nineteenth century as it was to the subsequent discrediting of Punjabi indigo and the suggestion that it was only suited to the markets of Persia, which was also the sink for inferior Bengal indigo.[77]

Fig. 4.3: Value of Bombay indigo re-exports[78]

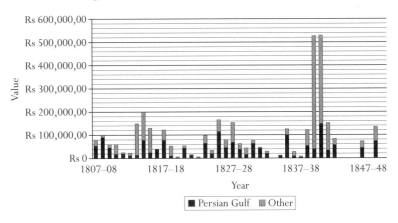

Bombay's re-export trade of indigo surpluses from Bengal and western India was directed towards Persia, suggesting to merchants that there was perhaps relatively little room for Punjabi indigo (Fig. 4.3). Yet, traders in western Punjabi markets asked the British Indian agents in 1836 for Bombay indigo prices in order to establish a direct trade with the presidency, presumably to provide an outlet for Punjabi goods via the Sindhi ports of Alaiyar, Hyderabad, and Karachi, thus circumventing the expensive and insecure journey via Rajasthan.[79] At the same time, Ranjit Singh became desirous of opening commerce between Punjab and Bombay, much to the chagrin of the Bombay government, which thwarted the project via a number of objections, some offered by the Bombay Chamber of Commerce, which knew little of Punjabi goods but believed there was no market for them.[80] Four years later, however, lists of previously alien north-west Indian imports and exports were published in the *Bombay Government Gazette*, capturing the interest of the formerly unenthusiastic Bombay Chamber of Commerce.[81] Indigo, in particular, was considered particularly promising: 'there can be little doubt but that the produce of the Khyrpore, Bhawulpore & the Punjab combined, will form a staple return commodity for merchandise to be transmitted from the [...] presidency.'[82]

Following the stereotype of the peddler, rooted to the earth and almost pathologically afraid of the sea, the British thought the expansion of the Karachi-to-Bombay trade unsuited to the inclinations of the Afghans. From 'their inland position', the Afghans only learned of the 'wonders and terrors [of the seas] by report'; thus their reluctance to 'avail themselves of the more expeditious mode of transport' by steamship and their 'complain[t] of the loss of life, time, and property to which the voyage to Bombay and back subjects them.'[83] Far better and cheaper, thought the commissioner of Sindh, Bartle Frere, that the Bombay merchants—'even after paying themselves handsomely for expense, time, sickness, etc'—trade with the Afghan traders in Sindh than 'if the Afghan merchants came all the way to Bombay.'[84] Of course, some Afghans did voyage by sea between Bombay and Sindh, much like the community of Afghan maritime traders on the Coromandel coast, whose trade took them along the peninsula and around the Bay of Bengal.[85]

Whether 'sea-fearing' or not, the re-expansion of maritime commerce did not incentivise the Afghans of Kabul and Kandahar and Multan to establish a network of settled agents linking Bukhara, Multan, Shikarpur, Karachi, and Bombay. Such factors as costs and competition, inexperience and information asymmetries, and a sense of home and belonging in Afghanistan perhaps worked to inhibit the establishment and entrenchment of business branches and agents across India, although these factors had not prevented generations of Afghans from settling across north India. More important, therefore, was the fractured and fragmented state of the subcontinent in the decades before 1850, worsened by the Company's exclusionary policies. Of course, indigo was only one of several commodities that could be transported and traded across India, but tracing the disconnections between Punjab, Bengal, and Bombay reveals much about the weak incentives for Afghan traders to develop trade and financial networks on the subcontinent, and about Afghanistan and central Asia's vital importance as markets for Punjab indigo between 1750 and 1850.

Afghans under Durrani Patronage

While the English East India Company prepared for war in Bengal in 1757, the Dutch merchants Brahe and Mahuij, during their impromptu stop in Sindh, were busy doing business with Afghan traders, including two named 'Gopierammie and Radja Runal'.[86] From their names, these men were perhaps Khatris procuring goods for the markets in Afghanistan in which they were settled or frequented each season. But, as the above analysis has highlighted, the Dutchmen made no mistake about the presence and prevalence of other sorts of so-called 'Afghan' traders in north-west India. When the English opened their factory in Thatta in the following year, trade prospects were pinned on Afghans and their interests in the Company's wares, especially woollens.[87] Through the factors' efforts to entice Afghans—mentioned more frequently than the 'Multan' and 'other up-country merchants'—the Company officials at Bombay learned of men such as Yusuf Khan, to whom the factors hoped to sell woollens in 1767–8 for onward trade towards Kandahar, and Mirza Mendi, to whom they sold woollens worth Rs 20,000.[88] In fact, opportunities in long-distance overland trade widened for Afghans following the withdrawal of the Armenians and Persians on the one hand, and the establishment of the Durrani Empire and its injection of cash into the trading world on the other.

The patronage of the Afghan state proved durable, continuing into the late nineteenth century. Such continuity belies the competition for the receipt of patronage and notable shifts in the support extended by the Durrani amir between different commercial groups involved in caravan trade. Timur Shah moved the Durrani capital city from Kandahar to Kabul in 1772. Although the Durrani polity remained relatively polycentric—with Kandahar remaining an important trade town, as a destination en route to Kabul or Herat, and as a commercial centre in its own right—Kabul developed as *the* political and economic epicentre of the emerging 'state' of Afghanistan over the following century.[89] Gradually, as the main axis of trade shifted towards the Khyber routes, as a more centralised state slowly came to replace the earlier polycentric polity, as Kandahar was subordinated to Kabul, and as the Ghilzai tribes' share of political power increased, the traders around the southerly routes and the environs of Kandahar were marginalised.[90]

At the same, there was a shift from the Lohanis, who were estimated to be the 'great carriers of the Afghan trade' by the British in the first half of the nineteenth century, to other Powinda trader-migratory groups by the second half of the century.[91] As Afghanistan was transformed into a markedly more centralised polity during Abdur

Rahman's reign, often through the brutal suppression of the outlying provinces and at the expense of political and commercial centres in the south, there was a further shifting of the flow of trade towards the north, with the Nasir Powindas from the Khyber–Derajat area assuming foremost importance in overland trade.[92] In contrast, the *Gazetteer of the Peshawar District* (1884) reported that 'most of the Bokhara trade [...] is carried by Kabulis, Tajiks, and Shinwaris who employ their camels in this manner,' shifting focus from tribal to geographic origins, and highlighting how the changing choice of routes had privileged particular groups.[93] Increasingly, the 'Iron Amir' used the extension or withdrawal of state support as a means of asserting his authority. The Shinwaris of Kohistan and the area around Kabul, formerly favoured with the task of toll collection in return for keeping the Khyber route open, suffered when Abdur Rahman reversed his policy in the 1880s, for example.[94] When the Ghilzais—the second major Pashtun tribal confederation after the ruling Durranis—rose against the centre in 1886 in response to the amir's heavy taxes, they suffered a similar fate.[95] After their defeat, the amir sought to snuff out their rebelliousness altogether through the economic impoverishment of the Ghilzai landowners, with deleterious effects on the Powinda trade.[96] Although Ghilzai tribes such as the Nasirs remained important, their relations with Kabul remained rocky, and the amir's dispute with the Nasirs in 1890–1 was attributed as a cause of the trade slowdown.[97]

For the cultivators and artisans of western Punjab, the Powindas and other Afghan traders remained the most important, if not the only, connection to foreign or faraway markets as late as the 1870s and 1880s.[98] The Multani and Shikarpuri firms remained recognisably important in overland trade to the turn of the century, with agents as far afield as Kerman, Meshed, and Yezd, if not further.[99] The 'merchants of Mooltan have firms of correspondents in all the cities of Panjab [...] and in most of the smaller towns having any pretence to an export trade,' stated the *Multan District Gazetteer* (1883–4), continuing that 'there is probably no large firm at Lahore, Amritsar, Peshawar, Jullundur, Pind Dadan Khan, or even Delhi and Bhiwani in the east, which has not its agents at Mooltan.'[100] But the report in 1861 of the committee entrusted with establishing a commercial fair in Peshawar was silent on the trader-financier firms of Multan, noting instead that trade was 'carried on in the usual manner by resident firms of Amritsar, Lahore, Peshawar, Kabul, and Bokhara, and by the well-known trading tribe of Parachas of Afghanistan and Peshawar.'[101] And intelligence and trade-related sources also reveal the names of men such as Rohidar Khan of Kabul and Mullah Ghulam Kadir of Peshawar who, together with traders from central Asia and Punjab, petitioned the Russian administrators of Samarkand in 1869 over new imposts disadvantaging trade from British India.[102] Merchants such as Qutb-ud-din of Peshawar and Imam Bakhsh of Bhera were already 'men of great wealth [...] their business [...] flourishing' around the mid nineteenth century, their operations thus decentralising the subcontinental centre of overland trade and intensifying the extent of commercial competition in western Punjab.[103]

Their activities would suffer from the effects of changes in trade policy north of the Khyber, however.[104] There were few signs that trade was threatened or being squeezed before the beginning of the Second Anglo-Afghan War (1878–80), and trade bounced back after the short wartime slump, at least according to the reports from newswriters in Kabul and Kandahar. After 1880, however, heavier trade exactions, extortions, and the unsettled state of life in Afghan cities were the constant complaints of traders.[105] Abdur Rahman relied on trade taxes, and also dabbled in trade as earlier Durrani rulers were wont to do, necessitating the freeing of trade from brigandage, the construction of caravanserais, and so forth.[106] Unlike earlier rulers, however, Abdur Rahman attempted to monopolise trade and finance, privilege collaborators, and squeeze out competitors. As Kabul's economy stagnated through the 1880s, Punjabi bankers and creditors were forced to the brink of insolvency, their assets in the city worth a fraction of the loans they had issued, with the smallest firms owed Rs 20,000 and the largest as much as Rs 100,000.[107]

By 1890, Abdur Rahman started to sideline these firms altogether. The British had subsidised the Durrani monarchy since the second reign of Shah Shuja (r. 1803–9, 1839–40), but Abdur Rahman's subsidies were larger and more regular than those received by his predecessors, and the amir disbursed the payments among specially selected expatriate Durrani officials in Peshawar and cities throughout India.[108] Through these officials, the amir purchased machinery for the modernisation of the economy and raw materials for finishing in Afghanistan.[109] Through his monopolies on this trade—in tea, fruits, and nuts, for example—Abdur Rahman squeezed out traders.[110] Of course, the family firms receiving the amir's support—especially Peshawari Hindkis such as the Sethis and Bakhshs—weathered and even benefited from the departure of other trading and banking houses. But in spite of their continued trade *with* Afghanistan, Russian interventions in Turkestan proved much more pressing and prohibitive on trade *through* Afghanistan, forcing further adaptation (analysed in chapter 8).[111]

Conclusion

Inspired by Tagore's story and its afterlives, not least the much-loved 1961 cinematic adaptation by Bimal Roy, Moska Najib and Nazes Afroz went searching for Kabuliwallahs in Kolkata (Calcutta) in 2012. Eventually, the journalist–photographer duo discovered a community 5,000-strong, many of whom lived as a distinct Pastho-speaking group dressing and observing festivities such as Eid in distinctly Pashtun fashion even though many had never set foot in their ancestral homeland.[112] Kolkata's Kabuliwallahs, Najib and Afroz discovered, were not from Kabul but from southern Afghanistan. They claimed to have been stranded in 1947 when, having no official documents, their return from India to Afghanistan became impossible, thus having to make Kolkata their home. These facts serve as a reminder of a recurring theme of this chapter, namely, the tremendous complexity of identities, origins, or belonging subsumed within such categories as Afghans or Kabuliwallahs or Pashtuns, and the differing specialisations and flux in the fortunes of the groups involved in trade. Yet, more than anything, the material presented in this chapter casts extreme doubt on the belief that a successful life as a Pashtun (man) involved eschewing involvement in commerce—conflicting, as scholars have claimed, with the ideals of *pakthunwali*—and which were thus supposedly to be left to Banias or Hindu and Sikh tributary clients.[113]

The biographies of the families of 'Kabuliwallahs' captured by Najib and Afroz reveal the history of a community of peddlers trading in dry fruits, spices, and *attar* (perfumed oil) who then settled into lucrative enterprises such as licensed moneylending. This chapter has similarly shown how certain Paracha or Indo-Afghan Muslim families, such as the Sethis, also rose from the ranks of peddlers to wealthy traders, a process supported by the rise of Durrani power and the extension of its patronage. This process should not be surprising, since each proves the other was not historically unique. This experience, furthermore, was not limited to Afghans. As the Sethis were reaping the benefits of extending an agency network into central Asia, the Chinese Muslim Tungan and Uighur merchants transformed their small-scale commercial circuits into geographically extensive and highly capitalised networks stretching from China to Russia.[114]

These processes were in fact part of a profound transformation of the continental interior, its societies and economies. Emin Khwaja's collaboration with the Qing in the conquest and integration of Xinjiang into the empire, for example, was the result of several factors, as so brilliantly shown by the work of Kwangmin Kim on Turfan in Chinese Turkestan.[115] In the first place, Qing imperial expansion into the interior from the fertile core facing onto the China Sea resulted in the transfer of some of China's silver liquidity—accumulated through its generally positive balance of trade—to the borderlands. The Qing war against the Zunghars in Xinjiang, lasting from 1690 to 1759, was tremendously expensive, cumulatively the second largest expenditure on a Qing military campaign to date after that associated with the suppression of the Three Feudatories Revolt (1674–81). The result was a massive silver influx into the oasis states in the eastern borderlands, received either in return for surrender or for service in the Qing army, otherwise in return for provisioning the Qing with military supplies such as horses, grain, livestock from the local economy, or regional trade networks.[116] Merchants in the Muslim oasis states thus profited both from opportunities for trade with the Qing and from the enhanced purchasing power of local people and their desire for goods from surrounding regions, and vice versa, lying as Turfan did along the arterial east–west Silk Road and a centre of jade and mineral extraction. Undergirding this relationship was the elites' reinvestment of their silver into land, stimulating an expansion of cultivation and specialised production analogous to the transformation in the decentralising eighteenth-century Ottoman and Mughal empires.[117]

The powerful group or guild of caravan merchants dominating trade between the Muslim oases of the Tarim Basin and other central Asian states, Kim notes, were not of local Kashgari or Yarkandi but of Bukharan, Andijani, or Indian origin. There were 220 such merchants residing in Yarkand in 1764, for example, indicative of the extant and increasing connection of continental trade networks.[118] Ultimately, the collapse of the Xinjinag elites' clientage to the Qing in the wake of the assault of the Opium Wars and subsequent domestic rebellions around the middle decades of the nineteenth century spelled a lull in the development of the economy and trade. Until the revival of Qing relations from the 1870s, the result was the deepening integration of Chinese Turkestan into central Eurasia, notably through servicing growing demand for cotton from Russia, indicative of the growing political and economic power of the Romanov Empire.[119]

Further west, in the Volga–Ural region, says Mustafa Tuna, the 'beginnings of the formation of a robust Muslim merchantry' can be dated to the mid eighteenth century, when the Russian state sought enrichment and consolidation of control on the Kazakh steppe borderlands where other imperial diasporic groups—namely, Jews, Armenians, and the Old Believers—seemingly struggled to gain a foothold.[120] This new merchant community was constituted of sedentary Muslims from the Volga and Kama basins, mostly of peasant backgrounds but also including some nobles, who settled in the Russian fortress towns established all along the borderland, including Orenburg, established in 1744. In support of their commercial enterprise, merchants such as Said Babay were offered tax breaks by the Russian state; later, they were entitled to enter guilds of merchants, marking their transition from peasants to peddlers to fully fledged traders, often with a diverse portfolio of activities, one family firm of fabric merchants also involved in property, construction, and transportation, for example.[121]

Ambitious merchants moved their kinsmen into new locales, such as Chinese Turkestan, resulting in the creation of long-distance networks akin to those outlined above, and the reaping of large fortunes. One prominent example is the firm of Ahmed Hüseyinof and Brothers, whose network entailed seasonal movement between Orenburg and the steppes (winter) and Kazan, Nizhny Novgorod, and Moscow (summer), as well as permanent agents stationed in Akmescit, Tashkent, Awliya Ata, Samarkand, Almaty, Simkent, and Tokmak.[122] The Hüseyinofs, like their counterparts from the Indo-Afghan region, crossed boundaries of community and confession, forming partnerships with Jewish and German merchants when these groups expanded their trade into Orenburg.[123] And, like their counterparts from south Asia, their fortunes suffered when the prevailing political, and thus business, environment changed towards the late nineteenth century—in their case as a result of fierce competition from Russian merchants supported by the tsarist state.[124]

Thus, from roughly the mid eighteenth century, with the establishment of liquidity-soaked Durrani power and the expansion of the Romanov and bullion-rich Qing empires into their borderlands, basically the Eurasian interior, a new terrestrially oriented imperial politics brought new commercial opportunities for entrepreneurs. In turn, as these newly minted mercantile communities spread outwards into the ever-shrinking space between the land-based empires, relocating as economic power relations were reconfigured, they were part and parcel of the deeper integration of the continental interior. Historians of trade, whether interested in its more economic or cultural dimensions, cannot be blind to the issue of race. Interrogating the sources reveals the contradictions in colonial knowledge and its information-gathering practices, not least in at once dismissing the importance of Muslims and Afghans and yet relying on them as spies and informants (the latter examined more closely and critically in chapter 7).

From the mid eighteenth century, several material factors supported the Afghan trade in such commodities as indigo to Kabul and Kandahar at the expense of establishing or entrenching networks of trade across India, not least the extent of trade taxation, the insecurity of cross-country travel, and the unsatisfactory state of transportation in that territory brought under the Company Raj. Historians of Indian Ocean trade and trade networks now emphasise that the 1750s to 1840s was a 'moment of "reconfiguration"' amidst the 'encroachment of empire'.[125] Rather than shrinking into insignificance, Asian trade networks weathered the storm of trade competition and changing circumstances around the turn of the century.[126] Although this maritime world was a more active set of sites of competition and confrontation between Europeans and Asians, the encroachment of empires—Asian as well as European—also effected change on the *terra firma*, reshaping networks of overland trade.

If the trauma of the eighteenth-century invasions caused the migration of merchant communities from (eastern) Punjab towards Company territory, where opportunities opened as the lower Gangetic valley was drawn into the economy of the British imperial world, the calm after the storm saw an almost counterintuitive deepening of (western) Punjabi traders' relations within the Indo-Afghan and Indo-central Asian world. In following traders (specifically, Multanis), historians have found considerable evidence for the former trend.[127] In following 'things' (goods, commodities), however, it is possible to see this second, alternative adaptation. Rather than being a backwater or a periphery of the emerging capitalist economy or modern world system, Punjab and the Indo-central Asian trading world might be better conceived as a vestige of the older Indo-centric world economy in which India was a sink for bullion and a core of economic activity and prosperity, even as it was transforming according to its own dynamics. Within this core, Punjab and the north-west were not antiquated as much as distant from, or else still to succumb to, the forces which had already absorbed and subordinated the coastal regions of India.

Yet, as in Tagore's story, the arrival and departure of the Kabuliwallahs was part of the annual cycle of life across north India, and his wares—even modest handfuls of dried or fresh fruits and nuts—were part of the material culture of town dwellers into the twentieth century. The next chapter examines more closely some of the 'things' brought through the networks of caravan trade and their role in the social life of south and central Asia.

5

MATERIAL CULTURE

Fig. 5.1: Muhammad Khan Shaybani

This portrait (Fig. 5.1) captures the likeness of Muhammad Khan Shaybani (d. 1510). He carved for himself a new polity in part of the vast space stretching across Eurasia that was fragmenting in the wake of the death of Timur. In 1500, Muhammad Khan conquered Samarkand, ousting Babur, thus precipitating the process that would lead to the establishment of Timurid Mughal power in south Asia in 1526. In 1506, the Shaybanid ruler conquered Bukhara, establishing the polity that—under the rule of his descendants until their over- throw in 1598—was the epicentre of the post-Timurid cultural and economic efflorescence. Sat against a bolster, dressed in an elegant sky-blue robe over a turquoise tunic and a finely wound turban of white muslin upon his head, his gaze resting upon a set of writing implements to his right, an inkpot to his left, Muhammad Khan Shaybani's portrait shows a man of letters, not a man of the sword, of courtly refinement rather than martial prowess. If wielding the instru- ments of hard power elevated and enlarged his political authority, the khan took pains to present that authority as legitimate within the estab- lished idioms of early modern sacred kingship, as revealed not only through the structure of the composition but the 'things' incorporated into the painting. What consumables, commodities, or goods mattered to the early moderns, including men such as this, his successors, and counterparts? Why did they treasure these possessions?

From the New World to the Kingdom of Naples, Britain to Tokugawa Japan, the early modern era of globalisation and the connected pro- cesses of 'domestic' market expansion within increasingly centralised and self-asserting states combined to create consumer societies. In these, novel forms of material culture and sociability reshaped what, where, and how people purchased and consumed and displayed their possessions, their worldly goods.[1] The economies and societies of south and central Asia were also undoubtedly connected to this wave of glo- balisation and the combination of macro- and micro- or household- level changes that followed therefrom. The latter consisted of 'industri- ous revolutions'—Jan de Vries' coinage for the redistribution of spending and reallocation of labour away from leisure, resulting in longer hours, growth of output, and thus increased income. If an indus- trious revolution underwrote the emergence of consumer societies in seventeenth- and eighteenth-century north-west Europe and north

America, where enhanced purchasing power chased a growing world of goods, then why not in Asia?[2] If there was deeper commercialisation and cash crop production on an expanding cultivable frontier worked by a population exhibiting only modest growth in Asia, then why is it hard to imagine a concomitant increase in consumption? Yet, consumption has been little studied in the context of premodern south Asia (and hardly at all amongst central Asianists), let alone the relationship of people to their possessions. India frequently appears as the locus of production of many of the novelties that transformed material culture in Europe, but seldom as a site where significant shifts in cultures of consumption took place in their own right.[3] A false implication to draw from this lacuna is that Indians either possessed no treasures or did not treasure their possessions.

Returning to the portrait of Muhammad Khan Shaybani, it is a reminder of the pains contemporaries took to (re)present themselves, both amongst contemporaries and for posterity. The production of this object, as much as the things consciously incorporated within the picture and associated with its sitter, demonstrate their power and importance to the early moderns. The picture thus serves as the point of departure for this chapter exploring the world of things and its connection to caravan trade. For contemporaries, what was the cultural significance of the goods procured through networks of overland trade? What does the meaning or manner of consumption of these goods suggest about early modern material culture within and beyond the trading world? To answer these questions, the first part of this chapter examines the self-fashioning of elite men not dissimilar to Muhammad Khan Shaybani. The remainder focuses on relatively quotidian consumption, in turn demonstrating how integral caravan trade was to the material and spiritual worlds of a wide range of actors.

Self-Fashioning

Muhammad Khan Shaybani had been a student of Islamic science during his youth in Bukhara at the time of the Naqshbandi ascendance (mentioned in chapter 1), although he was a devotee of the Yasaviya Sufi order. Thus, his portrait is that of the scholarly and princely *mirza*—not of the warrior who channelled control of *ghazis* to enlarge and cement his political authority.[4] Universally speaking, *ghazis* were neither wholly civilised into courtiers, nor was such a wholesale transformation desirable, a rough undercurrent that could be tapped by the *mirzas* remaining critical the exercise of power by the elite (as argued in chapter 4). But this only reaffirmed the importance to newly elevated or aspirant servicemen of distancing themselves from that which was most unseemly in early modern society. This entailed anything from dwelling furthest from the sources of foul stench on the one hand, to taking pains to perfect the fine art of self-presentation on the other. If a sense of the self is a central characteristic of early modernity, there is no doubt that this was a development not confined to Europe.[5]

In the seventeenth-century Indo-Persianate world, model manliness had taken the form of the *mirza*, often a high-ranking *mansabdar* or imperial serviceman.[6] Following the swelling of the ranks of the Mughal imperial elite from the reign of Akbar to the death of Aurangzeb, as well as its increasing ethno-cultural heterogeneity, the upper echelons of Indian society became more complex as the boundaries were blurred between royal and commercial power over the eighteenth century.[7] For this elite stratum, especially the steady stream of newcomers—or those who hoped to hold on to status and ranks in a changing world—social assimilation or elevation was sought through self-improvement and 'self-fashioning'.[8] Gentlemanly conduct was connected (in north India, certainly) to the Islamic gentrified or '*ashraf-*style' of right conduct and outward observance, in contrast to 'Hindu conceptions of "inner rightness"—purity and restraint', so that the fashioning of the self involved, in part, the practice, performance, or patronage of certain forms of consumption, including those relating to dress, diet, literary and leisure activities, art and artistic appreciation, and so forth.[9]

Guiding this self-fashioning was a wide range of educational materials and institutions circulating within the 'shared world of scholarship' of the Indo-Islamicate world, not least through the connected curricula of the *madrassas* (Islamic schools), where elite non-Muslims were also educated and Mughal cultural norms inculcated.[10] A range of texts and traditions were extant in south Asia, many in Persian or translated into Persian, concerned with correct conduct and deportment, focusing on moral and social behaviour, bodily practice, and consumption choices; namely, *nasihat-namas* (literally 'letters of advice', akin to Mirrors for Princes) and *Mirza-namas* (Books of the Prince).[11] Within these texts, it is striking how central horses, horsemanship, equestrian culture, and equine connoisseurship were to the life of the ideal Mughal nobleman or gentlemen, the imperial elite thus fashioning themselves into an image of which the emperor was the epitome.[12] While non-*mansabdars* could aspire to be or behave like a *mirza*, the *mirza* ideal was closely connected to what was within the reach of higher-ranking imperial postholders.[13] By the end of the seventeenth century, therefore, the Mughal elite was enmeshed within an equestrian-centred cultural complex—an entangled, self-reinforcing, and strongly hierarchical system of governance and culture, horses and horsemanship, reward and refinement.

Just as Rajput rulers fashioned themselves as Mughal *mirzas* whilst pupils in *madrassas* or when in attendance at the imperial court, so the successor-state princelings and the growing cadres of grantees to revenue rights or gentry elites fashioned themselves in similar manner, making use of texts in Persian, or else an increasingly vernacularised literature.[14] Amongst the texts read by north Indian elites were those that helped distinguish good from bad horses, those that serve their master well—on the battlefield, on the polo ground, on parade, on long marches. With such knowledge, the king is set apart from the pretender, the nobleman from the commoner. In India, the *Faras-nama* (Book of the Horse) genre emerged and developed within this context, a fusion of the Sanskrit *asvasastras* and the Arabo–Persian *Furusiyya* literature on equine management—the former part of the corpus of ancient Indian technical treatises on statecraft, the latter belonging to the wider Islamic texts on 'wonders and marvels' (*aja'ib al-makhluqat*).[15]

The content of these texts encompassed the best breeds, auspicious marks and colours, common defects, illnesses and cures, and breeding advice—indispensable reading for Indian noblemen maintaining sizeable stables. Joseph Earles' *A Treatise on Horses, entitled Saloter, or, A Complete System of Indian Farriery*—to take an example with a long genealogy and a geography of circulation that extended to the Company's territories—was translated and published in 1788, from an earlier translation into Persian in the seventeenth century by Abdullah Khan Bahadur Firuz Jang, who himself drew on a text written by Sultan Hashimi (Zain al-Abidin ibn Abi i-Husain) in Gujarat in 1520.[16] Monica

Meadows, in her study of the genre from the sixteenth to the eighteenth century, has revealed that the advice in these texts shifted as a reflection of changing circumstances: the incorporation of non-Islamic groups, such as the Rajputs, into the Mughal polity; the rise of new regional courts and centres of consumption; the altered availability of foreign horses as trade and trade routes shifted; and the changing character of cavalry warfare with the emergence of Maratha light cavalry. Of the surviving texts from this period are the well-known works of Muhammad Abdullah and Rangin (Sa'adat Yar Khan).[17] The wide circulation of these texts involved recensions, manuscripts changing hands, the copying of some or parts of some into other works, and the translation of several into vernacular languages.[18] Whether in Persian or other languages, these manuals most likely had a wide and growing readership amongst the gentrified and literate elites, including Afghan or Rohilla state-builders in north India.[19]

Besides seeking inspiration within these texts, the successor-state elites also commissioned portraits of themselves as powerful, princely equestrians.[20] Often self-aggrandising, these portraits reflected the outward image that the successor-state elites were fashioning for themselves.[21] The Afghan mercenary Muhammad Amir Khan (1768–1834), for example, commissioned an equestrian portrait shortly after leaving the service of Maharaja Man Singh of Marwar (r. 1803–43).[22] Having forged a career through jobbing in the wider military market, he had risen in the Marwar ruler's ranks, but was then expelled following intrigue at court, retreating to the land—Tonk—he had been allotted by a former master, installing himself as its nawab.[23]

The sometime mercenary resembles a maharaja in his equestrian portrait: his body, and the body of his beautifully caparisoned horse, enlarged as a reflection of his status, and flanked on either side by retainers.[24] Whether for private or public inspection, such pictures show the eighteenth-century elites as they saw themselves: refined, royal, powerful, and warrior-like.

'The Sikhs are such Turks', asserted Victor Jacquemont.[25] Becoming Mughal, however, ran much deeper and wider than political power struggles in the absence of primogeniture that Jacquemont observed in the twilight years of the Sikh Empire. Being outsiders to the Mughal court was no obstacle to the appropriation and adaptation of Mughal styles, symbols, and rituals. In contrast to earlier Sikh histories that emphasised the distinctiveness and distance of the Sikhs from the Mughals and other Muslim rulers, Louis Fenech has situated the court culture of the Sikh gurus in the sixteenth and seventeenth centuries within its 'Indo-Timurid' or 'Islamicate' context, thus linking the Mughal and Sikh courts.[26] Focusing on textual sources, Fenech has highlighted how the fondness for hunting of the sixth guru, Hargobind (1595–1606), was justified in the Sikh *rahit-nama*s (manuals of conduct) as training in self-discipline and preparation for battle in ways that paralleled the advice of the Persian Mirrors for Princes texts.[27] If a distinctly Mughal-inspired royal and courtly culture had emerged by the time of Hargobind, who was known as the *saccha padshah* (true emperor), then the next transformation occurred during the leadership of the tenth and last of the Sikh gurus, Gobind (1666–1708). Unlike his predecessors, Gobind's steadily expanding court at Anandpur was filled with imperially trained poets and artists—Hindus and Muslims as well as Sikhs—who had first-hand familiarity with the textual and artistic styles and conventions of the imperial court.[28] Gobind, however, sought not 'to transform his court [...] into an earthly paradise as those courts [... found] throughout northern and southern India, but rather to establish the divine court on earth, the court of God in the human world whose members adhered to a much higher ethical standard than all others.'[29] At Gobind's court, therefore, use of the Mughal idiom was integral to the process of legitimation in the eyes of the Mughal centre on the one hand, and the precepts and devotees of the Sikh faith on the other.

Gobind's larger legacy to the Sikhs was the establishment in 1699 of the Khalsa, the united body of the initiated. Of importance to understanding the culture of the new Sikh elites, who rose from peasant to princely status, is the work of Purnima Dhavan, who shows how the norms and ideals of the Khalsa brotherhood were continually contested and transformed in the eighteenth century. This was often through a complex process of negotiation in which hostile relations with 'rivals'—such as the Mughals and Afghans—hung in tension with the accommodation or appropriation of rival military traditions, claims to sovereignty, and styles of kingship.[30] Indeed, the Sikhs, like the Rajputs, 'viewed kingship as an attribute that acquired legitimacy only through the acknowledgement of powerful rivals.'[31] In the early eighteenth century, when Sikh power was relatively weak, the Sikhs made ceremonial offerings to the Mughals in a bid to strengthen their political position, or else worked in the service of Mughals and Afghans.[32] Once Sikh political power was stronger, the Khalsa chiefs expected to receive obeisance from, rather than offer prostrations to, their rivals, including in the neighbouring—and competing—Sikh courts. New ceremonies created by the Sikh chiefs based on Mughal or Rajput precedents, such as the exchange of turbans or public celebrations of rites of passage, reflected the continued development of Sikh court culture and the continued drawing upon the symbolic and cultural capital of the Mughal Empire to validate fresh conquests and newfound courts.[33]

This is the context to the competitive consumption and self-fashioning of the Sikh elites in the eighteenth and early nineteenth century. Several Sikh chiefs commissioned equestrian portraits akin to those of their Mughal and Rajput counterparts.[34] Ranjit Singh (r. 1801–39), who united these petty rulers into the short-lived Sikh Empire, even established a Persianate court in Lahore, filling it with all sorts of Mughalia, including costumes, jewellery, paintings, and weaponry, while also continuing to adapt Mughal court customs.[35] Painted with a nimbus, with royal symbols such as the *chattri* (parasol) mounted on a white stallion caparisoned in jewelled collars and surrounded by soldiers, Ranjit Singh's equestrian portraits fused Mughal and Punjabi Pahari styles of painting, and regionally rooted and imperial ideals of authority and kingship.[36] In commissioning similar equestrian portraits of the gurus, especially the warrior-leader Gobind Singh (1666–1708), Ranjit Singh was invoking 'the name of the Guru and the military brotherhood of the Khalsa' to counter the 'populist *arriviste* aspect of Sikh society'.[37]

Equine connoisseurship and display were central to Ranjit Singh's authority, as also for his contemporaries, such as Maharana Swarup Singh of Mewar (r. 1842–61); both rulers commissioned pictures of their inspections of prize horses, for example.[38] Visitors to the Lahore court were invited to watch the procession of the maharaja's horses, which dripped diamonds, emeralds, rubies, turquoises, pearls, and coral. Their bridles alone were worth tens of thousands of rupees, according to European insurers instructed to value two sets ahead of their transportation to London for the Great Exhibition of 1851. The glitter included a selection of the most magnificent gems—including the Koh-i-Noor, which had passed from the Afghans to the Sikhs— famously captured in a sketch by Emily Eden in 1838.[39] In 1839, the governor general instructed Major Gwatkin of the Hauper Stud to select horses for the maharaja.[40] Gwatkin duly selected suitable specimens, informing the governor general that the horses had been chosen 'with reference to those feathers or marks upon which Native Gentlemen set such a value', referring to the sorts of auspicious signs described in the Indian equine literature, and indicative of the extent of its circulation.[41]

Thus, horse traders and horse-mounted *ghazis* working within the subcontinent's economies of violence were connected with the competitive and conspicuous self-fashioning of men into the world of the *ashraf* and the *mirza*. Even when their treasured possessions had perished, the affections of their owners and the importance of horses in the cultural life of politics were signalled in the textual records of ritual display and gift exchange, as well as in articles of complementary consumption, such as ornate trappings, fine miniature paintings, and equine manuals. Fashioning the self in accordance with the available advice literature and manuals did not mean only sameness of individuals and lack of individual differentiation, observes the cultural historian Peter Burke.[42] In the Indian context, equestrian manuals and equine advice literature were evolving, producing contradictions and variety rather than stability and homogeneity, not least because these texts were not alienated from material and political realities. Instead, they were crystallisations of cultural hegemony predicated, in turn, on access to resources which were shifted and redistributed between the seventeenth and the nineteenth century. Because equestrian culture was constituted through the 'consumption' of horses and horse-related material culture, and as the latter was a meeting ground for the imperial and the regional or vernacular in terms of norms, styles, and techniques, the result was variety.

Fashion

Globally, Indian cotton cloth stimulated both 'consumer revolutions' and producer rivalries.[43] The reaction and response of the English textile sector to the rising tide of Indian imports, and its relationship to industrialisation, is now well known. The textile industries of other parts of Europe, as well as the Ottoman Empire, also attempted to compete with Indian goods.[44] As these 'extra-Asian' consumer centres were connected to maritime India, their innovators and industrialists were responding to the textile manufactures of Gujarat, Coromandel, and Bengal.[45] Eventually, western European technological innovation turned the tide against India, as demand declined for Indian cottons and was supplanted by European textiles in markets from the first decades of the nineteenth century. In these new narratives of India's global textile trade, therefore, Indian society is positioned as a space of production rather than consumption, certainly not linked to any 'consumer revolution' or 'consumer society'. Textile centres located in the subcontinental interior receive short shrift, their role in these changing patterns of global trade and the shifting of global production ignored, if known at all. But what was the place of cloth in the material culture of societies connected through caravan trade? And how were they affected by European industrialisation?

Just as Indian rulers could choose between horses brought through overland or overseas routes, so, too, were wearers of cotton cloth able to exercise a degree of choice. India's comparative advantage in the production and trade of cotton textiles never obliterated cotton cultivation and weaving in central Asia, so that the networks of caravan trade were a sea of variety: Gujarati brocades, Bengali muslins, Punjabi calicos and chintzes, Bukharan *kindyak* and *vyboika* and *zenden*, for instance. Affordability was one factor informing choice, particularly in the market for plain cloth. Durability was another. Design, however, serves to differentiate otherwise relatively homogeneous substitutes to undercut the price competitiveness of a rival's product, while design innovation arouses novelty and produces discernible changes in fashion. The importance of design and fashion are evident in the consumption of chintz. Colours, chromatic combinations, figural motifs, and patterns were not timeless and fixed but showed considerable flux and, thus, the attentiveness of textile manufacturers in stirring the interest of buyers of cloth.

Within this context, the influx of English textiles into the markets of the Indian Ocean world represented the widening of choice available to buyers and an intensification of competition for weavers. Whatever the Company's agents declared about the deleterious effect of the cheapening of English chintzes, the conclusion that Punjab's textile sector entered a phase of 'deindustrialisation' is as far-fetched as reports of the strength of demand for British textiles.[46] The flow of English cotton cloth to markets was extremely limited before colonial annexation and the inauguration of railway transportation, and demand. A Rajasthani trader of a firm from Churu, writing to agents at Bombay in 1825, for example, noted the slackness of initial demand for English cloth at Delhi and Amritsar, instructing no purchases to be made for fear of making a loss.[47] Other evidence into the next decade suggests that demand for these cloths was driven by novelty born of unfamiliarity, rather than their becoming a ubiquitous staple.[48]

A number of commercial channels were opening, but only slowly, and the types of fabrics imported meant that the flow of European textiles into Punjabi bazaars and entrepôts was in no immediate danger of overwhelming artisans. Re-exports of British cloth upriver from the port of Karachi contributed modestly to the stock available in the major marts of Sindh and Punjab.[49] British goods were also re-exported from Calcutta via either Delhi or Ludhiana, where the Company had maintained troops and a cantonment since 1809, and also—but less significantly—from Bombay via Pali, on the road through Rajasthan between Punjab and Gujarat.[50] Only a fraction of these textiles was re-exported to overland markets, however, alongside Rs 500,000 worth of cloth purchased by Powinda traders in Calcutta, Benares, and Farrukhabad, which were probably assortments of Bengali and English textiles.[51] The qafilas departing Kabul for Bukhara carried British textiles from Bombay which were sold at a profit and in increasing quantity by the early 1840s.[52] But if British textiles were 'highly esteemed in the bazaars of Bokhara', as exclaimed by Burnes, the most famous of the Company's agents working in the Indo-Afghan frontier at this time, these had to be sought, such was their scarcity at the northern terminus of the Indo-central Asian caravan trade.[53]

Driving the efforts of men such as Burnes was the search for markets for British manufactures on the one hand, and the threat of Russian commercial competition on the other. Such commercial rivalries were muted but long-standing. The English had doggedly sought outlets for woollens—principally perpets and broadcloth, their only premium textiles—since their first arrival in Asia. Although never particularly profitable, the English had few other manufactures to sell. Nevertheless, through networks stretching north–south from Moscow to Murshidabad, and east–west from the Caspian to China, Indian merchants carried Dutch and English broadcloths to central Asia before the re-establishment of the English Company's factory on the Indus delta in the mid eighteenth century.[54] When news came in 1760 that the Afghans had conquered Delhi, the Resident, Erskine, eagerly anticipated the Afghans' arrival, thinking they would not only stimulate local trade but also expand the trade in English woollens.[55] The Afghans, after all, were 'the great Purchasers' of woollens and, more than the Multanis, were where English hopes rested.[56] Such sentiments aroused interest in Bombay. Where were the Afghans getting their woollens?

Musters of broadcloth were requested from Sindh, from whence came the reply that the only broadcloths imported into Thatta were the Company's. The factors referred their masters in Bombay to their earlier, now lost, note on woollens dated 14 November 1760.[57] Perhaps this note referred to the woollens manufactured in Kashmir, Punjab, and Sindh from foreign or local wool.[58] Perhaps the note referred to the Afghan and Persian merchants' English woollen purchases in Bandar Abbas.[59] Unknown at this time, however, were details of Russia's involvement in the broadcloth trade in central Eurasia. Company officials only learned later, from 'a very intelligent Persian', that large quantities of woollens were brought 'from Astracan over the Caspian sea to Balk & Bukhara in Tartary, & from thence to Meshed, Herat & Candahar', underselling English broadcloths and surpassing them in their depth of colour.[60] Around that time, Russian traders sought monopoly rights on trade from Russia to Persia and central Asia akin to those sought by western European traders and trading firms in the seventeenth century. Although these enterprises were probably short-lived, their establishment demonstrated the extent of Russian enterprise and commercial interest in central Asia, and the rationale for the Russian conquests that were to follow. With the East India Company's factory a failure, and Russia advancing in central Asia, Russian broadcloth was without serious competition in the marketplaces of the continental interior into the nineteenth century.[61]

Russia was already ahead of Britain in the textile trade with central Asia and Afghanistan, broadcloth being a case in point. The effects were replicated in the case of cotton textiles, which became the chief object of Anglo-Russian commercial rivalry in the region.[62] Alongside cottons imported from India via central Asia, Russia imported Indian cottons brought by the English and Dutch trading companies to Europe through the seventeenth and eighteenth centuries.[63] By the mid eighteenth century, import-substituting initiatives were under way in the villages surrounding Moscow, where peasants produced printed linen known as *hamovan*.[64] Without native cotton-cloth manufacture at this time, Russian flax cloth was used alongside some cotton cloth from western and central Asia in the printing industry in the Moscow–Vladimir area of central Russia, especially Ivanovo, situated 185 miles north-east of Moscow.[65] Ivanovo, and the outlying villages to which weaving work was farmed out, specialised in production for peasants of the Volga region, Siberia, and central Asia, and was especially famous for chintz.[66]

Meanwhile, Britain's textile manufacture was mechanised, and more and more English plain and printed calicos were exported to Russia from the late eighteenth century, initiating competition between Russian and English chintzes.[67] The Moscow–Vladimir printing industry withstood the crisis, however, turning to manufacturing calicos with raw cotton from Bukhara. Although central Asian cotton cultivation for Russian industry boomed *after* 1850, Russian manufacturers' demand for raw cotton was earlier apparent in Khokand, for example, where trade with Russia increased tenfold between 1758 and 1853, especially in cotton.[68] When Napoleon invaded Russia and burnt Moscow in 1812, ruining its industry, Ivanovo's printers responded by increasing output and modernising production, using the technical know-how and pattern books brought from France and England.[69] Born in Germany, and educated in textile technology in Manchester before founding his business in Russia, Ludwig Knop was instrumental to the initiation of Russia's industrialisation.[70] Banned before 1842, English spinning machinery introduced by Knop enabled better thread to be made in Russia, thereby reducing the reliance on English yarn imports, fuelling the expansion of Russian cotton-cloth manufacture.[71] Such was its success and expansion that Ivanovo later became known as the 'Russian Manchester'.[72] The response of Russian manufacturers to the influx of English cottons, which was itself a response to the influx of Indian cottons into Britain, is thus closely comparable to the now well-known efforts of Ottoman and western European manufacturers.

With the domestic market still small, coarse and cheap cotton canvases hand-printed in Russia found their way towards Persia, central Asia, and China.[73] These were called *vyboika*, in imitation of the chinted textiles formerly brought from Asia to Russia. A number of late-eighteenth- or early-nineteenth-century samples of *vyboika* and *bakoika* (block-printed cottons) survive in the Muzei Sitsa (Museum of Chintz) in what is now the Ivanovo State Museum.[74] Nevertheless, unable to compete with the finest white cotton cloths woven in north-west India, Russian exports towards central and south Asian markets in the 1830s to 1850s largely consisted of fancy textiles or coloured calicos of thick texture.[75] From Astrakhan, Russian broadcloths and brocades, chintzes and coloured cottons, silks and velvets went onward to Afghanistan via Bukhara and Balkh or Meshed and Kandahar.[76] Despite Britain's technological lead, its commercial penetration into north-west India was slower and later than in maritime south Asia. As far as overland trade was concerned, Britain's technological advantages were eroded by Russia's territorial foothold and first-mover advantages in central Eurasia.

While European chintz was 'considered a present for a Chief' in Bukhara, Russian rather than British chintzes were the more amply available of European textiles north of the Indus.[77] Such was the novelty or prestige of European chintz, and the dominance of Russian chintz among European chintz imports, that 'He wears Russian Chintz' had become 'the proverbial expression in Sinde [Sindh] for a very well dressed man.'[78] Russian chintzes and cottons, moreover, were well suited to these markets. In texture, they were favoured for 'having less starch [...] and being much more durable than English Chintz which is of a very thin texture and lasts not even a year while the former remains [...] used for 2 or 3 years.'[79] Russian cottons were closer to the thick Punjabi textiles which, the Company's agents noted, 'in a cold Country [...] accords with the inclinations of the people and will induce them to adhere to their own fabrics.'[80] Punjabi and Russian cloth, consequently, were better value than the flimsier, cheaper chintzes manufactured in Britain, and were worn across the lower and middle stratum of Afghan and central Asian society.[81]

In pattern, Russian chintz hand-printers copied, adapted, and innovated designs from Kashmiri shawls and Punjabi chintzes in fashion in Russia and central Asia.[82] In contrast, British Indian agents were only able to recommend which English chintzes might be suitable, the recommendation taking some time to reach the Lancashire mills—if they were transmitted onward at all.[83] Initially, the anxiety that Russian manufactures were reaching Punjab was allayed through the British agents' inquiries into the articles available in the main bazaars in the 1830s and early 1840s.[84] Although Russia's limited import penetration into India was welcome news, the widespread availability of Russian manufactures north of the Hindu Kush took the British Indian agents aback. Unhindered, Russian textile manufactures moved progressively southwards, with growing cargoes of cloth reaching Punjabi and Sindhi bazaars by the later 1840s.[85]

Whereas the Company's factors on the Indus delta had earlier sent musters of cotton cloths to Bombay for consideration as trade items in Europe, the Company's agents in the 1830s and 1840s collected musters and price lists so that Russian textiles could be copied in Europe or analysed in India.[86] Scarcely any of these specimens survive. But specimens of Russian and central Asian textiles—collected in Shikarpur and forwarded to the Court of Directors in London in 1844–5—resurfaced in the course of J. Forbes Watson's ethnographic study of Indian textiles in the 1860s, and were incorporated into his sample books for distribution in Britain and India.[87] Russian thick, twilled cottons—called *naukr* in central Asia—were readily available and 'universally used' amongst the middling and poorer people in Bukhara and Kabul according—Watson noted—to further investigation conducted in 1852.[88] Finally, therefore, on the eve of the Indian Rebellion and the death of the Company, its Court of Directors recognised that British cloths hitherto sent towards the north-west were 'worse in quality, and less suited to the tastes of the consumers, than those supplied by Russia'. They were 'very inferior to Russian fabrics of the same description, being flimsy and not wearing so well', having earlier been deemed too dear, aesthetically inferior, and desired merely as trifles or luxuries.[89] Putting pride in underselling their Russian rivals aside, Company grandees and officials recognised the importance of meeting central Asian, Afghan, and Punjabi consumers' distinctive tastes.[90]

The extraordinary durability of Russian cottons was attributed to the manner of weaving: 'The English Chintz is made in the manner called plain weaving—that is with warp and weft, consisting of single threads', whereas Russian chintz was 'double woven much in the manner of the cloth called here American Drill.'[91] The implications were twofold. First, if true, Russian chintzes were considerably cheaper and better value than English chintzes, using much more material but only undersold by around 15 per cent, a remarkable indictment of Britain's technological advances. Second, to compete successfully, English manufacturers ought 'to change the mode of weaving' and accept that this would raise cost and reduce profitability.[92] Like the Russian broadcloths described to the Company's factors in Sindh in the 1760s, these textiles were also favoured for their brightness. The British believed this brightness faded fast, Russian manufacturers using natural dyes which gradually oxidised or otherwise darkened with exposure to sunlight.[93] Seeing a similarity with the colours and dyes used in Coromandel, Russian chintz samples were sent there so that the distinctive designs could be copied and improved.[94] The outcome of these experiments is no longer documented, but they did not (as chapter 8 shows) help British manufacturers gain any edge over their Russian competitors in interior markets.

Devotion

The life of the first Sikh guru, Nanak (1469–1539), was enmeshed within that of the trading world in numerous respects. His life, in the first place, is typical of the highly mobile itinerant: Nanak travelled to eastern and southern India, into the Himalayas, and—most notably—followed the caravans over the Hindu Kush to the shrines and tombs of the Shi'a saints in Safavid Iran, continuing onward to the holy city of Mecca in Arabia. One incident from these travels relates to his capture by Pashtuns for sale into slavery, a component of caravan trade that flourished in the early modern era and survived into the nineteenth century.[95] Nanak's teachings, moreover, were rooted in the great wave(s) of devotionalism and the simplification of spirituality during the global Reformation. He was, after all, a contemporary of Martin Luther, but also of those numerous wandering mystics and saints (*qalandars*)—Sufis, as well as Hindu *bhakti* devotionalists—who gained popular followings from the fifteenth century across post-Timurid west, central, and south Asia as they challenged the authority of mosque or temple-based religiosity and ritual. Nanak's teachings, in fact, drew heavily on those of his 'competitors' within this increasingly crowded spiritual marketplace, fusing Islamic and Hindu devotional practice into what would later be distinguished as Sikhism.[96]

Nanak was also a contemporary of Muhammad Khan Shaybani. Much like the portrait of the Bukharan khan, early likenesses of the guru depict a man dressed in blue robes, the *topi* (cap) and *seli* (black cords about his waist) of the Sufi *qalandar* distinguishing his piety and poverty from the temporal power and riches of princes.[97] None of these pictures were painted during the life of the guru, some of the earliest dating from the beginning of the eighteenth century, when Sikh rulers began to establish their own courts and engage in acts of princely patronage. Francisco José Luis has traced the Sufi and Shi'a visual references in an example from 1840 contained within a Sanskrit text on the zodiac, *Sarvasiddhantatattvacudamani* (The Jewel of the Essence of All Sciences), which are consistent with what is known about Nanak's spiritual journeys and influences.[98] Indeed, whether or not these are accurate likenesses of the guru, a set of visual and chromatic associations were established around the early eighteenth century, if not earlier. The similarities—within the pictures of Nanak and between the representation of Nanak and Muhammad Khan—are certainly more intriguing than the differences. What, then, is the significance of blueness in all of these pictures?

Blue was reviled in much of south Asia, where indigo was associated with *nazar* (the evil eye), to the extent that Bengali peasants had to be forced to produce the dye for European planters from the late eighteenth century, for instance.[99] Yet, western and central Asia were dotted with what Arash Khazeni has termed 'blue cities', their blueness dating to Timurid times, if not earlier: Samarkand, Tabriz, Isfahan, and Mazaar-i-Sharif.[100] And, moreover, blue-coloured precious stones—lapis lazuli and turquoise from Iran and Afghanistan—had a longer history of circulation through the worlds of nomads and courtiers, and were worn as amulets and rings, inlaid on swords and shields and bridles, and ground for medicinal use, or used to dust precious texts. These were 'imperial and sacred objects' in the material cultures of those states connected by caravan trade and tribute exchange.[101] The most intimate and prevalent chromatic encounter, however, came through the use of the blue textiles produced and consumed across central Eurasia.

Blues and greens are celestial colours, the colours of the Islamic Paradise, closely associated with the clothes of the heavenly as well as with the Prophet Mohammed.[102] In central Asia, attitudes to blue reflected the accretions and amalgamation of the Mongols' view of blue as auspicious and the Islamic view of blue as a protective colour, so that the body—shrouded in bright blue cloth—protected the wearer from wicked spirits, misfortune, or failure.[103] In addition, Sufis believed that blue was the colour indicating the renunciation of worldly concerns, wearing a blue or bluish-black cloak signifying this stage of spiritual awakening, with blue preferred to black, the latter too close to darkness and too far from awakening and light.[104] Sufis were critical not only to the entanglement of religious and commercial life (sketched in previous chapters), perhaps the most tangible consequence of which was the growth of the shrine-town of Multan—itself glimmering with blue and white tiles tinged with green and violet—as a major commercial centre. They also brought the chromatic dimensions of their devotions more deeply into the lives of central Asian Muslims, as well as Pashtuns and Sikhs, as the influence of their thought and practice diffused far and wide with the spread of the Naqshbandiyya and other Sufi orders to north India, as well as the connection of Sufi blessed men to the Afghan tribes.[105]

Unsurprisingly, in this context, blue was widely worn on the body. Samarkandi men and women wore blue and white *khilats* of pure or mixed silk.[106] In the 'Khorasan market', remarked a rather hyperbolic Company agent in the 1830s, 'there is a great demand [for indigo] on account of all the natives wearing nothing but blue trousers', as also amongst Pashtuns[107] Throughout the eighteenth and nineteenth centuries, Afghan traders bought blue ready-dyed woollens and cottons in India, complementing cloths dyed with indigo brought back from

Kandahar, Kabul, and Peshawar; bought from peddlers trading throughout Afghanistan; or bought directly from the marts of western Punjab.[108] While travelling through Afghanistan in 1836, the English traveller Godfrey Thomas Vigne sketched and painted people encountered in the Khyber Pass, Kabul, and Ghazni, his watercolours awash with blue-clothed or blue-turbaned wrestlers, Persian Shi'i Qizilbash military generals, and Pashtun tribesmen.[109] The Hazaras—the non-Pashtun tribes of central Afghanistan—were also drawn into Indo-central Asian trade through peddlers and traders from Kabul and Kandahar, from whom they purchased indigo to dye the blue velvet gowns worn by women, for example.[110]

If some strict Punjabi Hindus eschewed cloth dyed with impure and polluting indigo, the same was not true of Sikhs.[111] From the eighteenth century, if not during the lifetime of Nanak and his successors in the sixteenth and seventeenth centuries, blue started to symbolise to the Sikhs some of these same protective and spiritual qualities.[112] Uch, in Bahawalpur, ranked alongside Multan as an important Sufi centre, both famous for their blue-tiled Sufi shrines thronged by pilgrims even today. To escape the Battle of Chamkaur in 1704, Guru Gobind hired the services of Afghans, who set off only '[a]fter dressing him in blue in the style of Afghans of that region', and who would stop passers-by to ask whether they thought 'he's the son of a *pir* [the head of a Sufi order]'—an event recounted over 200 years later in a work of Afghan historiography, all the more remarkable given that this work is otherwise almost exclusively focused on the political narratives of the Durrani state after 1747.[113] Whether on orders or in remembrance of the guru, the orthodox Sikh warriors known as Nihangs or Akalis took to wearing blue turbans, tunics, and trousers as an outward sign of their faith over the eighteenth century.[114] And, under Ranjit Singh, the regular infantry of the Khalsa army were clothed in indigo-dyed tunics.[115]

The glorious greens and blues of such shrines and mosques and *madrassas* were the products of grinding cobalt and copper ores, but indigo was needed to produce these colours in the papers and cloths consumed across central Asia and Afghanistan. Unlike lapis lazuli or turquoise or even cobalt, moreover, indigo was much more widely available, partly because it was not a sacred or ritual substance in its own right, but also because of its lower cost of production. From the eighteenth century, a number of sources attest to the preference for Punjabi indigo over other sorts, whatever Company officials and Bengali planters might have opined about its rudeness of manufacture and impurity.[116]

Indigo soaked not only into cloth but also into the paper used in central Asia and Afghanistan, this paper imparting a fascinating story of interleaved circulatory flows, for the regional economy of blueness was linked into the global. Indigo gave greater strength and durability to the finished sheet and had been used to colour paper since pre-Islamic times, these blue papers used as writing paper, medicine wrappings, manuscripts, and religious texts.[117] From Asia, the technology of blue-paper production spread to Europe via Venice, where it was used for packaging sugar, the blueness making the sugar appear whiter and indigo's colour fastness preventing spoilage during long trans-oceanic or transcontinental voyages.[118] Following the establishment of the first sugar factory in Russia in 1719, Russian imports included the blue sugar-packing papers. With the establishment of an 'import-substituting' industry in the early eighteenth century, St Petersburg's mills were producing papers tinted blue with an Indian vegetable dye—undoubtedly indigo—by the 1740s.[119] The expansion of the mills resulted in the export of paper, not least the so-called 'Oriental' or 'Muslim' or 'Bukhara-style' blue books and sheets of paper sent via Astrakhan and Kazan to Persia and central Asia.[120]

In 1789, Mashitov, a Tatar Muslim in the Vyatka (Kirov) Province north-east of Moscow, produced around 400 reams of blue paper for export via Astrakhan to the east, a fact also indicative of the vibrancy and diversification of Tatar Muslim commercial activity (described in the previous chapter).[121] So conspicuous was the consumption of these materials in Bukhara or Kabul that it took aback British Indian agents visiting through the 1820s to 1840s.[122] Despite thinking Russian paper poor quality and easily eliminated by British trade via Bombay and Kabul, British agents recognised that the texture was well suited to the calligraphic 'reed used by Asiatics in writing'.[123] In fact, Russian blue sugar paper and writing paper were not supplanted by British substitutes in the nineteenth century.[124] Indigo was not an intrinsically spiritual substance, therefore, but the blueness it imparted was an integral element—alongside the blues of other substances—within a distinctive material culture of devotion encompassing the domains of the body, the book, and the built environment.

Status

In what is perhaps the most famous portrait of Nanak, the guru is portrayed not as a lithe mendicant but as an elderly stoic, wearing not a cap and blue robes but saffron robes and a turban. The work of the renowned twentieth-century artist, Sobha Singh, reproductions of this picture dangle over car dashboards and adorn the walls of temples and homes of diaspora Sikhs worldwide. The picture has gained a sort of hegemony in portraiture of the guru, a reference for his physical appearance. What is most striking is the difference of the earlier paintings to these more recent pictures, revealing a transformation in the visual and material culture of the Sikhs. The alteration is rooted in eighteenth- and especially nineteenth-century socio-economic changes in Punjab and their impact, in turn, upon Sikh (and Hindu) doctrine relating to religious orthodoxy and such institutions as caste.[125] How were caravan trade in raw silk, Punjabi textile manufacture, and material and spiritual shifts entangled with the patronage and consumption of silk cloth?

'If the city of Multan were not supplied with silk by central Asia,' wrote Mohan Lal, the *munshi* and traveller initially accompanying Burnes in the 1830s, 'it would not become the rival of the markets of Hindusthan, the Panjab, and Khorasan. The whole of the Panjab, and even the country of Sindh, wear cloths of silk and thread, which are fabricated only there.'[126] While historians have examined nineteenth-century cloth consumption in the Sikh courts, and European interest in shawl wool and the shawls of Kashmir, this is no reflection of the extent of textile production and consumption in north-west India, as Mohan Lal so acutely observed.[127] Multan was the hub of Punjab's textile economy by the later eighteenth century, but its weavers' wares complemented and competed with those of other production centres. Urban centres such as Dera Ghazi Khan, Dera Ismail Khan, Bahawalpur, Lahore, and Amritsar were entrepôts or emporia for wares from other specialist centres of production. But they were also typical as *qasbahs* where the gentry and nobility patronised artisans, not least in turning yarn into silk cloth.[128] In Sindh, Shikarpur and Thatta were also weaving centres of some repute. Both Bahawalpur and Thatta were well known for their pure silk or mixed cotton-silk *lungis*, a plain and often uncoloured sort of cloth, found for sale locally, across north India, in Afghan and central Asian bazaars, as well as in Persian Gulf markets.[129]

If Muslims were compelled by religious authorities to avoid the worldly luxury of silk, which was thought to distract the wearer from his full and proper submission to God, such injunctions were observed more casually in the early modern era when silk cloth consumption was widely patronised by secular as well as spiritual leaders in the Islamic world.[130] The Muslim rulers of Bahawalpur, for example, patronised fine silk-cloth production through to the mid nineteenth century, if not later.[131] And where the wearing of silks against the skin was still forbidden or frowned upon, wearing silken outer garments was commoner.[132] By 1750, wearing mixed silk-cotton cloth was *mashru* (permitted), including in western Punjab, where Multan was a major centre of *mashru* silk production for the predominantly Muslim population.[133] Multan's silk production probably also served the needs of pilgrims. Sudipta Sen writes of marketplaces in the pilgrimage centres of eighteenth-century Bengal and Benares as 'sites of display—places of worship, prestation, beneficence, and consumption', where '[o]fferings and prayer […] involve buying certain specialised goods at the nearby marketplace and their ritual redistribution.'[134] In Multan and throughout western Punjab, too, pilgrimage, the purchase of ritual goods such as textiles to be laid upon saints' shrines, and redistribution to the poor, ahead of marriages or other rites of passage, continue today. Amongst the Naqshbandis, silk thread even has a metaphorical meaning as the *suluk-e-sufiya* (the path of the Sufis).[135]

Amritsar became a rival centre to Multan for it, too, was a major pilgrimage centre and thus the locus of artisanal patronage by gentry elites. The city is famous for the Harmandir Sahib (the abode of God, the Golden Temple) and as the centre, therefore, of the Sikh faith. Built in the sixteenth century, the temple and the city were twice devastated by the Durranis between 1747 and 1767, although rebuilt thereafter. From 1765, Amritsar was the seat of the Sarbat Khalsa, the assembly of the Sikhs, with some of the *misldars* constructing their own *katras* (residences with markets) within the city.[136] Such endowments in public infrastructure were part of their self-fashioning, for the establishment and patronage of new marketplaces was an important marker of authority, civility, and virtuosity, at the same time cementing relationships with powerful commercial elites that had the resources (as chapter 4 showed) to make or break political authority.[137] Yet, more subtly, for those Sikh *misldars* who were establishing themselves in eighteenth- and nineteenth-century Punjab, silk-cloth consumption and the patronage of silk-weaving workshops were also part of their self-fashioning as magnanimous refined rulers in the Indo-Islamicate mould, and as heirs to the Mughals.[138] The apotheosis of these *misldars* was Ranjit Singh, who went as far as collecting Mughal clothes, despite dressing rather modestly.[139]

The city's expansion is well documented in the decades after Ranjit Singh's absorption of Amritsar in 1805, serving thereafter as the maharaja's summer capital. As Amritsar continued to draw the Sikh chiefs, there was a further phase of urban residential and commercial development in the south of the city.[140] The houses of Amritsar's richest traders and financiers were four-storey brick-built constructions, whitewashed and covered in frescoes on religious themes—conspicuous signs of wealth and the piety that was expected to accompany worldly riches.[141] 'There is more movement and life in Amritsar than in any town in British India,' wrote Victor Jacquemont at the end of the 1820s, 'and it is the first city I have seen showing obvious signs of expansion.' For Jacquemont, Amritsar was the Benares of Punjab. The residence of the Sikh elites was also understood in the same sense as the rich Bengalis residing at Benares.[142] Despite its 'very trifling' exports—'the inhabitants only manufacturing some coarse kinds of cloth and inferior silks'—Amritsar was already 'the resort of many rich merchants [...] the residence of bankers [...] and considered a place of great wealth and opulence' in the early 1800s. According to another reporter, it was gaining ground over the Sikh maharaja's winter capital, Lahore.[143] In contrast to Lahore, Amritsar's population was 'much more mixed' and included sizeable communities of Afghans, Kashmiris, and Persians, according to Jacquemont, indicative of its growth as a centre of long-distance trade.[144] The expansion of shawl weaving was closely connected not only to the relocation of artisans from Kashmir but also to state patronage.[145] Silk weavers were also drawn to Amritsar, serving the Sikh chiefs and their courts, as well as pilgrims. Within the city, certain areas and bazaars became famous for their silk dyers, winders, and weavers, their names indicative of their resident industries, such as Kucha and Gali Daryai Baffana.[146]

Political change brought social change not only for those who now found themselves at the top of the chain of command, but also into the upper reaches of village society, where the signalling and consolidation of newfound status was likewise achieved through shifting patterns of consumption and adopting what were often new forms of material culture. *In toto*, these processes were characteristic of the casteisation of Indian society in the post-Mughal period sketched by Susan Bayly.[147] In the first place, there was the 'rebirth' of arriviste eighteenth-century rulers as Kshatriyas (warrior caste) through the services of Brahmins (priestly caste), as well as the employment of literate Brahmin specialists within the revenue-administrative apparatus of their new states. In Punjab, this was evident in the 'spirit of imitation' amongst the Hindu and Sikh peasant leaderships of the eighteenth century who drew on the power of Indo-Islamicate or Mughal idioms of royal authority as much as the appeal of Kshatriya or Rajput status, some of whom would eventually establish dynastic principalities of their own.[148] In turn, the result was the elevation of Brahmins and Brahminic rituals within an increasingly hierarchical conceptualisation of caste relations, even— Bayly notes—in Ranjit Singh's Sikh polity.[149] As such ideas gained traction, there was a more widespread appeal to 'upper'-caste identity and the emulation of Brahmin and Kshatriya behaviours and mores by Indians—ever deeper into village society, often to the level of the peasant. The push was to claims over material resources, especially in times when economic hardship drove competition for cultivation or revenue rights, for instance. Outside urban centres such as Amritsar, the first signs of these changes were evident at the *pargana* level, for Sikh rule in Punjab from the eighteenth century gradually led to the replacement of the Muslim Rajputs or zamindars with Jats or local landed cultivators as the main revenue payers.[150] For the Jats who came to think of themselves as being at the apex of local society, it was necessary to uphold or else appropriate the customs and consumption habits of those they came to replace, and simultaneously to restrict the consumption choices of their social inferiors.

The profundity of these changes becomes apparent when considering the extent to which this new caste ideology sharpened the sense of social difference, defined through the purity/pollution or auspiciousness/inauspiciousness of consumption choices, such that consumption now articulated or even determined the inclusion and exclusion of individuals. In spite of the 'flatness' of caste in Punjabi society, and the far from straightforward relationship of caste to Brahminical Hinduism relative to the Hindi belt, caste was not irrelevant, and was important to social and occupational organisation amongst Hindus, Muslims, and Sikhs in rural and urban areas.[151] There was considerable exchange within these societies, across boundaries of caste and religion, with the Hindus of the plains worshipping local Muslim and Sikh saints and vice versa, for example, such popular religious practices often continuing well into the twentieth century.[152] If ritual notions of pollution affected consumption choices and habits amongst Hindus, these might also have affected their Muslim brethren, especially those who considered themselves of equal social standing, as well as Hindus converted to Islam or Sikhism, who remained concerned about the 'loss' of caste despite the religious injunction against casteism.[153] Ultimately, ritual notions of pollution were probably weaker in early-nineteenth-century Punjab than the Hindi belt of north India, in the westernmost districts than the eastern parts of the province, and in the agricultural villages than the urban pilgrimage and commercial centres.[154]

But notions of purity and pollution were not absent from Punjabi society and were, in fact, strengthening over the nineteenth century at the same time that boundaries differentiating religious identities (*qua* ideologies and praxis)—Hinduism, Sikhism, Islam—were being erected, as Harjot Oberoi has forcefully argued.[155] With the gradual rise to hegemony of Khalsa Sikhism came a new material culture of rites, not least those revolving around ritual objects. These included the *kirpan* (dagger), *kanga* (comb), and *kachera* (undergarments) on the person of Khalsa initiates—revealing the intersection of casteist concerns for purity with the martial ideology of this dominant sect of the Sikhs. This confluence of ideas also shifted the significations of silk, and the sorts of hierarchical relationships the patronage and wearing of silk cloth conveyed, from an article expressing political or material rank and refinement to a ritual good indicating the wearer's status within the moral order of caste society. In other words, material culture—including of silk cloth—was critical to the ethnogenesis or collective self-fashioning toward what would become 'upper'-caste Sikhism some time before colonial ethnography concretised such identities.

Silk, like the saffron colour worn by Nanak (in pictures discussed in the opening to this section), came to be favoured for its auspiciousness amongst caste-conscious Sikhs, as also their fellow Hindus. Moreover, as silk could be woven much more tightly and densely than coarser cotton or woollen yarns, the greater extent of its impermeability offered Hindus greater protection from the entrapment of pollution from spiritual and worldly impurities, also negating the need for regular washing of the fabric.[156] Silk was thus the textile of choice among the royal and priestly elites. It was worn more widely in society at festive and ceremonial times, or as a mixed fabric on these and other occasions, especially throughout eastern Punjab and Hindustan where Multani and Amritsari silks found sale amongst Hindus and Sikhs.[157] The Victoria and Albert (V&A) Museum's collection contains some of the earliest surviving examples of Punjabi silk fabrics and garments, dating from the 1840s and 1850s, giving an invaluable glimpse of the sorts of textiles worn on the eve of the British annexation of the province.

In 'upper'-caste urban society, popular pure-silk textiles included *gulbadan* and *daryai*. *Gulbadan*—a striped silk of two colours, such as pale green and scarlet, purple and yellow, or crimson and white—was 'much used for the [...] pyjamas worn by the wealthier classes of Hindoos and Sikhs'.[158] These trousers varied from voluminous vertically gathered trousers, such as a pair of pantaloons stitched in Peshawar from Lahore silk cloth, to narrow horizontally gathered trousers, such as a pair of trousers stitched in Sindh.[159] *Daryai*, a silk shot with two colours, such as red and green, was 'used by Mahomedans & Hindoos for shirts, caps, etc & by females for Petticoats'.[160] 'Light and shade', or *dhup-chaon*, was the term for the effect of such shot silks, which were worn as turbans in Punjab, including an example in the V&A woven from silk and silk-wrapped gold thread.[161] Outside the towns, and despite their more modest means, the wealthier landed Jats were known to wrap such silks around a cotton turban or trim their shawls with silk.[162] Despite being 'almost exclusively a military and agricultural people,' the Sikhs wore 'scarves [...] usually trimmed with a coloured silk border, and sometimes scarlet shawls, or other showy fabrics' to display their elevated status to the artisan and menial castes of their villages.[163] The Jat soldiery, too, sought to distinguish themselves through their dress, donning brightly coloured *daryai* turbans and tunics, for example.[164]

Collected by the Lahore Central Committee and sewn into a leather-bound book shortly after the annexation of Punjab, sent to London accompanying samples for the International Exhibition of 1862, and finally transferred to the South Kensington Museum (now the V&A) in 1881, are around eighty samples of silk fabrics manufactured in mid-nineteenth-century Lahore.[165] The Committee distinguished the samples as pre- or post-annexation patterns, with the former representing roughly two-thirds of the swatches. The pre-annexation patterns are further distinguished according to the religious rather than ethnic, age, or gender origins of the buyers—typical of the categories employed by the emerging 'ethnographic state' in colonial Punjab—with three-fifths attributed to Hindu consumption and two-fifths to Muslim consumption.[166] The rationale for this classification is confusing, however, for there are few differences in terms of texture or colour between fabrics purportedly bought by Hindus and by Muslims.[167] Nevertheless, the swatches show the variety of silk yardage woven in Punjab. Unlike the large collection of *lungis* or finely finished fabrics that were collected by colonial officials and survive in museum collections or pattern books, these silk swatches are relatively plain but brightly coloured pieces of cloth, and are probably the earliest extant examples of such silk cloth from Punjab. Aside from a few samples of *daryai*, most of the swatches of the older patterns are *gulbadan*, of which there are three main types. The commonest are broadly spaced stripes of one colour on a plain, sometimes shot, background of a contrasting colour. Also common are silks of alternating narrow stripes in two colours, known as *ulwan*.[168] Amongst the least common are the plain-backed silks with broadly spaced stripes of a contrasting colour, and periodically placed bars of block colour, sometimes of gold thread. Additionally, several striped silks introduced during the reign of Maharaja Sher Singh (r. 1841–3) are evidence of the innovation and introduction of new patterns to cater for changing fashions through to the closing years of Sikh rule.

Other evidence suggests yet further varieties of silk textiles. Fancy cloth included *atlas* (satin) and *kinkhab* or 'brocade of the Punjab', deemed 'inferior to that of Bengal and Guzerat' by Burnes, although perhaps ideally suited to the tastes of consumers in north-west India.[169] Some textiles, such as *lungis*, were woven as silk, *mashru*, or cotton cloths, often plain fabrics with coloured or embroidered borders. While silk *lungis* were 'not so much worn for head-dresses as the cotton lungis', they were worn as a sort of wrap-around skirt, and also 'much admired for scarves and waist-belts or sashes.'[170] Weavers of cotton *lungis* with silk-bordered ends made use of middling to cheap sorts of silk thread, such as *charkhi* from Bukhara, for more affordable embellishment.[171] Whereas cotton-silk textiles were widely worn, mixes of silk and wool were worn for warmth as shawls and cloaks.[172] Alongside fabrics woven for clothing, silk also adorned domestic spaces in the form of cotton-silk bed covers (*khes*) and wool-silk carpets.[173] Although raw-silk yarns of varying fineness were imported into Punjab, generally these were woven into thick textiles, reflecting the thickness of central Asian silk compared to the Chinese or Italian silks in vogue in Britain.[174]

If ritual or other notions of status guided the growing demand for silk cloth, provenance also played a part in the formation of preferences for silks woven from central Asian yarns, evident by the early nineteenth century. Unsuited to the market in Europe, British officials observed that cloth woven of central Asian yarn 'is greatly preferred by the Native [Punjabi] consumer, to the Bengal or other kinds, being much stouter and stronger'.[175] Such was the reputation and reverence of Bukharan silk that textiles would sometimes be woven with a strong Bukharan silk warp and a cheaper and weaker silk or cotton weft.[176] Although traders brought few finished central Asian silk textiles to India, their purchase and usage suggests the significance of provenance to those elite or courtly buyers in the north-west who bought them.[177] Worn by Sindhi women as a loose head covering, Bukharan silk sheets (*chaddar*) available in the bazaars of Hyderabad were 'used only on occasions of marriages or in the houses of the wealthy', unlike less-expensive and locally woven *lungis* which were in far greater demand for the same use.[178] Similarly, Bukharan *gulbadan* was sold on a small scale alongside similar Punjabi varieties, probably purchased for dowries or ceremonial occasions.[179]

Conclusion

Once gracing the ceiling of the East India Company's Revenue Room at its London headquarters, Spiridione Roma's painting of the Orient giving up its riches to Britannia is typical of a genre of pictures—from engravings in books to oil paintings and frescoes—produced in early modern Europe.[180] Such images are a boon to global historians, many of whom remain more entranced by east-to-west exchanges than the impact of globalisation on the world of things in Asia or Africa, for these pictures personify the emerging geopolitics of new material cultures while illuminating the imperialism of new materialist mentalités in Europe and the Atlantic world. In contrast, especially outside 'cosmopolitan' royal courts, Asian societies tend to be seen as relatively impervious to things, the sink for bullion brought through networks of global trade rather than global goods.[181] If India and China were the workshops of the world, then it is remarkable how little attention has been paid to the relationship of ordinary Asians with the things they produced, not least because Asians manufactured goods wanted by Europeans long before the latter started to buy them on any significant scale. Consumption was, in fact, as integral to material and spiritual life in south and central Asia as in Europe. As the material presented in this chapter demonstrates, moreover, the period from the eighteenth to the mid nineteenth century was a time of considerable political, social, and economic change, in turn shifting even the most quotidian patterns of consumption and transforming the relationships of relatively ordinary people to things in ways analogous to other societies. How alike or dissimilar was Asia from Europe, continental interiors from their maritime rimlands?

The early moderns were highly mobile, the course of their lives a cycle of different sorts of movement and exchanges (as earlier chapters have highlighted). In their day-to-day lives can be seen a microcosm of this mobility, for those dwelling in urban centres certainly travelled to hear and to share news, to shop or to be shaved, to eat and to bathe. Melissa Calaresu's study of street vendors of snow, sorbets, and ice creams in eighteenth-century Naples draws attention to the ephemerality of consumables and services, and, in turn, the ephemerality of so much—but especially plebeian forms of—early modern material culture and sociability.[182] Many of the goods brought by the caravans into the bazaars of south or central Asia certainly exhibited some sort of perishability or evanescence: they were depleted through 'use', whether dyestuffs such as indigo—dissolved so its blueness could be imparted upon cloth—or drugs and dry and fresh fruits disappearing upon ingestion.[183] Snow and ice, incidentally, were also brought from the Hindu Kush and Kashmir to Mughal Delhi and other urban centres, not only for the imperial elite and gentryfolk (who tended to store their supplies in the underground basements of their private residences), but also to be made available more widely in the summer months.[184] Other commodities, such as cloth, were worn until they disintegrated, not to mention the animals and slaves who worked until they died, were freed, or were of no further use. Of the small number of goods that were more robust, survival through to present times depended upon their consideration as worthy of collection and preservation or documentation. Such attitudes were unfortunately far too rare, as revealed in the collection and subsequent archival burying of the scrap-books of early-nineteenth-century Punjabi silk and cotton cloth. The reasons for forgetting about these textiles were rooted in the aesthetic and historical sensibilities of late-Victorian colonial officials (to which chapter 8 returns).

Whatever the difficulties of studying the social lives of things in premodern south and central Asia, this chapter shows that there can be no doubt about the importance to contemporaries of the world of goods brought by or built around caravan trade. Well into the nineteenth century, far from being a trade in trinkets and trifles, Indo-central Asian trade remained integral to the material cultures of diverse social actors and groups who tapped into these exchange networks: kings, noblemen, and gentry; nomads, peasants, and soldiers; Muslim, Hindu, and Sikh holy men and lay people, both of higher- and lower-evaluated caste, and orthodox or more mystical and devotional practice; men and women, many of whom sought to harness the opportunities brought by social and political change in the period to escape or elevate their standing. In Safavid and Qajar Iran, Rudi Matthee has argued, tea, coffee, and opium were not considered 'luxuries'—even if they possessed this status in western Europe—and so it would be wrong to analyse them as such.[185] In similar vein, some of the things examined in this chapter were conspicuously expensive but consumable in small quantities (such as a small piece of protective turquoise), or only occasionally (such as precious stones or other substances ground as a medicine), or else were available in cheaper varieties (not least cotton cloth).[186]

The variety of source materials discussed in this chapter is testament to the rich material cultures of early modern south and central Asia: texts written for or by the actors connected to the trading world and writings by travellers, the remains of things, the vestiges of a world in which such things circulated or were represented (not least courtly patronage of artisanal production and painting). Put crudely, some 'commodities' were 'raw materials' to be transformed through processing or manufacture—indigo and silk yarn into protective cloth, for example. Often, a particular object or commodity could have multiple lives or uses as a thing; the horse *qua* warhorse or as a prize specimen for ritual gifting or spectacular public display, for instance. The existence of variety enabled purchasers to articulate their sense of fashion, taste, and connoisseurship, and thus to self-fashion their identities, differentiating themselves from others and, often, elevating their rank or status in so doing. In this respect, the actors examined in this chapter were part of a world where fashion mattered, much like their contemporaries and counterparts in Damascus or the Dutch Republic, and where foreign goods played an important part in the performance and presentation of oneself and one's taste.[187]

Yet, ethno-religious, communal, sectarian, or other sorts of difference were neither wholly manufactured by the colonial authorities nor simply the result of the clash with modernity. A sense of difference existed in earlier times, transcended or concretised, dissolved or reconstituted as actors saw fit. In the case study of blueness, for instance, is a story at once of crossing categories of difference as the significations of sacred or protective colour were diffused, and, yet, also of the articulation of boundaries between different social groups. That is, because blue did not universally—in the world of caravan trade—become a colour to be worn on the body, eschewed by 'upper'-

caste (if not also 'lower'-caste) Punjabi Hindus; blueness also signified the existence of difference and separation. In the case of silk-cloth consumption can be seen how differentiation also entailed exclusion—namely, of the lower castes by upper castes—and the attempt to escape from exclusion by the emulation of 'upper'-caste practices when materially possible. In due course, this led to the elaboration of hierarchical orderings of people and personal relations within Punjabi society that made more real and more rigid the sense of social difference. These moral economies of consumption were of differing degrees of inclusiveness, but, crucially, inclusion always operated hand-in-glove with exclusion. The emergence of such moral orders, as much as their erosion (examined further in chapter 8), indicates that they were probably not permanent and certainly not timeless.

And, finally, the things examined in this chapter highlight the interconnections not only across space, but in the world of things itself. Just as the *Faras-nama* literature fused with other learning on equine care and management to produce an eclectic body of equestrian advice and texts by the early modern period, so, too, did *Javahir-nama* (Book of Stones) texts infiltrate other sorts of writings on the properties and significances of precious stones for literate elites, Arash Khazeni has shown.[188] Precious stones of the *haft rang*, the seven celestial colours—turquoise blue, night blue, black, green, red, ochre, and white—of Persianate tradition had become 'embedded in the culture of kingship and empire across Islamic Eurasia and known as [victorious stones] adorning conquerors and kings.'[189] The Turki horses in Ranjit Singh's stables were thus caparisoned in heavily studded bridles of diamonds, emeralds, rubies, pearls, coral, and, of course, Iranian or Afghan turquoise—the colours of the *haft rang* associated with the preeminent stones of the *Javahir-nama*. Horses and stones, kingly advice and beliefs in the divine, all were brought to India through trade networks stretching into central Eurasia. Traffic flowed in the other direction, too, not least in indigo used to impart its blueness upon cloth worn by Afghan pastoralists and Qizilbash soldiers, Sufi *pirs* and their Bukharan royal patrons, the successors to the dynasty established by Muhammad Khan Shaybani. Ultimately, caravan trade was the vector for the emergence of a shared, interconnected, or overlapping cultural and spiritual world. This world is evinced tangibly through things—and the beliefs about their temporal materiality or immanence—ranging from the provenance of knowledges contained within equine manuals, to the widening and deepening of a culture of blueness across the trading world.

Whatever the literate elites of the imperial heartlands might have penned about the barbarism of the frontier, this shared world of meanings and dispositions towards things serves to integrate the oft-forgotten interior or inner continental spaces into the study of material culture. While fashion or taste are alien and ahistoric concepts, they speak to the concerns of early modern selves and societies for performing or producing identity by harnessing the power of things, thus providing a language with which to connect Europeans and their Asian contemporaries.[190] Moreover, fashion—as a concept—has been analytically productive in this chapter, for it implies the appearance of novelty that prompts steady shifts in the nature or form or appearance of a particular good. In this way, fashion stands in contradistinction to the notions of 'traditional' or 'customary' consumption that continue to bedevil the study of non-European societies, making the relationship of people to things appear much more fixed than in European societies, thus manufacturing the notion of Oriental alterity in the material sphere. At the same time, processes of self-fashioning and emulation—even as individuals sought to subtly differentiate their individual or lineage identities, for instance—were framed in relation to the pull of some hegemonic centre or role model. In this way, the case studies examined in this chapter are a reminder that the ecological and economic distinctiveness underpinning the interdependence of the dry and wet zones was also a factor making for their integration and the flattening of cultural or social differences.

But all was not alike, and differences—of the north Indian plain to the dry zone stretching from the Indus to the Oxus, of Asia from Europe—are also discernible. The global turn in studies of early modern material culture has not been tinged with Eurocentrism, scholars consciously focusing on the ways in which Asian novelty held European consumption to ransom in an Indo-Sinocentric global economy. This developing body of work, however, is markedly Eurotropic, the stock of scholarship focusing predominately on those connections and exchanges that mattered to European material culture (either crowding out or coming at the expense of studying east–east connections, for example).[191] In other words, globally minded scholars of material culture have tended to reproduce the networks of imperial power and patterns of domination, thus reifying and giving new life to the Iberian, Dutch, French, and (especially) British empires in the present.

A growing body of work, however, has started to address the role of overland connections with Siberia and China, Iran and central Asia, in shaping Russian material culture. The long-distance tea trade—and the westward travel of the associated material culture of tea consumption—'domesticated' China in Russia, for example, highlighting the terrestrial alternative to early modern east–west exchanges through maritime channels prevailing in the scholarship.[192] Tea, rhubarb, and ginger were replaced in importance by other goods as these terrestrial networks developed in the nineteenth century (chapter 8 thus briefly returning to tea in examining Russia's impact on caravan trade in the final decades of the century).[193] Russia's Pacific Ocean trade, finally, shaped material cultures on islands comprising what could be called an 'oceanic interior'—another oft-overlooked space at a distance from the networks entangling the dominant actors of the early modern Atlantic world.[194]

As this and earlier chapters have shown, caravan trade looped into or overlapped with other commercial circuits, including those stretching further across India or Iran, into the Indian Ocean world and onwards to the Atlantic Ocean and Europe, and into the expanding Russian Empire. Overland trade between south and central Asia was thus enmeshed into a vast terreaqueous world. The argument is not that these inner spaces were more or less connected than the maritime rim of Afro-Eurasia; rather, it is that the geography of their connectivity was probably more complex than that linking western Europe with seaboard India or China, for instance, instead reaching outwards—perhaps necessarily—into *all* directions. If the seas offered the path of least resistance in an age of sail—when long-distance shipping became ever faster and cheaper—the land offered challenges that had long been surmounted by peoples who found no need to suddenly empty out of continental interiors. The vindication of terrestrial connectivity can be seen in the journeys of blue paper and textile motifs from Asia to the West, and back again, via Russia. This chapter has also shown that

Russian manufacturers and traders were already more responsive—even if only implicitly—to the dispositions and demand of consumers within these interior spaces by the early nineteenth century, and perhaps earlier. On the eve of the British and Russian colonial conquest of north-west India and central Asia, respectively, therefore, Russians were more intimately connected to the world of goods and people circulating across this space than other Europeans. This would have profound consequences for the transformation of caravan trade in the later nineteenth century, and it is to the impact of colonialism that the remainder of this book turns.

6

COLONIAL CONQUEST

By the 1830s, the first age of global imperialism was coming to its conclusion, as the British and French empires shifted from a phase of vigorous expansion to consolidation, not least in Asia.[1] Beyond the well-watered coastal regions and river valleys of the Indian Ocean world, however, the Durrani, Qing, and Romanov empires were pushing from all directions deeper into the Eurasian interior after *c.* 1750. The result was the enrichment of the dry-zone economies, their increasing integration through long-distance trade that channelled liquidity and goods through this space, and the concomitant ascendance of new merchant groups that took advantage of this burst of commercial opportunity (as analysed in previous chapters). These developments proceeded partly according to their own dynamics, disconnected in some respects from the rumblings of change emanating from the Atlantic and Indian ocean arenas, yet drawing some of their vitality from the bullion wealth accumulated or continuing to flow therefrom.

By the 1830s, the global economy was also in the midst of depression. In part, this was associated with the aftershock of the Napoleonic Wars in Europe, particularly the weakening of Spain that precipitated the struggle for independence in Spanish America, in turn disrupting the mining of New World silver. The effects of the contraction of global liquidity and global trade were palpable in China and India, formerly the world's sink for bullion. For, despite the conquest of much of the subcontinent by the East India Company by 1818 and the access, therefore, to India's vast revenues, the Company still relied on imports of silver to fuel some of its commercial activities as it bungled from one revenue-cash crisis to another.[2] On the one hand, the effects of this crunch in the modern world economy rippled through the archaic networks of caravan trade, whether in the Indo-Afghan frontier or Turkestan. Here slowdown in trade was accompanied by a wobble in the ruling lineages of the dry zone, including the transfer from the Sadozai to Barakzai line in the Durrani polity, the internal political conflict in Xinjiang studied by Kwangmin Kim, and the relatively inglorious reign of the Khokand ruler Madali Khan (r. 1822–42), whose career has been described in detail by Scott Levi.[3] On the other hand, the interior seemed a rich prospect to Europeans. Exploration of this uncharted El Dorado was the first step, often preceding conquest or the establishment of political relations (usually of a rather asymmetric or suzerain sort).[4] Exploitation of commercial opportunities—trade in manufactures, the sourcing of raw materials, including minerals as well as primary inputs such as cotton—followed. Thus, no sooner had the dust settled on the first age of global empire, than a second age of global empire was well in motion from mid century, culminating in conquest of the continental interior of Afro–Eurasia by the 1880s. Through colonial conquest, the territories and sphere of influence of British India were extended to Sindh and Punjab (1843–9), of Russia to Khiva, Khokand, and later Bukhara (1847–95), while Afghanistan was reshaped and subordinated to the British Empire.

Although the Marxist or Hobsonian–Leninist view of imperial expansion as the search for new markets has been extensively critiqued, economic interests and the exploration of commercial possibilities did play a part in the backdrop to colonial conquest in a much broader sense, while economic imperatives subsequently shaped colonial policy in both south and central Asia.[5] Aside from access to raw materials from central Asia, Russia sought markets for its manufactures, as well as areas of settlement for migrants from the land-hungry European domains of the empire.[6] Limiting the central Asian states' market potential was population size, which was too small to serve any useful long-run role as India served Britain.[7] Although India was three and a half times the size of the oasis states of central Asia, its total population was over forty-one times that of the latter, and its average population density about twelve times greater.[8] Russian ambitions were fixed upon India and China. To a lesser extent, protecting and promoting the flow of English and Indian goods to Afghan and central Asian markets was where British 'counter'-interests were formulated.

Anglo-Russian rivalry was thus rooted in the threat of territorial aggression and acquisition, but largely because markets could either be penetrated peacefully or broken open by force. Despite the attention 'Great Game' historians have given to the military, strategy, and security concerns, the most active arenas of competition and contestation were not the battlefields but the bazaars of central Asia and Afghanistan.[9] British commercial interest in central Asia grew tremendously through the nineteenth century, with the opening of trade with Turkestan debated as an economic policy in Parliament from the late 1850s.[10] Governmental interest culminated and crystallised in R. H. Davies' *Report* of 1862 on Indo-central Asian trade, a compilation of facts, figures, and findings from William Moorcroft's travels to Davies' own investigations for the information of the provincial, Indian, and metropolitan governments in Lahore, Calcutta, and London.[11]

Before mid century, the networks and exchanges of caravan trade shaped the societies and economies they connected: patterns of production and specialisation, urban–rural relations and marketing, power and state revenues, finance and financial markets, trade and trade networks, and consumption and material culture. But the incorporation of north-west India and central Asia into the British and Russian empires pushed and pulled caravan trade in different directions—some supporting and others obstructing trade in new or existing goods, some entrenching established routes and others assisting the growth of alternative economic geographies. Alongside the still-considerable traffic across the Hindu Kush, three other routes rose to prominence in the second half of the nineteenth century. First, trade up and down the length of the Indus—outward across the Arabian Sea and inward within Punjab—was again possible thanks to the opening of the river to steamships and the construction of a railway network. Second, trade through Kashmir to Chinese Turkestan was encouraged and expanded from the 1860s, offering an alternative route to Khokand and Bukhara.

Third, trade through the central Asian deserts and wastelands was boosted by railways constructed in the late nineteenth century, connecting Asia with the fringes of Europe. The aim of the remainder of this chapter is not to evaluate the motivations for, and the process of, colonial conquest. The aim is to sketch the broad changes in economic geography, mobility, and commercial opportunity that resulted from the extension of colonial rule, providing an anchor for the subsequent chapters examining the entanglements of colonial rule with the boom and subsequent decline of caravan trade in the latter half of the nineteenth century.

Across the Arabian Sea

Almost half a century after the departure of the English factors from the Indus Delta in 1775, and a few decades after the brief renaissance in British interests in Sindh between the 1790s and the 1810s, British interests in commerce re-emerged in the 1830s, this time with central Asia via Sindh, the province seen as a sort of springboard into these markets.[12] For the optimistic and opportunistic British, the Indus was seen as a channel for the flow of European manufactured goods upstream towards Punjab and beyond, an ambition that was realised after the conquest of Sindh. Karachi was occupied by the Company in 1839 on the eve of the Anglo-Afghan War and, following a string of conflicts with the Talpurs—Sindh's ruling family—the province was annexed in 1843 and incorporated into the Bombay Presidency in 1847.

The promotion of trade and economic enterprise increased in importance thereafter, to render remunerative territories neither London nor Calcutta had desired.[13] After surveying the bazaars of Shikarpur and Hyderabad, the British turned their attention to 'freeing' trade by integrating it into the customs system of Company territory and negotiating the reduction of the 'vexatious transit and trade duties' with the 'native princes' that they deemed detrimental to the success of Karachi as an inlet for the flow of European goods towards Afghanistan and central Asia.[14]

Without transport of sufficient capacity and efficiency—roads, riverboats, and railways—trade would remain expensive and extremely small in scope, however. The prelude to the conquest of Sindh was marked by examinations of existing ports and—ultimately unsuccessful—attempts to open the Indus to navigation.[15] Although a weekly steamship service was used to carry mail throughout the 1840s, the river was too shallow and shifting, and the currents too strong for fast and reliable service by steamships.[16] Thus, human-, animal-, and wind-powered boats outcompeted not one but four public- and privately-funded efforts to launch regular steamer services on the river, while later also holding their own against the railway traffic, carrying a significant proportion of the growing cargoes being ferried from Karachi to upstream Sindhi and Punjabi marts, and vice versa.[17]

The railways made a more significant impact on interior-to-coastal transportation, nevertheless. Under the Sindh, Punjab and Delhi Railway Company (SPDR), the construction of 32 miles of railway between Lahore and Amritsar was completed in 1862, and the 218-mile Lahore–Multan line laid in 1864.[18] By 1870, it was possible to make the 490-mile journey from Lahore through Amritsar to Delhi.[19] Following the establishment of the Indus Valley State Railway in 1878, it was no longer necessary to take steamer transport between Karachi and Lahore, finally cutting out the most dangerous parts of the steamer journey.[20] And, by 1883, the Punjab Northern State Railway connected Lahore with Peshawar. Thus, Punjab's main mercantile towns—Amritsar, Lahore, Multan—were linked by routine services to inland entrepôts as well as ports.

Aside from the expansion of trade from Sindh to the Persian Gulf across the sea, and to Baluchistan and southern Afghanistan across the land, the most important effect of Sindh's commercial opening was the emergence of Karachi as a conduit between Bombay and Punjab. Both mediating and moulding this transformation were local traders: Parsis, Memons, Jews, and other trading communities from western India.[21] A number of Afghan merchants made the journey to Bombay from Karachi, with countless others content to trade in Sindh.[22] A considerable number of Babis, a Yusufzai tribe, and other traders from southern Afghanistan and Kalat were involved in trade between Kandahar and Bombay.[23] It was from Kalati merchants such as Ghulam Muhammad, Abul Ahmed, and Abul Azur, therefore, that Sindh's colonial administrators sought information about the scope and scale of trade to

Bombay.[24] Persians were also to be found in Karachi and the Sindhi hinterland, although their commerce was directed westward rather than northward to central Asia.[25] For Punjab and Sindh's commercial classes, therefore, Karachi served as the springboard for the establishment of overseas trade networks to the Persian Gulf and north Africa, to the west, and south-east Asia and Japan, to the east.[26] But the impact of this new pattern and geography of integration would also be felt within the economy of caravan trade, for the activities of merchants trading via Karachi helped funnel imports from new locales, some supporting the expansion of Indo-central Asian trade, in goods such as tea, others undermining the productive economy upon which it was based, such as the influx of east Asian silks.

Across the Karakoram

Rising from the foothills in north India, the Himalaya and Karakoram ranges run in parallel, a double divide separating the Punjab plains from the Tarim Basin in Xinjiang or Chinese Turkestan, at the westernmost edge of the Qing Empire. This is Eurasia's 'pole of inaccessibility', its rivers running into no seas or lakes, its epicentre farther from the oceans than anywhere else across the entire land mass. Higher than the Hindu Kush passes, open only once a year between December and January, and alien to the camel, traders relied on small mountain ponies to traverse these routes, decanting their wares from ponies onto hairy yaks when the cold became bitter and burning, or when crossing the passes that remained glaciated even in summer.[27]

The annual traffic of traders and pilgrims took one of two main routes between north-west India and western China. Choosing between these two routes was to trade off efficiency and economy on the one hand, and security and safety on the other. The shorter and cheaper route ran roughly west of what is now the Karakoram Highway. Setting out north-westward from Lahore, the route arced north from Peshawar, and then north-east through Chitral, the Wakhan valley, and the Pamirs to Kashgar and Yarkand, taking traders thirty-seven days from Peshawar and a few more from Lahore, which was even accessible to loaded carts and caravans.[28] But there was 'great[er] danger to person and property on that route', which cut through 'the territories of numerous independent tribes.'[29] And, so, these routes were 'confined to certain adventurous Afghans'—from Badakhshan, such as the 'reputable and constant trader' Muhammad Rahim, as well as Kabul and other trading towns—and almost never traversed by Yarkandis.[30] The costlier, slower, but safer route steered eastward from Lahore to Palampur and Kullu, then northward through Lahoul and Leh to Yarkand and Kashgar, taking almost twice as long at sixty-four days.[31] From Chinese Turkestan, a trek across the Pamirs took the trader into the Fergana valley.[32]

Journeying across the Himalaya and the Karakoram ranges was arduous and dangerous, but traders profitably carried cloth and comestibles, drugs and dyestuffs, and other valuable goods including gold and silver.[33] There are scant sources on the traders themselves, many of whom were probably Tibetans, Yarkandis, and Kashmiris who met in Leh, Ladakh's entrepôt, to exchange goods. Since few of the goods bought and sold in China or India were from Ladakh, Ladakhis benefited from trade taxes and the passing of traders, rather than productive activities per se.[34] Just as some of the Powindas earned a living through the organisation of the caravans across the Hindu Kush, some Ladakhis (known as *kiraiyakashi*) rented their horses or ponies to the trans-Karakoram traders.[35] The Ladakhis linked the Yarkandi or Tibetan-dominated northward trans-Karakoram circuit, and the Kashmiri or Punjabi-dominated southern trans-Himalayan circuit, which were probably otherwise separate.

Shortly after the conquest of Ladakh in the 1830s by Zorowar Singh for the Jammu maharaja, Gulab Singh (d. 1857), however, Leh's northward trade tilted from Tibet towards Turkestan, with Ladakh assuming an unprecedented economic and political importance.[36] Gulab Singh later sided with the British in the First Anglo-Sikh War, receiving Jammu in return, the treaty signed with the Company outlining his sovereign rights, including the freedom from intervention, the right to raise revenues, and the right to impose customs duties.[37] Quickly, Gulab Singh established monopolies over Kashmiri manufactures—including ironwares, saffron, shawl wool, and wheat—and exacted or extorted trade-related dues.[38] As the British responded to the problems posed by the initial treaties, they realised that pursuit of free trade could usefully serve as a means to curtail the political power of the maharaja while simultaneously protecting their political and commercial interests in central Asia. An opportunity arose when Yarkandi merchants lodged petitions with British officials in Kashmir against arbitrary exactions made by the maharaja's *diwan* (treasurer), Basti Ram.[39] But Basti Ram's unwillingness to journey to Lahore to answer the complaint, the mysterious deaths of three of the four remaining Yarkandis, and the reluctance of the fourth to come forward, entailed little effective change.[40] According to Dr Henry Cayley, who was posted as 'Officer on Special Duty' at Ladakh in the 1860s, the authorities continued to extort traders, while also ignoring the agreed rates of duties as published in the 'Tariff of Transit Duties' (1867).[41] Only in May 1870 did Gulab Singh's successor, Maharaja Ranbir Singh (r. 1857–85), sign the treaty with the British that relinquished his right to levy any transit duties between British India and Chinese Turkestan. Trade via Ladakh was privileged at the expense of trade via Badakhshan, traders traversing the former route paying one-third of the charges on the latter route.[42]

The British also tried to open trade with Chinese Turkestan, sending two trade and diplomatic missions in the 1870s. Under Yakub Beg, the commander-in-chief of the Khokandi army who seized Xinjiang from the Qing in 1867, styling himself Atalik Ghazi or 'Champion Father of the Faithful', Chinese Turkestan was conceived by the British as an independent buffer between north India and Russia.[43] Within a few years of the mission's dispatch, in 1878, Xinjiang was reconquered by the Qing, ending British endeavours in Chinese Turkestan.[44] This included the termination of associated undertakings; namely, the construction of the Hindustan–Tibet Road. The road had begun in February 1827 as a 'means of communication between the Sikh Plains and the frontier of Chinese Tartary', and made use of hundreds of thousands of *begar* (indentured service) labourers supplied under duress by the rulers of the local hill states. For all this, the project was hugely expensive despite the continued growth of trade.[45] Instead of further costly infrastructure projects, the Government of India settled for the installation of a British joint commissioner in Kashmir for eight months of the year.[46] Alongside Cayley's reports, this agency produced the trade statistics, trade reports, and commercial diaries from which it is possible to piece together a picture of the growing trade between India and Chinese Turkestan via Ladakh.

Although trade between the plains and hills of Punjab had a history prior to the colonial conquest, the Punjabi Khatris had little commercial connection with Xinjiang before mid century.[47] Testing the waters in 1868 was a Punjabi merchant, followed in 1869 by 'Tara Singh, a Sikh merchant of Rawulpindi, and 2 merchants of Simla, who went last year to Yarkand.'[48] Their experimental expedition had been a success, at least for Tara Singh, whose enormous profits were largely made on exports of green tea from the new plantations in Kangra (Punjab).[49] Goods such as silk were probably part of mixed cargoes, although some Hoshiarpur merchants—who formed a distinct colony at Leh from mid century—preferred to travel through Kashmir to buy silk directly from Yarkand, doubtless bringing back animals loaded almost entirely with raw silk.[50] Alongside Hoshiarpur were other trading towns, such as Khanpur and Thanda, home to six 'big firms of Khatris and Bhabras' trading to the Hill States and Ladakh, which were possibly the competitors rather than the agents of the Multan or Shikarpur trader-financier firms.[51]

Despite the enthusiasm for establishing markets for British and British Indian goods in Turkestan, Indo-central Asian trade was seen as the task of peddlers and 'Asiatics'. Without steamship or railroad transportation, or even well-built roads, brute animal and human effort was required to transport goods over long distances in inhospitable conditions. For these efforts, trade prospects and profits were relatively meagre, on the basis of the small and easily saturated market, although later reports suggested sizeable profit potential.[52] Without an armed escort or expensive military presence, profits were easily snatched by bandits and thieves from easy targets unfamiliar with the terrain, a risk that restricted European involvement in overland trade.[53]

'The difficulties to contend with are great', summarised the lieutenant governor of Punjab in 1863, after reading Davies' report. 'The nations [through which trade passed] are for the most part in a semi-civilised state, on the border land, as it were, of nomad and settled life, bigoted adherents of the Mahomdean religion, and inaccessible to European influence.'[54] For R. H. Davies, however, Islam was not the problem per se; rather, the Muslims who dwelt north and north-west of British India were 'the rear-guard of the Mahomedan host' who, without influence from Europe, differed unfavourably from Muslims in 'the

Turkish and Persian nations'.[55] Excluding the Europeans were fundamental differences of civilisation—unimpeachable barriers of race and religion, culture and economy, rather than topography and geography. The 'indomitable mercantile energy' needed to transcend these difficulties was distilled in the Asiatic—'an energy which [...] in oriental fashion [was] crystallised, as it were, and made hereditary in certain tribes'—a dismissive view of the Indian and Afghan traders who had so successfully organised and orchestrated long-distance trade and finance.[56] Thus, the European saw himself as the manager, manufacturer, or shipper of superior goods; he hoped to break into the central Asian market without doing the breaking himself, he harboured desires of outcompeting and ousting the Russians even though this sort of trade was 'evidently more suited to the[ir] semi-Asiatic, pedlar-like genius'.[57]

Eccentric was the Englishman, therefore, who adventured across the Karakoram with wares for sale in the manner of the Asiatic. Trade with Xinjiang grew—albeit interruptedly—following Qing westward expansion and the stabilisation of the Khokand Khanate.[58] In the words of R. B. Shaw—tea planter, explorer, first Englishman to visit Kashgar, and subsequently installed by the British with the designation Political Agent on Special Duty—Chinese Turkestan however remained an 'Eldorado [...] closed to Europeans.'[59] Aside from Shaw, who himself vastly overestimated the market potential of Chinese Turkestan, Thomas Russell established the Central Asian Trading Company (CATC) in Hoshiarpur in 1873, where he hired an agent, Andrew Dalgleish, and an assistant, Abdul Samand.[60] They made their maiden adventure in 1874–5, taking a caravan comprising mostly English cotton cloth.[61] Receiving official sanction for trade with Chinese Turkestan via the Karakoram routes—the Calcutta government happy for private enterprise to help counter Russian commercial expansion—Russell found sales of piece goods much slower than his rivals selling Russian goods (with a much lower markup) in February 1875.[62] By April, Russell had departed, having sold half his caravan to a merchant named Burhan Bai, in whose hands the goods sold quickly and at a profit.[63] Dalgleish continued to dabble in trade until his assassination, but there is no other mention in the correspondence from Kashgar or Ladakh of the CATC, reflecting both its failure and that of British enterprise in Turkestan at large.[64]

Across the Desert

The British envisioned their empire as neo-Classical, inherited from the empires and civilisations of the Greeks and Romans.[65] At the most grandiose, the opening of central Asia to European goods through India was seen as an Alexandrian endeavour by both government officials and lay people alike, a task befitting the Macedonian's heirs, the British, even though Alexander had approached the subcontinent from central Asia.[66] From the British perspective, the conclusion of the Second Anglo-Sikh War in 1849 brought the borders of British India to the Khyber. The result was the resumption of Punjab's integration, which was initiated earlier, with the reform of transit duties in Ambala in 1824 and the rebuilding of roads up to the Company's north-western frontier with the Sikh Empire.[67] The Sikh fiscal system cast a fairly wide net over trade, taxing almost everything, and taxing the same cargoes at several points of transit or sale.[68] John Lawrence, newly installed as the officiating Resident at Lahore, simplified the external duties, abolished the internal duties, and abolished or lowered duties on specific trade goods in 1847, extending the system to the territories west of Lahore after 1849.[69] Of course, trade was never entirely free. Although the financial commissioner pensioned off Amritsar's revenue collectors in 1853, Davies turned first and foremost to the city's octroi farmers for information when trying to estimate the extent of raw-silk imports almost a decade later.[70] The 'somewhat medieval octroi system' remained the mainstay of municipal taxation through to the twentieth century in Punjab.[71] In Amritsar and Multan these transit duties were levied at rising but relatively low rates, starting at 0.5 per cent in 1850, rising to 1.5 per cent before 1883 on goods for local consumption or re-export.[72]

Preceding the river and railway developments, a rapid phase of road-building was initiated by the Punjab government, the cost of construction passed onto Indian rulers to spare the Company much of the bill.[73] First came the reconstruction of the Ludhiana–Karnal section of the arterial road, then the reconstruction of the Grand Trunk Road from Lahore to Peshawar, together allowing traders to proceed to the Afghan frontier via Dera Ismail Khan in the 1850s, rather than the circuitous routing via Multan.[74] In the next decade, Punjabi towns were connected to the expanding railway network of British India. Within this development, Amritsar was connected earlier onto the lines stretching towards Bombay and Calcutta, and had a one-stop proximity advantage over Lahore and Multan on the respective onward lines, privileging Amritsar as the new industrial and commercial centre of colonial Punjab. Further north-west, Peshawar was eventually connected to the rest of Punjab by both these new road and rail developments, and was a stone's throw away from the Khyber Pass, facilitating its rise from a small but steadily expanding town under the Sikhs, to the trade and financial centre most closely connected to Kabul and Bukhara after 1850.[75] When the British tried to encourage trade by organising commercial fairs, it was in Peshawar (for the trans-Hindu Kush trade) and Palampur (for the trans-Karakoram trade) that the fairs were established in the 1860s.[76] While Punjab's more easterly entrepôts were integrated into the economy of British India and the British Empire, Peshawar thus served as the way station between the older terrestrially oriented economy and the new imperial economy. The shift of production sites connected to caravan trade towards the north-west frontier as a result of these transportation developments on the one hand, and the growing obsolescence of caravan trade to Punjab's rapidly reorienting economy as a result of its new patterns of integration into British imperial markets on the other, are analysed closely in chapter 8.

Yet, it was for Russia, not Britain, that the task of opening trade through central Asia to India and China was manifest as a truly Alexandrian project of developing overland links between Europe and Asia.[77] Indeed, the changes emanating from the expansion of Russian power into central Asia were perhaps more profound than those from British India. In 1864, eight years after the end of the Crimean War (1853–6), which had preoccupied Russia, the tsar's generals commenced the conquest of Turkestan, taking Tashkent in 1865. The tsar was uninterested in Bukhara, fearing what would happen to Anglo-Russian relations.[78] But the Bukharan amir, Muzaffar al-Din, came to blows with the Russians as a result of his misguided ambitions towards enlarging the emirate. Defeated, the amir pressed for peace in 1868. The resultant treaty ratified the reduction on trade taxes on Russian goods to 2.5 per cent, unobstructed passage for Russian merchants through the emirate, the creation of commercial agencies, and the ceding of territories, including Samarkand.[79] With the resumption of fighting and defeats in 1869, and the subsequent treaty of 1873, Bukhara and Khiva were reduced to protectorates of the Russian Empire. In 1876, Khokand was liquidated, the territory reconstituted as the Fergana Province of Russian Turkestan.[80] Already transforming central Asian trade in the mid eighteenth century, the markets of the oasis towns were now laid bare before Russia.

The year 1881 was important for Russian economic expansion in central Eurasia. To the east, in Chinese Turkestan, Russia gained great privileges following the signing of the Treaty of St Petersburg with China, including four consulates in Xinjiang.[81] Russian traders were freed from the payment of *likin*, for example, the transit tariff imposed by the Chinese, advantaging Russian commerce through central Asia to Xinjiang at the expense of Chinese and Indian trade and traders.[82] Through the eventual establishment of the Russo-Chinese Bank (1895–6), which opened for business in central Asia in 1902, and through the customs house at Kashgar, which simplified the payment of taxes and the examination of goods at the frontier, east–west trade across the Pamirs was extended.[83] Russian commercial penetration and political power in Xinjiang were slowly and systematically to undermine trade towards British India via the Karakoram, especially under the efforts of Nikolai Petrovsky, the Russian consul in Kashgar, 1882–1902.[84]

To the west, there was the opening of the inaugural line of the Trans-Caspian Railway towards Khiva. The railways facilitated trade and economic expansion (or exploitation), with the line further extended to Samarkand in 1888, skirting Bukhara, at a distance of only twelve kilometres from the city. From Samarkand, the line was extended to Tashkent and Andijan in 1898. And, in 1906, the line connected Bukhara with Moscow and St Petersburg. The economic impact and importance of the railways was tremendous. Despite the delays brought by sandstorms and the costs created by banditry, the railways reduced transport time and transport expenses between Bukhara and Orenburg by over 300 per cent, these charges including insurance as far as Moscow.[85] The railways also facilitated the transformation of Turkestan into a net exporter of raw materials and net importer of manufactures from Russia, for Russo-central Asian trade remained proportionally rather small to the tsarist economy before 1880.[86] As far as the fate of Indo-central Asian trade was concerned, however, the new railways represented the final and fatal blows rather than the root cause of decline.

Whereas the British scoffed at personal participation in overland trade, though salivating over the market opportunities in central Asia, Russians (or Russian subjects, and those that passed themselves off as such) were much more proactive. Following unsuccessful efforts at establishing trading companies in the mid eighteenth century, Russian traders confined themselves to Astrakhan and, later, Orenburg and other fortified trade towns.[87] Despite the establishment of the Orenburg Trade Company (1823) and the Moscow Trade Company (1858) in a bid to circumvent Asian middlemen, Tatar, Kirgiz or Kazakh, and Bukharan agents, as well as some Indian and Afghan traders, intermediated most Russo-central Asian trade.[88] Journeying to Khokand on behalf of the Government of India in 1860–1, Mullah Abdul Majid met with 'Nazir Khyroola, the great merchant of Bokhara' and noted that some merchants were men of 'considerable capital', at least in central Asia, and given the appellation 'Bai' as a mark of respect.[89] Merchants such as Mahomed Darvesh Bai of Bukhara operated an agency network that extended to Orenburg and as far as Moscow, suggesting that some of the Bukharan traders were at least as adept in the art of profitable long-distance commerce as the merchant-moneymen of Multan and Shikarpur.[90] Some of these merchants also had stakes in the trade with India, or were willing to stand side by side with Afghan and Indian traders when Russian administrators attempted to restrict trade with British India shortly after the conquest of Tashkent.[91]

Their efforts, however, were in vain. From 1873, Russians started to stream into Bukhara as staff, construction workers, and traders.[92] Whereas the residents of south Asian origin in Bukhara and other trading towns dwelt in distinct quarters, Russian 'new towns' mushroomed across central Asia to accommodate the new arrivals, spatially segregating the European and Asian populations.[93] Buoyed by Russian protectionism, prohibitions, and preferential access, Russians and Russian subjects successfully competed with established traders from south and central Asia.[94] Complementing the policy of positive discrimination towards Russo-central Asian trade and traders was negative discrimination against Indians. As early as 1866, the Indians' reinvestment of trade profits in agricultural loans caught the attention of Russian administrators, who saw them as usurers and parasites.[95]

But the Indians were British subjects. Rather than evicting them, and thereby attracting consternation and conflict from British India, the Russians focussed their efforts on the difficult and drawn-out process of limiting their moneylending activities.[96] First, Indians were forbidden from securing loans against land. Second, the 'indigenous' inhabitants of Russian Turkestan in the position of debtors were given greater legal protection. Third, the Russian State Bank opened in Tashkent in the late 1870s, and the first savings and loans banks opened in 1879, soon spreading throughout Turkestan, with a branch of the Imperial Russian Bank opening in Bukhara in 1899.[97]

Together, these interventions and initiatives restricted the scope and profitability of the south Asian trader-financiers' operations in central Asia.[98] From 1890, the number of Punjabi traders travelling to central Asia declined, although the trading community only disinvested their assets after 1914, making losses in the meantime.[99] From a trading community of thousands, only 857 Indians remained in Russian Turkestan in 1882, their number entirely depleted in the colonial city of Tashkent by 1896.[100] As Russian institutions, influence, and authority slowly seeped into Chinese Turkestan after 1881, the mid-century opening of opportunities in Xinjiang went into reverse, with the Ladakh–Yarkand trade collapsing in the late 1930s, affecting yet more adversely the opportunities for Indians.[101]

In nominally independent Bukhara, Indian out-migration was slower, and many adapted to changed circumstances, serving as middlemen and agents for Russians, if not continuing as retail traders and moneylenders.[102] When Bukhara entered the Russian customs system in 1895, nevertheless, Indo-central Asian caravan trade in cotton cloth, raw silk, and indigo was already in the throes of decline. While the coming of the first age of global imperialism had pushed south Asia's trading communities into closer connection with central Asia, the second age would see some of them thrust out of the Eurasian interior for the first time in over four centuries.[103]

Conclusion

In the second age of global empire, the mechanisation of transportation precipitated a steady shift in the extent and character of trade and mobility, the impact perhaps most profound in the continental interior, where the transformative impact of the prior age of sail had of course been felt only secondarily. On the one hand, the infrastructure developments in this epoch prefigured those of the twentieth century. In 1959, almost a century after the termination of construction of the Hindustan–Tibet Road, for example, the governments of Pakistan and China initiated work on the Karakoram Highway (colloquially, the Friendship Highway). The work was completed in 1979, the highway forming not only a major commercial artery between the two nations, but also a funnel for Chinese investment to counterbalance or erode India's geostrategic power in Asia. On the other hand, nineteenth-century railways rather directly formed the basis for modern connections, not least the trans-Eurasian network upon which the emergent 'new' Silk Road economy is partly predicated. In this respect, the period of colonial conquest from the mid nineteenth century marked the beginning of the end of premodern caravan trade and of the Indo-central Asian exchanges that form the focus of this book, but also the beginning of a new phase in the history of the Silk Roads and the integration of the Eurasian interior.

The second age of global empire culminated in the conquest of what contemporaries saw as 'those parts of the globe which remain in a state of barbarism or semi-barbarism'.[104] Civilisational progress provided a powerful logic, if only in rhetorical terms, for the deeper and broader intrusion into colonial societies in the delivery of moral improvement and modernity, not least technological modernity. At the same time, the human manifestation of colonial power was often increasingly thin and fragile the greater the distance from imperial centres, to the extent that modern infrastructure or technology substituted for the physical presence of institutions and officials in the bringing of interior spaces under colonial control—what Patrick Carroll has termed 'technoterritoriality'.[105] Yet, even in proximity to the seat of colonial power, the technoterritorial enterprise could be foiled by local ecology or local agency, as the failure of steamboats on the Indus demonstrates, and chapter 8 thus examines more closely the impacts upon caravan trade of those innovations most closely associated with the New Imperialism. The next chapter returns to the issues of mobility and violence, examining their changing relation in the context of the expansion of the colonial state and the development of colonial knowledge.

7

KNOWLEDGE

Winter in Peshawar, 1855. A flurry of notes in a foreign hand are about to fall into the lap of Major H. B. Edwardes, the East India Company's commissioner and superintendent stationed in the city. The first is brought on 15 November by a Peshawari banker requesting payment from the Company to the tune of Rs 1,000. The chit, he claims, was a bill drawn by an Englishman and cashed at his banking house in Kabul. Edwardes' suspicion now aroused, he sends the fragment—which he suspects is written in Russian—to a translator in Layyah, a town at an important river crossing on the Indus lying roughly equidistant between Dera Ismail Khan and Multan. This is the sort of place to find men whose business has taken them along the Silk Roads into central Asia and Russia—but so is Peshawar, and it can only be assumed that Edwardes hopes to gain the upper hand by keeping his inquiries secret from the Peshawari merchant community. Sultan Ali, the translator employed by the local district commissioner, states the bill is for 1000 roubles, equal to Rs 2000—twice what the banker claimed was cashed and thus arousing further suspicion about both the veracity of his demands and the identity of the 'foreigner' who drew on the bill of exchange in Kabul.[1]

Two weeks pass before a Kabuli merchant named Gholam Mohiuddin also comes forward to press for compensation, bringing three more Russian notes, each duly translated. Of these, the third scrap is the most enigmatic, being a list of an assortment of banal but random and unconnected items—to be procured, perhaps, but for whom? And why? Or is it a coded message?[2] '4 bottles of lime juice. 2 boxes of tobacco. 6 pen knives. 50 vessels of stone ware. 1 ton of spirits. [unspecified amount of] bread.'[3] The other notes more clearly reveal a deception, possibly sinister. 'Tell me,' Edwardes most likely asks, 'who was the man behind these mysterious notes?' The merchant replies: 'He is certainly a Sahib; but says he is a Nooggaie. The Nooggaies are subjects of Russia. He talked very big; and said all the countries of Toorkistan and Afghanistan were in effect his; and Ameer Dost Mohamud Khan might be regarded as a mere "locum tenens".'[4]

A *sahib?* An Englishman gone native, or a British officer secretly stationed in central Asia, drawing on the Company's benevolence upon resorting to Kabul in distress?[5] Yes, Gholam Mohiuddin replies, there are in fact a number of Englishmen settled in central Asia. The Kabuli merchant's business has taken him to Tashkent and elsewhere across central Asia, where once he saw another Englishman in Khokand going by the name of 'Imamoordeen' and yet another in Khiva whose name escapes him. The Englishman at issue, however, has returned to Bukhara or Russia from Kabul via Balkh with Afzal Khan, the Afghan *sardar* (governor) of the last-named city—although not before Gholam Mohiuddin advanced the foreigner Rs 14,420, assured by the s*ardar*'s insistence to the Kabuli authorities that he would care for the foreigner and that the latter was a bona fide Englishman.[6]

Edwardes becomes convinced the foreigner was a Russian emissary pretending to be an Englishman in disguise as a Nogai—an almost comedic double bluff, the stuff of Shakespearean drama. Yet, the absence 'of annoyance at being cheated', which both the Peshawari banker and the Kabuli merchant had displayed, 'excite[s] a suspicion' in his mind 'that there was a perfect understanding between them and the foreigner, and that they had either not made any advances of cash to him, or else had good security for its repayment.'[7] Edwardes, meanwhile, writes to correspondents in Kabul with instructions to trace this man's movements and locate him through the auspices of the Balkhi *sardar* to settle the matter. Afzal Khan is the son of the Afghan amir, Dost Mohammad Khan (r. 1826–39, 1843–63), brother of the heir apparent—Sher Ali Khan (r. 1863–5/66, 1868–79)—from whom he would seize the throne in 1865 and reign until his death in 1867, and is the father of Abdur Rahman (r. 1880–1901).[8] It is reported the foreigner had arrived in Afzal Khan's train and, after a stay in Kabul, was 'got rid of with the least offence possible to the British and Russian Government', indicative of some connection of the court to this man and some collusion in his return.[9]

As this vignette from the Lahore archives shows, the movement of money and goods constituting the networks of caravan trade was closely related to other sorts of mobility: of persons, including diplomats and spies—but also those holy men and healers who figure in earlier chapters—and thus of information and knowledge. A reputable trader or traveller in need of cash in Bukhara or Samarkand could draw credit from Multani or Peshawari banking houses (or use the certainty of such option as a ruse), for example, the sum settled at a later date at one of their 'branches'. While money was something that moved—attested by the availability of a variety of coin throughout the trading world, including Venetian and Dutch ducats, Spanish dollars, Bukharan gold *tillas*, roubles, rupees of different mints—more common was the movement of *hundi* (bills of exchange), or information relating financial transfers or instructing the settlement of accounts.[10] There were numerous other sorts of information flow, not least about prices, demand, supply, credit conditions, or other relevant factors, such as political circumstances. Where commodity money was not used to settle accounts, the confiscation and sale of goods or the confiscation of rentable real estate generated cash income to maintain liquidity—and thus mobility—within the system.[11]

Insofar as there was a Great Game—the nineteenth-century 'cold war' between Britain and Russia for control of the Eurasian interior and the security of their imperial positions in Asia—it was a game played on the nerves of paranoid and distrustful British, just as the Kabuli merchant and the Peshawari banker had attempted to play Edwardes.[12] Indeed, as the vignette reveals, the knowledge nexus of the trading world was invaluable to political actors but, ultimately, was not so much a resource they could capture and command as a superstructure lying above any particular state authority.[13] The degree to which a ruler could tap into these networks of political and commercial intelligence was linked to the success of his relations with regional rivals. The British struggled to gain the degree of mastery they desired, oftentimes remaining susceptible to what they otherwise (dis)regarded as 'rumour', at other times wilfully ignoring reliable intelligence they had gathered; the causes and consequences of such contradictory practices are examined in this chapter.

The larger ramification of Said's *Orientalism* has been the investigation of the accumulation of 'colonial knowledge' and its transformative impact upon colonised societies.[14] This chapter tries to think across space but also across time, using caravan trade as a lens through which to examine long-run changes and thereby evaluate more precisely the transformative impact of colonialism and its knowledges upon the trading world. Ann L. Stoler's fruitful suggestion that the colonial archive be read not only *against* but also *along* the grain has helped foreground emotions, epistemic anxieties, and their generative potential in producing material or substantive change beyond the walls of the state's repositories of knowledge (a theme taken up in recent work cited in this chapter).[15]

As brought to life at the beginning of this chapter by reconstructing the passions within Edwardes' office, emotions thus play an important part in the analysis. The first half, on the 'security state', is concerned with the changing role and status of the agents involved in the networks of caravan trade to the production of colonial knowledge, highlighting how the drive to systematise knowledge only led to epistemic anxiety and feelings of paranoia and vulnerability. The second half focuses on the 'ethnographic state'. It looks at how the production of knowledge about the people inhabiting the dry zone—deemed some of the most fearsome and restive inhabitants of India—led to their transformation into sedentary yeomen or their channelling away from free transhumance, thereby curbing mobility to mitigate anxiety over threats from the ungovernable and unconquerable frontier.

The Security State

Edwardes acted with some urgency to translate the scraps he received, interrogate the two men before him, and collect further information. Even though the foreigner had departed, Edwardes duly collated the information and despatched it to his superiors in Punjab in early

January 1856, from whence it was transmitted to Calcutta. The matter was closed shortly thereafter.[16] Both the alacrity with which Edwardes performed his duties on the one hand, and the seeming disinterest of the higher authorities in Calcutta on the other, are explicable in light of events still relatively fresh in the Company's memory.

Winter in Kabul, 1837. A Russian diplomatic mission led by Count Vitkevich arrived in the Afghan capital and was received by the amir, Dost Mohammad Khan, accompanied by a motley crew of men from the West, among them Alexander Burnes and Josiah Harlan, a Scot and an American. Russia had been behaving aggressively with the Qajars in Persia, precipitating a wave of Russophobia in Britain and British India. Fearing tensions between the Afghans and Sikhs, as well as an Afghan–Russian alliance to invade India—this the product of the filtering and selective reading of intelligence sources—the governor general resolved to launch an offensive attack.[17] There ensued a minor witch hunt, the results of which, no matter how inconclusive, only seemed to legitimise and fuel the underlying fear. One incident involved laying suspicions on a group of Armenians mistaken for Russian spies in winter 1838; for, despite their long-standing repute in the Bombay trade, Armenians were now seen as subjects and allies of Russia.[18]

As preparations were made in 1838 for the British campaign into Afghanistan, Russia simultaneously launched an invasion of Khiva. Both campaigns proved disastrous.[19] Of the former, William Dalrymple estimates the cost at £15 million (or £50 billion today), 'exhausting the Indian treasury, pushing the Indian credit network to the brink of collapse and permanently wrecking the solvency of the East India Company; [...] losing maybe 40,000 lives, as well as those of around 50,000 camels; [... and] alienating much of the Bengal army.'[20] In a broader context, the failed invasion was begun little over a decade after the costly campaign in Burma (1824–6), was concurrent with the First Opium War (1839–42), and was soon followed by the conquest of the Sikh kingdoms, all within the midst of a protracted depression in the north Indian and global economies. Thus, while Edwardes was executing his duty with diligence in submitting his information to his superiors, it is unsurprising that the Company's government in Calcutta failed to be roused by the flimsy rumour of a foreigner—perhaps Russian—in Kabul.

The Limits of the Early Modern Information Order

In a yet broader sense, the campaign launched in 1839 was the culmination of the first age of global empire, showing the limits not only of British expansion, but also, to some minds, the limits of its associated 'information order' which lingered at the frontiers of British India. C. A. Bayly's landmark *Empire and Information* defined knowledge production and knowledgeable people as part of a social formation—the information order.[21] Given the needs and norms of early modern Indian kings and kingship, intelligence networks were informal and labile, idiosyncratic yet specific in purpose, often intersecting with a wide array of knowledges and their practitioners (including geographers, genealogists, and astrologers, for example), as opposed to the general and constant policing of action. The sophistication and efficiency of this information order notwithstanding, 'Kings and their officials collected and deployed knowledge in unstandardised forms because what should be known was not yet determined by any dominant notion of a critical bureaucracy or public.'[22]

The Company necessarily inserted itself into this information order as it began to build its Indian empire from the mid eighteenth century, with conquest bringing into its service those learned specialists, newswriters, runners, envoys, and so forth, formerly employed by Indian kings. Of course, the precolonial information order was subtly transformed through the inflection of Hastings' notions about India's political 'constitution' and the search for true information from those who understood it, to take one example.[23] In this way, from the outset, one of the primary concerns of the colonial authorities was what sorts of informants could be reliably trusted to produce true knowledge; in the realms of religion and politics, this search empowered the Brahmin, while in the mercantile sphere the Bania was elevated at precisely the time when other ethno-religious actors were forging an enlarged livelihood for themselves through commerce in other parts of Asia (to return to one of the arguments of chapter 4). At the same time, the information order was enlarged through the creation of specialist posts and intelligence units by the army.

Yet, if the Company was generally effective in appropriating and commanding indigenous bodies of knowledge, informants, and intelligence and communications networks within the wet zone as it deci-sively expanded its power there by *c.* 1818, the same was not true further afield in the dry zone, where the information order was roughly similar in its elaboration but the Company's success in drilling down into it fatally limited.[24] In the late eighteenth century, north-west India was *terra incognita*; and British or 'colonial' knowledge remained fairly fragmented as the Bombay Presidency competed—rather than co-operated—with the Company's government in Calcutta.[25] As com-mercial and political motives elided to prompt intelligence-gathering missions from the 1790s, therefore, new information was neither sys-tematically nor centrally archived, a fact that made more challenging the 1839 campaign to Kabul.[26] Henry Pottinger's tour through Baluchistan and Sindh in the early nineteenth century only skimmed the lower reaches of the Indus en route to Persia.[27] Pottinger and his companion, Charles Christie, travelled disguised as horse dealers employed by Sundarji Sivaji, a contact they had made in Bombay in consequence of the Hindu merchant's role as supplier of the Bombay and Madras armies with cavalry mounts procured from central Eurasia. Unsurprisingly, they were rumbled by Afghans in Sindh.[28] Ultimately, although the Company knew more about traders than society else-where at this time, in the words of Thomas Metcalfe in 1808, 'beyond the Jumna, all [... remained] conjecture'.[29]

Before becoming governor of Bombay, the Scottish Enlightenment Orientalist Mountstuart Elphinstone served as the Company's first envoy to the Durrani court in 1808. In Bayly's analysis, Elphinstone's mission gleaned much new information that could supplement what was known about Afghanistan through Pashtuns settled in north India or serving in Indian armies, for instance, but suffered in ways symp-tomatic of the Company's knowledge gathering in this region in the face of social institutions and social organisation perceived as differing from that in the wet zone. In effect, the more diffuse nature of the state and the tribal or clan organisation of society meant the information order was subtly different, and colonial officers struggled to identify and reach into its distinctive epistemic wells, especially when rulers such as Ranjit Singh were able to closely guard the intelligence sources with which they were more familiar.[30] Building on this work, Benjamin D. Hopkins has interrogated the ontology of colonial knowledge in

Afghanistan, pinpointing within the information collated by the Elphinstone mission the origins of chronic misunderstandings of the Afghan state.[31] Elphinstone had never set foot in Kabul, instead staying south of the Khyber Pass in the Durrani winter capital of Peshawar, and imposing the Romantic model of the history of Scots clansmen onto his analysis of Pashtun 'Highlanders', for instance.[32]

On the one hand, Elphinstone's mission was nevertheless a turning point in British knowledge of India beyond Delhi, narrowing the information gap and blazing a trail for further exploration: that of William Moorcroft and Mir Izzat-ullah, the veterinarian-cum-spy and his *munshi* (interpreter), from 1819; and then of Alexander Burnes and his *munshi*, Mohan Lal, alongside Conolly, Leech, Masson, Trevelyan, and others in the 1830s and 1840s.[33] In the later exploits, intelligence gathering and route mapping were complemented with inquiries into trade and the prospects for British commercial penetration beyond the Indus, this 'soft' commercial policy intended to thwart Russian advance in central Asia.[34] On the other hand, the 'Elphinstonian episteme', although flawed, acquired a sort of hegemony within the stock of colonial knowledge of Afghanistan, subsequently only tweaked through minor critique by men such as Alexander Burnes and Charles Masson (who also differed in opinion amongst themselves), and narrowed in the face of the bureaucratisation of the Company's ranks.[35] Dalrymple has shown how decision-makers' inability to fathom the importance of tribal patronage—namely, through the distribution or confirmation of land rights and subsidies, or else the recruitment and payment of tribesmen for military service—offended and jeopardised relations with the very tribes contingent to the production of political stability and necessary to guaranteeing the security of the British presence.[36] Dalrymple thus traces the doomed invasion of 1839 to the disregard for the more sensitive judgment proffered by men embedded within local society—such as Masson or Burnes or Rawlinson—by Company men in Calcutta. Dalrymple effectively pitches the conflict as one between representatives of the information order of the early Company state versus its critics.[37] With slightly different emphasis, Alexander Morrison argues that Burnes' voice *was* heard, but at the expense of indigenous voices such as Mohan Lal's, whose intelligence was superior but only deemed valuable when aligned with the sentiments of his white interlocutor(s).[38] In either respect is evident the reckless downgrading of Asian informants and Asian knowledge.

Ultimately, as the first age of global empire drew to a close, the reliability of precolonial intelligence networks was being called into question, not least because of the unease from certain quarters during the Age of Reform of the 1830s–40s regarding the dependence upon indigenous informants and the use of rumour.[39] Yet, for all the peculiarities of the beliefs held by Europeans about Indian society, history, and knowledge, it would be unwise to assume that the information order of north India was altogether alien to the Company's servants in either the later eighteenth or early nineteenth century. In fact, precolonial intelligence networks in India were fairly typical of those possessed by other early modern states, in which private and public office, commercial and political interest and expertise were entangled, and where men of practical experience could be elevated to the status of learned experts. The relative novelty yet acceleration of long-distance movement in the period meant that geographic mobility made for occupational mobility, the career of the adventurer or traveller, or even a pirate or corsair or soldier, thus often overlapping with that of the merchant, and vice versa.[40] In these respects, national interests frequently elided with those of mercantile bodies or individuals, while the Company and its servants were themselves deeply enmeshed within networks of intelligence, even drifting between the supply-side and demand-side of information exchanges.

Only after the Restoration in 1660, Alan Marshall contends, were intelligence gathering and espionage determinedly institutionalised within the English state itself. The mainstay of the state's intelligence apparatus remained the fairly sophisticated yet relatively loose networks of educated but untrained diplomats, spies, informants, interceptors of communications, and pools of casual and undirected sources (often transmitting rumour or misinformation to settle personal vendettas).[41] Where the phase of bureaucratic centralisation characterising many early modern polities—from England and Venice to the Habsburg, Ottoman, or Mughal empires—produced changes, the differences were a matter of degree rather than fundamental character, and could certainly not be delineated along the lines of Occidental versus Oriental forms of knowledge.[42] Whatever continuity was established through the gradual embedding of part of the state's intelligence gathering within the bureaucracy, this neither resulted in professionalisation and the creation of educated experts, nor energised the state out of its predominately passive receipt of information to a more active stance—those developments being a nineteenth-century phenomenon. In such respects, it ought not to be remarkable that the information order of precolonial India was so similar to the intelligence networks within which the Company was already embedded before *c.* 1750; if some officials found it bewildering, it is more likely the result of their having little political experience as the patrons (rather than clients) of intelligence operations, and less because of any innate peculiarities.

None of this is intended to deny the distinct position of the British—compared to their predecessors—in south Asia. To a far greater degree than Indian rulers, the Company's servants were heavily reliant on an intermediary layer of translators and linguists (not to mention runners) between themselves and their informants. This added to the anxiety about what was being 'lost in translation' and what was being manipulated by multiple layers of wily and possibly duplicitous indigenous actors, the very colonised peoples over whom they hoped to exert dominion.[43] But in emphasising the precolonial to colonial transition in south Asia, as per Bayly's *Empire and Information*, for example, it is easy to overlook the roughly comparable state of knowledge and information gathering in precolonial India to contemporaneous European or Asian polities, or to isolate the colonial transition in epistemic practices in south Asia from like changes in Britain or other parts of the British Empire over the long nineteenth century.[44] Given this, the aim of the foregoing discussion has been to shift the emphasis from the colonial and local to the global context, for the desire to replace unstandardised knowledge practices with more systematic intelligence gathering was neither unique to, nor originated in, colonial south Asia. Arguably, the Crown's loss of the American colonies after 1776 precipitated this shift in imperial governance and information, and the Company's building of an Indian empire and its gradual submission to greater oversight from Parliament fed these developments as much as they followed therefrom.[45] Overall, in fact, the drift was one from early modern to modern forms of knowledge rooted within a fundamental modernisation of the aristocratic-patrimonial into the bureaucratic state and the types of information to be produced for its efficient functioning.

A Modern Information Order and the Imperial Security State

Here the recent work of James Hevia is particularly valuable. Over the nineteenth century, new military technology combined with the emergence of a new military technocracy to professionalise and rationalise armies with a discipline common to that of industrial capitalism. This new military–epistemological–institutional complex emerged first in Prussia around the 1820s, so that, from the 1860s, men such as Richthofen and Hedin (whose careers were briefly described in the introduction to this book) were pioneering the scientific exploration of the ancient Silk Roads of inner Eurasia, well beyond the frontiers of their own states. This complex then spread further afield in continental Europe, and to Russia and Britain, and from the latter to its empire, including British India.[46] The changes in the second half of the century in Britain, Hevia argues, 'produced intelligence as a military discipline and as a specific form of knowledge [...] directly connected to the development of a new imperial state formation', believed by reformers to be less patrimonial and more aligned with reason and the values of meritocracy.[47] The emergence of schools of the 'scientific corps' for engineering and artillery officers was especially significant, for these graduates were believed best suited to military intelligence work. The influences of these developments not only flowed from Britain to India, but also vice versa, with the professionalisation of the Indian civil service after 1853 prompting a like change back in Britain, Hevia argues.[48]

Of particular importance was the quartermaster general's department, wherein military logistics was organised, in turn requiring 'specialised kinds of information for classifying, processing, storing, and retrieving' knowledge.[49] In India, Charles MacGregor served as first head of the Intelligence Branch in Simla, from 1878, then as Quartermaster General, 1880–5, and was instrumental to discussions about the creation of a more robust intelligence entity staffed by men who were knowledgeable in 'surveying and drawing reconnaissance, fortifications, languages, telegraphy, photography, Military history and geography, strategy and statistics.'[50] In fact, MacGregor's work was started as early as 1868, when he began compiling information on the region from the North-West Frontier into central Eurasia, the dangers of the enemy raising an army in this space to invade British India animating much of his career.[51] Indeed, this project demonstrated the deficiency of military intelligence in the non-European context, thus serving to flesh out an agenda for the closing of the information gap once in office: namely, the need for more language training, statistical surveying, cartographic mapping, analysis of the kinds of warfare expected in these less familiar regions, and the centralisation and archiving of all available knowledge.[52]

'As Asia was being constituted as a geo-strategic space' because of the shortfall of information about central Asia and other interior spaces, the effect—although not one adduced by Hevia—was to reify the significance of a threat emanating from central Asia in the manner typical of the circular and paranoid character of the colonial mind.[53] In part, this was because an analogous Russian imperial security state emerged through the work of Russian scientific-military professionals, that is, geographers and surveyors, statisticians and engineers.[54] As these imperatives simultaneously propelled Russian and British advance deeper into the interior spaces, the two powers became locked into a situation where they were ever more aware of the other's presence but seemed to possess ever more deficient or insufficient knowledge about the other's motivations and expansionary strategy. 'Paradoxically,' as Kyle Gardner observes, 'the more that became known about [the] frontier, the less "secure" it would become.'[55] Viewed within this inter-imperial context, therefore, the security state took on a self-fulfilling logic while perpetuating the anxieties that entrenched the underlying thirst for systematic intelligence gathering and knowledge formation.

The advance of Russian forces towards the Afghan border and the fear of Russian alliance with Afghanistan prompted the transformation of Afghanistan into a British Protectorate through the militarisation of the Indo-Afghan frontier and the establishment of fortifications, as well as the installation of an amir—following the Second Anglo-Afghan War (1878–80)—who relinquished considerable control over foreign policy to the British. As the joint Anglo-Russian (or Afghan) Boundary Commission worked from 1884 until 1886 to delineate the Afghan border with Russian Turkestan, MacGregor pressed the need to close what was clearly an information chasm in the context of Russia's aggressiveness toward India's landward neighbours, proposing the 'organisation of an improved news agency on the Russo-Persian Afghan frontier'.[56] Existing sources of intelligence were inadequate, for translations of old Russian newspapers, 'stray reports' from emissaries in Berlin and St Petersburg, information from 'native agents' such as Afzal Khan in Kabul, and bazaar *gup* (gossip) from Peshawar was far from systematic.[57] MacGregor dreamed of a denser network of informants stretching from western Europe to western China, from high-born emissaries to humble travellers.[58]

In a memorandum to the Government of India of 1886, MacGregor outlined the following sources from which he wanted to systematically collect information:

1. Military Attachés in Berlin, Vienna and St Petersburgh [*sic*].
2. Foreign Office employés in Russia, Turkey, Persia.
3. Secret European agents at Tiflis, Astrakhan, Orenburg.
4. Known European agents at Astrabad, and on the Perso-Afghan frontier. These to have secret agents where possible.
5. Secret Asiatic agents at Tashkand, Samarkand, Ush, Petro-Alexandrovski, Ashkabad, Krasnovodsk, Kila Panj, Faizabad, Balkh, Karki, Panjdeh and Sarakhs.
6. Known Asiatic agents employing secret agency where possible at Kabul, Herat, and Kandahar.
7. Steps to be taken to elicit all information obtainable from travellers, especially from Russian territory passing Leh, Srinagar, Peshawar, Kohat, Bannu, Dera Ismail Khan, Pishin and Kalat.[59]

In other words, stationary and mobile informants, both European and Asian, were essential to the regular flow of news that supplemented the unchanging or static sorts of information gathered through mapping and surveying. At the same time, Asian merchants—who had long supplied information to the colonial state—were to be briefed and disciplined to the agenda of the Intelligence Department. Elsewhere, non-European merchants who had supported the Company's expansion were being removed from positions of proximity to the state as they were pushed out of their roles in finance and revenue management once the Company had forged its hegemony, but on the fringes of the empire they remained critical even as late as the 1870s.[60] At stake, therefore, was neither their indigeneity per se nor their mobility, but the necessity of the transformation of this indigenous epistemic community to serve the needs of the modern information order. A list of British subjects trading in central Asia was duly drawn up—the roll of seventy-seven traders analysed in chapter 4—but there is no indication of whether they were recruited, let alone whether they were suitably bent into the service of MacGregor's vision.[61]

Information Panic and the Predicament of Mobility

From around the second quarter of the nineteenth century there came a shift from an early modern information order in which much knowledge was embodied, often by indigenous practitioners, to one both modern *and* colonial in its characteristics, where knowledge was both vested in institutions and institutionalised even as it was made abstract. The extent of transformation was greatest at the upper reaches of the state but only partial or negligible further down into Indian society, or farther away from the heartlands of imperial rule, where the older and more decentralised epistemic communities continued and were weakly or slowly integrated (if not rejected) by the newer.[62] The more 'modern' the training and institutional exposure of successive waves of British recruits into colonial service, the more distant they often were from Indian society and the greater their difficulty of interaction with the pools and practitioners of indigenous knowledge.[63] 'It was in the zone of ignorance where the knowledgeable colonial institutions met, but failed to mesh with, the sentiment of the knowing people of the locality,' says C. A. Bayly, that 'the information panics which periodically convulsed expatriate British society in India' arose.[64] Ironically, therefore, the result of modernisation was the colonial state's increasing susceptibility to rumour and its liability to information panics.[65] Because mobility had the effect of making indigenous society a shifting sands, information panic was more likely in contexts with higher degrees of movement, so that mobile groups were pinpointed as the Achilles' heel of colonial security.

Cartographic surveying was not new in the 1860s–70s, but men freshly trained in novel techniques or else imbued with the new imperatives of the security state gave mapping a new lease of life. Martin Bayly has shown how Afghanistan went from *terra incognita* to *terra nul-*

lius, the memory of the violent ejection in 1842 shaping British ideas about her northward neighbour as a violent and uncivilised space of sedition and intrigue. This was where—according to theories of positivist international law in vogue at the time—diplomatic relations were relatively impossible, the British Indian state thus shifting from intervention to non-engagement, from a 'forward policy' of extending imperial influence to the delimitation and closing of the border as the means of defending the empire in south Asia.[66] Yet, this territorialisation of Afghanistan within the political and spatial fixities of a sovereign nation-state were not always realised in practice. From 1873–4, twenty years prior to the commencement of the demarcation of what would become the Durand Line, efforts to increase the colonial state's fiscal capture by taxing the caravans at newly established customs posts was undermined by the ease of evasion along an incredibly leaky border.[67] Because caravan trade was impossible to police robustly, and since Afghans also moved relatively freely across the border in search of seasonal employment as agricultural labourers, or else enlisted in the military, nowhere did the very real changes brought to Afghan lives over the nineteenth century ever correspond fully with the increasingly rigid contours of the Afghan polity being mapped by the colonial state.

Nevertheless, a contradiction of British rule emerged from the disconnect between imperial rhetoric and the frequent vocalisation of pride in principles of liberty—liberty in justice, the 'liberty of locomotion', for example—versus the practice of policing colonial subjects' exercise of these liberties and the legal instrumentalisation of paternalism in the interest of colonial rule.[68] If the Indian Rebellion of 1857 unleashed an unappeasable anxiety about the fragility of British rule, this combined with the fear of *thuggee* and banditry, as well as the feeling of vulnerability to Russian invasion via Afghanistan, to spotlight the perils of unchecked mobility.[69] Itinerant and transhumant groups were viewed with growing suspicion as vectors of sedition—the Banjaras (nomadic pack-bullock carriers) believed to have spread the cry of rebellion in 1857, for example. The colonial state thus tried to settle these groups or undermine the basis of their mobility through such means as restricting access to common land.[70] In fact, snatching the means of livelihood of bona fide pastoralists was more likely to turn them toward criminality, if not sedition, but that was only another instantiation of the self-fulfilling logic of British rule in the nineteenth century.

At stake, therefore, was the principled promotion of the right sorts of mobility and the vigorous policing and restriction of the movement of undesirable persons. On the one hand, the transhumance and mobility associated with caravan trade, if channelled into the service of the state as MacGregor and others hoped, undergirded rather than undermined the security of British India. On the other hand, here lay another contradiction. British understandings of mercantile groups were more than tinged by ideas of race and racial difference, which were seemingly inconsistent yet made perfectly absurd sense within the hierarchical conceptualisation of Asian peoples and societies that had come into being by the second half of the nineteenth century. These attitudes could be schematised as follows: much of the trans-frontier trade was of a peddling sort and thus suited to 'Asiatics' rather than Europeans; Afghans were the 'rearguard'—the most primitive—of Muslims to the extent of being particularly suited to peddler trade; but the true trading class of the Asiatics were not peddlers—and, thus, were not Afghans—but Hindu Indians of some considerable financial and commercial skill (and cunning).[71]

At the same time, the fear of Muslims was being articulated much more sharply, for the spectre of Wahhabism loomed larger over the nineteenth century as Islamic societies assertively confronted European colonial regimes across the world, or else the Ottoman Empire became a co-ordinating centre—imaginary, if not real—of pan-Islamic uprising.[72] Those 'rearguard' Muslims living in the rugged environment of the frontier were especially feared, moreover.[73] In part, this was the legacy of the slaughter of 1839–42 and the recasting of Afghanistan as a violent space (described above). This bled into what became a more persistent anxiety about Pashtuns in the context of their continued hostility to the British presence in the mountains.[74] This hostility seems to have been the product of careless policy, such as the increase in the salt tax, as well as the ignorance and despoiling of the Pashtuns' sacred geography of shrines (ziarats), of sacred burial and pilgrimage sites associated with Sufi pirs, and of healing places in the process of surveying the physical geography of the Indo-Afghan region.[75] In part, this was also the product of ethnography and the fantasy of 'mad mullahs' and fanatics, seemingly vindicated and thus gathering traction as a result of violent attacks by Pashtuns and Punjabis on the colonial authorities (examined in the British and Russian empires in Asia in the next section).[76] The worst of these fears for the colonial body politic as a whole were vindicated in the (apprehended) Silk Letter Movement of 1916, whereby Muslim 'fanatics' returning to India from the Hejaz conveyed letters written on silk inciting rebellion to conspirators in Kabul with the view to forming an Indo-Afghan alliance with the Ottomans and Germany to overthrow British imperial rule in south Asia.[77]

Unsurprisingly, therefore, there was some unease from certain British Indian officials about the sorts of persons—Muslims, and Pashtuns, no less—who were free to move, were employed as informants, and upon whose honour and loyalty the security of British India thus rested. And, yet, just as Fakir Mahomed of Kabul returned from Moscow in 1841 bringing a bounty of information for Alexander Burnes about Russian trade with central Asia, so did Muslims continue to act as the most important intelligence agents and informants relating matters beyond the Hindu Kush, rather than the more esteemed Hindu merchants.[78] For supplying news about central Asia to the British, Nasir Khairullah, a Kabul merchant but otherwise mysterious figure, was granted a government pension in 1855 and, even more remarkably, was publicly presented with honours—including a *khilat*—in 1856.[79] And, there was Faiz Buksh, the 'F. B.' of several archival letters and printed pamphlets connected to Afghanistan and Turkestan.[80] He is better known for his assistance to the Forsyth Mission to Yarkand, but this engagement was consequent upon his earlier experience and travels to Bukhara and Khiva in 1856.[81] It was this well of contradiction and confusion, ignorance and fantasy that precipitated information panic.

In 1839, as the Company readied itself to move on the Durrani state, intelligence was received of the apprehension of Afghans 'under suspicious circumstances in the Deccan'. A few years earlier, the Company had garnered valuable information about Khokand from a Khokandi official, Khoja Bahadur Khan, while he passed through Bombay en route to Mecca.[82] Men such as Masson had also proved adept at integrating themselves into networks of pilgrims and *pirs* during reconnaissance and intelligence-gathering work, suggesting some familiarity or even an ability to detect imposters.[83] Yet, in the build-up to the Afghan invasion, such knowledge of religious mendicants and travellers seems to have been suppressed as British officials chose to amplify more instrumental forms of information.[84] The alarm that India was infiltrated by spies acting on Russia's behalf to undermine British rule proved unfounded, for the men were discovered to be 'miserably poor and illiterate'. One claimed to be returning to Afghanistan via India from Mecca, having no money and thus resorting to begging his way back, while the other had travelled overland on the outbound leg of the pilgrimage.[85]

A far larger proportion of the *hajjis* not subject to Britain yet passing through British India were central Asians and Afghans.[86] Until the Trans-Caspian railway was constructed and Russia's involvement in organising the Hajj for its subjects developed towards the *fin de siècle*, it was far more efficient for pilgrims to travel with the caravans to the first railhead—depending on which route they took, but most likely Peshawar—and then by train to British ports such as Bombay, transferring onto steamship services to the Hejaz.[87] On the one hand, the flow of pilgrims provided a useful stream of news: when government solicited information on the prices and profitability of Indian goods (tea, indigo, muslin) in 1882, for example, the authorities in Peshawar turned first to an Indian trader, supplementing his evidence with fresh information of recent price fluctuations received from newly arrived pilgrims.[88] On the other hand, the movement of central Asians and Afghans was troubling, for neither were expected to show loyalty to the British, the former more likely to be Russian subjects. So difficult was policing or prohibiting their movement across a porous landward border, or else isolating them within the train of the *qafilas*, that their 'threat' only became palpable at a distance from the marts of caravan trade where they were relatively conspicuous. More often, however, the real headache resulted from their being genuine pilgrims who had become destitute and unable to return home, or else the fear of plague and other disease epidemics, as John Slight has so cogently argued.[89]

Yet, information panic emerged even where the knowledge gap ought to have been smaller, such was the generative potential of mobility when faced with the nervous disposition of the proportionally tiny, and thus perpetually nervous, British population. So extensive were the Afghans' commercial operations in north India, so fungible were Afghans from western Punjabis or north Indians to the expatriate layman, and so paranoid was the colonial population about spies and foreign invasion, that efforts to identify and isolate Afghans could ripple terror through Indian society.[90] When the *Behar Herald* published a piece stating that some Kabulis were selling cloth on credit without security in February 1878, for example, the news spread rapidly, a similar story soon appearing in the *Indian Tribune*. Quickly, the police entered the fray, and reports flooded in that Kabulis, thought to be Russian spies, were scattered all over eastern India. Following a lengthy and, ultimately, unnecessary investigation, the police revealed that the men were bona fide traders, not Kabulis but Khojas of western Punjab working for Marwari firms in Delhi and attempting to extend their trade eastward.[91] In such cases, however, is evidence of the fundamental difficulty of policing movement, for the deficiency of knowledge about suspect types—let alone distinguishing red herrings from genuine threats—made it difficult to identify precisely who was to be thwarted in either British India or Russian Turkestan.[92] This is not to say that the colonial state was not producing new knowledge about Indian people in a bid to identify dangerous elements within Indian society, and, so, it is to colonial ethnography and its connection to the trading world that the next section turns.

The Ethnographic State

Under two years after the flurry of Russian notes fell in Peshawar, toward the other end of the Grand Trunk Road the high-caste Awadhi, Bengali, and Rajput sepoys recruited in the Company's army rose against their masters in rebellion. Mutiny turned into a general uprising as news spread from the cradle of events in the garrison town of Meerut, for Indians of vastly different rank, occupation, caste, and confession felt united by their various grievances against a foe identified in common: the British.[93] The Indian Rebellion of 1857 brought an end not to British—only to East India Company—government in the subcontinent, however. The result of the events of 1857–8 was not so much a radical departure in the institutional form of colonial government, therefore, but rather the amplification of the pathological anxiety about both the precarity of colonial rule and the danger to expatriates' personal safety. This fear of a hostile and vengeful population haunted colonial rulers through to 1947.

Just as the imperative to 'know the country' and the origins of the imperial security state were rooted in prior changes within Europe, so, too, was the ethnographic state a product of the late eighteenth or early nineteenth century. And here, too, there was feedback from the colony to the metropole and back again in fine-tuning the colonial state's ethnographic gaze and the modern information order overall. The work of Company Orientalists from the closing decades of the eighteenth century played an important part in propelling European understandings of Asian—specifically, Indian—peoples, at once also sharpening the developing sense of Occidental identities. The commencement of regular census operations in Britain in 1801 and the larger 'statistical movement'—the use of statistics to study society and formulate social policy—that began taking shape between 1780 and 1830, but truly came into being thereafter, was one of the new contexts to the collection of data about Indian peoples that exhibited greater vigour in the Victorian era.[94] The Rebellion, however, had the effect of ramping up the importance of 'knowing the people' as well as defining the more precise imperatives—such as the identification of criminal or semi-criminal 'types' or those who might resist colonial rule. This was required for the new technologies of the census and photography, thus marking the beginnings of a new and distinctive moment in these longer-run processes.

The origins of ethnographic photography are traceable to the entanglements of photography in capturing Indian peoples, places, and architectural sites from the 1840s.[95] With regard to portraits—as photography captured external characteristics, and because these were said to betray perceived political and cultural characteristics in turn—there was considerable momentum to the expansion of ethnographic photography after 1857.[96] Much as the aims of colonial intelligence were not merely to collect information but to construct new knowledge through the use of novel techniques or the new processes at work within the archives, so, too, did photography not so much reveal underlying facts as construct new 'truths', not least about racial types.[97] Nevertheless, in the early 1860s, the Foreign Department requested from provincial governments 'likenesses of "characteristic specimens" of each tribe within their jurisdiction', the culmination of which was the eight-volume *The People of India*, edited by John Forbes Watson and J. W. Kaye, and published between 1868 and 1875.[98]

The *Turkestanskii Al'bom* (encountered in previous chapters) was only briefly antedated by this analogous project in British India. The album was compiled in 1871–2 on the instructions of the first governor general of Russian Turkestan, K. P. von Kaufman, for the express purpose of updating existing knowledge and acquainting Russians and Europeans with life in central Asia in the 1850s and 1860s, and as a record for posterity, presumably to show the advances subsequently brought by Russian rule.[99] Divided into four parts—'Archaeological', 'Ethnographic', 'Trades', and 'Historical'—the album is a rich documentary resource on the lives and livelihoods of the various communities that inhabited central Asia, while also betraying the interests and understandings of central Asian society held by Russian contemporaries. The album was one element of a much larger collection of ethnographic and scientific knowledge of Russia's new lands in the service of the modern information order. General von Kaufman recruited Orientalists as well as naturalists, surveyors, statisticians, artists, and other scholars—including, most famously, Alexei and Olga Fedchenko—to investigate and produce new knowledge on central Asia.[100]

Recent work on Russian Orientalism has highlighted the relationship of imperial power to the study of Oriental languages, religions, societies, and history, and vice versa, bringing the Russian Empire into the study of colonial knowledge and the associated ethnographic state.[101] By the time of von Kaufman's recruitment of learned specialists, education in Oriental studies was well established in Russia.[102] Tsarist interest in Asia stimulated inquiry from the early eighteenth century as the empire expanded southward into the Caucasus. But it was in the nineteenth century that the establishment of new Oriental institutes—including the Kazan Theological Academy (first established 1798), the Oriental departments of the Kazan Imperial University (opened 1805, its chairs in Oriental studies transferred to St Petersburg in 1854), the Moscow University, and the academies in the imperial capital—brought the teaching of languages and the production of new knowledge on the

Islamic world and Asia into Russian intellectual life proper. After the conquest of central Asia, a further wave of Russian interest was stimulated, of which that of the Nalivkins was typical in character but relatively unique in methodology and depth of understanding, being the product of prolonged residence amongst relatively ordinary Muslim households, to take one example.

The tsarist state's instrumentalisation of ethnographic knowledge to facilitate colonial rule over Turkestan was less considerable than in British India, however. This was signalled by the tardiness of its first revenue-agricultural survey (conducted almost four decades after the conquest and of doubtful accuracy) and the lower degree of classification and codification in such undertakings as the (only, yet incomplete) empire-wide census of 1897. In part, this resulted from its fear of intervening too deeply in an alien and hostile society in ways that might provoke rebellion. But this also resulted from its weak control over both the nature and the use of ethnographic knowledge products.[103] That said, it was neither the case that the ethnographic state in British India was a monolithic and hegemonic entity, nor that British ethnographers were always handmaidens servicing the intellectual agenda and information requirements of the colonial state, as Zak Leonard has argued.[104] Rather, much of the production of ethnographic knowledge played a more general role in 'scientifically' substantiating existing policy prejudices and directions or else influencing the contours of policy rather broadly in south Asia (and also, perhaps, in central Asia). With these caveats in mind, therefore, in what ways did these states' ethnographic inquiries or use of ethnography impact the peoples or spaces connected through caravan trade?

Martial Races and Military Recruitment

Originating in the late nineteenth century, the theory of the martial races—in reality neither a formal nor even an internally consistent or codified doctrine—developed after the Indian Rebellion of 1857. After 1857, the British turned to Punjabis (Sikhs and Punjabi Muslims, Pashtuns, and other Afghan groups) and Gurkhas who had demonstrated their loyalty and military prowess during the Rebellion, and who were subsequently celebrated in the British Indian military establishment—and also in novels, the press, and popular culture in Britain—alongside the Scottish Highlanders with whom they had subdued the uprisings. The growing dominance of Punjabi soldiers was gradual at first: their initial recruitment is traceable to the first half of the century, including the Company's extension of the Sikh recruitment of Yusufzais soon after the conquest of Punjab in 1849, and was increased in the wake of the mutiny-rebellion in 1857 of the then-favoured Rajput and Brahmin soldiers from Bengal and Bihar, before accelerating dramatically after *c.* 1880.[105]

'The meaning of the "race" in "martial race"', Heather Streets argues, 'was both flexible and fictitious even as it used the language of fixed immutable racial binaries that claimed so much contemporary currency.'[106] While there is some debate about racially restrictive recruitment in practice, what is not disputed is the currency of the discourse of military racialisation—that is, martial races theory—by the later nineteenth century, and the intensification of recruitment amongst these groups in the last quarter of the nineteenth century.[107] In particular, the threat of a Russian invasion of India transformed martial races recruitment 'from a minority to a hegemonic position within the Indian military administration' for 'each crisis on the northwest frontier, [meant] the ideology of martial races gained greater credibility and influence'.[108]

The connection of race to military fitness within colonial India was complex and predates the Rebellion and the emergence of martial races ideology (and, in fact, the establishment of colonial rule), as other scholars have shown.[109] What is at stake, however, is the relation of new ideas about race and a newfound importance of ethnography in the formulation of new ideas of military fitness, even if its clearest manifestations were retroactive.[110] Tony Ballantyne notes, in his study of Orientalism and Aryanism, that Scots—both at home and abroad in East India Company service across the Indian subcontinent—were central actors in the projects of comparative philology and historical ethnography in the later eighteenth century from which emerged theories of Occidental development and Oriental degradation.[111] These studies also 'revealed' that India and Britain were inextricably linked by their common origins in the Aryan 'race'. But, whereas Britain had marched into progress and prosperity, India had declined and degraded, not least because of the degrading effects of the hot climate and of the intermixing of Aryan invaders from the north with the Dravidian peoples of the south of the subcontinent. In those areas where Aryans had first arrived into India, at greatest distance from Dravidian populations, such as Punjab and the North-West Frontier, the Aryan body and character were best preserved.[112] Thus, from roughly the mid nineteenth century, the textual and oral investigation of Punjabi and Afghan ethnogenesis gained currency as a means of fine-tuning, corroborating, or challenging the accumulation of anecdotal evidence.[113]

In effect, the British shifted their recruiting grounds to the dry zone, retaining its importance to the production of hard power in south Asia (to return to the argument of chapter 3). Yet, there were significant discontinuities. In the first place, the dry zone was understood in racial terms. Of course, the distinctive ecology—namely, the harsh and rugged landscape—of the dry zone led to the production of particular traits found in the martial races through ethnographic 'study'—evinced in Elphinstone's *Account*, for instance—such as strength, ferocity, and valour.[114] In this respect, early accounts of Sikhs and Afghans dating from the late eighteenth and early nineteenth century (discussed in the previous section) were often inflected with Romantic notions of tribe and clan, drawn in analogue with the discourse of the ruggedness of the Scottish Highlands and the Scotch Highlander as a 'noble savage' that developed from the second half of the eighteenth century.[115] In the words of Richard Temple, for example, the frontier tribes were 'noble savages [...] not without the tincture of virtue and generosity, but still absolutely barbarians nevertheless.'[116] When inquiries turned to ethnogenesis or origin narratives, discussion of mountains as a natural barrier assumed a crucial role in explaining how the Aryan descent of the Afghans was preserved in the face of such 'degrading' factors as the hot climate or miscegeny with subcontinental peoples.[117] But all such connections were novel, for Mughal ideas about the incivility of Afghans, for instance, were traced to their location outside the centres of urbanised civility rather than in the landscape they inhabited per se, and certainly never produced anything even as crude as the 'martial races' ideology.[118]

Secondly, and more significantly, the colonial state attempted to pacify the dry zone—or Punjab and the Indo-Afghan frontier, at least—just as they turned Punjab into a 'garrison state'.[119] In other parts of India, pacification through patronage of loyalists as well as more fickle mobile warrior groups was already part of the Company's post-conquest strategy around the turn of the century, if not earlier.[120] Yet, there was something distinctive about the Punjabi experience, for the inhabitants of the very province that had so decisively supported the colonial state in its darkest hour were, paradoxically, subject to some of its most draconian laws. Mark Condos' recent analysis provides a key to this conundrum: the problem with the martial races was precisely that they were 'warlike' and 'turbulent'. Despite their loyalty in 1857, the Sikhs had been difficult to defeat during the wars of conquest in the 1840s, demonstrating the threat they posed if not pacified or properly incorporated into the colonial military and transformed into subjects whose loyalty was foremost to the colonial state. In fact, the memory of one event weighed particularly heavily on the formation of any easy relationship of the colonial community with Punjabis and Pashtuns: the Siege of Multan in 1848–9.

Following the revolt of the Sikh-appointed governor of Multan over the payment of dues to the British, two British officers were violently murdered in a surprise mob attack, an 'outrage' from the British point of view that required a sharp and swift response. Additionally, there were concerns that 'various chiefs throughout the province and even the Afghans might seize upon any sign of British weakness or hesitation' to undermine British rule over central Punjab, annexed in 1846.[121] The result was the protracted Second Anglo-Sikh War and the annexation of western Punjab.[122] Under this 'permanent siege mentality', the need for violence was the product not of strength but of perpetual insecurity and perceived vulnerability. The events of 1848 and 1857, Condos argues, had highlighted that the British had much to fear even in (what became) the most loyal and prosperous province of their Indian empire.

As the state's ethnographic gaze evolved in the contexts of new intellectual and technological influences, it nevertheless contributed a steady stream of information to the corpus of colonial knowledge that valorised Punjabi Sikhs and Pathans (encompassing Pashtuns and other Afghan groups, including Hazaras), even as some of those qualities that made them most suitable to military careers were a source of anxiety in civilian contexts.[123] At the same time, puncturing the archive were instances of '"murderous outrages", "fanatical outrages", or "*ghazism*", [...] crimes that typically involved a sudden, seemingly unprovoked, and murderous assault against British personnel or their Indian subordinates', as well as cases of agitation or aggression more generally.[124] Centrepieces in Condos' study of these occurrences include: the 'Kooka Outbreak' of 1872, when forty-nine Namdhari Sikhs attacked a Muslim princely state in Punjab, seen as an open rebellion against overarching British authority and resulting in the men being blown from the mouths of artillery guns; the assassination of Viceroy Mayo by a Pashtun 'fanatic' in the Andaman Islands in the same year; and the violent (but not fatal) attack on the family of the station master of the Peshawar Cantonment railway within their home by a 'ghazi' in 1919. The result was the Murderous Outrages Act of 1867, whereby special tribunals without juries or appeals processes were used to mete out immediate executions or transportation for life, so that colonial law in Punjab came to embody arbitrary power by enshrining the absolute power and dispensation of 'justice' by those colonial officials who perpetually quivered with fear for personal safety in the presence of their subjects.[125]

If government in India could be characterised as 'military despotism tempered by law', government in Punjab was thus tantamount to military despotism through the law.[126] The situation in Russian Turkestan was comparable, for military rule prevailed until the fall of tsarism in 1917 and the Bolshevik conquest in 1918, and was likewise rooted in notions about the local peculiarities of its Muslim inhabitants. In the Volga–Ural region, Muslims were Russian subjects in the fullest sense, for they could be conscripted into the tsarist military and also benefited from access to some of the same rights as non-Muslims, judicial (trial by jury, for instance) and legislative (namely, self-government through the *zemstvo*). In Turkestan, by contrast, there were no *zemstvos* and the state's concern revolved largely around the maintenance of law and order or the furtherance of its—rather than the indigenes'—interests.[127] In the Russian mind, official and non-official, the local population of Turkestan was sometimes deemed as comprising 'aborigines' or a 'separate species', such was the sense of the distinctiveness of indigenous society and its backwardness relative to other parts of the empire.

Much as the events of 1848 and 1857 terrorised expatriate society in British India, so the long Russian war in the Caucasus (of which the Crimean War of 1853–6 was but one episode) was formative. It served not only as the prelude to the advance into Turkestan but also encouraged the belief that most Muslims were 'fanatics', a fire stoked by the polemical tracts of such writers as M. A. Miropiev and Agafangel Krymskii.[128] In turn, von Kaufman opted to maintain a light touch in matters of the state's involvement in Muslim life for fear of provoking a revolt—a strategy similar to that of the first chief commissioner of Punjab, John Lawrence, who preferred 'masterly inactivity' over close involvement in Afghan lands for fear of destabilising the frontier.[129] Instead, as Daniel Brower notes, his ethnographic projects were 'specifically intended to help construct a barrier to Islam' by classifying and ordering those '"bigoted, hypocritical, and corrupt Muslim holy men, mullas, judges, pilgrims, saints, and dervishes"' who otherwise would go unidentified in the Sart population.[130] The introduction of a new civil code in Turkestan in 1886 changed little, for the law continued to be administered by military courts and the military remained heavily involved in administration. Efforts toward reform, Morrison notes, were regularly stymied by those officials who saw 'Muslim "backwardness" and "fanaticism" or new pan-Turkic and pan-Islamic threats' as justification for the maintenance of military rule.[131]

This impulse was amplified in the wake of the Andijan Uprising of 1898, when armed men from Fergana attacked the Russian forces, killing twenty-two and wounding a further eighteen. The result—recently exposed in brilliant detail by Morrison—was an information panic, fed by existing prejudice and rumour amongst Russians about their Muslim subjects in place of sound knowledge of the moral leadership of a Sufi, Dukchi Ishan, who led the uprising. An eighteen-month-long wild goose chase ensued as the fear of Sufi fanaticism was warped by paranoia into the quest for a larger pan-Islamic plot, in which it was suspected that the Afghan amir was colluding. These investigations were perhaps guided by a local grandee who hoped to capture the fears of Russian officials and thereby authorise action against his local enemies. But possibly such speculation merely reproduces the sense of uncertainty and paranoia contained in the colonial archive, akin to that revealed upon reading Edwardes' correspondence.[132] Whether in

Punjab and the North-West Frontier or in Turkestan, nevertheless, the blurred ethnographic gaze of the British and Russian colonial states played a part in making more rigid than ever before the relationship of the state to the people.

Colonies of Sedentarisation

In spite of the preponderance of Pathans and Punjabis within the British Indian army and police, this channelling or relocation of their martial power into units away from their home territory was only one strategy of subduing their restive and violent potential.[133] Significantly, the transformation of the (male) labour market went hand-in-glove with the wholescale transformation of the land and the widespread drive to disarm and sedentarise mobile peoples in the dry zone. After the conclusion of its wars of conquest in Punjab, the British disbanded the Khalsa army and disarmed the countryside, channelling Punjabis into agriculture.[134] But as agricultural output increased, prices and living standards fell, fuelling disaffection. To placate its newest subjects, the state increased the availability of irrigation in the 1850s–60s to enlarge the extent of arable available to households, the aim being to enhance household revenue.[135] This was complemented with lower rates of land tax and preferential military enlistment in the province to provide alternative and lucrative employment to Punjabi men.[136] Together, the result was the transformation of Punjabis into wealthy yeomen, while the British also relied more heavily for military labour on those same restive and martial groups they distrusted and had only lately disarmed.

In the third quarter of the century can thus be found the precursor to the much larger project of constructing the 'canal colonies', the largest investment in irrigation technology anywhere in colonial India. The new Chenab, Jhelum, Lower Bari Doab, Upper Chenab, and Upper Jhelum colonies were in western Punjab, 'greening' the otherwise more arid lands of the region relative to central and eastern Punjab.[137] In the main, the recipients of the new land were drawn from the 'dominant' landed castes—often non-cultivators, but generally social elites, including Jats, Kambohs, Arains, Syeds, Shaikhs, Afghans, and Rajputs—rather than 'menial' landless castes.[138] And many of these recipients of land were recruited and migrated from central Punjab, causing a population growth of over 100 per cent in Jhang, Multan, Shahpur, and Sheikhupura, 219 per cent in Montgomery, and a phenomenal 2,215 per cent in Lyallpur.[139] With such numerical increase, sheer scale marked the departure of Mughal, Durrani, and Sikh irrigation investments and creation of arable (discussed in chapter 4) from the British schemes. In this new 'hydraulic society', as Imran Ali has termed it, agriculturalists laboured to produce wheat, cotton, and sugar—primary products then commanding high prices on metropolitan and international commodity markets.[140]

The basic logic of these policies was also extended north of Jhang to the Peshawar valley, where lower revenue demands and the infrastructural developments re-stimulated the expansion of cultivation from mid century.[141] In fact, this phase reflected the acceleration and culmination of a long process stretching back to the Mughal period, at least, of what Robert Nichols describes as 'settling the frontier' to exert imperial dominion. In the late nineteenth century, these developments included the Swat Canal, the newly irrigated lands from which attracted (oftentimes as seasonal labourers) Mohmand and Bajauri tribesmen. Nichols states that there were 96,618 immigrants in the later nineteenth century, of whom at least 48,309 were independent Afghans or under the Afghan amir's rule.[142] Ultimately, through receipt of the higher salaries payable to soldiers (relative to the peasantry) as well as army pensions, and the additional incomes from cash-crop production for imperial and world markets, households were flushed with cash in return for being tied to service of the empire. Punjabis and Pashtuns were thus recompensed with economic prosperity in exchange for a relatively backward economy, this backwardness maintained through colonial policy around agriculture rather than industry. The impact of this transformation was felt most decisively in the area around Multan, undermining that part of economic activity connected foremost to caravan trade (as examined more closely in the next chapter).

The colonisation of western Punjab by central Punjabi agriculturalists under the aegis of the colonial state was part of a 'worldwide process of frontier colonisation', with contemporaries comparing it to the same under way in north America and Australia, as well as China and numerous other locales.[143] It was certainly comparable to changing patterns of land ownership and land use in Russian Turkestan. The tsarist state's policy of *perselenie* (resettlement) to ensure optimal use of arable land within European Russia was *kolonizatsiya* (colonisation) in what were deemed the empty lands of Asiatic Russia, 'where supposedly there were no valid prior claims to the soil, and settlement could be linked to a civilising mission.'[144] From the late eighteenth century, Cossack peasants commenced their movement first into the recently conquered Kazakh hordes, continuing their creeping colonisation further east through the nineteenth century. From the mid nineteenth century, Cossacks thus started to settle in Turkestan, but—as in other colonial settler societies, including contemporary French Algeria—the hopes of their setting a good example to bring 'civilisation' to the 'natives' were always undermined by the sense that they were 'poor whites' rather than cultural pioneers, better hidden and hardly the stuff of imperial propaganda.[145]

In fact, early settlements were strategically located on the post roads to Tashkent to bolster the Russian presence, often established under the direction of individual officers. Where Cossacks settled in Turkestan proper, they often encroached on irrigated lands of seasonal (winter) Kazakh settlement, for most 'free' land was arid. Turkestan was closed to colonisation in 1897, such was the difficulty of placing migrants on previously unsettled land, but the decision was reversed in the wake of the Andijan Uprising of 1898, for the resumption of colonisation would, it was argued, bolster the Russian colonial presence against the native population.[146] In this, therefore, are broadly comparable patterns of changing land use, colonisation, and overall sedentarisation. In both colonial contexts can be traced a concern, albeit fraught, over encouraging 'good' sorts of settlers to move into the hotbeds of recently conquered land to diffuse (or even displace) indigenous 'fanatics' or more restive elements of the population, at the same time undermining the economies of caravan trade and its angst-making mobilities.

The impact of colonial policy with respect to sedentarisation was not restricted to the human actors and spaces of habitation connected to caravan trade, however, for there were also efforts to 'sedentarise' the breeding of animals long connected to the economy of pastoralism and overland trade. In spite of the shift in preference toward thoroughbreds, fascination with the Turki continued into the second half of the nineteenth century. Official interest and inquiry resurfaced at times of acute supply shortage, not least after the Indian Rebellion and around the time of the Second Anglo-Afghan War.[147] In both instances, the obtainable specimens fell short of demand or of desired quality.[148] Ultimately, central Eurasian stocks were in such short supply and of such poor quality that the Afghan amir was reluctant to issue passes to traders bringing Persian and Afghan horses through the southerly passes.[149]

Pastoralism was already in rapid retreat across north India in consequence of changes in land rights and land use as well as the state's anxiety about nomads' circulation.[150] With the establishment of the canal colonies, the colonial state was able to replace the remnants of the mobile breeding operations of (semi-)nomadic pastoralists with fixed and more 'modern' breeding grounds than Indian breeding and the failed Pusa stud farm in Bengal, its successor being the stud at the Government Cattle Farm in Hissar, Punjab.[151] Imran Ali has elaborated the numerous connections of the canal colonies to the military. Complementing the grant of land to ex-soldiers, for instance, were extensive settlement schemes for the breeding and maintenance of camels for military use.[152] A far larger enterprise was the establishment between 1900 and 1920 of cavalry horse runs on land in the Jhelum and Lower Bari Doab canal colonies—building on similar schemes dating from the 1890s, at least—that was granted to Indian cavalry regiments for the breeding and rearing of their own horses and mules. In theory, this removed the need for the purchase of horses and the budgetary crunch this would precipitate in the context of short supply and high prices.[153] Yet, just as horse breeding had earlier failed in south Asia, so the greening of the dry zone and its use for breeding operations brought the criticism that these schemes resulted in a massive opportunity cost and financial loss to government and people.[154]

Overall, then, what were the effects of the transformation of land and labour upon caravan trade? Precolonial Indian rulers had also channelled the unpredictable and highly mobile power of men of arms from the dry zone into their armies while making use of the animal power brought into the wet zone by pastoralists and horse traders. Colonial recruitment, however, regularised and fixed the footlooseness of men of arms into the stationary regiments of the standing army or the police, even as they were mobilised into service across south Asia and the British Empire. At the same time, if the (slow) shift from cavalry to infantry warfare undermined what was left of the horse trade, the (generally unsuccessful or insufficient) efforts to breed horses within Punjab signalled the desire to shut out or cut off the remnants of the archaic pastoral economy and replace it with more modern breeding operations *in situ*. In this way, as the colonial state became the monopsonist in the market for violence, the connection of the dry zone's ecology, the economy of pastoralism and seasonal migration, and service by Pathans and Punjabis of the economies of violence was subject to profound transformation in a direction that undermined part of the overarching logic of caravan trade and its mobilities.

The consequences for caravan trade were mixed, however. In the first place, the result was to decisively sever the relationship of the larger economy of caravan trade to the production of hard power, although the Company's establishment of its hegemony by *c.* 1818— following its victory in the third and final war with the Marathas—had effectively shut down the demand for mercenaries from Indian rulers beyond the Sikh kingdoms several decades prior to the creation of the hydraulic society. Rather than the merchants or organisers of the caravans securing the service of dominant tribes to protect the train, necessitating another sort of interaction between actors in the economy of trade and those with a foot in the economy of violence, the state supplied the caravans with an armed guard—itself another aspect of pacification of the trading world.[155] Frontier tribes were also paid allowances or subsidies to protect the region and the main routes, a strategy seen from the state's perspective as cheaper than the extensive use of military power, although the amounts were small and their significance was in forging the goodwill upon which security was predicated.[156]

Yet, the enrichment of Pashtuns—foremost through military employment, supplemented by incomes received as subsidy or through the sale of their productions (including animal products, fruit, and nuts)—enhanced purchasing power along the Indo-Afghan frontier.[157] The result was to sustain caravan trade, supporting the enlargement of the trade of certain goods, including cloth, toward the frontier, even as the rationale for the production of other goods was being eroded. The old economy of caravan trade briefly boomed and then shrank to survive on a smaller scale, but was ultimately hollowed out (a process analysed in more detail in the next chapter). At the same time, since the larger aim of sedentarisation was pacification, the project was only partially successful, for there was a steady increase in both the quantity and quality of firearms on the Indo-Afghan frontier.[158] The Mughals had armed the tribes in the seventeenth century, and a burst of prolific fighting and bloodshed in the early eighteenth century was part of the turbulence with which Ahmad Shah had to deal.[159] The British further weaponised this interior space, not least following the strategic security alliance struck with Dost Muhammad Khan in 1855.[160]

At the same time, the stipulations of the Indian Arms Act of 1878—making licences necessary for owners or traders in arms—did not 'apply in its entirety until later decades in some districts along the Indo-Afghan frontier', with local production established at Dera Ismail Khan.[161] Evidence discovered by the British during the Second Anglo-Afghan War threw into relief the networks connecting 'European firms, Indian merchants, Zanzibari commercial agents, Hindu bankers, and Armenian, Parsi, and Iranian intermediaries' in moving European arms to 'markets along the Gulfs of Persia and Oman.'[162] The movement of Afghans by dhows and steamers towards Muscat, an important mart in this arms traffic, gave greater cause for suspicion of Afghans purporting to be on pilgrimage, for some Afghans 'purchase[d] [...] hundreds (in some years, thousands) of rifles, revolvers, and packets of ammunition that would then be smuggled by *qafila* from the Persian Gulf to Afghanistan and beyond to the Indian frontier.'[163] The market in Kabul and at other places was vast and lucrative, the mark-up ten times or more on the purchase price. Aside from demand serviced through this channel, arms were sometimes stolen from Indian army garrisons, while 'artisans along the frontier and in Iran [...] perfected the art of counterfeiting European weapons, even down to the manufacturer's stamp.'[164] In spite of state efforts to disarm its colonial subjects and exert a monopoly over violence, therefore, the ease of smuggling combined with legitimate flows of arms and munitions and the thinness of the colonial presence on the frontier to undermine the exertion of colonial power.[165]

Conclusion

Set in the aftermath of the Second Anglo-Afghan War, and capitalising on popular hysteria about the Great Game, Kipling's *Kim* (1901) is an encrustation of much common and some secret knowledge of British India and its relations with neighbouring powers along the Silk Roads.[166] Predictably, for example, there is a Pashtun horse dealer, Mahbub Ali, employed as a British spy—a practice stretching back to the beginning of the century, even if British officials pretending to be Afghan horse traders were fooling no one by the century's end.[167] There is a lama, whose spiritual quest takes him along the trans-Karakoram trade routes, which were becoming busier in the second half of the century (as the previous chapter outlined). And there is a conflict with Russian intelligence agents in the Himalaya—presumably Chinese Turkestan, where the Russians were, in fact, more successful than the British in establishing their authority—and the seizure of Russian documents.

As the vignette that opened this chapter demonstrated, the appearance of mere scraps of paper in Russian script could palpitate colonial officials, who saw them as manna from heaven. Yet, as that vignette also demonstrated, the trickery could work both ways, and double deceptions and decoys could be used to play—and prey—on the colonial mind.[168] Such confusion, doubt, and dismissal are characteristic of what Stoler has termed the 'hierarchy of credibility' evident in the colonial archive.[169] Moreover, such instances were not isolated but systematic: sandwiched within the archives between the genuine news of a Russian in Kabul in 1837 and the rumour from Peshawar of 1856 was at least one other (albeit uneventful) case; that of a man claiming to be a Russian artillery lieutenant, who arrived in Peshawar in 1850 while Edwardes was receiving a hero's welcome in Britain for his role in the annexation of Punjab.[170]

If the figures discussed in this chapter are all male, it is because colonial intelligence networks—like the popular imagination of colonial espionage—were skewed along the lines of gender and race, at least at the point when pen was put to paper.[171] On the frontier, and beyond it, furthermore, much direct intelligence was gathered in the course of campaigns to the extent that Hevia describes this as a 'wholly masculine form of imperial knowledge', while, in time, Afghanistan (or

Kabul, at least) would be reconfigured as an essentially male space only suitable for fit and robust men, as Maximilian Drephal has argued.[172] Yet, for all this exclusionist gendering of space and knowledge (by men, no less), women had been important political and commercial actors in precolonial courts, where they had commanded information networks of their own in support of their business ventures or for the political candidacy of male relations in the process of *fitna* (faction- and alliance-building towards the formation of new political authority), as Bayly laid out clearly but few scholars have since elaborated.[173] Women acted as spy masters, were spied upon, but were also employed as informants in settings where they had (relatively) free mobility, not least those midwives (*dais*) who entered elite households, in counter-part to barbers and eunuchs.[174]

'Women's role in government', Thomas Wide has noted in a study of Afghanistan, 'could also extend to intelligence work, the British Agent at Kabul remarking on the hiring of large numbers of female informants by Habibullah Khan's brother, Nasrullah, in 1912', for example.[175] Within the heartlands of British India, in the other milieus of intelligence gathering and the archives in which knowledge was produced, madams and prostitutes, alongside their pimps, earned extra money as informants, one madam and her girls asked to spy on insurgent Afghans in the early twentieth century, for example.[176] One might also ask how much of Burnes' intelligence flowed from the lips of the Kabuli women of whom he was so fond.[177] Outside the evolving colonial or modern information order along the Indo-Afghan frontier, but perhaps within it to a greater degree than is obvious, women therefore continued to play a part in intelligence gathering and politics.

This chapter has examined the relationship of information to the mobilities engendered by caravan trade in the colonial context. On the fringes of empire and into the trans-imperial realm, commercial actors were vectors for the regular flow of news and the accumulation of knowledge for the maintenance of imperial security, remaining long after the colonial state rebuffed its closeness to merchant groups in imperial administration. Beneath any seeming continuity, however, was a shift from an early modern to a modern information order that fundamentally altered the imperatives of intelligence gathering. This shift was connected to the innovation of new technologies and techniques of statecraft and military power that seemed to call for new practices (institutional, behavioural) of producing or collecting, collating and archiving knowledge. The result was the rise of the imperial security state. The frontier was a site critical to this development, in turn: it was at once the space that required protection because it was initially such *terra incognita* and because adversaries' motivations and military capabilities were so difficult to know—and, yet, it was where the knowledge chasm was so difficult to close. The consequence of this, finally, was the perpetuation of the security state's underpinning mentalités—anxiety, paranoia, vulnerability—which were especially acute in the colonial context, as this chapter has sought to foreground, building on the work of other scholars.[178]

The ambivalence about trans-frontier mobility—which could as easily help close the knowledge gap as contribute to the overthrow of colonial rule—aroused suspicion and feelings of vulnerability. Meanwhile, the production of an evolving body of ethnographic knowledge about Punjabis and Afghans supported the transformation of land and labour north-west of Delhi. Massive investment in irrigation facilities opened new tracts in the formerly relatively parched lands of western Punjab all the way to the Indo-Afghan frontier. By opening this land to colonists from further east, and incentivising cash-crop production or animal breeding, the state slowly undermined the demographic, social, and economic bases of the archaic networks of caravan trade and its underpinning mobilities. The processes of pacification, sedentarisation, and peasantisation were probably the most profound transformations to afflict the material lives of Indians over the nineteenth century. Ironically, sedentarisation was not wholly successful as a means to pacification, however, for new transportation technologies combined with the newfound economic gains of sedentarised groups to empower a geographically vast and quantitatively significant arms-smuggling operation into being.

In focussing on the evolution—as opposed to the disjuncture—from precedent in the British Indian state and its information order, as well as the back and forth flow of influences between Asia and Europe in the development of colonial power and the colonial episteme, this analysis has aimed not to dismiss but to fine-tune the recent interest in these areas. There is a notion in common circulation that the colonial state's foremost problem relating to matters on or beyond its frontiers was one of unprecedented *mis*information as well as information gaps, itself the product of various sorts of ignorance, and that its blunders—not least three wars with Afghanistan—continue to plague the modern states of Afghanistan, Pakistan, and India.[179] These notions are rather close to historical actors' own concerns with the reliability and robustness of the available information, so that the recent work on the colonial archive and the ontologies of colonial knowledge actually draws its agenda or else actually reproduces—even as it seeks to interrogate—the epistemic anxieties driving knowledge production within the colonial state.[180] And, moreover, these notions are also too simplistic, for many of the strategies employed by the colonial state to deal with those social groups perceived as most turbulent were comparable to the strategies of their Mughal and Sikh—and even more tellingly, their Durrani—predecessors. These included the payment of subsidies or grant of *jagirs* to the frontier tribes and their co-optation into imperial service thereby, the channelling of men of arms into seasonal military campaigns and the hire or purchase of beasts of burden brought by nomadic pastoralists, punitive expeditions to pacify recalcitrant or hostile tribes, and so forth.

There was certainly something distinctive about the colonial episteme, for the effects of colonial forms of knowledge on land and labour, freedom of movement and the exercise of hard power were to alter these fundamentally. There is something intriguing, furthermore, about the parallels between policies regarding land and labour in the northwest frontier region to those in the north-east, where plantations and tea gardens replaced jungle tracts, and the use of indentured labour from other parts of India altered local demographics.[181] The work of Benjamin D. Hopkins demonstrates an even larger, *global* impact of the nineteenth-century transformation of the Indo-Afghan frontier, albeit viewed from a slightly different angle—that is, through the lens of the law, governance, and 'hard power'.[182] The Indo-Afghan frontier was, he argues, a 'laboratory' for the concoction of distinctive forms of control that were subsequently translated to colonial Africa and the Middle East. These he calls 'frontier governmentality', which involved not conquest and assimilation, but the physical and cultural containment and enclosing of the frontier and its inhabitants, who were perceived as violent, uncivilised, and bonded into collectivities (such as 'tribes') by the supposedly timeless precepts of 'custom' and 'tradition'. The state privileged certain groups—for instance, the elite men of particular tribes—over others, sanctioning them to rule on its behalf with reference to local customs and traditions of their own definition. The result was a highly personalised form of governance; it can perhaps be described as neo-patrimonial and hence archaic, to link it to ideas examined in this chapter. This was part of an overall strategy, complementing the processes of pacification, sedentarisation, and peasantisation.

Clearly, therefore, this assault on multiple fronts—the north-western and north-eastern frontier of British India, from thence to colonies in the Middle East and in Africa—distinguishes nineteenth-century developments from precolonial precedents, if they can be called thus. But it would unwise to imbue the colonial state with particularly powerful historical agency—rendered unique in its supposed exceptionalism or unprecedentedness—simply because the ontology and uses of precolonial Indian knowledges or early modern European knowledges have been subject to less interrogation than the colonial, or else ignored. And it would be unwise to assume that this was entirely the product of relations of colonialism, as opposed primarily to developments in the technologies of the modern state or the forces of the modern economy, for instance.[183] The institutions of the ethnographic and security states in British India, their knowledges, their intelligence-gathering and archival practices, were technologies of power both modern and colonial in character. Their impact, in this instance, was to reconceptualise and transform physical space and peoples' relation to the land on a scale and with a vision that distinguished it from precolonial precedent. Their impact, moreover, was deepest within British India itself, rather than neighbouring Afghanistan, no matter how novel the territorialisation of the Afghan polity might appear (on paper). But these technologies of power neither operated unequivocally, instead producing contradictions and inconsistencies, nor was there co-ordination between the British and Russian colonial states in ways that might have made possible the policing of mobility, for example. And they were predicated upon other technologies, including photography, signalling the importance of the later Victorian period as a conjunctural moment when manifold innovations came together to precipitate change in the physical world and the human imaginary. The final chapter thus turns to the impact of the hallmark technologies of the era of the New Imperialism upon Indo-central Asian trade.

8

TECHNOLOGY

Railways. Steamships. Telegraphy. Now synonymous with the time–space compression that accelerated circulation and globalisation in the nineteenth century, these were also among the premier technologies of the New Imperialism, of empire building by the Great Powers in the uncharted or unclaimed continental interiors. So integral were these technologies, in fact, that historians have coined the term 'techno-imperialism' to describe the design and use of technology in pursuit of imperial ambitions in this period.[1] There were, however, variations in the degree of direct control states exercised over what were, them-selves, technologies of control: telecommunications technologies were wholly a state enterprise in late-nineteenth-century Japan but in the hands of private entrepreneurs in the United States, for instance.[2] There were also differences in the domains within which techno-impe-rialism operated. Railways tended not to cross boundaries between empires, but railway construction is classically linked to strategies of British informal empire in Argentina, to take one example.[3] The British used steamships as an instrument of informal imperialism in Ottoman Iraq, while co-operation was necessary in the provision of ancillary technologies such as lighthouse facilities in British and Dutch-controlled south-east Asia. Presumably this is because lighthouses belong (unusually) to the class of pure public goods, with all the prob-lems of free riding and all the benefits of imperial prestige and improved safety deriving from concern for shipping and shipmen.[4] These examples highlight the variously formal or informal, imperial, inter-imperial, or trans-imperial contexts of these technologies' operation. Unsurprisingly, while their impact was everywhere apparent in the imperial metropoles, and palpable even in the farthest corners of empires, the precise effects of these technologies were often difficult to pin down with precision, let alone to predict before their inauguration. These were at once instruments of governance and, yet, were themselves unruly, capable of producing alternative logics of power or mobility to those desired by the coloniser. Were investments in these technologies buttressing imperial political and economic power and prestige? Were they being exploited by rivals or enemies of the state?

In this context, the Punjab government deputed Captain H. Grey in 1872 to determine more precisely the impact of British rule in northwest India upon the annual caravan trade. Grey duly engaged three Powinda merchants from the Khel and Kharoti tribes: Behar Khan, Khoedad Khan Zakori, and Muhammad Khan Kharoti. He began by asking them: 'Has the Gomul trade increased since the commencement of British rule, and what are the causes?' Khoedad Khan Zakori replied that 'profits under former rules were larger than now, as the telegraph now keeps everyone informed of the prices existing in other places, and special heavy prices are not, therefore, to be obtained'.[5] The telegraph was not mentioned again in either the interview transcript or the report; after all, there was no Peshawar–Kabul line, and the Afghan amir vehemently refused the laying of the line into the late 1880s.[6] But the point was taken up, albeit briefly, by Grey: 'This is a matter which cannot be interfered with, and may be expected to act as much in favour of as against the trader.'[7] Whereas the Afghan merchants considered the telegraph a threat to their livelihoods, the British thought trains and steamships would supplant caravan trade through Afghanistan.[8] Grey, however, was right to recognise the ambiguity of technology, the fact that it could as easily help as hinder the maintenance of the status quo. Technologies operated on several, sometimes overlapping, scales: local, regional, national, imperial, trans-imperial, global. Their impact was determined in interaction and in conflict with state authorities on each of these—sometimes competing—scales, and varied according to whether the state acted as predator, protector, or promoter of either continuity or change. But these were, above all, 'precarious' and 'vulnerable' technologies put to the service of empire—to borrow from Camille Cole's brilliant analysis of the environmental and societal challenges to the smooth functioning of British steamboats on the Tigris in the late nineteenth and early twentieth century.[9]

Inspired by Cole's work, this chapter emphasises the ambiguity of technologies and the frictional resistance to their operation from their particular contexts. It considers the relationship between technological change and the transformation of the trading world when new technologies, as well as new types of goods, people, and policies, moved more deeply into this space. The first half examines the impact of new transport technologies, the second focuses on change in productive technologies, with each also addressing the intervening role of policy. The conclusion broadens out to compare the transformation of interior spaces in the era of the New Imperialism and thereby connect the arguments of this chapter to the larger themes of this book: space and environment, economic geography and processes of economic change. What role did technological change play in the production of connection and disconnection, continuity or decline? What, in the end, precipitated the decline of trade and those relationships—personal, commercial, cultural—engendered through long-distance exchange?

Transport Technologies

Rather than subordinating or sweeping away indigenous networks of commerce and capital, the impact of the transportation revolution was the reinvigoration of Asian merchant networks and the redeployment of the Asian 'bazaar economy', the indispensable silent partners of Western capitalist and commercial enterprise.[10] But what was the fate of trade networks in the inner spaces, where more 'modern' transport and communications technology arrived later or penetrated less deeply? By the end of the century, confident in the transformative power of these technologies, the Government of India wished to know whether Peshawari merchants were diverting their trade to Bukhara from the overland routes via Kabul to road, rail, and sea routes via the Persian Gulf or the Suez.[11] The British and the Afghan amir both believed that Punjabi traders also remitted gold from Bukhara via

Moscow and Bombay, their interest aroused by the rumour of one Habibulla of Makhad remitting cash realised on merchandise sales in this way in 1886–7.[12]

Abdur Rahman interrogated traders in a bid to recover revenue 'lost' through this alternative, circuitous channel of remittance, while British officials examined the Bombay sea-trade returns, within which they found no evidence of these transfers taking place.[13] In the absence of certainty, a questionnaire—translated into the 'vernacular' by the Peshawar district commissioner's office—was distributed to the merchants of Peshawar and Nowshera.[14] The merchants replied that goods were not sent via Bombay and Moscow due to the heavy transport costs, acknowledging, also, that overland trade from British India was unable to compete with Russo-central Asian commerce.[15] Nor did the Peshawari trading firms send their goods via Bombay and the Persian Gulf, contrary to certain reports.[16] For all their complaints against the Afghan amir's heavy imposts, those levied by Persian officials were also 'intolerable.'[17] The route through Afghanistan was shorter, the profits higher, and the goods arrived quicker in Bukhara than through the alternative routes via Persia.[18]

If modern transport technologies had not revolutionised and routed the networks of the caravan trade in Asia by the late nineteenth century, their impact upon the trans-Saharan traffic was graver, Lydon suggests.[19] In both cases, Asian and African, nevertheless, the caravan circuits had long interlaced regional and global networks of trade at nodal points—riverine or coastal ports, entrepôt towns and capital cities—and were thus connected to the rhythms of European commercial and political penetration after c. 1500 that rose to a crescendo in the nineteenth century. Over several centuries, Asian and African merchants transformed 'threats' into 'opportunities', suffusing their networks with novel goods brought from Europe and carrying indigenous manufactures (and slaves) from the interior to the coast for overseas markets, while also shifting their routes in response to the expansion or contraction of particular settlements or commercial hubs and exploiting the synergies made possible through technological change in transportation. In this respect, even before the era of the New Imperialism, the evolution in transport technology that enabled the expansion of European mercantile activity and imperial penetration exerted both trade-creating and trade-substituting effects.

In the anxieties of British Indian agents in the 1830s and onwards regarding the availability and competitiveness of Russian exports—textiles including chintz, velvets, and lace, as well as manufactures such as various sorts of hardware, paper, and sugar, for example—in central Asian and Afghan bazaars, is evidence of trade creation and the durability of caravan trade.[20] In similar spirit, Abdur Rahman's expenditure of a large proportion of his subsidy from the British on industrial goods and technical expertise as well as raw materials for finishing in Afghanistan, meant the growth of trade in new goods from or through British India, generally under the agency of state-appointed brokers connected to overland trade.[21] Yet, as analysed throughout this chapter, there was something distinctive about the era of the New Imperialism; namely, the role of policy in fine-tuning, mediating, or moulding the transformative effects of technological change—railroads and steamships, in particular—thus stymying the extent of trade creation.

More complex but more prevalent were the trade-substituting effects of technology. Where newly available consumer goods or commodities replaced existing articles, one of two different impacts was likely. If exportables originating in A (e.g. north India) for markets in B (e.g. central Asia) were now imported from C (e.g. Britain) into A, their re-export from A to B did not precipitate a decline in trade so much as harm the local productive economy in A to the advantage of C; this is the so-called 'deindustrialisation' effect, the transformation and erosion of the relationships between producers and consumers encapsulated in exchange. If exportables originating in A for markets in B were now exported from D (e.g. Russia) directly to B, then deindustrialisation *and* an immediate decline in (that branch of) caravan trade was likely. The overall effect was the severance of extant exchange networks, hurting producers and traders, but perhaps also affecting consumers where the substitution was driven not by demand but by policy changes, not least prohibitions or protectionism. While the effect of both types of substitution was the production of disconnection and, in some cases, the abrogation of moral economies, the process was most pronounced in this second case. The remainder of this section turns to the examination of cotton cloth, for the textile trade between south and central Asia was significant not only in scale as well as significance to the Punjabi manufacturing or secondary sector as a whole, but also in exhibiting both types of substitution effect in its demise.

'Deindustrialisation'?

'If hand-loom weaving is dying', pronounced the author of the Delhi *Gazetteer*, 'it must be admitted it is dying hard in the Punjab.'[22] In Punjab, weavers withstood the effects of the influx of English machine-made textiles to a greater extent than elsewhere in India. In the first place, this resulted from the later integration of the province into British India and the degree of insulation this afforded artisans relative to their counterparts in the three presidencies, where artisanal livelihoods were being undermined in a long process stretching back to the late eighteenth century.[23] From the assertion of Company hegemony in the procurement of textiles around the turn of the century, which eroded weavers' negotiating power and depressed prices, to the appearance of machine-made textiles in the nineteenth century, which could be manufactured and transported cheaply enough to substitute for handloom manufactures, the cumulative impact of this trajectory lay in the twin evils of 'peasantisation' and 'deindustrialisation'.[24] Thus, when the rail network was extended, with the effect of deepening the penetration of English imports within the interior, and when the cotton famine hit textile manufacturers in the 1860s, Punjabi artisans suffered, but were not as embattled as their counterparts in other regions of India.[25]

Yet, around the mid nineteenth century, weavers across the subcontinent—where they survived—were becoming more proactive in ways that would stem the torrent of deindustrialisation.[26] Recognising the non-homogeneity of cloth as a manufacture, and that imported cloths were of middling quality, weavers either 'upskilled' to produce cotton cloths of higher thread count, silk cloths, and cloths embellished with metallic thread, tinsel or embroidery, or else wove 'coarse' cotton cloths of low thread counts for the bottom end of the market.[27] A complementary response involved switching from Indian to English cotton yarns, thereby outsourcing part of the productive process while taking advantage of cheap and more uniform inputs to sustain the role of weavers at the expense of carders and spinners, reelers and winders.[28] Although each of these strategies was employed in Punjab, the fate of Punjabi artisans has received little attention from historians of Indian textiles, including those interested in deindustrialisation.

Interrogating the causes of this neglect reveals what was distinctive about Punjab; namely, its specialisation in coarse-cloth manufacture for buyers in domestic and overland markets, and, thus, the role of caravan trade in artisanal survival in the nineteenth century in the face of supposedly more efficient productive and transport technologies.

In part, this neglect simply stems from the weight of scholarly attention on the presidencies, especially the debate over deindustrialisation in Bengal and the study of modern mills emerging in Bombay. In part, it stems from a relative (but not absolute) evidentiary deficit, itself reflecting not the death of Punjabi industry but the peculiarities of colonial practices of collecting. Fearing that industrialisation would wipe out India's traditional arts and crafts, colonial officials such as John Lockwood Kipling—principal of the Mayo School of Arts and curator of the Lahore Museum—adopted what Saloni Mathur terms a 'salvage paradigm' or 'preservationist' agenda, to collect, salvage, display, and promote 'those forms of traditional culture perceived to be threatened by imperial contact'.[29] Of course, tradition was a misnomer, for the artisans—compared to their predecessors in precolonial times—were gradually shifting towards working with different raw materials, within different locales as a result of migration and movement, for different 'masters' as a result of the changing organisation of production, and for different consumers as a result of the changes in the market.[30] These, however, were trivialities to the 'preservationists'. In their eyes, moreover, not all endangered traditional textiles were worthy of preservation. Unlike some of the finer types of cotton and silk textiles, coarse-cloth weaving was neither especially endangered nor considered worthy of salvage and scarcely given much comment, hardly an *art* in the eyes of the preservationists.[31] The sorts of cloths that Kipling and others collected, and that survive in museums, therefore, reveal these historical misunderstandings and aesthetic judgements, while reproducing the productive and consumptive geography of urban Punjab—for that was where the preservationists found their 'true' artisans, as opposed to ordinary weavers—ignoring the new towns that were emerging as major weaving centres, and the consumers who clothed themselves in the fabrics of their manufacture.

Compiled by the Lahore Central Committee to accompany the finer cotton fabrics forwarded to London for the International Exhibition of

1862, and as a companion to the volume of silk swatches discussed in chapter 5, is a sample-book of seventy-one 'cotton fabrics worn by the agricultural population of the Punjab'.[32] Compiled because the peasantry—which was increasingly seen as the bedrock of Punjabi society—'for the most part clothe themselves in coarse homespun clothes', the samples are unique and unlike the collections of costumes and textiles of finer quality that were collected, copied, exhibited, and survive in museum collections today.[33] Such cottons were not worthy of inclusion in the eighteen-volume collection of swatches, *The Textile Manufactures of India*, for example, which the ethnographer John Forbes Watson compiled in the 1860s at the same time as the *Peoples of India* albums.[34] Yet, a similarly 'ethnographic' gaze runs through the sample-book, for the swatches are classified according to the purported racial or religious origins of those who were their likely buyers. In texture, they vary from the better to rougher sorts of coarse cloth, the former of which represent the greater proportion of the samples, the latter generally loosely woven and heavy weighted. In spite of their coarseness, not all of the textiles are unbleached and undyed and unpatterned; many are dyed in darker and earthier colours, such as indigo blue and burnt orange, madder red and emerald—rather than the bright limes, roses, purples, and scarlets of the silk swatches—for these stood well against discolouration from the dirt of rural life. In pattern, the cottons show much greater similarity to the silks, especially in the prevalence of striped textiles as well as checked, resist-dyed, and roughly embroidered cloths.

Kipling observed that coarse-cotton weaving of this sort 'still thrives in all villages and back streets of towns notwithstanding the cotton imports from abroad.'[35] Although woven throughout Punjab, export production of these textiles was relatively urban-centred, taking place in some of the same trade towns noted in the journals of Henry Bornford or Alexander Burnes: Rahon, Nurmahal, Kartarpur, Ludhiana, Jalandhar, Firozpur, and Lahore in eastern Punjab, all lying along the east–west axis of the Grand Trunk Road.[36] Alongside these commercial centres, however, were other towns now enmeshed within an intra-provincial if not interregional network of coarse-cotton cloth production and distribution. In the towns of the Shahpur, Jhang, and Kohat districts of western Punjab, for example, the extent of coarse-cloth weaving was considerable.[37] The growth of coarse-cotton weaving in Punjab was supported by the boom in cotton cultivation from mid century, and the rise of a class of middlemen who procured coarse cloth from the towns and larger villages for sale, while the shift towards the west of the province was connected to the expansion of agriculture in the Peshawar valley, and, arguably, the commercialisation of village production.[38]

But the rise of these towns also affected the larger commercial centres. There were several sorts of coarse cloth, of which *khaddar* was the commonest.[39] Generally woven of homespun thread, *khaddar* was not a single sort of coarse cloth; instead, 'it has different names according to the width, *chousi* being *khaddar* with four hundred threads in the width, *painsi* five hundred, and *chassi* with six hundred.'[40] Where coarse-cotton weaving continued in cities such as Multan and Lahore, it tended to be of the better sorts of *khaddar*, rather than the roughest sorts with the lowest thread counts.[41] Dera Ghazi Khan and Bahawalpuri weavers turned out better sorts of coarse coloured and chequered cloth (*khes*), often blue and white or white and red, rather than unbleached and unpatterned cloth.[42] Between Ludhiana and Jalandhar, weavers switched from the coarser sorts of cloths to the better sorts of thick textile, such as *ghati*, a glazed and fairly fine cotton cloth.[43] With the advent of faster and cheaper railway and riverine connections relative to local forms of non-mechanised transport, importing the cheaper sorts of cloth was cost-effective, allowing a greater degree of specialisation between towns.[44] Realignment was, therefore, taking place: villages were increasingly importers rather than self-supporting producers of coarse cotton cloths; mid-size towns were centres of low quality but large-scale *khaddar* weaving; and the trade towns were producing the better sorts of thick textile as well as fancy fabrics.[45] And, furthermore, western Punjab predominantly produced coarse cottons, whereas eastern Punjab—which was earlier and more extensively exposed to British textiles—predominantly produced finer cotton fabrics.[46]

Competing with English cloths, the weaving of some types of textile—such as chintzes, muslins, and *rumals* (handkerchiefs)—was in decline.[47] But this was a far from straightforward story of substitution of European for Indian cloths. Multan continued its role as a centre of chintz printing, the inflow of Manchester chintzes representing a slow process of attrition rather than a short, sharp blow to the industry.[48] Juxtaposing the Punjabi chintzes in the sample-book of Punjabi cottons with the 'European' chintzes collected from the Peshawar trade fair of December 1869, it is clear that European and Punjabi chintzes were strikingly different in texture and design, the correspondence of design motifs notwithstanding.[49] The precise provenance of the textiles collected at Peshawar remains unclear, but it seems most likely they were re-exported from (rather than manufactured in) Kabul and were of Russian (rather than English) origin.[50]

The cleanness of print, brightness of colour, fineness of texture, and the adaptation of Indian motifs into novel designs are all markedly different from the Punjabi chintzes. Remarkably, Punjab's chintz printers survived in the face of Russian and English competition. There is little price data, but more anecdotal evidence suggests that Punjabi cotton cloth was cheaper than European substitutes until the final quarter of the nineteenth century, at least, and affordability and durability remained important in determining the consumption choices in overland markets.[51] A small surviving sample of so-called 'central Asian' chintzes shows marked similarity in terms of texture and pattern to the chintzes from the sample-book of Punjabi cotton cloths, suggesting that Punjabi chintzes reached as far as the bazaars of Bukhara after mid century, or that designs were copied or were common across the Indo-central Asian trading world.[52] The price differential was small and shrinking fast, however, indicating that these textural characteristics rather than custom, conservatism, or price per se sustained demand for Punjabi cloths at home and abroad.[53]

Reorientation and Survival: Weavers in Western Punjab

In review, two types of technological change affected Punjab's textile industry: first, those related to the mechanisation of manufacturing, which reduced the cost of English textiles, and, second, those undergirding the transportation revolution by which the English (and, later, Indian) cost savings deriving from factory production could be passed on to Indian consumers. These changes made English cottons more competitive than their closest Indian substitutes of handloom manufacture, leading, in turn, to the displacement of labour from certain aspects of the productive process, not least as English cottons now penetrated more deeply into north Indian markets as a result of the extension of the railways. Yet, artisans' responsiveness to these changes and the reorientation of textile manufacture across Punjab mitigated the extent of deindustrialisation.

What impact, in turn, did these changes have on caravan trade? Because coarse cloth—including dyed and chinted fabrics—had long been a Punjabi staple as well as a staple of Punjab's overland trade, the bulk of Indian cotton cloth exports to these markets remained unchanged in composition and provenance. And, since preceding generations of Asian traders had procured finer muslins and *malmals* from Gujarat or Bengal, the influx of middling to finer-textured English cloths and their re-export to Afghanistan or central Asia were like a continuation—after the lull of the later eighteenth and early nineteenth century—of this 'outsourcing' of fine-cloth production to textile centres outside Punjab. Reflected in the trade statistics, therefore, is this bifurcation between exports of lower-value Indian coarse cottons on the one hand, and re-exports of higher-value English medium-quality cottons on the other.

Before the arrival of the railways, imports of English cottons were relatively small-scale.[54] With the establishment of rail services from Calcutta via Delhi, from Karachi, and from Bombay, English cotton cloths streamed into Punjab from the 1860s, some for redistribution within the province and around three-quarters for re-export to markets in the Sikh States, Kashmir, Afghanistan, and Turkestan.[55] To construct the foreign trade returns for the years from 1869–70 to 1872–3, officials recorded and aggregated the trade of the major towns of Punjab.[56] On this evidence, Manchester weavers were gaining ground from those of Punjab. Punjabi weavers, however, were specialising at the cheaper end of the market, manufacturing non-import-competing coarser sorts of cloth, especially in the emerging textile towns in the west of the province. Maghiana was typical of these towns, its weavers relying on traditional techniques of production, their output of cloth bought directly by Afghan traders with smaller amounts sent towards Punjab, thus escaping the attention of civil servants stationed in the major commercial centres.[57]

The Punjab government was aware of the inadequacy of the early returns, though unaware of the extent of underestimation inherent in the earlier statistics.[58] From 1873–4, officials were stationed along the frontier, the returns better reflecting the nature and extent of trade.[59] Overland trade in cotton textiles was growing, contributing to the modest 'boom' in trade with central Asia after *c.* 1850.[60] In spite of the competition from English cloths, including in the re-export caravans, Punjabi weaving was 'still far from extinct' as late as the 1870s, precisely because it remained important to trade and, thus, the economy of many towns.[61] European cotton cloth re-exports were greater in value and growing in volume, but Indian cotton cloth exports remained relatively and absolutely larger in volume, reflecting the differences in the types of cloth produced in western Punjab and north-west England, as well as the aforementioned reorientations in the productive economy of the province.

The impact of these changes upon weavers' living standards was ambiguous, but trending downward in general. For the towns in western Punjab where weaving of coarse cloth for Afghan markets continued, the handloom industry showed signs of stability and expansion, despite earlier decline and the gradual retreat of *khaddar* consumption elsewhere in the province, although this trend could not continue indefinitely.[62] For chintz printers, the trend was more ambiguous still. Multani and other Punjabi urban printers were still only straggling towards unemployment in the early twentieth century—almost a century after British Indian agents first remarked that chintz printing was almost extinct—but were not about to be given a clean bill of health.[63] For the handloom weaver of simple cotton cloth, however, living standards were dire—as elsewhere in India—their meagre profits eroded by the interest repayments to moneylenders for advances of material, and their access to education extremely limited.[64] They survived solely by their ability to produce cloth of a range of textures and fineness, because of the belief that coarse cloth was more durable and better value for money, and, to a lesser extent, because of the state's attempts at promoting handicraft sales through craft shops, 'improving' the state of handloom weaving through instruction at 'model weaveries', and protecting the weavers through the establishment of co-operatives.[65]

If Punjab's artisans were struggling for bare subsistence, their survival pegged on the vicissitudes of demand in distant markets, then the signs ahead were troubling. Both types of technology implicated in the so-called 'deindustrialisation' of the Indian handloom sector—steam-powered productive and transportation technologies—were also diffused across imperial boundaries, from Britain and the British Empire into Afghanistan and the Russian Empire, for instance. Because the networks of caravan trade wove together a space that, by the later nineteenth century, was construed as an arena of trans-imperial rivalry and competition, the fate of India's textile trade became inextricably linked to the economic interests of those political powers in Afghanistan and central Asia precisely when they sought to harness the transformative potential of these technologies. It was worrying news, therefore, that trade from British India to Afghanistan showed signs of slight expansion from the second half of the nineteenth century through to the twentieth but onward trade from Afghanistan to central Asia was reportedly in decline.[66]

Was Afghan consumption 'crowding out' central Asian consumption or was increased consumption in Afghanistan taking the slack from reduced trade towards central Asia?[67] Sales of cottons to Pashtun tribes immediately across the frontier from British India were certainly increasing in consequence of enhanced incomes from subsidy payments, military employment, and seasonal labour opportunities in the Peshawar valley and elsewhere. Yet there was no shortage of cotton cloth in British India for trade to central Asia: European cotton cloth re-exports from Punjab were a small proportion of the total imports into Punjab from Europe, only one-eightieth in 1874–5, for example, and scarcely much more in the 1880s to 1900s.[68] Afghan consumption was thus not capable of crowding out the onward trade to Bukhara.

Contemporaries thought that the combined effect of Afghan and Russian tariffs on the one hand, and the establishment and extension of the Trans-Caspian Railway on the other, was the re-routing of Indo-central Asian trade through Kashmir and Yarkand.[69] But this is misleading. First, although trade towards Kashmir and Chinese Turkestan was expanding, the arduousness, added expense, and delay suffered on the Karakoram routes meant that they were never really a substitute for the Hindu Kush routes. Second, rail transportation did not absorb the larger part of the caravan traffic until well into the twentieth century, and its immediate effect was rather to 'ma[k]e it impossible to hope for any considerable extension of the market for Indian exports in Central

Asia.'[70] Third, the view of Abdur Rahman as a predatory ruler played well with British suspicions, and self-interested Indian traders were certainly wont to play to the prejudices of their contemporaries.[71] This portrayal of the amir, moreover, ignores his weakness *vis-à-vis* the Afghan and Indian traders.

The amir did pester traders to top up the state coffers, intervening in the valuation of goods to maximise customs receipts, for example.[72] Some of the Kuchis (nomadic camel drivers) even went on 'strike' in 1895 and 1896, reportedly redirecting their efforts from the Kabul–Peshawar routes towards the Kashmir trade, such was their discontent with the increase of export taxes.[73] But the amir was dependent on trade for tax revenue, and adjusted tax rates according to the flow of commercial traffic through the Khyber Pass.[74] When revenues were falling due to the decline in trade, he reduced levies to ensure enlarged revenue returns in future, and vice versa, the unpredictability perhaps more frustrating than the extortions.[75]

Ultimately, Abdur Rahman remained relatively powerless, and was unable to exercise effective control across all of Afghanistan. Taxation was heaviest in his home territory, the political and commercial centre in Kabul, while lighter levies were imposed by rulers of the outlying provinces, such as Balkh.[76] Although state-appointed *qafilabashis* were found throughout Afghanistan—their task being to organise, document, and tax commercial traffic—traders en route to Herat or Bukhara could re-route, via the Bolan Pass and Kandahar, for example, to avoid the tax demands made in Kabul.[77] When attempting to double duties on trade to raise revenues in the late 1880s, the Peshawari traders threatened to take an alternative route that skirted Kabul, forcing the amir to withdraw the new duty demand for fear of the collapse of customs revenues.[78] While the amir's demands disincentivised the expansion of trade, they were neither protectionist nor punitive—except in the case of taxes on those goods the amir attempted to monopolise—the sustainability of trade through Afghanistan being essential to securing future revenues.

The Decline of Indo-Central Asian Textile Trade

The combination of railway development with protectionism was the classic recipe of Listian economics of nineteenth-century import-substituting industrialisation. Sergei Witte, architect of imperial Russia's awakening from economic slumber and its industrial take-off in the 1890s, certainly subscribed to the ideas of Friedrich List. Witte's policies placed emphasis on the importance of Asian markets and were propelled by investments in the extension of the rail network, notably the Trans-Siberian Railway, as well as a regime of protectionist tariffs on imports.[79] Yet, the beginnings of mechanisation in Russian textile manufacture predated the Witte era by almost a century, while the threat posed by trade in British and Indian textiles to central Asia to the trade in Russian cottons was already apparent when Turkestan was conquered in the 1860s.

British intelligence sources—from the ambassadors in St Petersburg and Tehran, to Asian traders and customs officials in Afghanistan and central Asia, and the district commissioners in Punjab—reported on the prohibitions on British Indian trade and the protectionist tariffs to support Russo-central Asian commerce instituted in 1868.[80] Whereas Russian goods passed duty-free through the Romanov Empire, British Indian trade was subject to increasing taxes and tariffs in Russian Turkestan, in addition to those payable en route in Afghanistan and Bukhara. Indian trade to Bukhara could continue to Russian Samarkand, subject to the payment of *ad valorem* duty of 2.5 per cent (*zakat*) and an additional 5 per cent (the standard tariff on imports into Russia), certified by the customs officer. In April 1869, the cotton textile trade from British India to Russian Turkestan was absolutely prohibited, with traders caught contravening the order charged double customs and transit duties for the first offence, with confiscation in case of further offences, the goods then sold at public auction.[81] While Bukhara's consumption of cotton cloth did not decrease, and Bukharan traders continued to legally take these goods to Samarkand and onward to other trade towns in Russian Turkestan, the traders received reduced prices for their turban cloths and other muslins, being often forced to sell on credit, not cash.[82] As Russian muslins were unsuitable for their 'very flimsy [...] very thin and light' texture, the new prohibitions on muslins were lifted in the early 1880s, although still taxed very heavily.[83]

The real casualties of prohibition and protectionism were Punjabi and English plain cloths and chintzes, which were squeezed out of the market in Bukhara. Echoing the words of British Indian agents of the

1830s and 1840s, Russian cotton cloths were again judged to be 'better and cheaper, and [...] more durable than ours, and well suited to the climate of Afghanistan and to rough wear.'[84] By the final decades of the century, Punjabi cottons lost their cost advantage against similarly weighted Russian substitutes, so that consumption of Punjabi cloths seldom extended north of Afghanistan.[85] Earlier complaints that British chintzes were too dull, the patterns too infrequently altered, and the designs unsuited to the tastes of consumers in Turkestan were repeated in the 1870s and 1880s. Once again, a proposal was put forward to send samples to Indian and English chintz printers, so that 'they may more clearly appreciate what is wanted at such places', suggesting a view of tastes as static.[86] The British sense of the distinctiveness of consumer tastes and market potential was dulled by the way they saw one Asian bazaar much like any other—Trebizond as akin to Tashkent.[87] Industrialists from Ivanovo, however, recognised that the central Asian market was small but unique, and that to capture it necessitated not only close attention to peasant tastes, but the moulding of desires and demand through design innovation.[88] While it was true that central Asians preferred the Russian chintzes with their 'thick prints' to the intricate, fussy floral motifs of some of the English chintzes, these calls to imitate the Russian manufactures missed this fundamental fact.[89]

While the early Russian chintzes resembled rather closely the types that were imported from central and south Asia, technological change meant that the difference in design of Punjabi and Ivanovo chintzes widened more and more. Following Knop's introduction of English spinning technology in the 1840s, Knop and other Russian industrialists employed engineers, engravers, and mechanics from England, and continued to do so into the 1890s.[90] As roller printing replaced block printing in Russia, manufacturers innovated new and increasingly complex paisley patterns drawn from Kashmiri shawls, Punjabi chintzes, and central Asian silk ikats, while also offering new designs drawn from patterns popular in France and Britain adapted to the tastes of Asian consumers, incorporating calligraphy, and crescent moons and stars for the central Asian market or Chinese motifs for the markets of Xinjiang, for example.[91] Many of these chintzes were the work of textile designers trained at Moscow's Imperial Central Stroganov School of Industrial Design. The School was established in 1860 on the model of industrial art education in Britain by people interested in the work of William Morris, the Arts and Crafts movement, and the Art Nouveau.[92]

Uncompetitive in cost and aesthetic terms, British chintzes were not actually forbidden in Bukhara until it was incorporated into the Russian customs system in 1894–5, when importing Indian cloths (other than muslin, which was heavily taxed) became illegal.[93] Russian textiles then dominated the markets of central Asia and Afghan Turkestan, while British and British Indian textiles found their main market in Kabul, Kandahar, and along the frontier, fracturing the trading world into the two separate commercial circuits, at least in terms of the textile trade.[94]

Productive Technologies

In the era of the New Imperialism, recruits from Punjab were swelling the ranks of the army of British India, adding to imperial fighting power in arenas of conflict and conquest around the world. In fact, Punjabi soldiers were crucial to the campaigns into the interior spaces that typified this period, fighting in neighbouring Afghanistan (1878–80) and Burma (1885), but also in the new British Protectorate of Egypt during the Urabi Revolt (1882); coming to Britain's aid during the Mahdist War in Sudan (1881–99); in southern Africa during the Boer War (1899–1902); and in China, where Punjabi soldiers suppressed the Boxer Rebellion (1901).[95] In Punjab, as male relations served across the subcontinent and across the empire, the fruits of their military labour were reaped via remittances from their salaries, supporting the purchasing power of households that remained tied to the land and the production of global cash crops, itself a lucrative enterprise in the well-watered tracts of the canal colonies. The 'hydraulic society' was the fulcrum of the state's 'development of underdevelopment', for Punjab was famed as the land of five rivers and its numerous new canals that irrigated fields of cash crops—not factories and industrial modernity.[96]

By focussing on transport technologies, the previous section showed how their global diffusion made the distribution and control of the gains from technological innovation and investment more difficult to (pre-)determine. But it also showed that policy was a crucial intervening factor, manipulated to enhance or undermine cost savings in—or passed on through—cheaper long-distance transportation. At the heart of the story told in the previous section, however, was an underlying shift in productive technologies. This section foregrounds productive technologies to examine how they combined with policy to precipitate the cessation of overland trade.

Indigo

Just as the transformations in the labour market are traceable to the early colonial period, so, too, are those on the land.[97] In the 1840s and 1850s, Punjab's new rulers did not dream up the hydraulic society as it would concretise towards the end of the century. Rather, they took inspiration from available precedent, envisioning Punjab's economy centring on the production of higher value-added primary commodities—indigo, silk, opium, jute—to replicate Bengal's trajectory from the later eighteenth century. Such transformation was tied to primary products but also involved their processing (that is, light industry), the horizontal and vertical linkages resulting therefrom potentially providing fertile ground for other sorts of industrial development. Although hardly a radical vision of the province's economic future, it represented more of a departure than the provisioning role the province came to serve for British India and the British Empire in producing fodder for the battlefield (soldiers), the raw materials with which to cheaply clothe the empire's subjects (cotton), and cheap calories for the growing ranks of the global proletariat (wheat, sugar).

Indigo was thus of considerable interest to members of the Punjab government in the 1840s, especially as they tried to make remunerative and revenue-yielding their newly conquered lands, for extant cultivation could serve as the kernel of export production oriented toward world markets.[98] Initially, efforts focussed on the finessing of irrigation and taxation, which were fundamental to the profitability—and, thus, vitality—of indigo cultivation. The state inherited most of the main canals from the Sikhs, thereafter purchasing other large canals from the zamindars, such as the Massuwah and Fazlwah in Dera Ghazi Khan.[99] The newly created Irrigation Department's efforts to reform canal cleaning—namely, overhauling the *chher* system for a system of wholly tax-funded state-organised cleaning—proved unpopular, unsuccessful, and according to an official inquiry of 1874, unjustifiably costly.[100] The experiment also led to the decline of the indigo trade to one-tenth of its earlier value, prompting a return to the *chher* system in Derajat.[101]

Special attention was directed as early as 1847—a decade before the Rebellion, in which Punjabis demonstrated their loyalty to British India—to reducing duties on indigo, as these 'pressed heavily on the cultivators'.[102] Whatever its purported abuses, John Lawrence in fact sought to transform—rather than replace—the *kardari* and revenue collection, abolishing *abwab*, consolidating the revenue demand into one sum, reducing the land tax, and collecting payment in cash rather than grain in the First Summary Settlement.[103] Their fixity meant arrears soon stacked up, fluctuating with the vicissitudes of the harvest.[104] Instead, therefore, the First Regular Settlement of 1857 set rather light demands.[105] In Multan and Dera Ghazi Khan, the *tehsildars* (revenue officers) and *patwaris* (village accountants) reported that a 'great number of old vats [...] which having descended from father to son for some generations, are again becoming [valuable] property'—seen as symptomatic of the health of the indigo industry and the merits of the 1857 system over that of 1847.[106]

Overall, the available evidence suggests a secular expansion of indigo cultivation from the mid eighteenth century until the middle of the 1870s. Punjab's indigo output was second only to that of the Bengal and Madras presidencies in British India.[107] Yet, upwards of 90 per cent of all indigo cultivation was concentrated in only four of the districts in Punjab which, as a unit, now extended from Delhi to Peshawar.[108] Indigo cultivation remained rooted in the same well-watered tracts of Derajat where it had been established around a century earlier, which were now the districts of Dera Ghazi Khan, Bahawalpur, Muzaffargarh, and Multan.[109] From 1858, when the area sown with indigo stood at 39,796 acres in Punjab, almost entirely in Derajat, peasants continued to extend the area under cultivation until it peaked in 1876–7, when the indigo tracts stood at 99,363 acres.[110] Following inadequate rain and the subsequent spread of famine in 1877, Punjab suffered devastatingly heavy rains, ruining the year's harvest, and unleashing a disastrous malaria and cholera epidemic in 1878–9.[111] The collapse of indigo cultivation marked a turning point, cultivation never recovering and further retreating in extent thereafter (Fig. 8.1), indigo almost disappearing from Multan on the eve of the Second World War.[112]

Fig. 8.1: Indigo acreage in Punjab

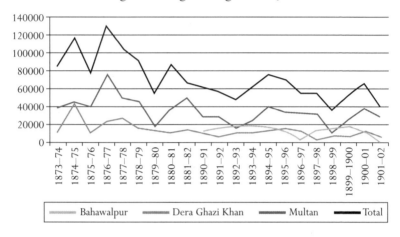

The Bengali precedent demonstrated that it was imperative peasants not only produce more indigo, but also process the plant better to improve the brightness, colour fastness, and purity of the finished dye-stuff to satisfy demand emanating from the Atlantic world. The favourable and unfavourable opinions of Punjabi indigo, both voiced from the 1830s, carried through to the 1850s and 1860s.[113] Unanimous were the calls for improvements or, at least, the implementation of modern methods of processing and 'the attention of European Capitalists'.[114] The district commissioners of Multan and Sialkot both suggested the establishment of a government-run model factory as a locus for the diffusion of techniques to peasants, to be profitably sold off once its impact had been absorbed.[115] The scheme was dropped, however, in favour of cotton-seed distribution in Punjab. Whatever its financial feasibility, the financial commissioner of Punjab thought in 1863 that there was 'little prospect at present of the native manufacture of Indigo being improved by any outlay on the part of Government', the quality presently produced sufficient for the main markets (Afghanistan and central Asia). He noted also the recent establishment of a European firm near Shujabad 'which will no doubt effect this matter more suitably and completely than the Government could do.'[116]

If the cash-strapped colonial government in late-eighteenth-century Bengal had avoided direct involvement in the cultivation and processing of indigo, there was even less likelihood that the central or provincial governments would take a hands-on approach around the mid nineteenth century. Shujabad, in the district of Multan, was well established in the cultivation and processing of indigo, its crop forming the greater proportion of Multan's total output, which was amongst the finest-quality dyestuff manufactured in Punjab.[117] When the Punjab government received a proposal from a Mr McIvor for the establishment of a modern indigo factory in Shujabad—backed by a Rs 10,000 loan from the state to be repaid in three years—its enthusiasm was unmatched by the comptrollers in Calcutta, who rejected the request.[118] The Government of India was perhaps dissuaded by the disaster of experiments along similar lines to establish a modern silk industry in the province, or perhaps disinclined to see indigo as a worthwhile investment.[119] The Indigo Revolt of 1859—the Blue Mutiny—was still three years away, but attitudes towards the indigo industry were changing, as was the market itself. The 1830s and 1840s had been straitened times for the government in Calcutta, and the collapse of the indigo houses, 1827–47, negatively affected sentiments about the indigo enterprise, the memory doubtless lingering into the equally squeezed years of the 1850s.[120]

Scarcely a few years after McIvor, Henry Spencer—backed by the Agri-Horticultural Society of Punjab—hoped to establish the Punjab Indigo Company in Multan.[121] Spencer's intentions were conveyed to the government in Lahore in March 1863, and a specimen indigo cake and six requests followed in November. The requests for 3,000 acres of tax-free wasteland adjoining the factory site, and for the cutting of a new canal for the dedicated use of the factory, could not be fulfilled.[122] The Punjab government claimed that the tract of wasteland was reserved for its fuel and grass, and that a preferential claim was extant from the zamindars of the surrounding villages. But it was the unfavourable report of the Bombay Chamber of Commerce, which thought the sample only slightly superior to 'Common Scinde' indigo and thus unsuitable for trade to Europe, that cemented the decision.[123] Attempts to secure skilled workmen to improve the indigo quality were futile, for the salary offered was 'not enough to tempt them so far from home.'[124]

If the indigo fields were expanding before the 1870s, therefore, there is no evidence to connect this development either to concerted state support for indigo processing or to any substantial changes in indigo quality. Of the indigo samples submitted to the Punjab Exhibition in 1864, for example, the jurors awarded the first prize to Messrs Skinner and Company and second place to Spencer's Punjab Indigo Company, but neither seem to have survived or made a mark on local manufacture.[125] Peasants remained responsible for most of the processing of indigo into dye, continuing to use the techniques and technologies from the precolonial period.[126] While Bengal's indigo processors could reap two to four times as much for their dyestuffs in the trade with Europe, Punjabis were reliant on purchases for the markets and consumers of Afghanistan and central Asia.[127] Rather than reflecting the peasants' ineptitude or inability to adopt new technologies, the continued production of 'inferior' sorts of indigo reflects the low incentives and high risks of attempting to enter the global indigo market.[128]

Was this relative backwardness injurious to caravan trade, therefore? Following the Russian trade mission to India after the opening of the Suez Canal, as well as the Russian advance in central Asia, the Government of India requested details of Russia's maritime trade in Indian cotton and indigo and Chinese silk from the Calcutta Customs House in 1871. Transported to Odessa under the agency of five Anglo-German firms, the findings reported that the needs of Moscow's burgeoning textile industry were being fulfilled by Bengal indigo (which had, in fact, been used in place of American indigo since at least the turn of the century), Madras indigo being rejected as inferior, and Punjabi and Sindhi indigo almost certainly never capturing any attention.[129] With this increase in dye imports to Moscow, and coloured-cloth exports from Russia to central Asia, it was thought that Punjab's indigo industry was on the road to ruin, Faiz Buksh writing from freshly annexed Samarkand to this effect in October 1869.[130] Yet, the scale of cultivation and exports expanded for almost another decade in

Punjab, suggesting that the circumstances of the late 1860s were unrepresentative of trade through the 1870s. Within overland markets, Punjabi indigo demand remained robust throughout the 1870s and 1880s, and even the 1890s, including in Bukhara.[131] There was no further notice of ready-dyed cloths in connection with depressing demand for Punjabi indigo until 1887, when it was alleged that cheapness resulted in their swamping the central Asian market.[132]

The retreat of the indigo fields after the mid 1870s was the direct result neither of burdensome transit taxes nor prohibitions on imports. True, Multani and Khairpuri indigo en route to Khorasan was subject to charges almost two-and-a-half times greater on the routes through southern Afghanistan than through Persia via the ports of Bushire or Bandar Abbas.[133] These impositions were reflective of the relative price inelasticity of demand for indigo, as well as the ability for traders to evade the Iron Amir's central authority which, in fact, was supple enough to have been impressed with a degree of lightness where and when due. There was a small indigo industry in southern Afghanistan for the Kandahar market, and the amir tried to encourage indigo (and sugar) cultivation and processing in the late 1880s as the basis for the development of light industry and trade, but this was unsuccessful and not supported by the institution of protectionist tariffs or prohibition on indigo imports.[134] In Russian Turkestan, similarly, Punjab indigo was without Russian substitutes.[135] Tax of 25 per cent *ad valorem*, however, was reportedly payable on indigo from 1868, rising to 6 roubles per pud of 36 lbs in 1882, equivalent to 16 per cent tax on the price of Bombay indigo, the tax burden even heavier on lower-valued Punjabi indigo.[136] Taxes were collected on the gross, not net, weight of the indigo, including packaging.[137] Consulting with a local trader, the commissioner of Peshawar, W. G. Waterfield, determined that the Punjab-to-Bukhara indigo trade was unprofitable, the trader typically purchasing 16 lbs of indigo for Rs 12, paying tolls and costs of carriage of Rs 13, selling in Bukhara at Rs 24, a loss of Re 1, with further charges of over Rs 7 to trade in Russian Turkestan.[138]

The retreat of the indigo fields, however, was abrupt and dramatic. So closely connected was Punjab's indigo economy with overland trade that the extension and retreat of indigo cultivation maps neatly onto the pattern of overland exports (Fig. 8.2).[139] The 'unseasonable rains', as well as the disruption of the Anglo-Afghan War, thus marked a turning point toward secular decline from the end of the 1870s.[140] The nominal value of overland indigo exports shrank to roughly half the size of trade a century earlier, or even less than half if accounting for the rise in prices.[141] In part, Afghan and central Asian duties disincentivised the expansion of trade and made merchants more risk averse: where previously traders took indigo freely for sale, in the 1880s and 1890s they only took indigo to fulfil existing orders in central Asia.[142]

Fig. 8.2: Punjab's indigo exports to Afghanistan and Turkestan

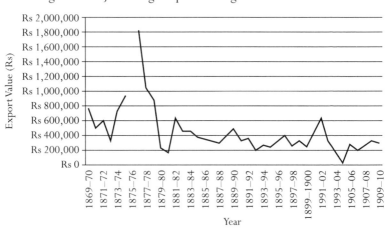

But the about-turn in indigo cultivation was connected to the wider transformation of Punjab's economy. In the first place, the development of anilines—artificial blue dyes—rendered indigo obsolete by the time they were manufactured on a mass scale after 1897.[143] Unlike natural indigo, artificial aniline dye was sold as a wet paste, thereby relieving the dyer of the task of grating and dissolving the dry indigo cakes. Kabuli dyers had long bemoaned use of the *kisht* (dry-brick) form of indigo, but traders seldom purchased indigo straight from the vats because of the added bulk (and, thus, cost) of transportation of the paste, preferring only to do so when prior shortages created opportunities to make high profits where traders could supply the market rapidly enough (that is, before it became overstocked).[144] Once anilines became sufficiently colour-fast, trade increased worldwide, initiating responses ranging from prohibition in 1885 to promoting the production of pastes of natural indigo through to the 1920s.[145]

There is no mention of the competitive effect of anilines in intelligence sources from central Asia, however, for sales took off only in the twentieth century. Rather, anilines made their impact in Punjab itself, where their growing use contributed to the shift in peasants' arithmetic about what to reap from their soil. Following the opening of the Suez, the rise in steamship traffic to Karachi, and the removal of export duties in 1873, the acreage cultivated with wheat in Punjab rose rapidly in response to the expansion of exports to Britain and western Europe, complementing and competing with American and Russian supplies.[146] The most rapid phase of expansion occurred after 1880, as the fruit of earlier infrastructural developments on the one hand, and as cultivating regions continued to be connected to the expanding rail network on the other.[147] If the cultivation of indigo was less alluring to experienced planters, then it was certainly of little interest to the new occupants of canal-colony land. Grain cultivation was a safer enterprise for the recipients of land since—although they tended to be drawn from the landed or dominant rather than landless or menial classes—some were not previously cultivators and others had rented out their land to tenant farmers.[148] Such cultivators had historically eschewed non-food crops, such as indigo, for *bajra* (millet) and *jowar* (sorghum) out of fear of food and income insecurity.[149] Because many were 'recruited' from central Punjab, outside the heartlands of indigo cultivation, the dyestuff was almost alien as a cash crop to the canal colonists, rather than a staple readily sown in the new tracts.[150] Instead, agriculturalists sowed wheat, as well as sugar cane and cotton.[151] So profitable were these crops that the government's revenue demand was set at Rs 10 to Rs 12.5 per acre on cultivated and canal-irrigated land—heavier than elsewhere in British India, the revenue-collection and canal-clearance expenses not exceeding 30 per cent of gross annual receipts—'making the [the canal colonies] among the most profitable in British India.'[152] Although Afghanistan and central Asia were formerly markets for the province's modest wheat surpluses, the massive exports produced by the end of the century almost bypassed these markets altogether, intensifying the disconnection.[153] Overall, the combination of factors making indigo less attractive as a crop, and caravan trade in indigo more difficult, shifted the odds against the dye as a lucrative article for either producers or middlemen.

Silk

'The soldier of the Khalsa no longer swaggers into the fight with his turban of *daryai*', commented (William) Malcolm Hailey, 'the bride no longer sends her father to the *banya* in order that she may appear with a fitting trousseau of Bokharan silks.'[154] Written at the end of the nineteenth century, Hailey's monograph on Punjab's silk industry was typical of the colonial state's belated concern over the state of India's traditional industries. Where earlier the state had fostered neglect through promoting free private enterprise—a euphemism for its self-serving but myopic non-interventionism—the growing financial burden of imperial rule and the imperial relationship with Britain necessitated a review of the structural imbalance of India's economy. This prompted provincial governments to commission inquiries—including Hailey's— into the state of various craft or cottage industries.[155] Viewed from Punjab's old textile centres, such as Multan or Lahore, both the wearing of silk and the weaving of Bukharan yarn into stout and stiff *gulbadan* and *daryai* were no longer in fashion.[156]

Yet, in consequence of the increasing availability of silk yarn, falling prices for finished cloth, and rising disposable incomes, the consumption of silk cloth was 'democratised' worldwide around the turn of the century.[157] In Punjab, too, the purchase of silks was increasing—at least outside the older centres connected to silk weaving—for the same constellation of factors were in play. The economic transformation that eroded the material basis of the indigo economy was also eroding the old economy of custom, a process that accelerated around the turn of the century.[158] The enrichment resulting from their harnessing of new employment opportunities in the military and on the land led the lower-evaluated castes to challenge the economy of custom precisely when the higher-evaluated castes sought to promote claims to ritual entitlements and rights. This challenge was made manifest through self-assertive forms of consumption, including the emulation of the customs, manners, dietary, and dress habits of their traditional caste superiors. Although this Sanskritisation often met with disdain, discouragement, and indignation from the higher-evaluated castes, thereby also reifying caste privileges and casteism where previously social relations had been much more flexible, the lower-evaluated castes continued to subvert 'subordinate' status through such novel forms of consumption.[159]

The better-off agriculturalists—and those who sought to emulate them—started to wear mill-made cloth, finer textured than the *khaddar* that previously constituted the main clothing fabric in Punjab.[160] The pace of change quickened after the 1880s. Formerly accustomed to a single change of clothes of coarse cotton, Punjab's soldiery was uniformed in silk and the finer-textured mill-made cottons. With their earnings from service and employment overseas, these men spent greater sums on clothing, eschewing turbans or waist-wraps of *khaddar*.[161] Only in the poorest districts, and amongst the poorest sections of village society, did dress remain unchanged.[162] Such consumption changes were not restricted to rural Punjab, however. Around the century's close, high-caste Hindus and Sikhs grew concerned they were being disfavoured by the colonial state while the lower castes were benefiting from the state's social levelling, or else converting to Christianity through the endeavours of various missionary societies in the cities.[163] 'Traditional' hierarchies of status and social privilege, it was thought, were being erased—even subverted.[164] The response from upper-caste Hindus and Sikhs was ambiguous: to reach out to the lower castes, to cross caste barriers, and even to condemn caste for fear of further conversions on the one hand, and yet to defend and cement casteism on the other.[165] This hardening of caste relations, effected both from above and below, was the context to the widening consumption of silk, a fabric formerly largely off limits to the peasantry or the menial castes and most closely associated with the nobility and the socio-religious elite.

For sericulturalists in central Asia, Punjab remained the major market for silk yarn until the turn of the century, if not later, for only select silks and only a small fraction of silk output were consumed in Russia in the 1870s and 1880s.[166] For Punjabi silk weavers, central Asian silks remained the major material with which they worked in the third quarter of the nineteenth century.[167] Of course, trade geography remained rather complicated, with weavers making use of silks from

'Kokand, Bukhara, Balkh, Khulm, Akhcha, Shibberghaum, Andkho' in central Asia, as well as from Kashmir, 'from Saidabad, Moorshedabad, Rampoor Baolia, and Radhanagari in Bengal; and from China, via Bombay.'[168] This import of raw silk was, as earlier, complemented with the import of a few finished silk piece goods from central Asia. A blue, yellow, and white printed silk purchased in Peshawar for the Punjab displays at the Indian Silk Culture Court in the Colonial and Indian Exhibition of 1886, for example, was believed to be a Bukharan specimen, so unusual was its pattern compared to Punjabi or other silk cloths commonly found in the province.[169]

Fig. 8.3: Punjab's silk imports from overland sources

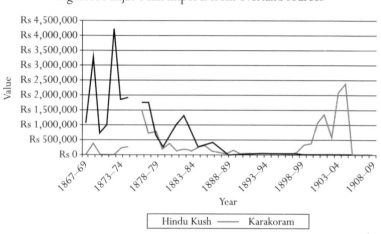

Whatever the problems of the early official trade returns from 1869–70, the data are more regular and reliable than the casual observations or estimations from the 1850s or 1860s, which nevertheless put more than half of Punjab's silk imports as originating in central Asia.[170] But the first regular returns from the Punjab government were not without problems of their own. If the earlier estimates are likely overstatements, based on casual observations, then those of 1868–9 are understatements. The mid 1860s was a troubled time for Eurasian silkworm rearers, as the spread of the pébrine disease from Europe—which afflicted silkworm larvae, preventing pupation and the spinning of silken cocoons—reduced raw-silk production.[171] Although the epidemic reached Persia, it is unclear whether the disease spread to Khorasan or Bukhara. The high prices of eggs in central Asia paid by Italians searching for disease-free eggs, to replenish southern Italian sericulture, suggested shortages.[172] The wars of colonial conquest also disrupted trade. Shortly after the good harvests of the early 1870s and the trade recovery of the later 1870s, however, trade peaked in the early 1880s, thereafter declining year after year (Fig. 8.3).[173]

Punjab's trade with eastern Turkestan showed signs of modest growth in the second half of the nineteenth century, and trade flows from Yarkand were slightly more swollen in years when the traffic from Bukhara or Khorasan was smaller than usual, as in the later 1870s.[174] The Karakoram routes were not capable of supporting the scale of traffic that flowed through the Khyber or Bolan, however, and the Yarkand silk route remained a small proportion of silk brought to Punjab by the caravans. More came from Kashmir, the pattern of imports closely following the successes and failures of the Kashmiri state's sericulture enterprise after 1869, this endeavour ending when an epidemic afflicting the silkworms broke out in 1878.[175]

The railway deepened the integration of Punjab into the economy of British India and the British Empire, and of central Asia into the economy of the Russian Empire. But this deepening integration neither supported the growth of the Indo-central Asian or the Punjab–Bengal silk trade, nor of technological transfer to central Asian or Bengali sericulturalists. The history of Bengal's struggling silk industry is relatively well documented and available elsewhere; a narrative of the rise to global dominance in the eighteenth century, followed by market stagnation and under-investment in technological improvement in the nineteenth century, its decline hastened by the disastrous outbreak of disease in the 1860s.[176] If the Bengal case is one of a failure to keep up, that of central Asia's silk industry is a failure to catch up. Unlike their counterparts in silk-producing centres such as Italy, China, or Japan, silk producers in the central Asian oasis towns and villages continued as they had in the early nineteenth century and earlier, isolated from technological change.[177]

V. F. Oshanin established a sericulture school in Tashkent, but the talented and famed Russian scientist and entomologist was also employed as curator of the Tashkent Museum, possibly to the detriment of the transformation of sericulture and silk production in Russian Turkestan.[178] Of seven filatures established for improvement in selecting cocoons and the reeling and winding of raw silk after 1867, for example, only one survived beyond 1872, turning losses until it was liquidated in 1875.[179] Although this last and longer-surviving enterprise was established by a Moscow merchant at the behest of General von Kaufman, it is unclear whether and how far Moscow's textile industry was calling for the improvement of silk production in central Asia.[180] Russia was consuming a considerable amount of silk from Italy and England, the latter presumably of Bengali or Chinese origin, alongside supplies from the Caucasus and western Asia.[181] Ultimately, technological transfer and improvement in quality were unlikely, since, first, sericulture remained dispersed and domestically organised; second, it largely supplemented supplies from other sources in Russian trade; and, third, the imperial state remained reluctant to foster the development of primary-processing industries in Russian Turkestan, except cotton-cleaning, which was nevertheless relatively backward.[182]

Rather, it was in east Asia—the historic home of silk—that the adaptation of new productive technologies combined with the harnessing of new networks of steamship and rail transport to advantage its silk industry and return it to pre-eminence in world markets. The loss of the Company's monopoly on the China trade in 1833 and the opening of China's silk export economy in 1842 catapulted the expansion of China's silk exports. In Punjab, silk imports from China were routed via Bombay, Chinese silk receiving a readier market there than in Calcutta.[183] If Multani and Lahori weavers could scarcely lay their hands on Chinese silk in the 1840s, the integrative effects of nineteenth-century transport technologies became readily apparent after mid century. Chinese silk was initially reshipped from Bombay to the new port of Karachi, and then sent by steamboat or rail to Multan, Amritsar, and Lahore. From 1841–2, when re-exports to Karachi are first recorded as separate entries in the *Bombay Commercial Proceedings*, the overseas silk trade rapidly doubled from around Rs 50,000 to Rs 100,000 by 1849–50.[184] Continuing the pattern and proportions established as early as the 1820s in Bombay's re-export trade, Chinese and Persian silk imports into the Indus delta ports exceeded those from Bengal, although a considerable amount was of unspecified origin.[185] But the route was circuitous, involving considerable break of bulk and repeated reloading of cargoes.

Once Punjab's trade towns were connected to the railway network in the 1860s, therefore, silk more readily and directly found its way from Bombay to Amritsar or Multan, often at the expense of trade via Karachi, where the port facilities were poor compared to Bombay.[186] Before the 1880s, the growth of trade was not so great that it represented the displacement of central Asian silks by those from east Asia. Although free from the pébrine epidemic in the 1860s, the Taiping Rebellion (1850–64) had disrupted and devastated the Chinese economy and, despite Japan's forced opening to the world after 1853, it would take some years before Japan was an effective player in the global silk market.[187] By the end of the 1880s, however, only 3 per cent of the freight of foreign silk by sea or rail was routed through Karachi, next to 96 per cent through Bombay.[188] Brought through the Bohra and Multani trade networks, which also organised weaving within Bombay, much of this was Chinese silk (and silk cloth).[189] Despite the increase in the trans-frontier trade to 1914, which was the consequence of increased imports of Kashmiri rather than Turkestan silk, the overland trade was dwarfed by the overseas trade from east Asia.[190]

Three interlinked changes contributed to the rising market share of east Asian silks in Punjab as in the world market, relating to the price, quantity, and quality of these silks. Over the nineteenth century, Chinese silk yarns steadily fell in price. Already, in the 1870s, the most expensive east Asian silks were half to one-third the value of the most expensive central Asian silks, the prices of which had remained relatively stable.[191] Until the introduction of modern methods of mechanised steam-reeling, east Asian raw silks were unsuitable for use on European powerlooms. In the first stage, the introduction (or reinvention) of European threadle and re-reeling technology in Shanghai and Canton, and from there to Japan, improved the texture and quality of these silks.[192] They first found markets in the networks of intra-Asian trade, within which Punjabi consumption was critical.[193] The readiness with which Punjabi artisans substituted Bukharan and Kabuli for Chinese and Japanese silks is partly explained by the convenience and cost-efficiency of working with east Asian relative to central Asian silks. Upon receipt, Turkestan silk was 'in appearance … quite dull and glossless, full of dirt' and, presumably to add weight for the profit of the trader, 'apparently […] steeped in some form of size or starch, giving it a coarse appearance like horse hair.'[194] To clean a *seer* (0.93 kg) of silk, it was 'put into an iron pan with 4 *chitaks* of soap and 4 *chitaks* of alkali', boiled and bleached, and 'well washed twice' until suitable for dyeing, all at an average cost of Rs 2 and a loss of 25 per cent of its initial weight.[195] But 'to make the Bokhara silk fit for the loom,' rewinding was also necessary 'at an expense of one Rupee per *seer* [one-fortieth of a maund], during which unwinding, a loss of from 3 to 5 tolas of refuse is incurred.'[196] Apart from the cost and inconvenience from readying the yarns for weaving, central Asian silk was also relatively more difficult to dye than Chinese and Japanese silks.[197] Thus, even Peshawari weavers in close proximity to the silk-producing peasants around Kabul switched to working primarily with Chinese yarns, easily and cheaply transported thanks to the railroad connecting the city with Bombay.[198]

Initially considered cheap and inferior, technological transfer prompted the revaluation of east Asian silks against central Asian and Indian raw silks.[199] In contrast to the 'improved' east Asian silks, 'the thread of Turkestan silk' remained 'much coarser than that of China and Japan.'[200] At the same time, the Punjabi market was widening, with new consumers whose preferences were flexible. On the one hand, the growth of east Asian raw silk and silk piece goods reified the 'prestige' of traditional styles woven of Bukharan yarns, which were scarcer and more expensive.[201] On the other hand, the influx of Chinese silk into Amritsar, Punjab's most rapidly modernising city, meant the end to the 'time when silk was worn only by nobles and courtiers,' with the emergence of 'a demand for less costly fabrics' following 'the increase in wealth, and rise in the standard of comfort', such that the 'wearing of silk has become much more general among all classes of natives'.[202]

In the twentieth century, silk cloth consumption widened further as the result of two factors, which highlight how marginal the old, overland world economy was to this new consumer society in Punjab. First, the substitution of east Asian for Punjab silk cloths, which were favoured for 'the lustre and finish […] and their immense range of colour and design.'[203] Second, the increasing substitution of imitation or artificial for genuine silk yarns—for the weft, warp, or both—as the new mercerised cottons and, in the twentieth century, art silk or rayon became available.[204] These were considerably cheaper and thinner textured than the silks of fifty years earlier: *daryai* of artificial silk, for example, cost around one-third the price of pure silk *daryai* woven from east Asian silk.[205] Thus, by the 1930s, the first mills manufacturing artificial silks from rayon had opened in Amritsar, marking the ultimate transformation of Punjab's silk industry.[206]

Conclusion

At heart, the New Imperialism reflected an impulse more profound than the grabbing of land by the status-anxiety ridden and rivalrous Great Powers—the *ancien regimes* of Britain, France, and Russia, as well as the rapidly ascending imperial states of Germany, the United States, and Japan—for it resulted in the projection of modern forms of power deep into the inner spaces of Eurasia, Africa, and the Americas. A multitude of modern technologies were central to these processes, for without technological innovation in weaponry and steam-powered transportation, medicines and mapping, successive waves of conquest and commercial penetration into the difficult terrain and disease environments of continental interiors would have been almost impossible.[207] In this respect, the era of New Imperialism was not uniquely a 'Western' phenomenon: alongside Japan, the Ottoman *reconquista* of the arid and desert zones—in north Africa, across the Arabian Peninsula, and in Transjordan and Iraq—was similarly predicated upon bureaucratic centralisation and extension, including improvements in cartography and the collection of census data (itself a new technology of the modern, ethnographic state).[208] In turn, however, the New Imperialists also relied on technologies associated with standardisation and acceleration—railways, the transportation of mail and goods and people, for instance—to consolidate control.[209] The Ottomans' expensive telegraphy and railway projects at the arid frontiers of the empire, Mostafa Minawi has shown, were inaugurated following the frustration of territorial ambitions in Africa during the 'Scramble' of the 1880s.[210] The investment in technological modernity was thus cause, response, and counter-response in the rivalrous inter-imperial arena during the era of the New Imperialism.[211]

'Machines', Michael Adas demonstrated very powerfully, became the 'measure of men' in the nineteenth century. If Western science and technology were central to conquest across the world, then, it was thought, Western rationality and intellect must be most closely aligned to the actual workings of the world. The extent of technological development or use of technologies served as instruments of conquest and control, but also as yardsticks with which to determine—to measure—the place of non-white peoples on the hierarchy of the races constructed by imperial rulers.[212] Those more proximate to or more distant from the West, in technological terms, were deemed more or less civilised, respectively. Space and the environment, however, are worthy of foregrounding in this argument, for the degree of civilisation achieved by a particular people was often proxied by the degree of technological modernity *visible* in the *places* they inhabited. The compilation of the *Turkestanskii Al'bom*—which was itself possible because of the development of the still somewhat new technology of photography—was rooted in such practices of visualisation and juxtaposition: the visual present of precolonial central Asia, represented in the snapshots of life and people and places in the 1870s, and appearing relatively backward in relation to contemporary Russia as well as the modern future of Russian Turkestan that was visualisable in the mind's eye. In turn, by juxtaposing outer and inner spaces, and translating them onto the binaries of advanced and backward, or civilised and uncivilised, the New Imperialists were impelled to bring technological modernity to the distant frontiers or deep interiors under their control. In this way, modern technology was intimately implicated in the *mission civilisatrice* of nineteenth-century empires, both as the benchmark against which to measure development and as the instantiation of the otherwise hollow rhetoric of imperial legitimation regarding progress, propagated by officials and laymen alike more motivated by the lure of profit and resource extraction.[213]

Inherent within Ottoman modernisation, too, was what Ussama Makdisi has termed 'Ottoman Orientalism', for the former also generated 'its discursive opposite, the [notion of the] pre-modern within the empire'.[214] The Ottoman Orient was conceived not so much as a frontier as the edge of a vast expanse of interior Eurasia where Islamic states and societies—stretching from Iraq and Lebanon to Afghanistan—displayed an abject (technological) backwardness. Afghanistan, Michael O'Sullivan notes, '[w]as a disconnected appendage of the Ottoman state' and as a space which could usefully receive Ottoman technocratic expertise in facilitation of Afghan modernisation.[215] From the perspective of the Afghan state, however, the despatch of technocrats in 1908 represented a continuation of experimentation with national modernisation stretching back to at least the reign of Abdur Rahman. As this chapter has shown, Abdur Rahman was not the petty despot, or the player of Great Game machinations, or the pawn in the hands of the British and Russian officials who dominate depictions of his rule.[216] Rather, the seeming 'arbitrariness' of the Iron Amir was perhaps a reflection of the pressures of trying to fashion a modern nation-state at a time of considerable flux. Transformation in society and economy in both Russian Turkestan and British India were undermining the flow of long-distance trade, and, in turn, undermining an important part of the Afghan state's sources of revenue. The amir ruled more flexibly than he is often credited with doing, his 'exactions' the consequences or symptoms rather than the primary causes of the decline of caravan trade.

Ultimately, whatever the role of these technologies as markers of modernity, and whatever the investment made by imperial powers in (usually, transport) technology, the result was far from a clean break with the past, for the 'modern' neither replaced the 'primitive', nor did the two jostle side by side.[217] Rather, a symbiosis emerged, evident at every railway station or port, and perhaps most dramatically around the Suez Canal, as Valeska Huber's study throws into relief. The Bedouin and their camels, she shows, came to be viewed as backward relative to steamships and the new canal which cut through the desert, and, yet, both the tribesman and his animal power remained integral to the functioning of the newer technologies and routes, used not only for moving goods around the ports and their carriage away from the canal zone but also for policing the new ports, which produced no new or 'modern' technologies of security of their own.[218] Mostafa Minawi and Camille Cole, likewise, have highlighted the agency of tribal societies from north Africa to western Asia in the process of technological modernisation.[219]

Cole, in particular, has shown that steamboats did not smash old political economies but were readily appropriated as a means of transporting 'traditional' products, such as ghee (clarified butter) and reeds, and integrated into the norms and politics of tribal raids. At the same time, the shallowness of the Tigris river and its competing use for irrigation made the operation of steamboats more difficult. While the material presented in this chapter has not emphasised the environmental vulnerabilities of technology, this is only because of the greater importance of other dimensions of technology's vulnerability and precariousness.[220] In turning to examine the silences and failures regarding such technologies, scholars have highlighted the limits and Achilles' heel of imperial power in particular contexts.[221]

Similarly, the Trans-Caspian Railway did reduce transport time and costs between Bukhara and Orenburg, accelerating central Asia's integration into the Russian Empire, but only when trains were not delayed by human or environmental disruption.[222] (By its necessity to unblocking the passage of trains caught in storms, and use by tribesmen in attacking carriages at speed, animal power prevailed over steam yet again.) The Russian investment in transportation technology, moreover, made its impact upon Indo-central Asian trade only from the late 1880s, by which time caravan trade was already in decline. This itself is a reflection of the spatio-temporal unevenness of the 'Great Transformation' in the Russian Empire—that is, the investment in and rolling out of technologies associated with the time–space compression—sketched in detail by Mustafa Tuna. Overall, and despite the deep roots of tsarist involvement in connecting the expanding empire, the greatest investments were made first and with most profundity in European Russia, only reaching Asiatic Russia to precipitate discernible changes towards the *fin de siècle*.[223]

Thus, although a process of technological modernisation was under way across the inner spaces of Afro–Eurasia, it was distinct from processes that undermined older forms of mobility and exchange. In south and central Asia, indigenous trade and finance were neither totally subordinated to the new transport technologies of the nineteenth century, as suspected by the British in the 1880s and 1890s, nor undermined by the new communications technologies, as feared by the Afghan traders interviewed by Captain H. Grey in the 1870s. Rather, the effects of the new transport technologies worked through existing economic geographies, so that their effects were never 'neutral'—on account of their profound endogeneity—so much as complex and contradictory. Seldom, after all, were these technologies inserted into uncharted terrain: the decision to establish or extend a railway or shipping line entailed enormous cost, which could reasonably be justified on the basis of future economic benefit only where the calculus derived from sound existing knowledge of the markets or resources that lay ahead (or of the worthiness of defending existing territory).[224] The result was frequently the overlaying of new connections onto old routes, or the linkage of existing centres in new configurations.[225] In turn, the effect was to amplify the advantages of existing centres but also to empower relatively more minor towns and cities, and vice versa. Outcomes, however, were often unpredictable because of the intermediation of a range of exogenous factors, rendering railways and steamships relatively more blunt instruments of imperialism than proponents of recent histories of 'techno-imperialism' might suppose.

'Mooltan [...] has no doubt a great destiny before it,' wrote J. H. Morris, settlement officer in the district in the late 1850s, believing the city would 'be[come] to Western, what Allahabad is to Eastern India'—the two cities sharing a significance as commercial centres and pilgrimage sites with existing connection via a great river to coastal ports, and, soon, as termini of railway lines that could channel produce from the interior to world markets.[226] Morris' prediction was remarkably accurate, for Multan became the productive centre of the new agrarian economy of Punjab, its population more than doubling due to the increase in irrigated agricultural land.[227] Multan's retreat into agrarianism was somewhat retrogressive: whereas Multani financiers possessed the requisite skills, and although some 'Multani' trader-financiers turned to the grain trade as moneylending activities were curbed by the authorities in Punjab and Russian Turkestan at the turn of the century, it was Amritsar that emerged as the centre of Punjab's futures market for wheat.[228] Amritsar was advantaged by its earlier connection to the railway line and its greater proximity to Bombay and Calcutta. At the same time, Multan's textile industry experienced a drift into stagnation and eventual decline, whereas Amritsar's workshops were faster to exploit the yarns imported from east Asia to become the dynamic new heart of Punjab's silk industry. More broadly, Punjab's textile sector did not 'deindustrialise': Punjabi weavers responded to the influx of English cotton yarns and cloth—as well as east Asian silk yarns and cloth—by shifting to the production of non-import-competing types of textile. Peshawar and the towns of western Punjab were, in this respect, empowered and enlarged by the greater connectivity that followed the extension of the rail network to the North-West Frontier—at least until their specialisation in coarse-cloth weaving for markets connected by caravan trade was undermined by protectionist policy in Russian Turkestan.

At the same time, however, imperial powers took little interest in other sorts of technologies besides roads, railways, and telegraphs in the interiors of their empires. Only those technologies that widened and deepened the state's authority or supported imperial interests were generally deemed worthy of investment—this being as true of British India or German Tanganyika as of Russian imperialism in late-nineteenth-century Turkestan or Japan's empire in Korea or Taiwan in the early twentieth century.[229] In this respect, the rhetoric of modernisation was rather superficial. In fact, 'modernisation' misrepresents the process of change in those inner spaces now opening outwards, for the disincentive or disinclination to invest in productive technologies meant the perpetuation of relative backwardness, at least in the economic sphere. Of note, moreover, was the role of *inter*-imperial rivalry for markets and prestige that drove territorial competition during the era of New Imperialism, itself the product of the porousness of empires and the *trans*-imperial flows and networks that were as capable of undermining as undergirding the empire project.

Russia's empire in central Asia was partially sealed off to trade from (but not to) British India. The effect was the more grave of the two forms of trade substitution sketched above. In accelerating the decline of Punjab's indigo economy and shutting out trade in cotton textiles, for instance, the final result was the secular decline in long-distance caravan trade as it had existed for several centuries. In effect, the trading world was fractured into two sets of exchanges, one between India and Afghanistan, the other between Afghanistan and Turkestan, even though the humans and animals moving through these increasingly separate circuits had earlier served to integrate south and central Asia.

If the latter circuit was more closely integrated into patterns of trade moulded by Russian imperial interests, the former was suffused with goods from the British Empire and the wider world. Afghanistan thus became a site of confluence, rather than a landlocked frontier space, as these commercial channels brought goods from around the globe: 'in addition to porcelain teacups, saucers, and pots arriving in blue and red patterns from Russia, […] [the caravans] hauled tea and cotton goods and matches "made in Sweden" and kerosene labelled "Standard Oil Co., made in U.S.A." and other goods stamped "made in Germany and Austria" and "made in Japan."'[230]

In hindsight, the rapid decline of trade as a result of the burden of trade taxes on the one hand, and the obsolescence that followed the growing use of anilines on the other, seem to vindicate the state's unwillingness to support a modern indigo industry in Punjab. Such arguments exhibit extreme myopia, however, ignoring the linkages cultivable through investment in light industry capable of supporting other industrial enterprises, and the economic development resulting therefrom. In contrast to the closedness of Russian Turkestan, the British Empire was much more porous, certainly in south Asia, to the extent that British economic hegemony was eroded in certain cases through the diffusion—whether by straightforward purchase or by imitation or adaptation—of British technologies. This impact of steam-powered productive and transport technologies, in particular, is apparent in the tale of east Asia's late-nineteenth-century resurgence in the world silk market while Bengali sericulture languished in the face of the state's indolence and, later, impotence. Ultimately, policy was the state's sharpest technology of control, at least when wielded decisively.

Thus, states were far from universally successful in increasing the suppleness, strength, and reach of their technologies of control in the late Victorian era. Merchants, furthermore, continued to outfox state officials in their efforts to restrict, regulate, and tax both the passage of the caravans and the despatch of particular (usually prohibited or protected) goods. Yet, the evasion of state authority was but one of the options available to traders; negotiating with the state's men on the ground—where power was more friable—was another. Viewed, in fact, from the bottom up, the distribution of gifts and payment of discretionary dues (bribes) reflected 'foreign' traders' agency and their ability to continue to shape the contours and contexts of economic activity. The formation of partnerships with indigenous merchants was another strategy that ensured the flow of goods along the caravan routes. In these ways, although policy changes produced uncertainty and transaction costs on a scale sufficient to accelerate the decline of caravan trade and an increasing disconnection of south from central Asia, and even of India from Afghanistan, they were not sufficiently powerful to extinguish this long-distance exchange altogether. The concluding chapter of this book offers a brief sketch of the trading world—as it was repeatedly transformed and reconfigured—through to the present.

CONCLUSION

Time

In Lahore, today, there are a number of Sikh Kabuliwallahs—Sikhs whose home was formerly in Kabul—who fled Afghanistan for Pakistan following the Taliban's seizure of power in the 1990s. In the course of research for this book, I met a group of these Afghans who worked as the custodians of Sikh monuments and temples. In part, their migration reflects the greater ease with which they could cross from Afghanistan into that part of Punjab incorporated into post-Partition Pakistan (rather than India), perhaps more so than any sense of returning to their 'homeland'. For, while history and historical memory, ecology and economic opportunity have all helped to maintain merchant networks and other forms of mobility across south and central Asia, there have also been numerous new beginnings, when circumstances have arisen to introduce new goods or new merchant communities or new ideas or new technologies. This has in turn precipitated not so much a rupture as an adaptation of exchange relationships, a reorientation of networks and routes, or a replasticisation of space itself.

In thinking *with* the Silk Roads, this book not only bridges spaces that have for too long been partitioned into the silos of different Area Studies categories (South Asia, Central Asia). It also integrates the divisions of historical time that have become ingrained in the scholarship. In Indian history, especially, the markers of 'precolonial' and 'colonial' segregate time and the activities of their respective communities of scholars. On the one hand, the effect has been to obscure those histories and historical experiences that do not neatly sit within the narrative of the 'colonial transition', a process starting in mid-eighteenth-century Bengal to then engulf other parts of the subcontinent. By the time of Punjab's conquest in the 1840s, the master narrative of colonial history has shifted to other matters.[1] But this fact occasions pause to reflect on this process from the edges of empires, such as western Punjab and the Indo-Afghan frontier. From this vantage point, the belatedness of the transition to colonialism produced its own effects; namely, the deepening integration of western Punjab and Afghanistan's economy into networks of overland trade toward central Eurasia, not least because of the exclusionary effects of Company policies in its new domains.

On the other hand, this partitioning of time has permitted the tendency to think of these periods in very different terms, the precolonial as a time of 'state-sponsored' cosmopolitanism and pluralism, the colonial era as one of 'state-directed' terror and violence. Take, for example, the experience of western Punjab, which is of crucial importance to the colonial history of canal colonies and martial recruitment (and failed attempts at animal breeding). This book highlights that these developments built on the long-standing relationship of the dry zone and the mobilities engendered by caravan trade to the subcontinent's economies of violence. It stresses the role of pastoralists and mercenaries within the annual transhumance, whose provision of animal and human power to Indian rulers coincided naturally with the campaign season, and whose channelling into fighting forces was crucial to the production of order and the exercise of hard power. In other words, there was something distinctive about channelling formerly mobile warrior groups into stationary regiments in the late colonial period, but this development can be situated within a much longer and larger history of the entanglement of mobility with the exercise of violence and the production of power. This book has also shown that the wave of state-building across south and central Asia in the wake of the Little Ice Age was marked by efforts to extend the area of cultivable land, which was sown with those crops that could be exchanged through the networks of caravan trade, highlighting the entanglement of power with political and material interests and trade. In fact, the extension of arable to increase revenue surplus and at once support powerful commercial interests was evident from at least Mughal times, suggesting the intensification of a process through the Durrani and Sikh eras, finally culminating under British rule. Yet, this approach does not aim to privilege continuity over change, so much as achieve balance by thinking across oftentimes arbitrary periodisations.

India and the Silk Roads concludes in the early twentieth century, not because trans-Eurasian trade had ceased to exist, but because a number of factors came together to change the character, significance, scope, and scale of Indo-central Asian trade more specifically. These included processes of socio-economic change that dis-embedded this branch of caravan trade from the material, cultural, and political worlds of participants, as well as policies that shut out particular goods or people from free circulation, while the growth of automobile traffic—especially British, American, or Russian trucks and lorries—over newly constructed roads steadily displaced a large part of the animal trains and altered the seasonal rhythms and temporality of long-distance circulation rather fundamentally.[2] In India, the Great War served to culminate the transformation of land and labour in Punjab, and its provision of much of the bran and the brawn of the British Empire at war. The experience of war, in turn, altered the tenor and debates of Indian political life, the result of which would be the birth of new nations—hostile neighbours with more rigidly controlled borders than before. In 1919, the new sovereign of Afghanistan, Ammanullah Khan, launched the Third Anglo-Afghan War, the remainder of his reign marked by efforts to modernise the nation-state.[3] And the 1917 Revolution eventually spilled over into the Russian Empire, the Bolshevik conquest of Bukhara in 1920 marking the termination of rule of the Bukharan amirs, the reorientation of the economy, the remaking of society, and the deeper integration of central Asia into the largely terrestrial 'Soviet world'.

While trans-Eurasian trade continued, its overall logic, proportional size, and shape were altered dramatically in the decades that followed, the analysis of which is well beyond the scope of this book, save to mention some of the broad contours and causes of the changes from mid century. The Great Partition of 1947 sharply reterritorialised the (political) economies of the Indian subcontinent toward the imperatives of the newly defined 'national interest', while the subsequent and enduring hostility between India and Pakistan has done little to support the trade networks or geographies examined in the preceding pages. On the contrary, holding up trucks crossing the border, and pestering drivers for their documentation or with inspections of their cargoes, has been a means of asserting state power, albeit passive-aggressively and for little tangible gain to any party. Another factor has been the steady intensification of the India–China rivalry since the 1960s—and even more acutely as they have vied for regional geopolitical hegemony following their respective economic take-offs—for China has sought a strategic partner in Pakistan. This spurred new patterns of interaction between Pakistan, China, and parts of central Asia—but to the exclusion of north Indian markets and actors. These effects may, in time, be accentuated by China's Belt and Road Initiative (BRI). But these enterprises have not been left unchallenged by India. Conceived a few years before the announcement of the BRI in 2013, the 'International North–South Trade Corridor' (INSTC) aims to cut transport times between the western Indian Ocean via the Suez to St Petersburg by using sea–rail–road routes from western Indian ports, through Iran, and onward to Russia. A commitment signed almost two decades ago has more recently been followed by a 'dry run' that has verified the cost and time savings of the INSTC. Aside from benefits to India, Iran, and Russia, the idea is for the INSTC to integrate neighbouring states in central Asia, the Caucasus, and around the Black Sea; Afghanistan and Pakistan are excluded. Thus, goods moving through the INSTC would circumvent, rather than revivify or reinvent, the geographies and mobilities examined in this book.[4]

India continues to be cleaved apart from Pakistan and Afghanistan, therefore, as indexed by the diminishing significance—in relative, if not absolute, terms—of its trade with the latter, and vice versa. Much of the core of this book's analysis, however, has been on that part of the historic 'India' that is now in Pakistan, and its integration with Afghanistan and central Eurasia. In this arena there are signs of a deepening integration, as well as new kinds of connection with—rather than a divorcing from—the larger Indian Ocean world, which has historically been an important backdrop toward terrestrial networks of exchange and circulation in the Eurasian continental interior. Magnus Marsden has shed valuable light on the more recent past of these networks, his research at once also serving to underscore themes examined in this book.[5] From Chitral, where he conducted his first studies, Marsden followed his 'friends' and 'informants' to trace a trading world of Afghan merchants across the Soviet and post-Soviet world, sedimented in multiple layers as successive waves of Afghans migrated across central Eurasia in response to changing opportunities, much like the mobilities that sedimented and constituted the early modern Indo-Persianate world. In the wake of the Soviet conquest of Bukhara and the New Economic Policy of the 1920s, economic opportunities opened for Afghans within the USSR. With the opportunity open to Communist party members to migrate for training in universities in the USSR—from the Ukraine to Uzbekistan—there arose prospects for trade in partnership with central Asian merchants. These were akin to partnerships in the pre-modern period, albeit in the context of radically transformed marketplaces, with many Afghans settling in their host states, forming the basis of new networks. Others had served as officials and officers in the security forces during the pro-Soviet Afghan government of the 1980s, and thereafter lived in Tajikistan and other central Asian republics since that government collapsed in the early 1990s, just as earlier communities of Afghan traders had made use of the political patronage of the Afghan state as a means to developing and deepening their commercial enterprises.

Marsden notes the much more rapid spread of Afghan networks in the last ten to fifteen years, no doubt because of the 'push' coming from the collapse of the USSR and political change in Afghanistan since the 1990s on the one hand, and the 'pull' of new opportunities in the capitalist 'West' and the rise of cheap consumer manufacturing to fuel its demands in China on the other. Of course, trade continues to take place at a range of geographic scales and levels of risk within this vastly expanded trading world, from the relatively 'local' cross-border trade between Afghanistan and Tajikistan, to the more 'global' trade of Chinese manufactures to markets from the Ukraine to the United States, from the trade in imperishables such as concrete, to the relatively risky transport of fuel from Russia to Afghanistan for the use of NATO forces or the international smuggling of hashish and heroin, for example. The Taliban, as Rashid Ahmed has highlighted, promoted the transit trade through Afghanistan in the period prior to 2001, so that

Afghan trade networks weathered this otherwise turbulent period.[6] In fact, Marsden shows, Afghans have also been able to adapt to the exigencies of altered economic and political landscapes in the aftermath of the 'War on Terror', with new groups continuing to relocate within and beyond Afghanistan for purposes of trade.

Empires and States

Afghans and Punjabi Muslims, as this book has brought to light, were not only mercenaries and pastoralists, nor merely petty traders—despite this characterisation in certain primary sources and much of the scholarship. In common with the Multanis who reinvested trade profits into real estate, high-yielding agricultural loans, and specialist services to host governments from the sixteenth to the nineteenth century, some Afghans and other Muslim groups in the continental interior were able to leverage their profits at particular conjunctures to establish well-capitalised long-distance exchange networks. In more recent times, too, Afghan heroin smugglers have reinvested their profits into other economic activities, 'partly to enhance their reputation with the local communities and state officials on whose support their "other work" (*kor-i-digar*) depends.'[7] Marsden's study suggests that Hindu and Sikh Afghans continue to specialise in finance alongside trade, complementing the business of Muslim Afghans. But his fieldwork also supports the notion that the latter have been able to rise to the ranks of big businessmen, that they have raised and reinvested considerable sums of capital, and that they reinvested in financial ventures akin to those of their non-Muslim brethren.[8]

To avoid being 'hassled' and 'held-up' by Tajik officials, the (Muslim) Afghan merchants studied by Marsden take pains to look less conspicuously 'Afghan'. Their sartorial choices are not subordinated to their commercial ambitions alone, however, for these traders also use their dress to distinguish themselves according to their outlook on Afghan politics, notably the more 'Western' dress of the 'democrats' and the more 'Afghan' dress of most *mujahids*, while at the same time articulating their religious, regional, and ethnic identities. Marsden argues these choices reveal 'multiple layers of information, both to other traders and those with whom [a trader] interacts more generally' about 'his capacity to trade and enter into partnerships, or [...] aspects of his inner moral state, commitment to work, and trustworthiness.' Collectively, these shape trading relations and partnerships, and, ultimately, the success of particular agents within the trading world.[9] At stake, therefore, is the way in which actors can traverse vast geographic distances, passing through multiple political domains, and, yet, go relatively unnoticed or else slip between different markers of identity.

Part of the reason for this invisibility, in the more modern context, results from the traders' exertion of their agency. Perhaps in the eighteenth and nineteenth centuries, too, Afghans and Punjabi Muslims favoured a low profile. Yet, colonial ideas about race inflected the sources surviving in the colonial archive, adding an extra layer of haze over the activities of certain commercial actors. The Hindu Bania was seen as the authority in matters of long-distance specialist trade and finance, whereas Muslim traders were no more than peddlers or petty merchants. The Punjabi or Pashtun was, furthermore, eventually seen as a sturdy yeoman or as one of the martial races—rather far from the calm and calculating magnate or merchant. The archives are thus full of information garnered from Afghan and Punjabi Muslims involved in caravan trade, and the simultaneous silencing or marginalisation of their testimony. Other sorts of privileging or prejudice are also evident in the sources. If there is considerably more material on the trade in indigo, silk, horses, or cotton textiles, for instance, it is because these commodities interested the colonial authorities in ways that the slave trade or the peddling of talismans and charms did not, prompting their investigation and rendering visible these flows. Navigating the archives with a critical eye, and reading the history of race or economic interests into the source materials to render greater visibility to particular actors and exchanges have been among the aims of this book.

By the same token, however, the colonial archives are peculiarly rich in material about caravan trade, precisely since understanding and controlling its flows of finance and goods, people, intelligence, and ideas were of importance to colonial security. Thus, while British and Russian policies cumulatively undermined the older logic of trade and cleaved the trading world into separate commercial circuits, the concern with Muslim fanatics or the restive power of the peoples inhabiting the trading world—not to mention the recurrence of information panic—reveal the fragility of colonial power and the fragile emotional state of the expatriate population. This book has shown that the mobilities and exchanges constitutive of caravan trade were as critical to the functioning of political authority as the state was to the vitality of caravan trade, and that the British followed their forebears by striving to integrate into these networks of animal power, mercenary power, finance, and information flows from the early nineteenth century, particularly from the commencement of their preparations for the First Afghan War. In so doing, this book has also shown that the trans-regional, trans-imperial networks of caravan trade were more durable than those fragile and friable states and empires they criss-crossed and connected.[10]

Moreover, this book shows that the challenge of the global compels a historical vision larger than that bounded by one or other empire, for the framework of much of the analysis in the preceding chapters has been trans-imperial in scope. Take, most significantly, the elision of 'British' India for the Indian subcontinent in the time of colonial rule, and the way this vests the policies of the British government—as rulers of much of south Asia, as well as the hegemonic power in the modern world-system—with a somewhat singular transformative agency. By focusing on north-west India and its connections to central Eurasia, the preceding chapters have emphasised that Russian imperial policy was as critical in shaping developments within the Indian domains of the trading world as those of the British Indian government. Russia's industrialisation of textile production might have been derivative of British innovation, but its first-mover advantage in central Eurasia meant Russian manufacturers outcompeted their British rivals in this space. In turn, the tariff policy on Indian goods and the restrictions on Indian subjects imposed by the government of Russian Turkestan served to decisively exclude the free movement of goods, people, and finance that sustained caravan trade. The result was the reorientation of terrestrial long-distance exchange networks, rather than their extinction, with certain continuities holding through such periods of political change.

Today, for instance, Afghan involvement in the trade in fresh and dried fruit between central Asia and India continues, one element of which is the tangerine trade from Sargodha (Punjab, Pakistan) to

Afghanistan, Tajikstan, and Iran.[11] Some merchants also trade asafoetida (*hing*)—another commodity of considerable historical significance—from Afghanistan to India for the use of traditional doctors.[12] Of course, there is a discontinuity in terms of the actors involved in this trade—presumably not the progeny of the Kabuliwallahs who inspired Tagore's story, but new groups that have won a share in the modern fruit wholesale business—belying any continuity. Yet, these processes of reorientation and reconfiguration of long-distance exchange networks, and the resultant persistence of terrestrial or overland trade, nevertheless point to their historical significance. If there is such an enterprise as the history of empires, then surely more attention is merited on the history of long-distance trade networks, as the comparison of Indo-central Asian and trans-Saharan networks in this book has striven to show.

In an impressive study centring on fieldwork in Dushanbe and Lahore, the anthropologist Aeron O'Connor has examined the cultural worlds of intelligentsia who travelled between central Asia, south Asia, and Russia from the late 1940s to the early 1990s.[13] O'Connor shows how they pay little explicit attention to the monumental political changes from the Great Game to the Cold War, from the transformation of life under Soviet rule to national independence. In their poetic recitations (*mushaira*) and repartee, in person or in correspondence, their lives seem to exist 'outside national-historical time' and in the more 'timeless' shared world of the Persian cosmopolis kept alive through their circulation, physical and intellectual. Whether or not this suspension of time is merely a form of escapism from the present, rendering it inherently political, it suggests how alternative conceptions of time and space—outside the nation-state and its history—have been mobilised to challenge the primacy of states and their events of supposed 'world-historical' importance. What is revealed, instead, are more invisible networks and mobilities that nevertheless transcend the history of empires and states, more akin to—and, in fact, drawing upon—the world forged by caravan trade studied in this book.

Space

The ease with which deserts can be thought of as seas, and vice versa, risks missing the source of their commonality: their 'interiority'—

their existence behind the littoral, their remove from populous agglomerations of human habitation. This book is about interior space, which has been so neglected by scholars even in the wake of the 'global turn' and its supposed breaking free of the hegemonies of empires and nations that have hitherto dominated historiographical production. This concern with space, spatial relationships, and spatial processes runs through the book. The distinctiveness of the different ecologies of south and central Asia has been a building block of this book's analysis, not least in understanding the interdependence of the dry and wet zones that gave impetus to the mobilities associated with the annual circuit of caravan trade. The attentiveness of environmental and technological change in shifting economic geographies of production and trade has shaped the analysis of change over time, including the shift in primacy from Lahore to Multan to Amritsar in Punjab's economy, or the westward drift of textile production that made the core of the trading world more compact, to take two examples.

Overall, *India and the Silk Roads* argues that scholarly neglect of the continental interior is neither to be confused for its inconsequential place in history, nor that it reflects this space becoming a backwater to the emerging global economy as populations slowly shifted to the continental 'exterior' along the coasts. Running through this book, therefore, is an alternative conception of the global history of south Asia; namely, one that does not reduce south Asia's global significance to the connections radiating outward across the Indian Ocean world alone. This book has not sought to show that the region stretching from Punjab into central Asia was straightforwardly part of the increasingly globalised world that emerged after *c.* 1500, however.[14] To be sure, as this book has foregrounded, the space under examination was subject to global-level phenomena, such as the climatic cooling of the mid-seventeenth-century Little Ice Age that triggered social upheaval and a burst of state-building through to the mid eighteenth century, the overall pattern characteristic of the General Crisis. The exploration of the relationship of people to the world of things brought through caravan trade suggests a consciousness of fashions, an awareness of the power of the self and its presentation, and of forms of sociability all characteristic of what is increasingly seen as a global early modern world.

None of this is to say that the states and societies studied in this book were directly connected to the modern world-system as it developed, for the connections from the Eurasian interior to the Indian Ocean world were oblique. The bullion influx that stimulated state-building and productive expansion in the Durrani and Khokand states, for instance, was not received directly from Europeans in exchange for the goods or resources of these states. Rather, it flowed into neighbouring economies—India and China—parts of which were more directly connected to the linking of the New World, Europe, and Asia through trans-oceanic routes after 1500. In this respect, the place of the Eurasian interior is subtly different to that of the African interior in the development of the modern world-system, as refracted by the histories of the slave trades. In the trans-Saharan context, the slave trade had connected the African economy to the economy of the Atlantic world and, in turn, to the emerging global economy from the sixteenth century onward.[15] In the trans-Eurasian context, however, the slave trade existed beyond the commercial horizons of the early modern maritime European powers and persisted despite British efforts to abolish slavery in the Indian Ocean world or Russian efforts in central Asia in the nineteenth and twentieth centuries.[16]

Globalisation

Thus, even as New World bullion flowed through India and China and onward into central Eurasia, or as new machine-made goods coursed through the networks of caravan trade, the impact of modern globalisation was highly uneven, affecting some commercial groups or the trade of certain goods or particular locales far more than others, some remaining relatively unchanged. There is little evidence of modern globalisation or more modern forms of exchange trumping and supplanting the archaic. Instead, the archaic was rendered modern, as the actors, institutions, technologies, and goods associated with modern globalisation necessarily interacted with those in the trading world. On these grounds, scholars should avoid hastily and simplistically ascribing everything as being 'global', for it lends the global and globalisation a singularising or totalising effect, flattening diverse experiences across different spaces with their differing temporalities. One further set of insights from Marsden's work serve to underscore this point.

The most remarkable feature of modern-day Afghan trade networks is their scale and spread through times of tighter controls on migration and movement across borders than in any prior period in the history of global trade. Of considerable importance to the 'success of being Afghan' is the ability to form and maintain relationships with bureaucrats and border guards, policemen and customs collectors through payment of bribes and other 'dues'—much as their forebears paid a range of 'customary' tolls and seemingly 'arbitrary' charges to hereditary chiefs or collectors—as a means of facilitating movement across borders without visas or passports. Overarching and structuring these Afghan enterprises are Afghan trade diasporas. In refutation of Philip Curtin's assertion of over thirty years ago that industrialisation rendered the cultural and commercial brokerage performed by such far-flung communities obsolete, Marsden shows how the trade diaspora continues to play a critical role in modern market-capitalist economies.[17] Prominent in Afghan trade today is a family firm—formerly pastoral nomads who entered the tea trade towards the end of the nineteenth century, thereafter repeatedly reinvesting in new ventures—which owns and operates big businesses involved in the sale of petrol, other fuels, and food products in Afghanistan, and is registered in the Virgin Islands. The Afghan trading world extends from the multinational Alokozay Group of Companies, to the cousins and nephews who rent properties from kinsmen to sell cheap consumer goods transported from China to Europe by other Afghans.

Returning, then, to where this book started: Bradsher's article on the revival of the Silk Roads. These recent developments are distinctive, reflecting an unprecedented power in the global economy never before exerted by China, as well as a scope, scale, and speed of exchange unimaginable in the heyday of the 'old' arterial east–west Silk Roads. But the BRI is predicated on existing technologies of connectivity, while many of the Afghans interviewed by Marsden are already involved in the overland movement—albeit by truck, rather than railway—of cheap consumer goods from China to Europe. At the same time, the shift of part of Chinese manufacturing toward the interior reflects a transformation of economic geography that is not entirely unprecedented. This is, in other words, a new development in an old and oft-forgotten story, not so much the resuscitation of something that lay undisturbed for half a millennia or so, but the augmentation of the steadily developing networks of terrestrial connectivity.

VARIETIES AND PRICES OF SILK

Table 1: Prices of Raw Silk per *Seer* Available in Bombay, 1802–3 to 1848–9[1]

| Year | Bengal[2] | | | | China | | | | Persia | |
| | Radhnagar | | Kasimbazar and Banack | | First Sort | | Second Sort | | Basra | |
	Max	Min	Max	Min	Max	Min	Max	Min	Max	Min
1802–03	6–3	7–0	6–0	6–2	10–0	11–0	9–0	10–0	—	—
1803–04	7–0	8–0	7–0	7–2	9–2	10–0	9–0	9–2	—	—
1804–05	7–0	8–0	6–0	7–0	11–0	12–2	9–0	12–0	—	—
1805–06	8–2	10–2	7–1	9–0	11–2	15–0	8–2	13–0	—	—
1807–08	9–1	10–2	7–2	8–2	11–1	12–0	10–1	11–0	—	—
1808–09	9–1	11–0	7–0	8–0	10–1	11–2	9–2	11–1	—	—
1809–10	9–2	12–3	10–0	13–1	10–1	12–3	9–3	11–3	—	—
1810–11	11–3	13–1	11–2	14–0	14–0	16–3	13–0	15–3	—	—
1811–12	12–2	15–0	15–0	18–0	16–2	19–0	20–0	25–0	—	—
1812–13	11–2	15–0	13–0	17–2	13–1	17–2	12–2	17–0	—	—
1813–14	9–0	12–2	9–1	14–0	12–0	14–3	11–0	14–0	—	—
1814–15	8–1	10–0	9–0	10–0	10–3	15–0	10–1	14–0	—	—
1815–16	7–3	10–0	8–2	10–0	11–0	14–3	10–1	14–0	—	—

Year										
1816–17	9–1	10–1	9–2	10–2	12–0	14–2	11–1	14–0	—	—
1817–18	9–2	11–0	10–0	11–0	10–2	12–0	9–2	11–2	—	—
1818–19	10–1	15–0	10–2	15–0	11–3	18–0	11–0	18–0	—	—
1819–20	12–1	17–0	12–0	16–2	14–0	18–0	13–0	21–0	—	—
1820–21	12–0	14–2	12–0	14–1	13–3	16–0	13–0	15–2	—	—
1821–22	12–0	14–2	11–0	13–2	13–0	15–0	12–0	14–0	—	—
1822–23	11–2	12–0	10–3	11–0	13–0	13–2	12–0	12–2	—	—
1823–24	14–0	15–1	12–0	13–1	15–1	16–2	15–0	15–2	—	—
1824–25	11–2	12–2	12–0	14–0	13–0	17–0	12–0	16–0	—	—
1825–26	9–0	14–0	8–0	12–0	12–0	14–2	11–2	14–0	—	—
1826–27	10–0	12–0	9–2	12–0	13–2	14–2	12–2	13–2	9–2	12–0
1827–28	10–0	12–0	9–2	12–0	12–0	14–0	11–0	13–0	9–0	11–3
1828–29	10–0	12–0	9–2	11–2	12–2	14–0	11–0	13–0	8–2	10–0
1829–30	11–0	12–0	11–0	12–0	11–2	13–0	11–0	12–0	9–0	11–0
1830–31	9–0	11–2	9–0	11–2	10–0	13–0	9–0	12–0	9–0	9–2
1831–32	8–0	12–0	8–2	11–0	10–2	15–0	9–2	12–0	8–2	12–0
1832–33	10–2	14–0	10–0	14–0	12–0	14–0	12–0	14–0	10–0	12–2
1833–34	9–0	13–1	10–0	13–1	11–3	14–0	11–0	13–2	10–0	13–1
1834–35	9–0	11–8	9–0	11–0	11–0	13–0	10–8	12–8	9–8	12–0
1835–36	9–0	11–8	10–8	12–0	12–0	13–8	11–8	13–0	10–0	12–0
1836–37	5–0	6–0	5–0	5–12	6–0	6–8	5–12	6–4	5–12	6–0
1837–38	4–8	10–0	4–8	11–8	6–0	13–0	5–0	12–8	5–0	12–0
1838–39	4–8	6–0	5–0	5–8	6–4	7–4	5–8	7–8	5–4	6–4
1839–40	5–0	6–0	5–8	6–4	6–0	7–8	6–0	7–8	4–0	6–0
1846–47	4–0	5–12	4–0	5–0	—	—	—	—	4–8	5–8
1848–49	3–10	4–10	3–8	4–12	4–2	4–8	3–8	4–4	3–8	4–8

Table 2: Prices of Raw Silk per *Seer* Available in Punjab in the 1830s–1840s[3] and 1870s–1890s[4]

Variety			1836 Multan	1837 Multan	1837 Shikarpur	1841 Shikarpur (price/assar*)	1847 Multan
Central Asia	Bukhara and Khokand	Charki	10–0 to 15–0	13–12	–	–	8–0
		Chilla	–	14–0	20–0 to 21–0	–	–
		Kokani	10–0 to 15–0	10–0	13–0 to 14–0	10–0	12–0
		Nawabi	–	15–12	18–0 to 19–0	14–12	15–0
	Herat	Herati	–	14–12	–	–	–
		Kaloochur	–	–	–	9–0	–
	Samarkand	Lab-i-Abi	10–0 to 15–0	–	–	–	–
	General	Chitta	–	17–0	–	–	–
		Kushikanee	–	7–0	–	–	–
		Lola	–	–	7–0 to 9–0	–	–
		Shal Bafee	–	–	–	15–10	–
		Sufarfeen	–	–	10–0 to 11–0	–	–
		Toonee	–	18–0	10–0 to 11–0	13–12	–
Persia		Ghilanee	–	6–0	–	9–0	–
China	via Bombay	Bat	–	–	6–0 to 7–0	–	–

* Note: 1 assar = Rs 90.25 Shikarpuri or Rs 88 Company.

	Variety	1870s	1890s		
		Amritsar	Amritsar	Peshawar	Unspecified
Central Asia	Akhcha	14–0 to 15–0	–	12–8 to 16–0	–
	Bahardhan	15–0 to 16–0	–	–	–
	Baf	14–0 to 16–0	12–0 to 12–8	–	–
	Charkhi	11–0 to 11–8	–	12–0	–
	Kokani	–	14–0	12–0	–
	Lab-i-Abi	–	14–0	–	–
	Nawabi	–	–	13–0 to 18–0	–
	Phulu	7–0 to 11–0	–	–	–
	Phulu of Shahri-Sabzi	13–0 to 15–0	–	–	–
	Tani	19–0 to 20–0	–	–	–
	Tani Kokani	18–8	–	–	–
	Wardan	–	18–0	18–0	–
India	Radhanagur—Charpaya	13–0	–	–	–
	Radhnagur—Gadhor	14–0 to 15–0	–	–	–
	Other	–	7–0 to 13–0	–	–

China	Hariar	6–0	—	—	—
	Mai Phul	—	—	—	10–0 to 11–0
	Mai Phul (best)	—	—	—	17–0
	Manchu	—	4–0	8–0	—
	Mathria	2–12 to 3–2	—	—	—
	Mathul	4–0 to 7–0	—	—	—
	Saddak	13–0	—	—	—
	Sikka	5–6 to 5–8	—	—	—
	Shishmahal	2–8 to 4–0	—	—	4–0
	Sultani	—	11–0	—	—

APPENDIX II

BRITISH SUBJECTS TRADING IN CENTRAL ASIA[1]

Serial No.	Name	Tribe	Native of	Now residing in	Remarks
1.	Muhammad Hasan		Nowshera		
2.	Khalil Rahman		Nowshera		
3.	Abdul Rashid	Paracha		Kabul	
4.	Muhammad Bakhsh		Attock		
5.	Muhammad Sadig		Attock		
6.	Muhammad Jan				
7.	Muhammad Bakhsh	Lakesar	Peshawar		Agent of Ilahi Bakhsh of Peshawar
8.	Muhammad Said				
9.	Khanimulla				
10.	Sufi-ullah				
11.	Shudi	Paracha	Nowshera	Tashkurghan	
12.	Sultan Jan				
13.	Muhammad Jan				
14.	Muhammad Said				

15.	Muhammad Shafi				
16.	Muhammad Amin				
17.	Ghulam Din				
18.	Ali Muhammad				
19.	Muhammad Sharif				
20.	Ilahi Bakhsh				
21.	Mir Husen				
22.	Abdul Karim				
23.	Muhammad Sadig				Brothers
24.	Muhammad Said				
25.	Abdul Rahman				
26.	Sharf-ud-din		Bhera		
27.	Muhammad Amin				
28.	Ghulam Jehani	Parach			
29.	Fakir Nur Ahmad		Peshawar		
30.	Rahim Bakhsh	Sethi			
31.	Muhammad Bakhsh	Matha			
32.	Abdul Rahman	Zargar			
33.	Ali Mulla	Bhati			
34.	Mian Kamr-ud-din	Paracha		Bokhara	
35.	Sabz Ali	Paracha Mang			
36.	Hosan-ud-din				Brothers
37.	Sadr-ud-din				
38.	Haji Muhammad		Nowshera		
39.	Muhammad Latif	Paracha			
40.	Hasan Ali				
41.	Umar Bakhsh				
42.	Nur-ud-din				

No.	Name				
43.	Sher Zaman				
44.	Muahmmad Zaman				
45.	Muhammad Hasan				
46.	Fazl Din	Bhati Paracha			
47.	Mir Hasan	Paracha			
48.	Shah Alam				
49.	Hasan Ali				
50.	Fazl Kadir				
51.	Muhammad Bakhsh				
52.	Umar Bakhsh				
53.	Muhammad Bakhsh	'Labdol'	Peshawar		
54.	Mulla Muhammadi				
55.	Shams-ud-din	Paracha	Attock		
56.	Hasan Ali				
57.	Haji Sharafdin Sigal		Bhera		
58.	Karm Din				
59.	Shekh Abdulla				
60.	Abdul Aziz				
61.	Mian Ghulam Jan		Mukhad		
62.	Muhammad Kasim				
63.	Gul Mai				
64.	Abdulla				
65.	Ghulam Kadir		Peshawar	Katta Karghan	
66.	Lala Majit				
67.	Muhammad Said		Bhera	Karshi	Brothers
68.	Muhammad				
69.	Nausher Zaman		Nowshera	Kolab	

70.	Ghulam Jan			Nowshera	Kolab	
71.	Muhammad Hafiz					
72.	Sher Zaman				Charjui	
73.	Muhammad Bakhsh				Yarkand	Agent of Mahesh Das of Peshawar
74.	Mir Ahmad	Sethi		Peshawar	Ourganj (Khiva)	
75.	Muhammad Rawar	Paracha				
76.	Ghulam Jelani	Sethi				
77.	Mokam Din					

APPENDIX III

VOLUME AND VALUE OF COTTON CLOTH EXPORTS FROM PUNJAB, 1869–70 TO 1909–10[1]

Year	Indian				European				Total	
	Weight		Value		Weight		Value			
	Maunds	% of Total	Rupees	% of Total	Maunds	% of Total	Rupees	% of Total	Maunds	Value
1869–70	1,319	15%	93,375	10%	7,311	85%	802,665	90%	8,630	896,040
1870–71	936	11%	53,597	6%	7,640	89%	832,319	94%	8,576	885,916
1871–72	1,485	18%	138,905	13%	6,603	82%	922,089	87%	8,088	1,060,994
1872–73	912	9%	74,813	6%	9,816	91%	1,269,860	94%	10,728	1,344,673
1873–74	37,511	77%	2,207,586	69%	11,494	23%	995,022	31%	49,005	3,202,608
1874–75	35,983	74%	1,282,485	28%	12,537	26%	3,330,746	72%	48,520	4,613,231
1875–76	–	–	–	–	–	–	–	–	–	–
1876–77	37,773	78%	1,071,985	53%	10,590	22%	957,136	47%	48,363	2,029,121
1877–78	36,385	73%	1,938,434	55%	13,775	27%	1,582,969	45%	50,160	3,521,403
1878–79	29,798	68%	1,355,708	42%	13,901	32%	1,896,550	58%	43,699	3,252,258
1879–80	46,177	68%	2,030,490	44%	21,543	32%	2,629,727	56%	67,720	4,660,217

Year										
1880–81	36,859	53%	1,831,212	32%	32,188	47%	3,935,520	68%	69,047	5,766,732
1881–82	53,532	66%	2,519,419	44%	27,366	34%	3,180,614	56%	80,898	5,700,033
1882–83	32,163	53%	1,475,289	35%	27,992	47%	2,782,123	65%	60,155	4,257,412
1883–84	24,464	56%	1,103,827	35%	19,206	44%	2,049,350	65%	43,670	3,153,177
1884–85	26,811	59%	1,228,022	36%	18,522	41%	2,228,710	64%	45,333	3,456,732
1885–86	36,444	64%	1,693,322	45%	20,607	36%	2,097,400	55%	57,051	3,790,722
1886–87	48,773	64%	2,280,336	46%	27,049	36%	2,688,545	54%	75,822	4,968,881
1887–88	38,420	54%	1,768,069	34%	32,569	46%	3,372,295	66%	70,989	5,140,364
1888–89	32,982	57%	1,565,501	39%	24,519	43%	2,452,941	61%	57,501	4,018,442
1889–90	45,821	54%	2,449,261	36%	39,589	46%	4,316,807	64%	85,410	6,766,068
1890–91	29,349	52%	1,453,119	35%	27,554	48%	2,702,991	65%	56,903	4,156,110
1891–92	39,006	51%	1,921,144	34%	37,396	49%	3,771,470	66%	76,402	5,692,614
1892–93	43,342	57%	2,246,159	40%	32,777	43%	3,309,961	60%	76,119	5,556,120
1893–94	32,304	52%	1,562,349	36%	30,101	48%	2,819,167	64%	62,405	4,381,516
1894–95	27,684	52%	1,264,054	34%	25,569	48%	2,421,100	66%	53,253	3,685,154
1895–96	25,585	52%	1,164,538	34%	23,159	48%	2,298,345	66%	48,744	3,462,883
1896–97	36,195	54%	1,619,652	37%	30,222	46%	2,752,033	63%	66,417	4,371,685
1897–98	44,839	71%	2,115,361	57%	18,625	29%	1,621,730	43%	63,464	3,737,091
1898–99	27,448	50%	1,227,405	34%	27,205	50%	2,347,887	66%	54,653	3,575,292
1899–1900	51,933	52%	2,240,186	37%	48,453	48%	3,833,503	63%	100,386	6,073,689
1900–01	49,175	55%	2,349,025	40%	40,098	45%	3,549,139	60%	89,273	5,898,164
1901–02	50,945	56%	2,440,002	40%	40,245	44%	3,611,664	60%	91,190	6,051,666
1902–03	42,575	51%	2,041,122	36%	40,752	49%	3,570,520	64%	83,327	5,611,642
1903–04	53,034	58%	2,383,196	39%	38,196	42%	3,730,014	61%	91,230	6,113,210
1904–05	53,237	52%	2,540,358	33%	49,849	48%	5,205,890	67%	103,086	7,746,248
1905–06	45,435	47%	2,168,765	29%	50,938	53%	5,431,962	71%	96,373	7,600,727

1906–07	52,403	49%	2,477,715	30%	53,475	51%	5,715,089	70%	105,878	8,192,804
1907–08	51,240	47%	2,329,020	28%	57,004	53%	5,857,665	72%	108,244	8,186,685
1908–09	40,574	42%	1,815,916	24%	56,788	58%	5,828,428	76%	97,362	7,644,344
1909–0	36,203	38%	1,581,658	22%	58,621	62%	5,585,571	78%	94,824	7,167,229

NOTES

INTRODUCTION

1. *The New York Times* (accessed 22 February 2018): http://www.nytimes. com/2013/07/21/business/global/hauling-new-treasure-along-the-silk-road. html?pagewanted=1&_r=1&adxnnl=1&adxnnlx=1397383363-CcBkx-AWjK%20klUp98HdPT4A

2. Adshead, *Central Asia*, Part III. Adshead, however, connected this shift in trade patterns to an epochal shift in central Asia, whereby the region transitioned from serving as an 'active' to a 'passive' place in the world. It is against this characterisation of the region as a 'backwater' that some historians subsequently situated their work, discussed below.

3. The arguments in this section are drawn from the material in the present book as well as three recent critical analyses of the Silk Roads: Millward, *Silk Road*; Levi, 'Early Modern Central Asia'; and Rezakhani, 'Road That Never Was'.

4. Sivasundaram, 'Towards a Critical History of Connection'.

5. McNeill, 'Environmental History', 29.

6. Wallerstein, *Modern World-system*. See also: Rezakhani, 'Road That Never Was', 426.

7. Green, 'From the Silk Road', 3.

8. See, classically, Steensgaard, *Asian Trade Revolution*. And, more recently: Beckwith, *Empires of the Silk Road*.

9. Levi, 'Early Modern Central Asia', especially 870–2.

10. Alam and Subrahmanyam, *Indo-Persian Travels*; Levi, ed., *India and Central Asia*.

11. Chaudhuri, 'Export of Treasure', 23–38. On Mughal, Safavid, and Uzbek commercial policies: Dale, *Indian Merchants*, 33–42.

12. For assessments of early modern overland trade in Soviet historiography: Golden, *History of the Turkic People*, 334–5.

13. Alongside the 'resurgent' kingdoms and the 'social movements' turned into

283

kingdoms, Bayly outlines two other types of eighteenth-century successor state: the Muslim conquest state and the Mughal satrapies. Bayly, *Rulers, Townsmen and Bazaars*, 17–27. For an alternative typology incorporating developments in the Ottoman and (former) Safavid empires: Sood, *India and the Islamic Heartlands*, 6–13.

14. Gommans, *Indo-Afghan Empire*, especially 50–1.

15. Levi, 'Fergana Valley', 213–32; idem, *Khoqand*, for an expansion of this thesis. On Khokand's relations with the Durranis: Newby, *Empire and the Khanate*, 47.

16. For a sketch of earlier work, during the Cold War era and the Indo-USSR Cultural Exchange more specifically, see: Shastitko, 'Preface', xxii–xxiii. A range of Russian facsimiles are archived in the Private Papers Collection of the NAI.

17. Dale, *Indian Merchants*; Markovits, *Indian Merchants*; and Levi, *Indian Diaspora*.

18. Stern, *Company-State*.

19. On what is commonly called the Indian 'depression' of the early nineteenth century: Bayly, *Rulers, Townsmen and Bazaars*, chapter 7. For bullion flows from Russia to Bukhara around this time: Hopkins, *Modern Afghanistan*, 125–6.

20. Findlen, ed., *Early Modern Things*, 11; Appadurai, *Social Life of Things*. For a review of developments in the wake of this volume: Gerritsen and Riello, *Global Lives of Things*, especially 1–13.

21. For example: Curry-Machado, ed., *Global Histories, Imperial Commodities*; Riello, *Cotton*.

22. Cohn, in his 'Renaissance Attachment to Things', has called for a similar approach. In contrast, historians of science have more rapidly engaged with 'the materiality of knowledge': Findlen, *Early Modern Things*, 14–15.

23. Khazeni, *Sky Blue Stone*, xiv.

24. Neumann, *et al.*, 'Future Coastal Population Growth', 1–34.

25. Beckwith, *Empires of the Silk Road*, chapter 9. Note the reference here to the 'new thalassology': Vink, 'Indian Ocean Studies'.

26. For example: Bose, *A Hundred Horizons*.

27. Sivasundaram, *Islanded*, 4. See, also: idem, 'Indian Ocean'.

28. Drayton and Motadel, 'Futures of Global History', 10.

29. Miran, 'The Red Sea', 156.

30. Hopkins, *Modern Afghanistan*, chapters 5–6.

31. Lydon, *Trans-Saharan Trails*. See also: Green, 'Africa and the Price Revolution'; Webb, 'The Horse and Slave Trade'.

32. For the boom associated with early modern globalisation, see the increasingly vast literature on the Great Divergence, indicatively: Broadberry and Hindle, 'Editor's Introduction'.

33. *Cf.* Ray, 'Asian Capital'.

34. On recent attention to friction and resistance, albeit within the more famil-

iar geographic spaces of global history: Drayton and Motadel, 'Futures of Global History', 9. On the layering of intensification of connections amidst disconnection in the Indian Ocean arena: Sivasundaram, 'Indian Ocean', 41–2.

35. Bayly, *Rulers, Townsmen and Bazaars*, especially 5–6, for an outline of these groups.

36. Alongside Bayly's work on inland areas of eastern India, Ashin Das Gupta's work on coastal areas of western India and Rajat K. Ray's work on the bazaar economy contributed to the larger but brief appearance of the merchant in the mainstream of Indian history in the 1980s: Markovits, *Indian Business*, 256–64.

37. The classic works on the domestic economy of early modern India are those associated with the 'Aligarh School' and its detractors, most characteristically: Habib, *Agrarian System of Mughal India*. A canonical work in Indian Ocean economic history remains: Chaudhuri, *Trade and Civilisation*. The revisionist views of the eighteenth century are discussed in chapter 4.

38. Notwithstanding what Bayly incorporated about Punjab in *Rulers, Townsmen and Bazaars*. See, for the weakness of the state in relation to merchants in Gujarat: Nadri, *Eighteenth-Century Gujarat*. Whatever the supposed strength of Ranjit Singh's state in Punjab, control over the westernmost territories remained relatively weak; see: Banga, *Agrarian System of the Sikhs*, 94, and also material in chapter 8 of this book.

39. Markovits *Indian Merchants*; idem, *Indian Business*, 187–92.

1. ENVIRONMENT

1. Parker, *Global Crisis*. Goldstone's *Revolution and Rebellion* was a prior attempt to synthesise the European with the Ottoman and Qing experience to challenge the Eurocentrism in the articulation of the General Crisis thesis.

2. Tezcan, *Second Ottoman Empire*; Struve, ed., *Ming–Qing Cataclysm*.

3. On the weakening of personal loyalties and imperial culture during the expansionist campaigns in the south: Richards, 'Imperial Crisis in the Deccan'. For the general consensus on the eighteenth century, which was once seen as an age of decline, see chapter 3 of this book and the references therein.

4. On rapid regime change in the years following Aurangzeb's death, and the power of the Sayyid brothers as 'king makers': Richards, *Mughal Empire*, 253–81.

5. Newman, *Safavid Iran*, chapter 7.

6. Levi, *Khoqand*.

7. Ibid., 4 and nn. 9–10. On the connection of the silver shortage with the weakening of the Ming, see, for example: Wakeman Jr., *Great Enterprise*, vol. I, 1–14.

8. Levi, *Khoqand*, 3.

9. Braudel, *Mediterranean World*. See, for a recent review of the Braudelian 'turn' and its aftermath in Indian Ocean scholarship: Sivasundaram, 'Indian Ocean'.

10. Sivasundaram, 'Indian Ocean'.

11. Rezakhani, 'Road That Never Was', 441.

12. On the former, see, for example: Alam and Subrahmanyam, *Indo-Persian Travels*. On Indo-Khorasan: Nejatie, 'Iranian Migrations'.

13. McNeill, 'Environmental History', 31.

14. Ibid., 32.

15. Singh, *Region and Empire*, 13–15.

16. Kessinger, *Vilyatpur*, 11.

17. On terminology: Kakar, *Government and Society*, xvi–xviii. See, for the history of the border agreements with British India and Russian Central Asia: Kakar, *Afghanistan 1863–1901*, chapters 10–11.

18. McChesney, *Waqf*, ix.

19. On the endeavour to avoid such slippages, and the problems that result from conceptual conflation: Nichols, 'Afghan Historiography', 2–4.

20. See, for a detailed discussion of these terms: Levi, *Indian Diaspora*, 8–12.

21. Monahan, *Merchants of Siberia*, especially 100–1, 271–2, and *passim*.

22. Bukhara features more prominently in the sources consulted when writing this book than, for example, Tashkent, a city that grew in importance with the expansion of Khokand, as revealed by Levi, *Khoqand*, 133–5.

23. Eden, 'Beyond the Bazaars', 936, for a statement of the difficulty of analysing Khiva's slave markets—due to the paucity of relevant sources—as illustrative of a wider problem.

24. Aslanian, 'Trade Diaspora', 288–98.

25. The Armenians, for example, came to the Sindhi port of Tatta in the later eighteenth century, but there is little mention of them in the hinterland: MSA–SILB, 1771, No. 25, Letter Nos 35, 69.

26. For the pattern and causes of the shifts in the Julfan Armenians' networks: Aslanian, *Armenian Merchants*, 44–52, 202–14. On the Armenian presence in Afghanistan: Hopkins, *Modern Afghanistan*, 118, 145; Kakar, *Government and Society*, 214. Levi states that the Armenians continued to use the overland route in the eighteenth century, although as a complement to their growing overseas activities: idem, 'Eighteenth-Century Transformation', 525.

27. This was true throughout the eighteenth as well as the nineteenth century. See, for example: Hanifi, *Connecting Histories*, 72; Nichols, *Settling the Frontier*, 197.

28. See, for a balanced evaluation of the effects of warfare in the eighteenth century: Bayly, *Rulers, Townsmen and Bazaars*, 68–73.

29. Coote and Morgan, eds, *Early Voyages*, vol. I, 88; Pallas, *Travels*, vol. II, 254–9; Gopal, ed., *Indians in Russia*; Dale, 'Indo-Russian Trade', 140–56; Dale, *Indian Merchants*, 56–60; Markovits, *Indian Merchants*, especially 37–39. Levi, *Indian Diaspora*.

30. Levi, 'Multanis and Shikarpuris', 35.

31. Ibid., 36–40.

32. Ibid., 47. Gujarati Khatris were also closely connected to weaving: Nadri, *Eighteenth-Century Gujarat*, 26.

33. Levi, 'Multanis and Shikarpuris', 47–49.

34. See, for a social history of the Multanis in Central Asia: Levi, *Indian Diaspora*, chapter 3; Dimitriyev, 'Indian Colony', 85–96.

35. Levi, *Indian Diaspora*, especially chapter 2, Markovits, *Indian Merchants*, 24; Markovits, *Indian Business*, 187–212, 234–35. See, also: Subrahmanyam, ed., *Merchant Networks*, xv, for a critical review of the literature applying the term diaspora. For a comparison of the Julfan Armenian, Multani, and Sephardi Jewish networks: Aslanian, *Armenian Merchants*, 1–22, 215–34.

36. Levi, 'Multanis and Shikarpuris', 54–5.

37. Ibid., 40–6.

38. Alam, 'Trade, State Policy and Regional Change', 214–15.

39. Davies, *Report on the Trade*, 4; Dale, *Indian Merchants*, 60–6.

40. On the history and use of these terms: Gommans, *Indo-Afghan Empire*, 9–10. See, for a discussion of the confusion concerning Lohanis as Afghan Muslims or Sindhis: Levi, 'Multanis and Shikarpuris', 41.

41. Gommans, *Indo-Afghan Empire*, 21.

42. Rose, ed., *Tribes and Castes [...] Vol. II. A.–K.*, 225; idem, *Tribes and Castes [...] Vol. III. L.–Z.*, 162, 233; Crooke, *Natives of Northern India*, 60. The nomenclature of 'confederation', 'tribe', and 'clan' follows: Tapper, 'Introduction', 9–10; Tapper notes that, within this tiered schema, sometimes multiple tiers exhibit the characteristics of a tribe—amongst the Ghilzai, for example—a confusion evident in the source material surveyed in this study. Note: tribe is not used to refer to non-state societies—for tribes formed the basis of states as much as they existed within states—but to those identities articulated in relation to rival or neighbouring groups, polities, and states. See, for the view of tribe as an 'ethnographic fiction', especially *vis-à-vis* their relationship to the state and statehood, and for an alternative approach and lexicon: Sneath, *Headless State*, especially 1–21.

43. Gommans, *Indo-Afghan Empire*, 21.

44. Hanifi, *Connecting Histories*, 60–8; Bayly, *Empire and Information*, 128–40. On Babur's encounter and engagement with the Lohanis: Dale, *Indian Merchants*, 62–3.

45. IOR/V/24/4167, ETP (1881–2), 9–11.

46. Noelle, *State and Tribe*, 282.

47. Rose, *Tribes and Castes [...] Vol. II. A.–K.*, 31, 225.

48. Hanifi, *Connecting Histories*, 67–72. See, for discussion of differences in the extent of hierarchical authority amongst the tribes of the dry and unirrigated lands from those of the fertile valley lands: Noelle, *State and Tribe*, 136.

49. NAI–F, Secret, 28.5.1858, Nos 8–11, 37–8.

50. Monahan, 'Siberian Trader', 222–9.

51. Noelle, *State and Tribe*, 63–4; Burton, 'Bukharan Trade', 3; Hutton, *Central Asia*, 269; Ferrier, *History of the Afghans*, 301, 320; Khanikoff, *Bokhara*, 71–2. For a rich reconstruction of Jewish life in nineteenth-century central Asia: Cooper, *Bukharan Jews*, 61–119.

52. Levi, 'Fergana Valley', 218; Burton, 'Bukharan Trade', 13, 15.

53. This sketch of the itinerary, routes, and passes is drawn from: Gommans, *Indo-Afghan Empire*, especially 21, 24, 80–1; Dale, *Indian Merchants*, 53; Markovits, *Indian Merchants*, 80. For a comparable scenario: Lydon, *Trans-Saharan Trails*, 220–2.

54. Dewey, *Steamboats on the Indus*, 216–21, describes the ferries and bridges of boats—and their respective economies—in the Sikh and early colonial eras.

55. Levi, 'Eighteenth-Century Transformation', 532–3.

56. On the fairs: Gommans, *Indo-Afghan*, 80–3. On the reinvestment in cloth: Hanifi, *Connecting Histories*, 53; Noelle, *State and Tribe*, 281–2.

57. Wink, *Al-Hind*, 13.

58. Dewey, *Steamboats on the Indus*, 17.

59. Ibid., 17.

60. Wink, *Al-Hind*, 15–16.

61. On the greater difficulty with navigability of the river over the eighteenth century: Hamilton, *New Account*, vol. I, 124. See, also, the testimony of the author of the *Khulasat-ut-Tawarikh* (c. 1695) in: Sarkar, *India of Aurangzib*, 71. On the resultant disconnection: Singh, *Region and Empire*, 229–30.

62. Moosvi, *People, Taxation, and Trade*, 93.

63. For a broader discussion: Lally, 'Introduction to the Third Edition', xxiv, n. 12.

64. Khazeni, 'Through an Ocean of Sand', 133–58.

65. Burton, 'Bukharan Trade', 12, 17–18, 41–2. Hanway, *Historical Account*, vol. I, 354; Pallas, *Travels*, vol. II, 223–4.

66. Dhamija and Jain, *Handwoven Fabrics of India*, 128.

67. Burton, 'Bukharan Trade', 41–2. The cost of living and wages were lower in India than Persia through to the nineteenth century: Stirling, *Journals*, 80–1.

68. Nomadic peoples often lived more comfortable lives than settled agriculturalists, however: Beckwith, *Empires of the Silk Road*, 76.

69. The landmark study was Digby's *War-Horse and Elephant*.

70. For example: Fazl, *Ain-i Akbari*, vol. I, 133, 215.

71. For the contrast with the diet and training in central Eurasia: Burnes, *Travels into Bokhara*, vol. II, 272; Ferrier, *Caravan Journeys*, 93–7.

72. Gommans, *Indo-Afghan Empire*, chapters 3 and 5.

73. Khazanov, *Nomads*.

74. Gommans, *Indian Frontier*, 31–4. See, also: Moorcroft, *Travels*, vol. I, 96–7.

75. Gommans, *Indian Frontier*, 34–9.

76. For parallels with Senegambia: Webb, 'Horse and Slave Trade', especially 221–2, 227–8.
77. Ali, 'Organisation of the Nobility', 232–3. On the sources of income from which *mansabdars* were to pay for the upkeep of horses: Trivedi, 'Share of Mansabdars', 411–21.
78. Irvine, *Army of the Indian Moghuls*, 61. Mughal-era changes were predicated on a shift slowly under way in regional kingdoms such as Marwar: Ziegler, 'Horses, Structural Change and Warfare', 194–201. On the strain placed on procuring and presenting the requisite number of horses as the *mansabdari* was transformed in the Aurangzeb era: Ali, 'Organisation of the Nobility', especially 236–8, 251.
79. Gordon, 'Symbolic and Structural Constraints', 159–63.
80. Ibid., 162–3.
81. Kolff, *Naukar, Rajput and Sepoy*, 71.
82. Gordon, 'Symbolic and Structural Constraints', 162–3. Generally, see: Gommans, *Mughal Warfare*, 204. On Jaipur and Kota: Desai, 'Timeless Symbols', 312; Sethia, *Rajput Polity*, 53–4; Singh, *State, Landlords and Peasants*, 144–7. On the Sikh kingdoms: Banga, *Agrarian System of the Sikhs*, 120–5.
83. Gordon, 'Symbolic and Structural Constraints', 170–1; Gommans, *Mughal Warfare*, 204; Gommans and Kolff, 'Introduction', 40–1, nn. 105–6.
84. Levi, 'Fergana Valley', 217–18.
85. On this historically long-standing divide between overland trade servicing demand in the north and overseas trade for the south: Digby, *War-Horse and Elephant*.
86. Gommans, 'Indian Warfare', 365–86.
87. Gordon, 'Symbolic and Structural Constraints', 172.
88. Ibid., 172–3.
89. On the centrality of cavalry to large and small retinues: Elphinstone, *Account*, 4; Alder, *Beyond Bokhara*, 110–11. On the Sikh system: Singh, *Military System of the Sikhs*, 38–65, 135–6; Grewal, *Sikhs of the Punjab*, 107. For evidence of the importance of horses to Sikh forces from Persian newsletters in Delhi: Grewal and Habib, eds, *Sikh History*, 187–203. Note that, as cash payments came to replace the distribution of *jagirs*, the incentives for the cavalry commanders to penalise troopers with inadequate mounts probably became stronger: Singh, *Army of Maharaja Ranjit Singh*, 29.
90. Yarwood, *Walers*, 24–7, 47–8.
91. See, also: Lally, 'H is for Horse'.
92. Ibid., 16, 28; Alder, *Beyond Bokhara*, 64, 102, 110–12.
93. *Press Lists of Old Records [...] Volume II*, 130; Gardner, *Memoirs*, 177; *cf.* Alder, *Beyond Bokhara*, 110–12.
94. Alder, *Beyond Bokhara*, 114, 122; NAI–M, 9.5.1808, No. 87. The Moorcroft mission was an intelligence-gathering expedition under the genuine guise of

the superintendent's search for better breeding stock; see: Bayly, *Empire and Information*, 107–40.

95. Alder, *Beyond Bokhara*, 314, 349, 352.

96. For breeding and breeders' attention to bloodlines and genealogy in England: Caton, 'Imperial Ambition'. See, also: Meadows, 'The Horse', 107–39.

97. Khan, *Travels in Central Asia*, 56, 58–9; Lal, *Travels*, 138; Fraser, *Marches of Hindustan*, 286; Gommans, *Indian Frontier*, 26; Levi, 'Fergana Valley', 219.

98. Khodarkovsky, *Where Two Worlds Met*, 28, 127, 153, 219. See, also: Monahan, *Merchants of Siberia*, 153, 186, 189, 192.

99. Khodarkovsky, *Where Two Worlds Met*, 28, 219.

100. Levi, 'Fergana Valley', 217–18.

101. Blanchard, *Russia's 'Age of Silver'*, 270. Levi notes that pastoral peoples were also displaced in Siberia and along the southern steppe as Russia expanded and erected its frontier fortresses: idem, *Khoqand*, 29.

102. On the transformation of tribute into trade from the mid eighteenth century: Golden, *History of the Turkic People*, 335; di Cosmo, 'Kirghiz Nomads', especially 355–6 and 366.

103. Levi, *Khoqand*, 63.

104. McNeill, 'Environmental History', 40.

105. Ferrier, *History of the Afghans*, 98–9, 312. See, also: Elphinstone, *Account*, 250, 297, 414.

106. Noelle, *State and Tribe*, 124, 165, 202, 268–9, 273–4, 276.

107. Elphinstone, *Account*, 142; Moorcroft, *Observations*, 274–5.

108. Khazeni, 'City of Balkh', 465–6; McChesney, *Waqf*, 218, 234.

109. Khazeni, 'City of Balkh', 469, 470–2.

110. See, for comparisons: Elphinstone, *Account*, 142, 297; Moorcroft, *Observations*, 274–5; NAI–F, Political A, February 1876, Nos 73–4, 2. *Cf.* Harlan, *Central Asia*, 31–2, 69.

111. Ferrier, *Caravan Journeys*, 95; NAI–F, Political, 6.3.1839, Nos 23–8, 60.

112. NAI–F, Secret, 2.8.1841, Nos 61–4; NAI–F, Secret, 22.6.1842, No. 3.

113. NAI–F, Political, 25.9.1837, Nos 87–96, 56. Trade remained small-scale thereafter, as evident from the numbers of horses reported in the import statistics in the *Punjab External Land Trade Reports* in the second half of the nineteenth century.

114. NAI–F, Political, 25.9.1837, Nos 87–96, 70–1; NAI–F, Secret, 28.5.1858, Nos 12–15, 28.

115. Yarwood, *Walers*, 49.

116. NAI–F, Foreign, 3.9.1852, No. 171, 4.

117. Metcalf, *Imperial Connections*.

118. NAI–F, Secret, 4.5.1842, Nos 4–7, 40; NAI–F, Secret, 26.10.1844, Nos 66–7; NAI–F, Foreign, 23.7.1858, Nos 14–16.

119. NAI–F, Foreign, 7.3.1845, Nos 99–100.

120. NAI–F, Political, 4.1.1845, Nos 67–8, 1–2.

121. NAI–F, Political, 4.1.1845, Nos 67–6, 1–5; NAI–F, Foreign, 26.1.1855, Nos 209–11, 5–6.

122. NAI–F, Political, 28.8.1837, Nos 25–6; NAI–F, Political, 1.11.1837, No. 10; NAI–F, Political, 27.12.1837, Nos 42–3; NAI–F, Political, 14.11.1838, Nos 49–50; NAI–F, Political, 25.9.1839, No. 140; NAI–F, General A, August 1866, Nos 26–9; NAI–F, General A, October 1866, Nos 20–5, 40, 70–2; NAI–F, General A, November 1866, Nos 2–3; NAI–F, General A, January 1867, Nos 8–9; NAI–F, General A, March 1867, Nos 3–10; NAI–F, Political A, March 1867, Nos 194–5; NAI–F, Political A, November 1867, Nos 136–7; NAI–F, Political A, February 1868, No. 198; NAI–F, Political A, March 1874, No. 33; NAI–F, Political A, September 1875, Nos 141–2; NAI–F, Political A, December 1875, Nos 76–8; NAI–F, A Political E, September 1883, Nos 106–22, 131–2; NAI–F, A Political E, January 1884, Nos 92–6. See, for the longer history of Ottoman prohibitions on exports of warhorse and weaponry: Reindl-Kiel, 'No Horses for the Enemy', 43–5.

123. Langley, *Narrative*, vol. I, 55–6.

124. See, for example: NAI–F, General A, March 1867, Nos 3–10; NAI–F, Political A, February 1876, Nos 73–4.

125. Yarwood, *Walers*, 16.

126. Ibid., 21.

127. Ibid., chapter 3.

128. NAI–F, Foreign, 8.6.1844, Nos 35–7; Yarwood, *Walers*, 15, 44.

129. Yarwood, *Walers*, 70–9.

130. For example: 'Punjab Characters Album', BL–IOSM, Add.Or.1357 and Add. Or.1396. Painters included Imam Bakhsh Lahori and Ghulam Ali Khan, the latter a notable painter of Afghans; one of his pictures of horse dealers, now in a private collection, is reproduced in: Dalrymple, *Return of a King*.

131. See, for instance, the album of pictures taken by Benjamin Simpson, an amateur photographer serving in the Indian Medical Service during the First Anglo-Afghan War. His pictures of Kandahar include a double full-length portrait of two Afghan horse dealers: National Army Museum, London, NAM.1951–01–43–29.

132. Roche, *Humeurs Vagabondes*.

133. Hamid and Khan, 'Introduction', 492.

134. On Afghanistan's place within the Indo-Persian world: Noelle-Karimi, 'Maps and Spaces', 142.

135. Nile Green's use of this term analogised the social life of religion to the market *vis-à-vis* its productive and consumptive aspects, and is used here thus with the additional sense that religious institutions became more deeply involved in the productive economy and the production of power thereby. Green, *Bombay Islam*.

136. Gross, 'Naqshbandiya Connection', 232–3.

137. Moin, *Millennial Sovereign*, 71, 97–100; Dale, 'Legacy of the Timurids', 184.

138. Levi, *Khoqand*, 112; Gross, 'Naqshbandiya Connection', especially 238–9.

139. Ibid., especially 245–6. On the efforts of the founder of the Khokand state to trace his lineage through Chamash Biy, a disciple of Lutfallah Chusti, a revered sixteenth-century Naqshbandi Sufi: Levi, *Khoqand*, chapter 5.

140. Ziad, 'Transporting Knowledge', 105 for citation. On the prior patronage of Sufism in Kabul: Dale and Payind, 'Ahrari *Waqf*'.

141. For a broader view of this Indo-Afghan spiritual world forged by mobile Afghans: Green, *Making Space*.

142. This is discussed in chapter 6, except that it needs to be highlighted here that the reverence of the Sufi, Shaykh Farid ad-Din, by the Sikhs was such that they incorporated his verses into their holy book, and that Sikh and Hindu reverence of the saint continues today. This is despite some conflict between Chishtis and Sikhs in the eighteenth and nineteenth centuries, as noted by: Ernst and Lawrence, *Sufi Martyrs*, 3, 108.

143. Green, 'Blessed Men', 326–7.

144. Gidwani and Sivaramakrishnan, 'Circular Migration'. I am grateful to Aeron O'Connor for directing me to this article.

145. Bayly, *Empire and Information*, 134.

146. There was no singular legal category of slaves as much as a continuum of bondage and multiple legal and social statuses across the Islamic and Indian Ocean arenas: Campbell, 'Servitude'. For a recent analysis of slavery in central Asia: Eden, 'Beyond the Bazaars'. For work focussing more closely on the world of Indo-central Asian caravan trade: Levi, 'Hindus Beyond the Hindu Kush'; Hopkins, 'Race, Sex and Slavery', 652–66; Newby, 'Bondage', 990–1. See, for the anxiety that British Indian subjects were being trafficked: PAL–P, 21.10.1854, Nos 32–4; PAL–P, 9.12.1854, Nos 1–2.

147. Blake, *Shahjahanabad*, 35–6, citations from 35.

2. EXCHANGES

1. See, for Ahmedpur, Bahawalpur, Multan, and Shikarpur: NAI-F, Political, 25.9.1837, Nos 87–96.

2. Compare, for example, with the bazaars of the Fergana valley: Nalivkin and Nalivkina, *Muslim Women*, 33–4.

3. Grover, 'Integrated Pattern', 229–30; NAI–F, Political, 25.9.1837, Nos 87–96, 45.

4. Grover, 'Integrated Pattern', 226.

5. The significance of these goods is expounded in the following chapters. For indicative evidence of their importance, see: Vigne, *Personal Narrative*, 68; Lal, *Travels*, 395.

6. Barak, *On Time*, citations on 5 and 7.

7. Riello and Roy, eds, *How India Clothed the World*, especially 1–27.

8. Naqvi, *Mughal Hindustan*, 155.

9. Riello and Roy, *How India Clothed the World*, 4.

10. See, for the Dutch and English share of trade, and the increase in production in Bengal: Prakash, *Dutch East India Company*, 234–47.

11. Parthasarathi, *Why Europe Grew Rich*, especially 89–182.

12. See, for example, the brief references to the Punjab industry in: Chaudhuri, *Trading World of Asia*, 240, 243–5. This citation is usually repeated in more recent work; for example: Riello, *Cotton*; Parthasarathi, *Why Europe Grew Rich*. See, also: Riello and Roy, *How India Clothed the World*; Riello and Parthasarathi, *Spinning World*, 22.

13. On the failure of the Company's efforts to sell Punjabi *bafta* in the Persian Gulf in 1644, the cloths considered unsuitable for Europe: Foster, ed., *India 1642–1645*, 204; idem, *India 1646–1650*, 13, 100.

14. Naqvi, *Mughal Hindustan*, 163–4.

15. Purchas, *Hakluytus Posthumus*, vol. IV, 272, for the observations of Richard Steele and John Crowther while travelling through Afghanistan in 1615. On the demand for Dacca muslin in Khokand: NAI–F, Secret, 24.11.1854, No. 19.

16. Naqvi, *Mughal Hindustan*; Bayly, 'Town Building'.

17. Foster, ed., *India 1637–1641*, 135–8; Moosvi, 'Economic Profile of the Punjab', 99; Naqvi, *Mughal Hindustan*, 18; Singh, *Region and Empire*, 173–90.

18. For Bornford's account: Foster, ed., *India 1637–1641*, 134, 136. See, also: Tavernier, *Travels*, vol. II, 5–7; Alam, 'Trade, State Policy and Regional Change', 205, 222. See, for the towns situated along the Delhi–Lahore road, according to the author of the *Chahar Gulshan* (*c*.1720): Sarkar, *India of Aurangzib*, xcviii–c.

19. Singh, *Region and Empire*, 180.

20. Garrett, trans., *Punjab*, 58.

21. See, for the decline and desertion of Lahore during 'the invasions of Ahmad Shah and the upsurge of the [Sikh] Khalsa' as well as the rejuvenation under Ranjit Singh after *c*.1800: Grewal and Banga, eds, *Early Nineteenth Century Punjab*, 115. See, also: Singh, *Region and Empire*, 230–1. For an alternative account, with revival from the end of the eighteenth century: Grewal and Sachdeva, 'Urbanisation in the Mughal Province of Lahore', 107–18.

22. Bayly, *Rulers, Townsmen and Bazaars*, 112.

23. Anon, 'Tour to Lahore', 433, 438–9.

24. Ibid., 429.

25. Thomas, *Military Memoirs*, 343.

26. For evidence of recovery: Sachdeva, *Polity and Economy*, 144.

27. Habib, *Atlas*, map OB.

28. Many pilgrimage centres served as trade towns, the two functions—commercial and spiritual—growing symbiotically as a result of road-building, marketing networks, footfall, and so forth; see, for comparable examples to Multan of Hindu and Muslim pilgrimage-cum-trade towns in eastern India and northern Afghanistan, respectively: Yang, *Bazaar India*; McChesney, *Waqf*.

29. Compare, for example, Multan's economy and trade with that of Lahore as described by John Griffiths (1794), reprinted in Singh, ed., *Early European Accounts*, 90, 93.

30. Sachdeva, *Polity and Economy*, 130; Moosvi, *Economy of the Mughal Empire*, 376. The under-used, uncatalogued, and almost inaccessible Persian records in the Punjab Archive and Library in Lahore present a potentially rich source of information, although even the provincial and local revenue records seldom say much about the nature and organisation of production, or about consumption; see, for a survey of precolonial revenue records and record-keeping in Punjab: Kessinger, *Vilyatpur*, 16–24.

31. An abridged translation of VOC document 2937 is published in: Floor, *Dutch East India Company*.

32. For example: Foster, ed., *India 1634–1636*, 126–33. The Dutchmen suggested that the English were engaged in ongoing private trade with Sindh, the Bombay governor sending two English agents ahead of the factory's establishment in 1758, trading in Coromandel chintzes, for example: Floor, *Dutch East India Company*, 72–4. They were perhaps referring to Company merchants who had left Bandar Abbas for Sindh, and from thence to Surat: MSA, Gombroon Factory Diary, 1756–57, No. 7/118, 25.2.1757, 275.

33. The establishment of rival Dutch operations are mentioned as early as 1769: MSA–SILB, 1769, No. 23, Letter No. 125.

34. MSA–SILB, 1760, No. 14, Letter No. 204

35. MSA–SILB, 1760, Letter No. 31. See, for Erskine's difficulties in collecting suitable samples: MSA–SILB, 1760, Letter Nos 60 and 154.

36. MSA–SILB, 1760, Letter Nos. 204 and 207. See, also: Floor, *Dutch East India Company*, 74–5; Hamilton, *New Account*, vol. I, 126–7.

37. MSA–SILB, 1760, No. 14, Letter No. 204.

38. MSA–SILB, 1760, No. 14, Letter No. 42; Floor, *Dutch East India Company*, 70.

39. See, for praise from the author of the *Khulasat-ut-Tawarikh* (*c.* 1695): Sarkar, *India of Aurangzib*, 72, 95–6. For demand in Rajasthan: Sethia, *Rajput Polity*, 297.

40. Chaudhuri, 'The Structure of Indian Textile Industry', 127–82.

41. Elphinstone, *Account*, 294. See, also: Thomas, *Military Memoirs*, 343–4.

42. NAI–F, Political, 25.9.1837, Nos 87–96, 45.

43. Ibid., 71, 82.

44. Thomas, *Military Memoirs*, 102; NAI–F, Secret, 16.4.1832, No. 9, 1161–2.

45. Khan, *Afghanistan and its Inhabitants*, 7–11.

46. Biddulph, *Tribes of the Hindoo Koosh*, 74. For details of periodic fairs, such as those held in Tashkurgan in the nineteenth century: Kakar, *Government and Society*, 203–4. For details of dress and types of textiles: Khan, *Afghanistan and its Inhabitants*, 69, 125, 249–50; Ferrier, *History of the Afghans*, 291; Rose, *Tribes and Castes [...] Vol. III. L.–Z.*, 178, 505. On the protective qualities of particular motifs: Baker, *Islamic Textiles*, 165; Sumner, 'Flowers of the Hearth', 27.

47. NAI–F, Political, 4.9.1847, Nos 26–30.

48. Garrett, *Punjab*, 12.

49. Although Harlow's 'swing to the east' thesis has been heavily criticised for ignoring the Atlantic world's continued importance to imperial concerns and configurations after *c.* 1750, the period did see greater exploration and expansion around the Indian and Pacific oceans: Hyam, 'British Imperial Expansion'; Bayly, 'First Age of Global Imperialism', 32; Marshall, *Britain, India and America*.

50. Chowdhury, *Commercial Agriculture in Bengal*.

51. Bayly, '"Archaic" and "Modern" Globalisation'.

52. See, most recently, for a fleeting mention of the import of Indian indigo (production site not specified) into central Asia and Russia (trade route and merchant network, ditto): Nadri, *Indigo in India*, 120–1.

53. A similar hierarchy of settlements and pattern of market activity was also evident in central Asia: Nalivkin and Nalivkina, *Muslim Women*, 34.

54. Grover, 'Integrated Pattern', 222–4. On the periodic fair at Turun Taran, Punjab, for example: Davies and Blyth, eds, *Report*, 68. See, also: Banga, *Agrarian System of the Sikhs*, 9.

55. Durrani, *History of Multan*, 98. From the outset, overland trade was extremely important to the state, as noted by: Griffiths, *Early European Accounts*, 89–90.

56. Banga, *Agrarian System of the Sikhs*, 168, 174–6, 180–3; Talbot, *Punjab and the Raj*, 16–17.

57. PAL–R, 8.9.1860, Nos 55–8, 5–7.

58. NAI–F, Political, 25.9.1837, Nos 87–96, 55–6.

59. Ibid., 2–3.

60. PAL–R, 8.9.1860, Nos 55–8, 5–6.

61. Morris, 'Appendix A.', 164.

62. Baden-Powell, *Hand-Book of the Economic Products*, 440; *Gazetteer Muzaffargarh District*, 105; Lal, *Travels*, 385, 392–3, 396–7, 404; NAI–F, Political, 1.8.1836, Nos 32–4; Ali, ed., *History of Bahawalpur*, x, xxiii; NAI–F, Political, 25.9.1837, Nos 87–96, 2–4.

63. Lal, *Travels*, 384–5, 413; NAI–F, Political, 25.9.1837, Nos 87–96, 2–3; *Gazetteer Muzaffargarh District*, 105; PAL–R, 8.9.1860, Nos 55–8, 5–6.

64. NAI–F, Secret F, June 1889, No. 142, 2.

65. NAI–F, Political, 25.9.1837, Nos 87–96, 55–6.

66. Rose, *Tribes and Castes [...] Vol. III. L.–Z.*, 33; Khanikoff, *Bokhara*, 88–91; Hutton, *Central Asia*, 229, 260, 289; Meakin, *Russian Turkestan*, 178; NAI–F, Secret, April 1882, Nos 132–5; Jews were also distinguished from other groups as indigo dyers in Fergana: Nalivkin and Nalivkina, *Muslim Women*, 32. See, also: Poujol, 'Bukharan Jews'.

67. Burnes, *Travels*, vol. II, 179; Khanikoff, *Bokhara*, 173–4. *Cf*. NAI–F, Secret, 25.11.1831, Nos 1–3; Pahlen, *Mission to Turkestan*, 27. See, for the advantages of dispersed production: Federico, *Silk Industry*, 14–15. See, for detailed insight into the productive cycle and organisation of central Asian sericulture, including marketing geographies and structures: Nalivkin and Nalivkina, *Muslim Women*, 107–9, and the introduction to this translated edition, which contextualises their life and work. See, for another, albeit largely second-hand, description of silkworm-rearing: Davies, *Report*, 14–15. Such was the importance of sericulture that a series of photographs documenting the process of thread production were included in the *Turkestanskii Al'bom*, which is discussed in chapters 4 and 7.

68. See, evidence from a later report of Bansi Lal and Ram Ratan, the octroi collectors of Amritsar: IOR V/24/4166, 'Note on the Trade Statistics of the Punjab for the Years 1871–72 and 1872–73', 5.

69. Ferrier, *Caravan Journeys*, 103, 124–5, 183; Lal, *Travels*, 107, 122, 272, 274, 277, 411; Burnes, *Travels*, vol. II, 227; Davies, *Report*, 25; Hutton, *Central Asia*, 337, 369.

70. McChesney, *Waqf*, 179, 200, 218.

71. This paragraph summarises (unless otherwise referenced) the information in: Maxwell-Lefroy and Ansorge, *Report*, vol. II, 65–6; *cf*. NAI–F, Secret, 27.9.1841, Nos 127–30, 42.

72. Baden-Powell, *Hand-Book of the Manufactures*, 57.

73. Cookson, *Monograph*, 5.

74. NAI–F, Political, 9.5.1836, No. 42, paragraph 23; *c.f.* NAI–F, Political, 25.9.1837, Nos 87–97, 10–11. See, also: Hopkins, *Modern Afghanistan*, 119–20.

75. Baden-Powell, *Hand-Book of the Manufactures*, 58.

76. For a description of the colours and costs of different dyed yarns: NAI–F, Secret, 27.9.1841, Nos 127–30, 41.

77. NAI–F, Secret, 27.9.1841, Nos 127–30, 41, 43–5.

78. Levi, *Indian Diaspora*, especially chapter 4.

79. Kashmiri silk output was almost entirely absorbed by the local weaving industry: Rizvi, *Trans-Himalayan Caravans*, 187. On the activity of the merchant networks in Iran: Levi, *Indian Diaspora*, 151; Dale, *Indian Merchants*, 66–75; Markovits, *Indian Merchants*, 99–104. For evidence of Persian silk in use in Kabul in the late 1830s: NAI–F, Political, 11.4.1838, No. 30, 17. And for Persian silk for sale in Shikarpur, albeit cheap and scarcely used: NAI–F,

Secret, 27.9.1841, Nos 127–30, 45. On Afghan production: NAI–F, Secret, 30.4.1858, No. 42, 2236–7. And in Sindh: Grover, 'Integrated Pattern', 235; Habib, *Atlas*, 16, and map 5B. Habib notes that Sindhi silk was deemed inferior by contemporaries.

80. MSA–SILB, 1762, No. 16, Letter No. 49, 116. On the activities of northwest Indians in Bombay *c.*1820: Anon, *Jan-e Bomba'i* (Calcutta, *c.*1820), referenced in Green, *Bombay Islam*, 10. On the trade via Rajasthan: Grover, 'Integrated Pattern', 229–30.

81. On the former: Floor, *Dutch East India Company*, 72–4.

82. Chaudhury, *From Prosperity to Decline*, 211, 233, 235–6; Bayly, *Empire and Information*, 136; Chaudhury, 'International Trade in Bengal Silk', 375.

83. Chaudhury, 'International Trade in Bengal Silk', 380.

84. Ibid., 382–3.

85. Ibid., 381.

86. Anon, 'Report on Raw-Silk', i–xxviii.

87. Davini, 'Bengali Raw Silk', 63. Bayly, however, has emphasised the growth of trade ties between the Gangetic valley and the Maratha states in the late eighteenth century: *Rulers, Townsmen and Bazaars*, 147.

88. Davini, 'Bengali Raw Silk', 63.

89. NAI–H, Public, 26.3.1788, No. 3, 2362–3.

90. Ibid., 2366–8. Bayly, *Rulers, Townsmen and Bazaars*, 378 (including n. 21), 411, 417–21, which highlights just how extensive was the existence of partnerships within family firms, and across kin, kith, and religion, as well as the reliance of Hindu traders on Muslims from the north-west in the trade of certain specialist commodities, such as shawls.

91. NAI–H, Public, 1787, Appendix VI.

92. Sen, *Empire of Free Trade*, 39–40, 119, 135–48.

93. NAI–H, Public, 1787, Appendix I.

94. Ibid., Appendix XI.

95. Bag, *Changing Fortunes*, 85–7; Chaudhury, *From Prosperity to Decline*, 246–7, 256–7.

96. See, for the Company's 'domination effect' until the Charter Act of 1813: Bhattacharya, 'Regional Economy—Eastern India', 287–8.

97. Davini, 'Bengali Raw Silk', 66; Davini notes that there was still some trade with Punjab, namely to the growing city of Amritsar, *c.* 1820, which is discussed in chapter 8.

98. Sen, *Empire of Free Trade*, chapter 2.

99. Washbrook, 'Comparative Sociology to Global History', 437.

100. Davini, 'Bengali Raw Silk', 64.

101. Ibid., 64.

102. Bag, *Changing Fortunes*, 243–4.

103. Davini, 'Bengali Raw Silk', 70; Ray, 'Silk Industry in Bengal', 353–4, 360.

104. For example: NAI–F, Political, 5.9.1836, Nos 9–21, 94–5.

105. For a brief history of Bombay *vis-à-vis* Surat, *c.* 1750–1850, and Bombay's rise to parity with Calcutta, *c.* 1830–60: Markovits, *Indian Business*, 129–30.

106. The data for Figs 2.2 and 2.3 are compiled from: BCP, IOR/P/419/39 [1801-1802] to IOR/P/419/90 [1848-1849].

107. IOR/P/419/51.

108. Ray, 'Silk Industry in Bengal', 350.

109. Appendix I, Table 1.

110. Appendix I, Tables 1–2.

111. BCP, IOR/P/419/48 [1811–12].

112. Nadri, *Eighteenth-Century Gujarat*, 24. In preceding decades, some silk cloth, rather than raw silk, regularly reached as far inland as Jaipur from Gujarat: Gupta, *Agrarian System of Eastern Rajasthan*, 111. Note that the external or overseas trade returns show a similar picture as the import trade.

113. BCP, IOR/P/419/46 [1809–10], for the collapse of these returns when war broke out in Kutch, reflecting its greater importance.

114. Carless, 'Memoir', 202; Hart, 'Report', 218.

115. NAI–F, Political, 25.9.1837, Nos 87–96, 18–22.

116. Ibid., 18–22; *c.f.* NAI–F, Secret, 27.9.1841, Nos 127–130, 41.

117. The sources concerning silk imports before this time tend to conflate silk cloth with silk yarns, and so silk was said to flow in both directions between Bengal and Bukhara through Punjab; see: Dale, *Indian Merchants*.

118. For the Orientalist gaze: Arnold, *Tropics and the Traveling Gaze*. Of course, these representations were also produced by other Europeans and Americans, and some feelings were more ambivalent, especially non-colonial ones; see, for example: Huang, 'Deodorizing China', especially 1093–4.

119. The Russian ethnographers Nalivkin and Nalivkina studied life in Fergana and described the local bazaar as a 'huge anatomy theatre', as a space containing all local 'life drama' unrivalled even by the theatre, and as a 'human opera'. Their *Sketch of the Everyday Life of Women of the Sedentary Native Population of the Fergana Valley* was originally published in Kazan by The Printing House of the Imperial University in 1886, and has been translated and published as *Muslim Women*, with these descriptions of the bazaar on pp. 112–3.

120. For a description of the changing nature of fruit cultivation (plots and orchards) from the countryside onto the approach of a city: Nalivkin and Nalivkina, *Muslim Women*, 32. Irfan Habib mapped sites of fruit production in north Afghanistan and around Lahore in the Mughal eras: *Atlas*, Maps 1A–B and 4B.

121. Sen, *Empire of Free Trade*, 82–6.

122. Baden-Powell, *Hand-Book of the Economic Products*, 69–74

123. Khazeni, *Sky Blue Stone*, 41–2. See, also: Hofmeester, 'Diamonds as Global Luxury Commodity'.

124. On the mechanics of moneylending and the collection of debts in the late-nineteenth-century Fergana valley: Nalivkin and Nalivkina, *Muslim Women*, 55–6.

125. Ibid., 53.

126. NAI–F, Political, 25.9.1837, Nos 87–96, 57; NAI–F, Secret, 5.9.1836, No. 9.

127. Elphinstone, *Account*, 294; NAI–F, Political, 25.9.1837, Nos 87–96, 57.

128. See, for the example of Uzbek elites' specialist demands: Alam, 'Trade, State Policy and Regional Change', 205–6; Levi, 'Eighteenth-Century Transformation', 531

129. Sood, *India and the Islamic Heartlands*, 97.

130. Rublack, 'Material Invention', 37.

131. Bayly, *Rulers, Townsmen and Bazaars*, here, 462 and 371, respectively.

3. POWER

1. See, for a fuller overview and interrogation of the 'tribal breakout' thesis: Lally, 'Beyond "Tribal Breakout"'.

2. *Panjab Notes & Queries. A Monthly Periodical*, 3, 34 (1886), 177; *Panjab Notes and Queries, A Monthly Periodical*, 1, 1 (1884), 6.

3. For a survey, see: Marshall, ed., *Indian History*. For an overview of comparable moves made in Ottoman historiography: Rizk Khoury, 'The Ottoman Centre versus Provincial Power-Holders'.

4. Alam, *Crisis of Empire*; Marshall, *Indian History*, 13–19.

5. See, for instance: Roseberry, *Imperial Rule in Punjab*, especially chapter 1.

6. On the nature of corporatist and associated collective—rather than individual—identities in the world of trade in this period: Sood, *India and the Islamic Heartlands*, 150, 248–50.

7. Eaton, 'Temple Desecration', citations from 255–6. See, also: Thapar, *Somnatha*.

8. For a survey: Ruff, *Violence in Early Modern Europe*.

9. This and the following paragraph draw on Thomson, *Mercenaries, Pirates, and Sovereigns*, here specifically, 1. This analysis has been criticised for taking the Weberian state model as an accurate reality—a point of departure from which to explain how states succeeded in monopolising violence to produce a world of Weberisn states—and, in turn, for producing a Eurocentric understanding of the historical territorialisation of violence: Barkawi, 'States and Armed Force'. In broad outlines, however, the picture of the pre-modern marketisation of violence and its steady territorialisation and de-marketisation accords with the processes discussed in this chapter and chapter 7.

10. The English East India Company is a pertinent example, its use of violence sanctioned by the state via its charter of operation: Stern, *Company-State*.

11. Tagliacozzo, 'Violent Undertowns'.

12. Colás and Mabee, *Mercenaries, Pirates, Bandits and Empires*.

13. Nadri, *Eighteenth-Century Gujarat*; Hasan, *State and Locality*; Yaycioglu, *Partners of the Empire*; Khoury, 'The Ottoman Centre versus Provincial Power-Holders'. See, also: Tezcan, *Second Ottoman Empire*.

14. Yaycioglu, *Partners*; Faruqui, *Princes*. This shift is part of a wider examination of horizontal bonds between various powerholders and (corporate) groups beyond the vertical or patrimonial bonds from the emperor or the centre to particular individuals that has preoccupied scholars: Mikhail, *Nature and Empire*, 23–5.

15. Kolff, *Naukar, Rajput and Sepoy*.

16. Gommans, *Mughal Warfare*, especially chapter 3.

17. Gommans, 'Embarrassment of Political Violence'; Elias, *Civilizing Process*.

18. Carroll, *Blood and Violence*, here, 330.

19. For a more concerted critique of a wide range of ideas shaping the narratives of human history as a linear progression from violence to the relative peace prevailing in our own times, see: Carroll, 'Thinking with Violence', including 30–1, for the problems of validating Elias' thesis. On the persistence of bloodfeud and vendetta in the face of ritualised peacemaking efforts: Cummins, *Governing Hatred*.

20. Note: this conceptualisation differs from that of 'an endless round of provocations and retaliations, or affronts and private, violent justice' where this '"economy" could be a matter of individual quarrels or of massive, collective uprisings', as defined by Greenshields, *Economy of Violence*, 1–2. For a similar conceptualisation, see: Robinson, *Bandits*.

21. Robinson, *Bandits*, 5, 163.

22. Richards, *Mughal Empire*, 86–7. For a comparison with disarmament and the danger of violent quarrelling in Venice: Laven, 'Banditry and Lawlessness'.

23. The Ottoman's reactive engagement with Portuguese sovereignty in, and their expansion within, the Indian Ocean world was the most direct but nevertheless short-lived: Casale, *Ottoman Age of Exploration*.

24. Although treatises and texts outlined princely duty, power and justice were subjects for kingly contemplation, some monarchs taking these issues especially seriously. Alam, *Languages of Political Islam*, especially chapter 2.

25. Dale, 'Empires and Emporia'; Sen, *Empire of Free Trade*.

26. For an example of a petition brought before the East India Company's government: NAI–H, Public, 26.3.1788, No. 3, 2362–3.

27. On the early modern world of passes and sovereignty: Benton and Clulow, 'Empires and Protection'.

28. Alam, 'Trade, State Policy and Regional Change', 221–2; Burton, *The Bukharans*, 444–7; Burton, 'Bukharan Trade', 3–4.

29. Burton, *The Bukharans*, 444.

30. See, for trade and theft in the caravanserais: ibid., 444.

31. On Iran, see: Good, 'In the Service of the Shah', 151–3.

32. For evidence of the precarity of the early-nineteenth-century Punjab–Rajasthan trade in the face of increasing insurance costs: Sharma, 'Ports of Gujarat', 204.

33. See, for evidence from Iran during the period of the first tribal breakout: Good, 'In the Service of the Shah', 152.

34. PSA–F, April 1872, No. 4, 204; Gommans, *Indo-Afghan Empire*, 24.

35. Naqvi, *Mughal Hindustan*, 231.

36. PSA–F, April 1872, No. 4, 204. See, also: Bhattacharya, 'Predicaments of Mobility', 182–3.

37. Rose, *Tribes and Castes [...] Vol. III. L.–Z.*, 392; Mackenzie, *Six Years in India*, 270.

38. *Press Lists of Old Records [...]. Volume VI*, 391.

39. Hunt, '1689 Mughal Siege', 157 and n. 34.

40. Murphy, *Materiality of the Past*, 22, 40–55.

41. Lafont, *Indika*, 358.

42. On the threats to postal runners, for example, and the role of various parties in producing fears regarding long-distance cross-country movement, see: Joshi, 'Dak Roads, Dak Runners'.

43. Wagner, *Thuggee*, especially chapter 7 for the Thugs' organisation and their modus operandi, which varied widely and was not restricted to picking off those travelling with the caravans.

44. Ibid., 111–14.

45. Hobsbawm, *Bandits*; idem, *Primitive Rebels*. See, for examples of this critical scholarship from across the early modern world (in addition to that discussed elsewhere in this chapter): Danker, 'Bandits and the State'; Moss, 'Bandits and Boundaries in Sardinia'.

46. Cummins, 'Enmity and Peace-Making', 169, notes that alliances with aristocrats were sometimes part of the latter's challenge to royal authority, indicative of the deep integration of violence within the drama of state power. See, also: Barkey, *Bandits*.

47. A sometime early-eighteenth-century toddy-tapper turned plunderer and state-builder is an exception, studied by: Eaton, *Eight Indian Lives*, chapter 7; Richards and Rao, 'Banditry in Mughal India'.

48. Such views are traceable to Elphinstone, but, for its expression by the premier ethnographer of late-nineteenth-century Punjab, Denzil Ibbetson, see his: *Panjab Castes*, especially 58. I am grateful to my student, James Price, for this reference. For the analysis of ideas of racial difference on the Frontier, and the Pathan as a 'noble savage' or 'martial race': Metcalf, *Ideologies of the Raj*, 145–8.

49. Richards, *Mughal Empire*, 246.

50. Green, 'Tribe, Diaspora, and Sainthood', 173.

51. Gommans, *Indo-Afghan*, 111.

52. Marino, 'Wheat and Wool', 885.

53. On the Yusufzais' migration to this 'frontier' and their fraught relationship with the Mughal Empire: Nichols, *Settling the Frontier*, 1–15.

54. Ibid., 40–1.

55. Richards, *Mughal Empire*, 170–1. On the significance of agriculturalists' sense of *relative* deprivation as a motivation for rebellion in the nineteenth century: Stokes, *The Peasant Armed*.

56. Blok, 'Peasant and the Brigand', 496.

57. Cummins, 'Enmity and Peace-Making', chapter 4.

58. Vartavarian, 'Pacification and Patronage', 1757. For a comparison with the career of Papadu, who wished to fashion for himself the life of the landed gentry, as a zamindar or raja, rather than a brigand or a revolutionary leader: Eaton, *Eight Indian Lives*, 164–5.

59. Blake, 'Patrimonial-Bureaucratic Empire'; Gommans, *Frontier*, chapter 4.

60. On the bleeding between the military campaign and sport, reality and visual culture, see: Lally, 'Empires and Equines'.

61. Gommans, *Indo-Afghan*, 17; Gommans, *Indian Frontier*, 111.

62. Richards, *Mughal Empire*, 92, 145–6. Sikh recruitment of Pashtuns continued well into the nineteenth century: Nichols, *Settling the Frontier*, 277.

63. Lal, *Memoirs of the Puthan Soldier*; Gommans, *Indo-Afghan*, chapter 4.

64. Noelle-Karimi, 'Abdali Afghans'.

65. Gommans, *Indo-Afghan*, 35.

66. See, for estimates: Gommans, *Frontier*, 167–8. Cf. Matthee, *et al.*, *Monetary History of Iran*, 158.

67. Some, including the nominally Mughal political elite in Punjab, and the Afghan state-builders in service of the Mughals, were less resolute; see: Lally, 'Beyond "Tribal Breakout"'.

68. Rose, *Tribes and Castes [...] Vol. III. L.–Z.*, 101; Gommans, *Indo-Afghan*, 109. See, for settlement of Pashtuns around Jullundar: Green, 'Tribe, Diaspora, and Sainthood', 191–2.

69. Rose, *Tribes and Castes [...] Vol. III. I.–Z.*, 101.

70. Evidence cited by Markovits states that Afghan Pashtuns also owned property in the Emirate of Bukhara in the late nineteenth century, perhaps belonging to traders, or else to exiled Afghan elites: Markovits, *Indian Merchants*, 90.

71. Chatterjee 'Collaboration and Conflict'; Yaycioglu, *Partners of the Empire*, 80–4, 95–7. Prince Murad Bakhsh (d. 1661) was advanced a loan by the Gujarati Jain merchant Shantidas during the war of succession, which was repaid by Aurangzeb following the former's execution: Truschke, *Aurangzeb*, 34. The role of bankers before the eighteenth century, however, has been the subject of vigorous debate; see: Leonard, 'The "Great Firm" Theory'; Richards, 'Mughal State Finance'.

72. *Cf.* Blake, *Shahjahanabad*, 110–12, for the habits and lifestyles of (Punjabi) Khatri merchants and their status within and relationship to the Mughal court in the imperial centre.

73. MSA, 'Scindy Diary. Commercing 1st of August 1762 & ending 31st of July 1763', entries for 25.11.1762 and 31.5.1763. Hughes, *Gazetteer*, 86–9, including a brief description of the small minority of Sikh traders.

74. Levi, *Indian Diaspora*, 163; Moorcroft, *Travels*, vol. II, 413–44.

75. Rose, *Tribes and Castes [...] Vol. III. L.–Z.*, 126–7.

76. Levi, *Indian Diaspora*, 143–4, 149–50.

77. Levi, 'Multanis and Shikarpuris'.

78. Levi, *Indian Diaspora*, 211–20.

79. Masson, *Narrative*, vol. I, 353–5.

80. For debate over the most appropriate descriptor of the organisation and operation of these businesses: Levi, *Indian Diaspora*, especially chapter 2; Markovits, *Indian Merchants*, 24; Markovits, *Indian Business*, 234–5. See, also: Subrahmanyam, ed., *Merchant Networks*, xv; Aslanian, *Armenian Merchants*, 1–22, for a critical review of the literature applying the term diaspora, and 215–34 for a comparison of the Julfan Armenian, Multani, and Sephardi Jewish networks.

81. Subrahmanyam and Bayly, 'Portfolio Capitalists', 413–23.

82. In fact, the Punjab governors' recalcitrance in remitting revenues to the centre had undermined Mughal operations on the frontier earlier in the century, paving the way for the growth of Afghan power: Alam, *Crisis of Empire*, 292–6.

83. Noelle-Karimi, 'Afghan Polities'.

84. Bayly, *Rulers, Townsmen and Bazaars*, especially chapter 1.

85. Gommans, *Indo-Afghan*, 28–9.

86. On the debilitating shortage of copper coin even in the wake of the Nadirid raids: Matthee *et al.*, *Iran*, 160.

87. Ibid., 172, n. 112.

88. MSA–SILB, 1761, No. 15, Letter No. 139; MSA–SILB, 1763, No. 17, Letter No. 201; MSA–SILB, 1765, No. 19, Letter No. 175; MSA–SILB, 1766, No. 20, Letter No. 2; MSA–SILB, 1767, No. 21, Letter Nos 108, 148; MSA–SILB, 1768, No. 22, Letter No. 25; MSA–SILB, 1769, No. 23, Letter No. 92; MSA–SILB, 1770, No. 24, Letter No. 179; MSA–SILB, 1771, No. 25, Letter No. 35. Note: The Company factors simply use the designation 'chuppar', which is understood here as 'agent'. Irvine defines 'chapars' as Ahmad Shah's 'Quick-riding horsemen' (*chupar* from the Turkish *capmak*, 'to gallop') in the context of the transmission of edicts to Rohilkhand and Farrukhabad following Ahmad Shah's arrival in Shahjahanabad; Irvine, 'Ahmad Shah', 13. But these horsemen were treated 'with all due ceremony', suggesting that, therefore, they were more than mere messengers and were, in fact, the personal agents of Ahmad Shah.

89. MSA, 'Scindy Diary. [...] 1764', entries for 10.12.1763, 15.12.1763, and 11.3.1764.

90. MSA, 'Scindy Diary. [...] 1763', entries for 31.8.1762.

91. MSA–SILB, 1771, No. 25, Letter No. 35; MSA–SILB, 1772, No. 26, Letter No. 254.

92. On the revisionism of such view of the Mughals: Faruqui, *Princes of the Mughal Empire*, especially chapter 3. On the investment in maritime trade by the immediate Mughal household: Findly, 'Mughal Women and European Traders'. The Mughal elite in Bengal, beyond the imperial household but at all levels of officialdom, participated in maritime trade: Prakash, 'Indian Maritime Merchant', 451. In contrast, the blurry boundary between private fortunes and fortunes amassed by virtue of position and status attached to imperial appointments was more actively contested by the Ottoman centre in the long eighteenth century, when the centre sought to alienate property and wealth from officeholders as it attempted to bridge its fiscal deficits, making private fortunes no less important but more precarious than in the Mughal Empire; see: Yaycioglu, *Power, Wealth and Death*.

93. Noelle, *State and Tribe*, 286; Wide, 'Astrakhan, Borqa', Chadari, Dreshi', 166.

94. MSA, 'Scindy Diary. [...] 1763', entry for 31.4.1763. The Durranis (and their successors) also continued the Mughal practice of confirming the *jagir* of the boatmen who maintained mobility along the Indus: Dewey, *Steamboats on the Indus*, 184.

95. This development was evident elsewhere, including Rajasthan and Company Bengal: Bayly, *Rulers, Townsmen and Bazaars*, 88; Sethia, *Rajput Polity*, 237–8; Singh, *State, Landlords and Peasants*, 65.

96. Lockyer, *Account*, 246, 249, 263. *Cf.* Hanway, *Historical Account*, vol. I, 354, vol. II, 20–3.

97. Singh, *Accounts*, 93; Morris, 'Appendix A.', 165.

98. Pallas, *Travels*, vol. II, 228; Masson, *Narrative*, vol. I, 390; NAI–F, Political, 14.12.1835, Nos 64–5, 8.

99. Morrison, *Russian Rule in Samarkand*, 201–3; Carrère d'Encausse, *Islam and the Russian Empire*, 8.

100. For a summary, see: Radkau, *Nature and Power*, p. 91.

101. Burnes, *Travels*, vol. II, 179; Khanikoff, *Bokhara*, 41–2. Khanikoff also offers detailed descriptions of Bukhara's fruits, vegetables and cotton crops.

102. Pahlen, *Mission to Turkestan*, 27, 87–90; Hutton, *Central Asia*, 264. This is also true of the Balkh region; see, for a detailed description of its hydrology and productive capability: McChesney, *Waqf*, 21–6.

103. PAL–R, 1.12.1860, No. 23, 7; Morris, 'Appendix A.', 161.

104. NAI–F, Political, 25.9.1837, Nos 87–96, 4; NAI–F, Secret, 27.9.1841, Nos 127–30, 50; Morris, 'Appendix A.', 161–2.

105. PAL–R, 8.9.1860, Nos 55–8, 4–5; Morris, 'Appendix A.', 164.

106. Morris, 'Appendix A.', 163.

107. Khanikoff, *Bokhara*, 41–2; Morrison, *Russian Rule in Samarkand*, 202.

108. For irrigation, see: Levi, 'Fergana Valley', 226; Morrison, *Russian Rule in Samarkand*, 12–13, 202.

109. Morrison, *Russian Rule in Samarkand*, 92–3; McChesney, *Waqf*, 146, 179, 184–5.

110. Levi, *Khoqand*, 75, 111.

111. Singh, *Ahmad Shah*, 353–6.

112. Durrani, *Multan*, 96, 116.

113. Nichols, *Settling the Frontier*, 56.

114. On Mughal irrigation infrastructure in the Peshawar valley: ibid., 50—and 90 for a flavour of Pashtun–Sikh hostility in the region from the late eighteenth to early nineteenth century.

115. Morris, 'Appendix A.', 165.

116. Ibid.; idem, 'Appendix B.', 167, 170–1.

117. PAL–R, 1.12.1860, No. 23, 7.

118. *Gazetteer Mooltan District: 1883–4*, 98. See, for indications of yields from the Deputy Commissioners of Ludhiana (17 *seers*/acre), Jalandhar (16 *seers*/acre) and Ambala (16 *seers*/acre), Dera Ghazi Khan (12 *seers*/acre): Baden-Powell, *Hand-Book of the Economic Products*, 441–2. See, for the results of 58 experiments in Multan (5 to 24 *seers*/acre, averaging 13–14 *seers*/acre): *Gaz. Mooltan District: 1883–4*, 97–8. See, for charges: Morris, 'Appendix A.', 164. *Cf.* PAL–R, 8.9.1860, Nos 55–8, 6–7.

119. *Gazetteer Mooltan District: 1883–4*, 123–4; *cf.* Banga, *Agrarian System of the Sikhs*, 90–1.

120. *General Report upon the Administration of Punjab Proper* (Lahore, 1854) quoted in: Banga, *Agrarian System of the Sikhs*, 94. Later, and in keeping with the Sikh precedent, Morris offered a further seven points in explanation of the light assessment proposed for the Multan District: Morris, *Report*, 3.

121. Banga, *Agrarian System of the Sikhs*, 110; Khilnani, *British Power in the Punjab*, 109–10.

122. Singh, ed., *Early European Accounts*, 62; *Gazetteer Mooltan District: 1883–4*, 124; Roseberry, *Imperial Rule in Punjab*, 15; Banga, *Agrarian System of the Sikhs*, 107–9.

123. Grewal, *Sikhs of the Punjab*, 110.

124. Morris, 'Appendix A.', 165; Roseberry, *Imperial Rule in Punjab*, 17.

125. Morris, 'Appendix A.', 165. See, for the *kardars'* responsibilities: Sachdeva, *Polity and Economy*, 70–1.

126. Morris, 'Appendix A.', 165; Morrison, *Russian Rule in Samarkand*, 240; Banga, *Agrarian System of the Sikhs*, 94.

127. Morris, 'Appendix B.', 171 2.

128. Ibid.; *Gazetteer Mooltan District: 1883–4*, 139; *Gazetteer Muzaffargarh District*, 129–31.

129. *Gazetteer Muzaffargarh District*, 129.
130. On the historical process by which the Khalsa acquired hegemony within the Sikh faith, see: Dhavan, *When Sparrows Became Hawks*.
131. Ibid., 75–6, 80–1; Malhotra, *Sikh History*, 39–40, 179. Such ideas represent a hardening of differences when compared to the *Zafarnama* (epistle of victory) addressed by the tenth Sikh guru, Gobind, to the Mughal emperor, entreating for peaceful relations and asserting that the call to arms was a last resort in the face of immoral oppression, for example. See: Malhotra, *Sikh History*, 24–5; Fenech, *Sikh Zafar-Namah*.
132. See, for a differing interpretation—albeit based on religious texts at the expense of political records: Malhotra, *Sikh History*.
133. Dhavan, *When Sparrows Become Hawks*, 99–100. See, also, for other Sikh chiefs' alliances with the Marathas against other Sikh rulers: Malhotra, *Sikh History*, 49–50.
134. Malhotra, *Sikh History*, 44. Note: the massacre also receives little analytical attention in Malhotra's volume. For a biography of Tahmas Khan: Singh, *Ahmad Shah*, 418–19.
135. Singh, *Ahmad Shah*, 280.
136. Ibid., 282.
137. Eaton, 'Temple Desecration'.
138. For the view that communal violence was a product of the modern period, see: Bayly, 'The Pre-History of "Communalism"'. For a view that traces communalism into the precolonial period, see: Kruijtzer, *Xenophobia*.

4. TRADERS

1. Tagore, *Short Stories*, 115.
2. These afterlives are discussed in the conclusion to this book.
3. Chaudhuri, *Trade and Civilisation*, especially chapters 1–2; Prakash, *European Commercial Enterprise*, chapters 1–2.
4. In Indian Ocean history as a whole, Indian and Chinese mercantile groups receive most attention. Ray, 'Asian Capital'; Tagliocozzo, 'Indian Ocean in Flux'. *Cf.* Aslanian, *Armenian Merchants*.
5. Tagliacozzo, 'Indian Ocean in Flux', explicitly 90–1.
6. Kapila, 'Race Matters'. For the deep roots of this process in the seventeenth-century Mughal Empire—namely, the integration of mercantile groups in what was increasingly seen as the business of imperial management—see: Subrahmanyam, ed., *Merchant Networks*, pp. xx–xxi. The argument, here, is about how contemporaries identified and reified 'commercial castes'. A distinct development—but one that has solidified the focus on Khatris and Banias, Marwaris and Parsis—has been their retroactive elevation through historiographical production by business historians who, working since the early twentieth century,

were keen to test the relation of caste (unique to India) to the peculiarity of India's development. For a recent summary and concise critique, see: Roy, *Business History*, 3–9.

7. See, for instance: Nalivkin and Nalivkina, *Muslim Women*, 55.

8. Sood, *India and the Islamic Heartlands*, 155.

9. MSA–SILB, 1762, No. 16, Letter No. 92.

10. Lal, *Travels*, 142; NAI–F, Foreign, 23.10.1847, Nos 44–5.

11. NAI–F, Political, 5.9.1836, Nos 9–21, 85; NAI–F, Political, 25.9.1837, Nos 87–96, 83; NAI–F, Secret, 28.5.1858, Nos 8–11, 38–40; Masson, *Narrative*, vol. II, 107–8. *Cf.* Steinbach, *Punjaub*, 89–90.

12. Nichols, *Pashtun Migration*, 38–58; Hussain, 'Jagirdari in the Eighteenth Century', 119–28; Gommans, *Indo-Afghan Empire*, chapters 4–5. See, for mention of moneylending by the Afghan gentry: Bayly, *Rulers, Townsmen and Bazaars*, 31, n. 98.

13. Nichols, *Pashtun Migration*, 68–71; Faruqui, 'At Empire's End', 20–36; Gommans, 'Afghāns in India'.

14. Dale, *Indian Merchants*, 56–66. Scott Levi follows Dale in drawing such a distinction: Levi, *Indian Diaspora*, especially 1–2, 104–5.

15. Markovits, *Indian Merchants*, 177–8, 261.

16. See, for example: Markovits, *Indian Business*, 191, 210–12.

17. Gopal, 'Indians in Central Asia', 8–9.

18. Markovits, *Indian Merchants*, 57, 250–1.

19. Kolff, *Naukar, Rajput and Sepoy*, 57–8.

20. Hanifi, *Connecting Histories*, 10.

21. Ibbetson, *Panjab Castes*, 253. See, for brief details of Rawalpindi's indigo and textile imports from western Punjab entrepôts: *Rawalpindi District, with Maps: 1907*. The Khojahs of Nowshera and Peshawar were involved in the textile trade after the 1860s, but this took them towards Delhi rather than Bukhara: Bhattacharya, 'Predicaments of Mobility', 172.

22. Ibbetson, *Panjab Castes*, 253.

23. Hanifi, *Connecting Histories*, 153.

24. Metcalf, *Ideologies of the Raj*, 145–8.

25. Tagore, *Short Stories*, 115. Chapter 8 returns to the 'martial races'.

26. Bayly, *Caste, Society and Politics*, 199, 234. See, also: Washbrook, 'Economic Depression'.

27. MSA–SILB, 1760, No. 14, Letter No. 60, 89; MSA–SILB, 1761, No. 15, Letter No. 91, 190.

28. MSA–SILB, 1762, No. 16, Letter No. 49, 116.

29. NAI–F, Foreign, 30.4.1852, Nos 40–5, 4–5.

30. See, for example: Pallas, *Travels*, vol. II, 254–9. Pallas even sketched one of the Hindu shrines in Astrakhan. In Afghanistan, too, despite the freedom to trade, Hindus suffered restrictions and prescriptions on their dress, making

them more visible; see: Rattray, *Costumes of the Various Tribes*, plate 9 and accompanying text.

31. Newby, *The Empire and the Khanate*, 130.

32. Brower, 'Islam and Ethnicity', 128–9. 'Sart' was often used interchangeably with other terms, although usage changed considerably, variously referring to settled people and town dwellers or Persian speakers before the colonial conquest, and the Tajiks or even the peoples of central Asia as a whole during the period of Russian rule; see, for further discussion: Morrison, *Russian Rule in Samarkand*, 44–6.

33. Compare, for example, with the turbans worn by the men painted by Vigne, discussed in the next chapter.

34. See, for their rebuttal of the peddler thesis, and their studies of Indian merchants: Nadri, *Eighteenth-Century Gujarat*, 53–76; Markovits, *Indian Merchants*; Ray, 'Asian Capital'. See, for broader study of 'Asian' commercial diasporas: Dobbin, *Asian Entrepreneurial Minorities*; Dale, *Indian Merchants*, especially 137–8.

35. NAI–F, Political, 10.8.1835, No. 29.

36. Markovits has noted a similar attitude towards the operations of the Shikarpuris in central Asia by the British at the supra-provincial and metropolitan levels of government, the relevant files retained at the lower levels of administration but only sporadically sent upwards and seldom read by administrators at higher levels: Markovits, *Indian Merchants*, 216–17.

37. PAL–R, 8.9.1860, Nos 55–8, 5–6.

38. *Press Lists of Old Records [...] Volume VI*, 391.

39. Ibid., 165–6. Connolly's account gives some context to the merchant's investment: House of Commons, *Report*, 132. See, also: NAI–F, Secret, 25.11.1831, Nos 1–3, 14.

40. See, for example, the response of the Shikarpur Collector to a request for information regarding overland trade via the Bolan Pass: PAL–P, 12.10.1861, Nos 37–9.

41. See, for an example of a Shikarpuri agency operation: NAI–F, Political, 25.9.1837, Nos 87–96, 27.

42. NAI–F, Secret I, 1870, Nos 90–6, 7.

43. NAI–F, Secret F, March 1886, No. 305. This roll, and the context in which it was compiled, is discussed in chapter 8.

44. Hanifi, *Connecting Histories*, 153–4.

45. Ibid., 160–1; Kaushik, 'Economic Relations', 81. See, for partnership and commenda: Dale, *Indian Merchants*, 118–20. On the Multanis' and Shikarpuris' roles as rural moneylenders, and the causes of the growth of this aspect of their operations in central Asia towards the later nineteenth century: Markovits, *Indian Merchants*, 93–4, 187–94.

46. NAI–F, Secret F, June 1889, No. 142, 2; NAI–F, Secret F, November 1889, No. 41, 3.

47. Bayly, *Rulers, Townsmen and Bazaars*, 31.

48. Hanifi, *Connecting Histories*, 53. For the dealings and dependence of the 'the Horse Merchants of Caval [Kabul] and Candehar' upon a dealer named Sunderji in western India in the early nineteenth century: NAI–M, 27.11.1813, No. 108, 390–1.

49. Anon., *Jan-e Bomba'i*, referenced in Green, *Bombay Islam*, 10.

50. NAI–F, Political, 25.9.1837, Nos 87–96, 55–6.

51. For the schedule of dues between Kabul and Multan: ibid., 54–6, 62, 84–5; *cf.* NAI–F, Political, 9.5.1836, No. 42, paragraphs 13–16.

52. Levi, *Indian Diaspora*, 51.

53. Grover, 'Integrated Pattern', 252.

54. See, for the Kota ruler's trade-promoting policy, for example: Sethia, *Rajput Polity*, especially 285–6. See, for the effects of the multiplication of state authorities in eighteenth-century north India, the testimony of James Browne (1787): Singh, ed., *Early European Accounts*, 17. *Cf.* NAI–F, Secret, 9.4.1832, Nos 6–8, 6–7.

55. Given the importance of princely redistribution and patronage to political authority, as described in the previous chapter, Punjabi rulers perhaps preferred to squeeze traders—generally those outside their kingdoms upon whom they were less reliant for finance—rather than peasant producers in the straitened times of the later eighteenth and early nineteenth century: Anon., 'A Character of the Sieks', 11.

56. Yang, *Bazaar India*, 204–5; Lafont, *Indika*, 349–50, 362.

57. The roots of this free-trade ideology are to be found in Wellesley's government and, in fact, the pace of liberalisation probably stalled subsequently as the government withdrew from economic management during the Age of Reform, which Bayly has also described as the Age of Hiatus; see: Bayly, *Indian Society*, 84, 123, 202–3; idem, 'The Age of Hiatus'.

58. *Press Lists of Old Records [...] Volume I*, 25; *Press Lists of Old Records [...] Volume III*, 490; NAI–F, Secret, 25.11.1831, Nos 1–3, 59.

59. *Press Lists of Old Records [...] Volume III*, 521–2; *Press Lists of Old Records [...] Volume VI*, 52.

60. Khilnani, *British Power in the Punjab*, 97, 99–100.

61. According to Henry Steinbach, one of Ranjit Singh's European soldiers, the roads through Punjab deteriorated after the maharaja's death: *Punjaub*, 86. See, for the general picture of transport infrastructure: Studer, 'India and the Great Divergence', 420; Deloche, *Transport and Communication*, 122; Kessinger, 'Regional Economy—North India', 247.

62. *Press Lists of Old Records [...] Volume IV*, 465; *Press Lists of Old Records [...] Volume I*, 361.

63. *Press Lists of Old Records [...] Volume VII*.

64. *Press Lists of Old Records [...] Volume I*, 371. The Government of India later

attempted to recover these costs from the Bahawalpur and Rajput states connected to this route: ibid., 372.

65. *Press Lists of Old Records [...] Volume I*, 373. *Cf.* Ali, ed., *History of Bahawalpur*, xxiii.

66. NAI–F, Political, 5.9.1836, Nos 9–21, 94–5. See, also: Kessinger, 'Regional Economy—North India', 258. Despite the faster flow of riverine traffic downstream, the time and expense involved in the upstream traffic and the break of bulk necessary to transport goods to Punjab doubtless dampened the expansion of Indus–Ganges exchange; see, for the vibrancy of trade *within* the later-eighteenth-and early-nineteenth-century Ganges valley: Yang, *Bazaar India*, 25–52.

67. NAI–F, Political, 5.9.1836, Nos 9–21, 94–5; NAI–F, Political, 25.9.1837, Nos 87–96, 84–5; See, also, for the relatively more meagre road network in western India than elsewhere on the subcontinent: Diverkar, 'Regional Economy—Western India', 339. Alternatively, the return cargoes were perhaps insufficiently remunerative, necessitating higher outward charges: Anon, 'Trade Beyond the Indus and Sutlej', 546, 550.

68. NAI–F, Political, 5.9.1836, Nos 9–21, 94–5. See, also: NAI–F, Ootacamund Political, 9.10.1834, Nos. 7–8, 1–5; Steinbach, *Punjaub*, 89–90.

69. Bayly, *Rulers, Townsmen and Bazaars*, especially 202–6.

70. Ibid., 156–60. Indeed, most trade in north India was local or regional, rather than trans-regional or cross-country, in its scope, *c.* 1700–1850: Studer, 'India and the Great Divergence', 393–437. See, also: Sethia, *Rajput Polity*, 280–1.

71. Morris, *Report*, Appendix F.

72. Shukla, *Indigo and the Raj*, 14–15; Kumar, *Indigo Plantations and Science*, chapters 1–2; Chowdhury, *Commercial Agriculture in Bengal*, 77.

73. See, for the expansion of production: Kessinger, 'Regional Economy—North India', 260.

74. The Bengal zamindars were not expressly excluded, rather, they opted out of establishing new enterprises in indigo; see: Chowdhury, *Commercial Agriculture in Bengal*, 80–1.

75. NAI–F, Secret, 27.9.1841, Nos 127–30, 51–2. See, also: *Gazetteer Muzaffargarh District*, 91; Carless, 'Memoir', 202. For the instructions and inventions availed to Bengali producers: Kumar, *Indigo Plantations and Science*, 108–10.

76. For the more positive evaluations: NAI–F, Secret, 27.9.1841, Nos 127–30, 49; Morris, 'Appendix A.', 164.

77. See, for the long history of the rhetorical creation of reputation and value: Kumar, *Indigo Plantations and Science*, 20. For indicative views of Punjabi indigo: Hart, 'Report', 64–5.

78. The data for Fig. 4.3 are compiled from: BCP, IOR/P/419/39 [1801–1802] to IOR/P/419/90 [1848–1849].

79. NAI–F, Political, 9.5.1836, No. 42, paragraph 5; NAI–F, Secret, 27.9.1841, Nos 127–30, 41; NAI–F, Political, 25.9.1837, Nos 87–96, 18–22, 83.

80. NAI–F, Political, 26.6.1837, Nos 3–5, 7.

81. NAI–F, Secret, 27.9.1841, Nos 127–30, 25–8.

82. Postans, 'Memorandum', 397–9.

83. NAI–F, Foreign, 30.4.1852, Nos 40–5, 4–5.

84. NAI–F, Foreign, 26.12.1851, No. 639, 36.

85. House of Commons, *Report*, 133; Thomas, ed., *Records of the Bombay Government*, especially 189–208, 341–61.

86. Floor, *Dutch East India Company*, 66.

87. See, especially: MSA–SILB, 1760, No. 14, Letter No. 94; MSA–SILB, 1761, No. 15, Letter No. 139; MSA–SILB, 1762, No. 16, Letter Nos 49, 92; MSA–SILB, 1763, No. 17, Letter Nos 17, 201; MSA–SILB, 1764, No. 18, Letter No. 202; MSA–SILB, 1765, No. 19, Letter No. 175; MSA–SILB, 1767, No. 21, Letter Nos 49, 64; MSA–SILB, 1768, No. 22, Letter Nos 14, 64; MSA–SILB, 1769, No. 23, Letter No. 24; MSA–SILB, 1770, No. 24, Letter No. 16; MSA–SILB, 1771, No. 25, Letter Nos 35, 208.

88. MSA–SILB, 1760, No. 21, Letter No. 42; MSA–SILB, 1767, No. 21, Letter Nos 64 and 108, 35, 214; MSA–SILB, 1768, No. 22, Letter No. 14, 30; MSA–SILB, 1771, No. 25, Letter No. 35, 68; MSA–SILB, 1772, No. 26, Letter No. 254, 355.

89. Hanifi, *Connecting Histories*, 6. See, for the British colonial state's construction of Afghanistan as a 'state': Hopkins, *Modern Afghanistan*.

90. Rose, *Tribes and Castes [...] Vol. II. A.–K.*, 31, 225; Noelle, *State and Tribe*, 123–4, 236.

91. The quotation is from the correspondence of the former Commissioner of Sindh, Bartle Frere: Andrew, *India and her Neighbours*, 311–12.

92. Kakar, *Afghanistan 1863–1901*, especially chapters 4–9; Davies, *Report*, 43.

93. *Gazetteer Peshawar District: 1883–4*, 154. See, also: Masson, *Narrative*, vol. I, 131. For the origins and trade of the Tajiks: Rose, *Tribes and Castes [...] Vol. III. L.–Z.*, 452.

94. On the location of the Shinwari populations: Biddulph, *Tribes of the Hindoo Koosh*, 9. See, for their treatment in the later nineteenth century: Kakar, *Afghanistan 1863–1901*, 72–3.

95. Kakar, *Afghanistan 1863–1901*, chapter 5.

96. Ibid., 94.

97. IOR/V/24/4167, ETP (1890–91), front matter, 2.

98. *Gazetteer Muzaffargarh District*, 104. Cf. *Jhang District, with Maps: 1908*, 115.

99. NAI–F, Foreign, 18.7.1851, Nos 15–20, 23–5, 156; NAI–F, Foreign, 12.8.1853, No. 126, 1–2; NAI–F, Frontier A, February 1889, No. 17, 2.

100. *Gazetteer Mooltan District: 1883–4*, 155.

101. See, for a reprinting of the report: *Gazetteer Peshawar District: 1883–4*, 154.

102. NAI–F, Secret I, 1870, Nos 90–6, 3. See, for Mulla Ghulam Kadir's re-appearance, in further correspondence relating to the tea trade: NAI–F, Secret A, August 1882, Nos 349–59.

103. Grewal and Banga, *Early Nineteenth Century Punjab*, 73.

104. See, for trade and trade policy prior to the reign of Abdur Rahman: Gregorian, *Emergence of Modern Afghanistan*, chapter 3.

105. See, for the amir's demands of security money, and the harassment of traders: NAI–F, Secret E, October 1882, No. 385. These restrictions were not terminated until 1896; see: NAI–F, Secret F, July 1896, No. 119, 2.

106. Kakar, *Government and Society*, 204–7.

107. NAI–F, Secret F, November 1889, No. 41, 3.

108. Hanifi, *Connecting Histories*, 97–102.

109. Ibid., 106, 114–20; Kakar, *Government and Society*, 220–3.

110. Hanifi, *Connecting Histories*, 105–6.

111. See, for the fortunes of the Sethis and Bakhshs, respectively: ibid., chapter 6; Kaushik, 'Economic Relations', 64–70.

112. Fifty photographs capturing the lives of the community formed the basis of a touring exhibition—'Kabul to Kolkata: Of Belonging, Memories and Identity'—staged in Kabul, Delhi, Dhaka, and Kolkata, and supported by Goethe-Institut South Asia and the India–Afghanistan Foundation.

113. Christensen, 'Tribesmen, Government and Political Economy', 174–5.

114. Millward, *Eurasian Crossroads*, 155.

115. Kim, 'Profit and Protection'. See, also: Kim, *Borderland Capitalism*.

116. Kim, 'Profit and Protection', 611.

117. Kim, *Borderland Capitalism*, especially 12, 20, 41–4, 74–82. Note: this book is an audacious expansion of Kim's earlier work, claiming that the oases were connected to global trade and, thus, the rhythms of global capitalism from *c.* 1600, to the extent that the commercial and political elite of Chinese Turkestan were poised to seize the advantages gained through alliance with the Qing following the latter's westward expansion, especially in the wake of the downturn associated with the Ming–Qing transition era that signalled their reliance on the Qing silver balance of trade in the maritime arena. This argument aims to bring the 'borderland' into the historical mainstream through connection to global phenomena—capitalism and globalisation—that are conceived, however, as singular and totalising. In turn, such conceptualisation renders the analysis somewhat insensitive to the coeval relationship of archaic and modern globalisation, for example. In Punjab, as argued above, agrarian expansion and the rise of new states and merchant groups was part of a capitalist transformation and fuelled by what had been expropriated from the Mughal domains (itself accumulated partly through trade with Europeans in the modern world system), but was oriented towards archaic networks oriented around caravan trade.

118. Kim, 'Profit and Protection', 616.

119. Kim, *Borderland Capitalism*, chapter 5.

120. Tuna, *Imperial Russia's Muslims*, 128.

121. Ibid., 128–30.
122. Ibid., 130–3.
123. Ibid., 135.
124. Ibid., 137–8.
125. Machado, 'Cloths of a New Fashion', 56. See, also: Machado, *Ocean of Trade*; Reid and Fernando, 'Shipping on Melaka and Singapore'.
126. For a recent expression of the 'continuity thesis', placing Indian Ocean history within a *longue durée* framework that, therefore, counters the long-standing tendency to fixate on post-1750 empire-building as ushering a sudden disjuncture, instead seeing a transformation brought by colonial rule only from the early nineteenth century: Parthasarathi and Riello, 'Indian Ocean'.
127. Bayly, 'Town Building', especially 485–6, 491–3.

5. MATERIAL CULTURE

1. Peck, *Consuming Splendor*, especially 11 and n. 34 for an overview of the pioneering work of Neil McKendrick, John Brewer, and J. H. Plumb on what became 'consumption studies', connecting social with economic change and macro with micro levels of analysis. See, for indication of the geographical reach of this 'material turn' in the historical scholarship: Findlen, *Early Modern Things*, 16, nn. 58–61; Gerritsen and Riello, eds, *The Global Lives of Things*. Of course, the exercise of choice could be involuntary, not least in the case of European missionaries coercing American natives into making use of 'civilising goods', for example. But this is merely to underline the need to be attentive to the ways in which asymmetries of power and hegemony within the global economy or exchange relationships filtered into the realm of material culture. See: Bauer, *Goods, Power, History*, especially chapter 4.
2. Bayly, *Birth of the Modern World*, 49–59.
3. For an explanation of the causes of this oversight, see the pioneering volume: Haynes, *et al.*, *Towards a History of Consumption*.
4. For the juxtaposition of the *ghazi* and *mirza* ideals, see: Gommans, *Mughal Warfare*, especially 39–40.
5. The autobiography of the Mughal emperor, Babur, is a well-known example of self-awareness in early modern Islamicate Eurasia: Rizvi, *Affect, Emotion, and Subjectivity*, including 7–8 on Babur.
6. O'Hanlon, 'Manliness and Imperial Service', 68; Gommans, *Mughal Warfare*, 51–3. See, for the Akbarid construction and representation of imperial service as the sole means through which men could develop their highest virtues: O'Hanlon, 'Kingdom', 889–923.
7. On the changing composition of the *mansabdari*: Richards, *Mughal Empire*, 19–21, 143–8.
8. Greenblatt, *Renaissance Self-Fashioning*. Of course, Greenblatt was not the first scholar to address this phenomenon: Burke, *Fortunes of the Courtier*, 2 and n. 3.

9. Bayly and Bayly, 'Eighteenth-Century State Forms', 67–68. O'Hanlon, how-
    ever, notes the importance of Sufi and Sanskrit traditions in the Mughal con-
    struction of the ideal of masculine virtue: O'Hanlon, 'Kingdom', 889–923.

10. Robinson, 'Ottomans–Safavids–Mughals'; Alam, *Languages of Political Islam*,
    128–40.

11. See, for an introduction to the Mirror for Princes genre in Mughal India, and
    for a Jahangir-era text: Sani, *Advice*. The *nasihat-name* are part of the wider
    tradition of *akhlaq* literature; see: O'Hanlon, 'Kingdom', 890–91; Alam,
    Languages of Political Islam. See, also: O'Hanlon, 'Manliness and Imperial
    Service', 50–1.

12. Aziz Ahmad, 'British Museum *Mīrzānāma*'. O'Hanlon, 'Kingdom', 901. This
    is not to say that the emperors did not continually refashion themselves for,
    in the first place, they were exposed during their education as imperial
    princes to such texts and traditions; and, secondly, they engaged with texts
    that were sometimes critical of their rule. See, for example: Sani, *Advice*. The
    emphasis here, however, is on deportment and public image rather than moral
    or lawful conduct.

13. O'Hanlon, 'Manliness and Imperial Service', 83–4.

14. See, for the limits to the Persianisation of early modern India, and the resis-
    tance from Muslim elites and those learned in 'local languages' alike: Alam,
    Languages of Political Islam, especially 141–51. Of course, such 'local lan-
    guages'—including Sindhi, Punjabi, and Bengali—were important to the
    wider dissemination of (mystical) learning through media such as poetry, sug-
    gesting that Persianisation and vernacularisation went hand in hand to some
    extent: Robinson, 'Ottomans–Safavids–Mughals', 165. This 'kingly style' of
    conspicuous consumption, and the associated patronage of production, was as
    much a building block of royal authority and gentry sensibility as it was
    important to the health of the economy and polity; see: Bayly, *Rulers, Townsmen
    and Bazaars*, 57–62.

15. Gommans, *Mughal Warfare*, 121; Khazeni, 'Through an Ocean of Sand', 145–6.

16. Gommans, *Mughal Warfare*, 121, n. 104; Hashimi, *Faras-nama*. For a detailed
    study of Firuz Jang's text, and its deviations from that of Hashimi: Meadows,
    'The Horse', chapter 2.

17. Khan, *Faras Nama e Rangin*. Abdullah's text is referenced by Phillott, the trans-
    lator of the *Faras Nama e Rangin*, xi.

18. Of course, 'copies' or recensions sometimes subtracted, added, or edited ear-
    lier material.

19. Khan, 'Awadh Scientific Renaissance', 281. Khan's research draws on the work
    of the nineteenth-century orientalist Aloys Sprenger, who catalogued the man-
    uscripts in the libraries of the Afghan chiefs and the Nawab of Awadh. See:
    Sprenger, *Catalogue*. For administrative handbooks, including those on farri-
    ery, produced in Safavid Iran after the Afghan invasions in the early eighteenth
    century: Rota, 'Horses of the Shah', 324 and nn. 9–11.

20. This paragraph, and the remainder of this section, should be read in conjunction with: Lally, 'Empires and Equines'.

21. For examples of pictures reflecting these developments, see: ibid., nn. 87–94.

22. Equestrian Portrait of Muhammad Amir Khan (unknown artist, Jodhpur, c.1815), Victoria and Albert Museum, London, IS. 143–1952. To view this picture, see: http://collections.vam.ac.uk/item/O433375/amir-khan-painting-unknown/[accessed: 27 August 2020]

23. Lal, *Memoirs of the Puthan Soldier*, especially 300–1, 321, 323, 440–1.

24. This use of scale, introduced in Akbar's reign, was popular in portraits of Rajput rulers. See, for the Akbari innovation: Asher, 'A Ray from the Sun'. See, for an eighteenth-century example: Crill and Jariwala, eds, *Indian Portrait*, 124–5.

25. Jacquemont, *Letters from India*, vol. I, 231.

26. Fenech, *Darbar of the Sikh Gurus*.

27. Ibid., 90–7.

28. Ibid., 136–68.

29. Fenech, *Sikh Zafar-Namah*, xii.

30. Dhavan, *When Sparrows Became Hawks*.

31. Ibid., 146.

32. Bayly, *Indian Society*, 15.

33. Ibid., 142–6; Alam, *Crisis of Empire*, 17.

34. See, for an example from Kashmir: 'Equestrian Portrait of Gulab Singh', Pahari, *c.* 1840, IOSM, Add.Or.707.

35. Melikian-Chirvani, 'Ranjit Singh', 66; Stronge, 'Court of Maharaja Ranjit Singh', 77.

36. Equestrian Portrait of Maharaja Ranjit Singh (unknown artist, Punjab Hills, c.1835–40) © Victoria and Albert Museum, London, IS.282–1955. To view this picture, see: http://collections.vam.ac.uk/item/O17682/maharaja-ranjit-singh-painting-unknown/ [accessed: 27 August 2020]

37. Bayly, *Rulers, Townsmen and Bazaars*, 22. See, for an example of an equestrian portrait of the tenth guru, Gobind Singh: Stronge, ed., *Arts of the Sikh Kingdoms*, 36. Ranjit Singh also commissioned equestrian portrait murals of the guru to adorn the Golden Temple, and such murals were once common throughout the city of Amritsar: Kang, 'Murals of Amritsar', 282, 289.

38. 'Maharan Sarup Singh Inspecting a Prize Stallion', Marwar (Jodhpur), Rajasthan, 1845–6, Metropolitan Museum of Art, New York, USA, Accession No. 2001.344. A picture of Ranjit Singh and General Hari Singh Nalwa inspecting horses, from the Toor Collection, is reproduced in: Madra and Singh, *Golden Temple*, plate 7. For discussion of two eighteenth-century equestrian portraits commissioned by Punjabi rulers in the Mughal topos: Canby, 'Persian Horse Portraits', 193–4.

39. Moorcroft, *Travels*, vol. I, 96; NAI–F, Foreign, 8.11.1850, Nos 54–7, 9–10;

Eden, *Up the Country*, 227 and the colour-plate reproduction of her watercolour sketch. *Cf.* Burnes, *Travels*, vol. II, 154.

40. NAI–F, Political, 20.2.1839, Nos 135–6; NAI–F, Political, 27.3.1839, Nos 103–6.

41. NAI–F, Political, 27.3.1839, No. 103; Steinbach, *Punjaub*, 84–5.

42. Burke, 'Meaning of Things', 9.

43. See, for the consumer or demand-side and trade-related revolution in Britain: Lemire, *Fashion's Favourite*. See, also: Lemire, *Dress, Culture and Commerce*. For the response of producers, innovators and industrialists: Parthasarathi, *Why Europe Grew Rich*, chapters 4–5.

44. On Ottoman responses: ibid., 116–25, 131–3.

45. Samuel Crompton's spinning mule of 1779, for example, 'made it possible to spin yarn as fine as that used in the Bengal muslins': Roy, *India in the World Economy*, 133.

46. NAI–F, Secret, 16.4.1832, No. 9, 1161–2, 1165–6. See, also: NAI–F, Political, 25.9.1837, Nos 87–96, 56.

47. Sharma, 'Ports of Gujarat', 204. Sales of British cotton cloth did not accelerate in interior north India until the later 1840s, and probably later in the parts of Punjab most closely connected to Indo-central Asian trade: Bayly, *Indian Society*, 120.

48. NAI–F, Secret, 25.11.1831, Nos 1–3, 14; NAI–F, Political, 4.6.1832, Nos 4–8; NAI–F, Political, 26.6.1837, Nos 3–5.

49. NAI–F, Political, 14.12.1835, No. 64, 9. For the limited volumes and value of goods transported this way: NAI–F, Political, 1.8.1836, No. 32; NAI–F, Political, 25.9.1837, Nos 87–96, 25; NAI–F, Secret, 27.9.1841, Nos 127–30, 24–7; NAI–F, Political, 4.9.1847, Nos 26–30.

50. NAI–F, Political, 25.9.1837, Nos 87–96, 56.

51. Ibid., 83.

52. NAI–F, Secret, 23.1.1837, No. 30, 12; NAI–F, Secret, 2.8.1841, Nos 61–4, 1.

53. NAI–F, Secret, 12.2.1833, No. 16.

54. Dale, 'Indo-Russian Trade', 150.

55. MSA–SILB, 1760, No. 14, Letter No. 42.

56. MSA–SILB, 1760, Letter No. 154; MSA–SILB, 1762, No. 16, Letter No. 109; Floor, *Dutch East India Company*, 70.

57. MSA–SILB, 1762, No. 16, Letter No. 1.

58. Hamilton, *New Account*, vol. I, 126–7; NAI–F, Secret, 4.5.1842, Nos 4–7, 38; NAI–F, Political, 25.9.1837, Nos 87–96, 26; NAI–F, Political, 4.9.1847, Nos 26–30.

59. MSA–SILB, 1762, No. 16, Letter No. 92, 245–6.

60. MSA–SILB, 1762, No. 16, Letter No. 109. See, for information on broadcloth exports from Russia via the Astrakhan customs house: Gopal, ed., *Indians in Russia*.

61. Elphinstone, *Account*, 294–5.

62. NAI–F, Foreign, 18.7.1851, Nos 15–25, 173.

63. See, for the trade via the White Sea to Archangel: Dale, 'Indo-Russian Trade', 154–5; Bushkovitch, *Merchants of Moscow*, 19, 34–6, 42, 44, 59.

64. Dale, 'Indo-Russian Trade', 149; Carlano, 'In Celebration', 31. See, for the testimony of a Marwari merchant in 1731 in Russian sources from Astrakhan: Gopal, ed., *Indians in Russia*, 180, 244. For the state backing of two Englishmen to develop chintz printing: Struve, 'English Tissue-Printing in Russia', 303–10.

65. Struve, 'English Tissue-Printing in Russia', 308–9.

66. Fitzpatrick, *Great Russian Fair*, 58–61. On the development of the industry in Ivanovo: Arseneva, *Ivanovskie Sittsy*, 5–30.

67. Struve, 'English Tissue-Printing in Russia', 307–8; Blackwell, *Industrialization of Russia*, 12–13.

68. Levi, 'Eighteenth-Century Transformation', 531; Levi, *Indian Diaspora*, 244; Levi, 'Fergana Valley', 226.

69. Carlano, 'In Celebration', 32. More recently, Alison Smith has zoomed in to examine the 1820s and the relationship of Ivanovo's owner, Count Sheremetev, and the serfs who produced its famous calicos: Smith, 'Ivanovo', 163–93.

70. Carlano, 'Russian Printed Cottons', 86. For Knop's contribution to the development of Russia's textile industry, and the history of Knop's business: Thompstone, 'Ludwig Knop', 45–73.

71. Blackwell, *Industrialization of Russia*, 12–13. Although the Alexandrovsk State Textile Mill was established in 1798, the ban on English machinery exports, the complication of circumventing the ban, and the reliance on Belgian or French machinery meant that there were few spinning mills in Russia before the 1840s: Thompstone, 'Ludwig Knop', 46.

72. Struve, 'English Tissue-Printing in Russia', 309. See, for the expansion of manufacture of Russian cotton cloth 1797–1803 to 1858–1861: Thompstone, 'Ludwig Knop', 47, table 1. See, as an index of expansion after 1850, the growing size of trade through the Nizhnii Novgorod Fair: Fitzpatrick, *The Great Russian Fair*, 57.

73. Blackwell, *Industrialization of Russia*, 12–13.

74. A number of examples of these textiles are usefully reproduced in: Arseneva, *Ivanovskie Sittsy*. These can be compared with early Mughal chintzes, including some which Veronica Murphy speculates may be of Punjabi or Kashmiri origin: Murphy, *Origins*, 19, 29.

75. NAI–F, Secret, 25.11.1831, Nos 1–3, 14; NAI–F, Foreign, 25.4.1851, No. 23, 1–2; NAI–F, Foreign, 18.7.1851, Nos 15–20, 23–5; NAI–F, Foreign, 22.2.1856, Nos 47–8, 3.

76. NAI–F, Political, 17.7.1839, Nos 22–4; NAI–F, Foreign, 23.10.1847, Nos 44–5.

77. NAI–F, Secret, 25.11.1831, Nos 1–3, 12–13; NAI–F, Political, 6.3.1839, Nos 23–2, 58.

78. NAI–F, Foreign, 18.7.1851, Nos 15–25, 156.

79. NAI–F, Political, 11.4.1838, No. 30, 14–15.

80. NAI–F, Secret, 16.4.1832, No. 9, 1165–6. Compare with the samples examined in chapter 9.

81. NAI–F, Political, 11.4.1838, No. 30, 14–15.

82. NAI–F, Foreign, 23.10.1847, Nos 44–5. This is evident from the earliest surviving samples, through which the design development is traceable: Arseneva, *Ivanovskie Sittsy*. Central Asian *khilat* makers continued to imitate Kashmiri designs into the late nineteenth century, as attested by the book of lithographs produced by the archaeologist N. Simakoff during an official Russian expedition in 1879: Simakoff, *Les Arts Decoratifs*, plate 8.

83. NAI–F, Political, 25.9.1837, Nos 87–96, 71.

84. Ibid., 27.

85. NAI–F, Foreign, 25.4.1851, No. 20, 1.

86. NAI–F, Secret, 25.11.1831, Nos 1–3, 14; NAI–F, Foreign, 25.4.1851, No. 20, 2; NAI–F, Foreign, 18.7.1851, Nos 15–25, 172; NAI–F, Foreign, 22.2.1856, Nos 47–8, 3.

87. Watson, *Textile Manufactures*, 145.

88. Ibid., 145.

89. NAI–F, Foreign, 25.4.1851, No. 20, 1. For earlier assessments: NAI–F, Political, 11.4.1838, No. 30, 14–15.

90. NAI–F, Secret, 25.11.1831, Nos 1–3, 14; NAI–F, Foreign, 25.4.1851, No. 20, 1–2; NAI–F, Foreign, 18.7.1851, Nos 15–25, 174–5.

91. NAI–F, Foreign, 18.7.1851, Nos 15–25, 166.

92. NAI–F, Foreign, 25.4.1851, Nos 19–24, 1; NAI–F, Foreign, 18.7.1851, Nos 15–25, 166.

93. NAI–F, Foreign, 25.4.1851, No. 23, 2. See, also: Fitzpatrick, *The Great Russian Fair*, 64.

94. NAI–F, Foreign, 25.4.1851, No. 23, 2–3; NAI–F, Foreign, 30.4.1852, Nos 40–5, 14.

95. Luis, 'Guru Nanak Shah Faqir', 283.

96. See, for instance: McLeod, *Guru Nanak*.

97. For a picture from 1733: IOSM, Mss.Panj.B.40, f.128. For an example from the Skinner Album of 1825 of a Nanakpanthi (devotee of Nanak) who has adopted all the elements of the guru's dress discussed here: IOSM, Add. 27255, f.426v.

98. Luis, 'Guru Nanak Shah Faqir'. The painting is from: IOSM, Or. 5259, f.9.

99. Eaton, 'Nomadism of Colour', 68.

100. Khazeni, *Sky Blue Stone*, 57–67.

101. Ibid., 3, 30–1, and here, 70.

102. Bloom and Blair, eds, *Diverse Are Their Hues*, 6, 10, 14–15; Mahmoud, 'Colour and the Mystics', 107.

103. Bloom and Blair, *Diverse Are Their Hues*, 16, 44.

104. Ibid., 24–5, 150. See, also: Rose, *Tribes and Castes [...] Vol. I*, 520.

105. See, for a fascinating indication of the pervasiveness of the apotropaic properties of blue, the local remedies for a variety of afflictions noted in: Nalivkin and Nalivkina, *Muslim Women*, 78.

106. Landsell, *Russian Central Asia*, vol. I, 606.

107. NAI–F, Political, 25.9.1837, Nos 87–96, 2–3. See, also: NAI–F, Secret, 25.11.1831, Nos 1–3, 42; Pottinger, *Travels*, 46, 64, 196, 324; Crooke, *Natives of Northern India*, 61. For representations, see: 'Rohillas' (unknown artist, Punjab, *c.*1838–9), IOSM, 'Punjab Characters Album', Add.Or.1365.

108. MSA–SILB, 1762, No. 16, Letter No. 92; NAI–F, Political, 11.4.1838, No. 30, 13–14; Khan, *Afghanistan and its Inhabitants*, 9–10, 249–50, 505. See, also: Rose, *Tribes and Castes [...] Vol. II. A.–K.*, 490–1; Rose, *Tribes and Castes [...] Vol. III. L.–Z.*, 127, 178.

109. G. T. Vigne (Afghanistan, 1836), V&A, Accession Nos SD.1109, SD.1116, SD. 1118, SD.1124, and SD.1126. See, also, for the blue *khilat* as a constituent of courtly dress in Afghanistan and amongst tribesmen: Rattray, *Costumes of the Various Tribes*, plates 3, 4, 6, 12, and 14; Moorcroft, *Travels*, vol. II, 422. For a survey of European artists in Afghanistan, including James Rattray: Falconer, ed., *Afghanistan Observed*. Note: Nejatie observes that Shi'i, Irani, and Persian were used interchangeably in works composed in Durrani political milieus: 'Iranian Migrations', 497.

110. Mousavi, *Hazaras of Afghanistan*, 101–2, 105–6; Harvey, *Traditional Textiles*, plate 137.

111. *Panjab Notes & Queries. A Monthly Periodical*, 1, 3 (1883), 26; *Panjab Notes & Queries. A Monthly Periodical*, 1, 12 (1884), 142.

112. See, for the popularity of blue clothes amongst Sindhi Muslims: Burton, *Sind Revisited*, vol. I, 46, 302, vol. II, 300.

113. Hazarah, *History of Afghanistan*, 52. Other sources specify the blue mantle of the Sufis of Uch: Rose, *Tribes and Castes [...] Vol. I*, 697, 709.

114. For the blue clothes of the Sikh Akalis: 'Punjab Characters Album', IOSM, Add.Or.1350 and Add.Or.1351. See, also: Malcolm, *Sketch of the Sikhs*, 117; Singh, ed., *Early European Accounts*, 17, 63; Francklin, *Reign of Shah-Aulum*, 77.

115. Steinbach, *Punjaub*, 95.

116. Pallas, *Travels*, vol. II, 228; Pottinger, *Travels*, 324; NAI–F, Political, 14.12.1835, Nos 64–5, 8.

117. Balfour-Paul, *Indigo*, 214–15; Bloom, *Paper before Print*, 69–70.

118. Porter, *Painters, Painting and Books*, 36–45; Anon., *Sublime Indigo*, 77–79.

119. Uchastinka, *Russian Hand Paper-Mills*, 17, 52–53, 72, 141.

120. On the raw-silk papers of Bukhara and Samarkand that these Russian papers imitated, see: Vambery, *Travels*, 423–524. On the mills exporting to central Asia, see: Uchastinka, *Russian Hand Paper-Mills*, 124, 149.

121. Uchastinka, *Russian Hand Paper-Mills*, 8, n. 23.

122. Khan, *Travels in Central Asia*, 68; Lal, *Travels*, 77–8. *Cf.* Burnes, *Travels*, vol. I, 145; NAI–F, Political, 11.4.1838, No. 30, 9–10; NAI–F, Foreign, 30.4.1852, Nos 40–5, 13–14; Schuyler, *Turkistan*, vol. II, 13–14. Russia was also instrumental in the introduction of printing and printing presses into central Eurasia: Green, 'Persian Print and the Stanhope Revolution'.

123. NAI–F, Political, 11.4.1838, No. 30, 9–10; NAI–F, Foreign, 30.4.1852, Nos 40–5, 13–14; Schuyler, *Turkistan*, vol. II, 13–14.

124. Vambery, *Travels*, 429; Fraser, *Marches of Hindustan*, 304.

125. Anne Murphy has masterfully studied the shifts in the relationships of material artefacts or relics relating to the Sikhs, the Sikh religion, and the Sikh understanding of the past: Murphy, *Materiality of the Past*. This work shows a more complex range of factors at play—although her focus is on devotional objects, and not the more mundane articles of everyday consumption studied in this book.

126. Lal, *Travels*, 395.

127. See, for an introductory survey: Crill, 'Textiles in the Punjab', 114–33. See, for a wider purview: Askari and Crill, *Colours of the Indus*.

128. While the production of silken textiles in Dera Ismail Khan was probably secondary to that of Bahawalpur, Lahore, and Multan, it was noteworthy, nevertheless, with samples of silks collected after the colonial annexation for exhibitions and inclusion in sample–books, for example: Watson, *Textile Manufactures*, 104–5.

129. Floor, *Dutch East India Company*, 74–5; MSA–SILB, 1762, No. 16, Letter No. 49, 115; NAI–F, Political, 9.5.1836, No. 42; NAI–F, Political, 25.9.1837, Nos 87–96, 24–5; NAI–F, Secret, 28.8.1847, Nos 106–17; NAI–F, Secret, 28.7.1848, Nos 9–11; NAI–F, Foreign, 18.7.1851, Nos 15–20, 23–5, 167–8. For an example of a silken *lungi* with gold thread woven in 1855 in Sindh: V&A, Accession No. IS 556.

130. Bayly, 'Origins of *Swadeshi*', 290; Liu, *Silk and Religion*, 158–78.

131. Nominally independent, Bahawalpur's rulers personally presented fine silk fabrics to British administrators responsible for collecting samples for exhibitions in India and abroad; see, for silk fabrics presented in 1855: V&A, *[India Museum] Slip Book Nos 2751 to 3000*, Nos 2937, 2967–8, 2972, 2978–9; V&A, *[India Museum] Slip Book Nos 3001 to 3251*, Nos 3122–3.

132. Such concerns were common in the Ottoman world: McCabe, *Shah's Silk*, 20–1.

133. Talbot, *Punjab and the Raj*, 18. See, for *mashru* production: Latifi, *Industrial Punjab*, 39.

134. Sen, *Empire of Free Trade*, 33.

135. Werbner, *Pilgrims of Love*, 203.

136. Bal, 'Amritsar in the Eighteenth Century', 73–4.

137. Sen, *Empire of Free Trade*, 43–4.

138. See, for Akbar's patronage of textile workshops in Lahore, and for the institution of the *karkhana*: Verma, *Karkhanas*, especially 27.

139. See, for Ranjit Singh's dress: Crill, 'Textiles in the Punjab', 117.

140. Singh, 'Amritsar During Maharaja Ranjit Singh's Time', 75, 80–2.

141. Garrett, ed., *Punjab*, 26. On conspicuous displays of piousness and the concern for spiritual merit in the fashioning of the 'middle-class' Indian family, see: Bayly, *Rulers, Townsmen and Bazaars*, chapter 8.

142. Garrett, ed., *Punjab*, 26.

143. Anon, 'Tour to Lahore', 430, 433, 438–9. See, also: Grewal and Banga, *Early Nineteenth-Century Punjab*, 133.

144. Garrett, ed., *Punjab*, 58.

145. *Gazetteer Amritsar District: 1883–4*, 39–40; Crill, 'Textiles in the Punjab', 118–29; Ames, *Woven Masterpieces of Sikh Heritage*.

146. Gauba, 'Amritsar', 352–3; Gauba, *Amritsar*, 70, 148–9.

147. Bayly, *Caste, Society and Politics*, especially chapters 1–2.

148. Sharma, *Artisans of the Punjab*, 107–9; Bayly and Bayly, 'Eighteenth-Century State Forms', 68.

149. Bayly, *Caste, Society and Politics*, 66.

150. Kessinger, *Vilyatpur*, 29.

151. Caton, 'Social Categories and Colonisation', especially 34–43. For analysis focusing largely on Hindu and Sikh communities: Ballantyne, *Orientalism and Race*, 63–4; Malhotra, *Gender, Caste, and Religious Identities*, 19. See, for a discussion of social stratification amongst Muslim communities in Punjab: Mir, *Social Space of Language*, 127.

152. Rose, *Tribes and Castes [...] Vol. I*, 115–16. See, also: Oberoi, *Religious Boundaries*, chapter 3. On Hindu–Muslim hostility and amity in Sindh: Markovits, *Indian Merchants*, 44–5, 49.

153. Malcolm, *Sketch of the Sikhs*, 137.

154. Garrett, ed., *Punjab*, 9–10; Crooke, *Natives of Northern India*, 93–4. See, also: Bayly, *Indian Society*, 157.

155. Oberoi, *Religious Boundaries*, especially chapter 1 for pre-nineteenth-century shifts in the Sikh 'episteme'.

156. *Panjab Notes & Queries. A Monthly Periodical*, 2, 23 (1885), 185; Bayly, 'Origins of *Swadeshi*', 289. For concerns about cloth containing illness and disease: Maskiel and Mayor, 'Poison *Khil'ats* in India', 97 and n. 4.

157. Edwardes, *Monograph*, 57–8.

158. Baden-Powell, *Hand-Book of the Manufactures*, 62–3.

159. V&A, Accession Nos IS 5548 and IS 6047 (respectively).

160. NAI–F, Political, 4.9.1847, Nos 26 30.

161. See, for example: V&A, Accession No. IS 5931.

162. Francklin, *Reign of Shah-Aulum*, 77; Masson, *Narrative*, vol. I, 434. Francklin

writes of a silk resembling a 'Scotch Tartan', presumably *khes*—see, chapter 8 for discussion of this textile.

163. Masson, *Narrative*, 434.

164. Steinbach, *Punjaub*, 95. See, also: Hailey, *Monograph*, 21.

165. V&A, *Samples of Silk Fabrics Manufactured in Lahore Shewing the Patterns &c Peculiar to Mahomedans, Hindus, Sikhs &c.* [*c*.1849–*c*.1862], Accession No. IS. 7915. The samples for the 1862 Exhibition were sourced in Lahore, as well as Multan, Bahawalpur, Amritsar, and Peshawar; see, for the provenance of the sample books: Dowleans, *Catalogue of the Contributions from India*, Section III, 10, 15. See, for the composition of the Lahore Central Committee: Dowleans, *Catalogue of the Contributions from India*, iv. The sample books are discussed in more detail in chapter 8.

166. See, for the 'ethnographic state': Dirks, *Castes of Mind*, 43–60. On the use of these categories by the colonial state in Punjab: Malhotra, *Gender, Caste, and Religious Identities*, 26–34. Of course, Punjabis—aware of the relationship of caste and tribe belonging to property rights—involved themselves in the crafting of these categories in the post-annexation period; see: Caton, 'Social Categories and Colonisation', 43–50.

167. Watson subsequently replicated this categorisation, taking 'the authority of the Lahore Central Committee' as an adequate basis for doing so: Watson, *Textile Manufactures*, 97 and footnote.

168. See, also: NAI–F, Secret M, 1870, No. 48.

169. NAI–F, Secret, 16 April 1832, Nos 8–10, 1161.

170. Baden-Powell, *Hand-Book of the Manufactures*, 62–3.

171. See: Appendix I, Table 2; Hailey, *Monograph*, 14–16.

172. Hamilton, *New Account*, vol. I, 126–7.

173. Askari and Crill, *Colours of the Indus*.

174. See, for finenesses and grades as reflected in prices: Appendix I, Table 2. See, for the texture of Punjabi silks: V&A, *Samples of Silk Fabrics*. See, for the unfavourable comparison of central Asian silks with European or East Asian silks: Baden-Powell, *Hand-Book of the Manufactures*, 57. See, also: Khanikoff, *Bokhara*, 174.

175. NAI–F, Foreign, 14.11.1856, Nos 222–3, 12.

176. The use of cheaper silk for wefts continued into the later nineteenth century; see: Hailey, *Monograph*, 14–15; Maxwell-Lefroy and Ansorge, *Report*, vol. II, 67.

177. For details of royal consumption and some of the varieties procured: NAI–F, Political, 25.9.1837, Nos 87–96, 71; NAI–F, Political, 11.4.1838, No. 30, 15–17; Baden-Powell, *Hand-Book of the Manufactures*, 66; Dowleans, *Catalogue of the Contributions from India*, Section III, 16.

178. NAI–F, Foreign, 18.7.1851, Nos 15–20, 23–5, 169.

179. NAI–F, Political, 4.1.1845, Nos 67–8; Hailey, *Monograph*, 21.

180. For an analysis of Spiridione Roma's painting: John McAleer, 'Displaying its Wares', 203–4.

181. On the cosmopolitanism of early modern Indian dynasties and their courts: Asher and Talbot, *India Before Europe*.

182. Calaresu, 'Ice Cream in Naples'.

183. For a lively description of street vendors and consumption in the bazaars of the Fergana valley: Nalivkin and Nalivkina, *Muslim Women*, 33, 113–14.

184. Such was its importance that the royal ice factory was raided during the Indian Rebellion, prompting concerns of shortages of ice when needed in Shahjahanbad: Farooqui, *Besieged*, 212, for a first-hand account of events.

185. Matthee, *Pursuit of Pleasure*. See, also: Dale, *Indian Merchants*, 21.

186. Bayly, too, casts doubt over the usefulness of 'luxury' as a descriptor of those goods traded over long distances in precolonial north India: Bayly, *Rulers, Townsmen and Bazaars*, 57.

187. Grehan, *Everyday Life*, especially 191–222.

188. Khazeni, *Sky Blue Stone*, especially chapter 2.

189. Ibid., here especially 14, 36.

190. Of course, as Burke notes, 'fashion' or 'la mode' only emerged as terms in the seventeenth century in Europe, although they often have conceptual and analytical purchase before gaining wider currency: Burke, 'Meaning of Things'.

190. Indicative, and arguably representative of these trends, for example: Berg, *et al.*, *Goods from the East*; Gerritsen and Riello, 'Spaces of Global Interactions'.

191. Gamsa, 'Refractions', which shows that there was friction to the fully reciprocal or two-way flow of this process, Russian goods making no comparable impact in China through the early modern period until as late as the close of the nineteenth century.

192. On rhubarb, see, most recently: Romaniello, 'True Rhubarb?'

194. Hellmich, 'Crossroads of the Pacific Ocean'.

6. COLONIAL CONQUEST

1. Bayly, 'First Age of Global Imperialism'.

2. Bowen, 'Bullion for Trade'.

3. Kim, *Borderland Capitalism*; Levi, *Khoqand*, chapter 5 and 182–3.

4. The reports from Punjab, Afghanistan, and central Asia utilised in this book are evidence of this commercial exploration in the period preceding expansion from the 1840s. Meanwhile, similar sorts of exploration were under way in other interior spaces soon to be conquered and absorbed into British India, not least the upper reaches of the Irrawaddy and the larger region of Upper Burma preceding the Third Anglo-Burmese War (1885). See, for example: Sladen, *Expedition to Explore the Trade Routes to China*.

5. For recent work interrogating this notion, as well as the alternative explanation affording agency to 'men on the spot' in the context of Russian Turkestan, see: Morrison, 'Camels and Colonial Armies'; idem, 'Fall of Tashkent, 1859–1865'; idem, 'Killing the Cotton Canard', 135–6. See, also: Morrison, *Russian Rule in Samarkand*, 30–6; Geyer, *Russian Imperialism*, 86–99.

6. The latter phenomenon is discussed in the next chapter. See: Morrison, 'Peasant Settlers'.

7. See, for the minority of central Asian traders, and the marginality of Russo-central Asian trade through the Nizhnii Novgorod Fair, the largest fair in the Russian Empire: Fitzpatrick, *Great Russian Fair*, 39, 113.

8. Morrison, *Russian Rule in Samarkand*, 41–2. See, also: Levi, *Indian Diaspora*, 233; NAI–F, Secret E, March 1884, Nos 202–5, 1.

9. For a revaluation of the Great Game: Yapp, 'Legend of the Great Game'.

10. See, for example: Ewart, *Settlement in India and Trade with Central Asia*.

11. Davies, *Report*.

12. Huttenback, *British Relations with Sind*, 110.

13. Ibid., 110; Wong, 'British Annexation of Sind'.

14. For the customs system: NAI–F, Foreign, 12.8.1848, Nos 45–6, 1. On the fraught negotiations with nominally independent rulers: NAI–F, Secret, 27.9.1841, Nos 127–30, 24–8. See, also: NAI–F, Foreign, 30.4.1852, Nos 40–5, 10–11. The Khan of Kalat's duties were seen as especially detrimental to trade from Sindh through Baluchistan to Afghanistan, although he acquiesced to British rates of duty demands in the early 1850s: NAI–F, Foreign, 3.2.1854, Nos 19–20.

15. See, for reports on Karachi, Sonmiani, and other Sindhi seaports: Thomas, *Records of the Bombay Government*. See, for the difficulties faced in the latter endeavour: Huttenback, *British Relations with Sind*, 26.

16. Bourne, *Indian River Navigation*, 20–6, 63–7. See, for a number of more reasonable reports on the geology of the Indus: Thomas, *Records of the Bombay Government*, Part II.

17. Dewey, *Steamboats on the Indus*.

18. Until 1869, the SPDR constructed the lines at its own cost, with government assistance. After 1869, new lines were constructed at the expense of the state, which purchased the SPDR and amalgamated it into the state railway in 1885. Berridge, *Couplings to the Khyber*, 22–3.

19. For distances: Slaughter, *Railway Intelligence*, 189, 211.

20. Berridge, *Couplings to the Khyber*, 21.

21. Unlike the routes through the Hindu Kush, which were numerous yet defined and fixed to the location of the mountain passes, trade through Sindh and Baluchistan to southern Afghanistan and Persia shifted like the sands underfoot. See, for the resultant difficulties in assessing the extent of trade through to the 1870s: NAI–F, Secret, 31.7.1847, Nos 75–88, 4; NAI–F, Foreign,

18.7.1851, Nos 15–20, 23–5, 54; NAI–F, Political A, April 1868, No. 135, 2; NAI–F, Political A, July 1871, Nos 474–6.

22. NAI–F, Foreign, 18.7.1851, Nos 15–20, 23–5, 55.

23. NAI–F, Political A, May 1864, No. 10, 3; NAI–F, Secret, 28.5.1858, Nos 8–11, 40–1; NAI–F, Foreign, 18.7.1851, Nos 15–20, 23–5, 175–6; Davies, *Report*, 4, 7.

24. NAI–F, Political A, May 1864, No. 10, 3; NAI–F, Foreign, 18.7.1851, No. 15.

25. Davies, *Report*, 41; Baillie, 'Sind', 88.

26. Markovits, *Indian Merchants*, especially chapter 4.

27. NAI–F, Political A, May 1864, No. 10, 3; NAI–F, Secret, June 1873, No. 133, 2; Rizvi, *Ladakh*, 108. The animal mortality rate was one in four and, consequently, the cost of carriage relatively high: Rawlinson, 'Trade Routes', 13. See, also: Bhattacharya, 'Predicaments of Mobility', 180.

28. NAI–F, Secret, September 1872, Nos 193–4, 24–5. See, for detailed descriptions of the stages and stopping points along two alternative roads through Badakshan between India and Chinese Turkestan: Hayward, 'Route', 122–30.

29. NAI–F, Secret, September 1872, Nos 193–4, 24; Hayward, 'Route', 127. See, for discussion of safety and attacks on the road: Montgomerie, 'Report of the Mirza's Exploration'.

30. NAI–F, Secret, August 1871, No. 22; Munshee, 'On Gilgit and Chitral', 130–3.

31. NAI–F, Secret, September 1872, Nos 193–4, 24–5. See, for specific routes and passes: Rizvi, *Ladakh*, 109–11.

32. See, for a description of Yarkand as entrepôt in the China–Bukhara trade: Davies, *Report*, 25. Khanikoff stated that Bukhara's trade with Khokand, Kashgar and Yarkand was fairly brisk: Khanikoff, *Bokhara*, 227–8.

33. Rizvi, *Ladakh*, 87, 96, 107.

34. Ibid., 103.

35. Davies, *Report*, 58; Rizvi, *Trans-Himalayan Caravans*, 241–60.

36. Before the reorientation, which culminated around the turn of the century, the Tibet trade was important as a source of shawl wool; see: Rizvi, *Ladakh*, 80–7, 98–103.

37. NAI–F, Revenue A, July 1864, No. 77, 1.

38. Huttenback, *Kashmir and the British Raj*, 25–6.

39. See, for Basti Ram's promotion of, and profit from, trade through Leh: Rizvi, *Trans-Himalayan Caravans*, 191–2.

40. NAI–F, Secret, 27.10.1849, Nos 37–46, 33; NAI–F, Foreign, 28.6.1850, Nos 21–2. See, also: Rizvi, *Trans-Himalayan Caravans*, 191–2.

41. NAI–F, Political A, October 1867, Nos 149–51, 2.

42. Hutton, *Central Asia*, 285; Gill, 'Trade of the Punjab', 303.

43. Rizvi, *Trans-Himalayan Caravans*, 19. See, also: Millward, *Eurasian Crossroads*, 117–23.

44. Huttenback, *Kashmır and the British Raj*, 44–5. *Cf.* NAI–F, Secret, June 1873, No. 133, 3.

45. *Press Lists of Old Records [...] Volume III*, citation 353. For other motives, especially those emerging as construction was under way and the colonial context shifted: Gardner, 'Ready Materials for Another World'. See, also: Gardner, 'Border Making', especially 128–84, which examines the Hindustan–Tibet road in the context of transport networks radiating out of—or through—Ladakh. The examination is part of a larger thesis about the transformation from indigenous to colonial ways of seeing this space, the resultant efforts to delineate or make a border to enclose territory that recast it as a frontier, and the legacy of these undertakings. On the termination of the Hindustan–Tibet Road project: NAI–F, Political A, April 1869, Nos 141–2, 2.

46. Huttenback, *Kashmir and the British Raj*, 48–9.

47. Gommans, *Indo-Afghan Empire*, 41.

48. NAI–F, Political A, December 1868, Nos 52–3, 1; NAI–F, Political A, September 1869, Nos 232–4, 1.

49. NAI–F, Political A, September 1869, Nos 232–4, 1.

50. Maxwell-Lefroy and Ansorge, *Report*, vol. II, 65; Rizvi, *Ladakh*, 87.

51. *Hoshiarpur District, with Maps: 1904*, 135.

52. NAI–F, Secret, July 1875, Nos 169–85, 10–11.

53. NAI–F, Political, 5.9.1836, Nos 9–21, 66; Bhattacharya, 'Predicaments of Mobility', 181.

54. NAI–F, Political A, May 1864, No. 10, 3.

55. Davies, *Report*, 3.

56. NAI–F, Political A, May 1864, No. 10, 4.

57. Hutton, *Central Asia*, 385.

58. Newby, *Empire and the Khanate*, especially 64, 130–44, 200, 213–15.

59. Shaw, *Visits to High Tartary*, 68.

60. Gill, 'Central Asian Trading Company', 182. See, also: IOR/V/24/4166, ETP (1873–4), 9.

61. Arms were also sold to the Kashgar ruler through the CATC: Frechtling, 'Anglo-Russian Rivalry', 483.

62. NAI–F, Secret, July 1875, Nos 169–85, 10–11.

63. Ibid., 24.

64. Of Dalgleish, Col. Mark S. Bell, deputy quarter master general, eulogised: 'The prestige gained to the Empire by such men of enterprise and morality is great. I cannot say much for the morality of the Russian shop-keepers I met with in China. They adopt the customs of the people, takes concubines of them, and when these can no readily be obtained, bazaar women are not beneath their attention.' NAI–F, Secret F, May 1888, No. 40, 10. Dalgleish did not deserve such 'praise', insofar as he had actually married a Yarkandi woman: Rizvi, *Ladakh*, 106. See, for a comparison with British entrepreneur-

ship in *fin de siècle* Afghanistan: Omrani, 'Making Money in Afghanistan', 374–92.

65. Metcalf, *Ideologies of the Raj*.

66. Certainly, British writers invoked Alexander throughout the century as exploration of Afghanistan and central Asia increased, or otherwise created lineal connections to the Macedonian general; see, for example: Pottinger, *Travels*; Andrew, *Indus and its Provinces*, 2–3; Holdich, *Gates of India*.

67. *Press Lists of Old Records [...] Volume I*, 25. Similar endeavours were under way in western India following the conclusion of the Third Anglo-Maratha War in 1818; see: Sharma, 'Ports of Gujarat', 208–11.

68. Khilnani, *British Power in the Punjab*, 116.

69. IOR/E/4/804, 834–5. See, also: Khilnani, *British Power in the Punjab*, 116–17.

70. See, for the roll of octroi farmers in 1853, and the details of their pensions: PAL–R, 29.10.1853, Nos 38–42; PAL–R, 3.12.1853, Nos 21–2. The competition for the right to collect octroi in Lahore and Amritsar under Ranjit Singh is described by Jacquemont in: Garrett, ed., *Punjab*, 59.

71. Badenoch, *Punjab Industries*, 55.

72. *Gazetteer Amritsar District: 1883–4*, 45; *Gazetteer Mooltan District: 1883–4*, 154. See, for octroi as a source of income to the Amritsar Municipality, its administration, and rates after annexation to the twentieth century: Gauba, *Amritsar*, 199–206, 210.

73. PAL–P, 19.2.1853, Nos 52–3.

74. Khilnani, *British Power in the Punjab*, 183, 212.

75. See, for the involvement of traders from Peshawar District in profitable trade from Punjab towards Chitral, Gilgit, and Badakhshan: Biddulph, *Tribes of the Hindoo Koosh*, 10, 66. For evidence of its relative insignificance earlier in the century: Steinbach, *Punjaub*, 7. For Peshawar's growth under Ranjit Singh: Grewal, *Sikhs of the Punjab*, 110.

76. For the rationale for a trade fair at Peshawar: Khan, *Afghanistan and its Inhabitants*, 20. The fairs were in decline by the early 1870s, however; see: NAI–F, Secret, September 1872, Nos 193–4, 25.

77. Bayly notes the justificatory reference to trade expansion concealed the needs associated with the expansion of the garrison state under Catherine II (r. 1762–96) and Alexander I (r. 1801–25): 'First Age of Global Imperialism', 37. For the plans to trade with central Asia through a terraqueous sea–land route proffered by J. P. Nixon, consul general in Baghdad, indicative of continued British interest (if not action): Anon., *Reports in Relation to Trade with Turkey*, especially 6.

78. Geyer, *Russian Imperialism*, 329.

79. Carrère d'Encausse, *Islam and the Russian Empire*, 38.

80. Levi, *Khoqand*, chapter 7.

81. Millward, *Eurasian Crossroads*, 133–6, 157.

82. Ibid., 157.

83. Fraser, *Marches of Hindustan*, 259, 266; Carrère d'Encausse, *Islam and the Russian Empire*, 42–3. For a history of the Russo-Chinese Bank, and a review of the scholarship on the subject: Yago, 'The Russo-Chinese Bank', especially pp. 145–7, 159–60, 162–4.

84. Rizvi, *Trans-Himalayan Caravans*, 205. *Cf.* Curzon, *Russia in Central Asia*, 99.

85. Carrère d'Encausse, *Islam and the Russian Empire*, 39–40.

86. Ibid., 42–3; Geyer, *Russian Imperialism*, 92–3.

87. Indian traders also frequented these military-cum-trade forts: Levi, *Indian Diaspora*, 224.

88. On the founding of these trading companies: Levi, *Indian Diaspora*, 246; NAI–F, Secret, Governor General's Despatch to the Secret Committee, No. 37 of 1858; NAI–F, Secret, Despatch from Secret Committee, No. 1922, 9.2.1858; NAI–F, Secret, 7.10.1859, No. 16. For the identities of the indigenous middlemen: Fitzpatrick, *Great Russian Fair*, 81–2; NAI–F, Secret, September 1872, Nos 193–4, 20. For Indian trade in Russian trade towns and Indo-Russian commercial relations: Levi, *Indian Diaspora*, 239–41.

89. NAI–F, Political A, December 1861, Nos 89–91. Abdul Majid offered 'brother' as a translation of *Bai*, although the term is more likely to be the local variant of *Bey*, meaning 'lord' or 'chief', and is thus indicative of their economic and social standing.

90. NAI–F, Secret I, 1870, Nos 90–6, 13.

91. Ibid., 3. It was not unusual for local populations to protest the effects of discriminatory policies on non-subject peoples, who they saw as their brethren as well as their 'colleagues'; see, for the protests following the Qing's expulsions of foreign merchant communities from Xinjiang in 1828: Newby, *Empire and the Khanate*, 137.

92. Carrère d'Encausse, *Islam and the Russian Empire*, 40–1.

93. See, for a description of the 'dual city' in Tashkent, with Russian and Asian segments: Landsell, *Russian Central Asia*, vol. I, 438–52. See, also: Logofet, *The Land of Wrong*, 8; Carrère d'Encausse, *Islam and the Russian Empire*, 40–1.

94. NAI–F, Secret E, October 1882, No. 385.

95. Levi, *Indian Diaspora*, 251–2.

96. Ibid., 252–3.

97. Kakar, *Government and Society*, 214.

98. Levi, *Indian Diaspora*, 256–7.

99. Markovits, *Indian Merchants*, 78–9, 220, who, of course, focuses exclusively on the Hindu merchants of Shikarpur.

100. NAI–F, Secret F, May 1888, No. 40, 11; Kaushik, 'Economic Relations', 69.

101. On the collapse: Bhattacharya, 'Predicaments of Mobility', 182. For details of Indian traders in Yarkand: Rizvi, *Trans-Himalayan Caravans*, 206.

102. NAI, Foreign Department, Secret F, February 1892, No. 160, 1; Levi, *Indian Diaspora*, 257–8; Kaushik, 'Economic Relations', 69–70.

103. With restrictions on moneylenders within Punjab after the turn of the century, some turned not only to trade within Punjab or finance-based opportunities outside India, but to financial markets elsewhere on the subcontinent. 'Punjabi' and 'Kabuli' bankers formed the bulk of the 'outsiders' who constituted the moneylending class in 1920s Muzaffarpur in Bihar, for example: Yang, *Bazaar India*, 242. Some Shikarpuris moved to Karachi, Bombay, south India, and Burma: Markovits, *Indian Merchants*, 105–6.

104. Anon., *Reports by Her Majesty's Secretaries*, 170.

105. Carroll, *Science, Culture*, 171.

7. KNOWLEDGE

1. PAL–P, 9.2.1856, Nos 1–2, 3.

2. Ghobrial, *Whispers of Cities*, 1, for details of Ottoman cryptic messages submitted as bundles of goods where each item rhymed with something significant.

3. PAL–P, 9.2.1856, Nos 1–2, 8.

4. Ibid., 4.

5. Note, however, that identities were easily mistaken: the French traveller J. P. Ferrier was repeatedly annoyed at being mistaken for an Englishman: Bayly, *Taming the Imperial Imagination*, 57.

6. Ibid., 4–5.

7. Ibid., 5–6.

8. For the political context surrounding Afzal Khan's posting in Balkh: Lee, *Ancient Supremacy*, especially 206–81.

9. PAL–P, 9.2.1856, Nos 1–2, 6.

10. On the mobility of money: Sood, *India and the Islamic Heartlands*, 46. On the variety of coins and specie flows: Crews, *Afghan Modern*, 95–6; Hopkins, *Modern Afghanistan*, 119–26. On *hundi*: Markovits, *Indian Merchants*, especially 186–9; and, Martin, 'Economic History of Hundi', for a detailed exploration of *hundi* as a legal-commercial instrument.

11. On the acquisition of land in return for debt, see: Levi, *Indian Diaspora*, 252–6.

12. The Great Game thesis has been much debated and mainly exorcised by historians from the analysis of imperial relations and the formulation of policy with regard to Afghanistan and the central Asian states. See: Bayly, *Taming the Imperial Imagination*, especially 10–16. *Cf.* Sergeev, *Great Game 1856–1907*.

13. This is akin to what C. A. Bayly was suggesting in writing that the 'information order' was 'not separate from the world of power or economic exploitation, but stands both prior to it and dependent on it [...] [with a degree of autonomy from politics or economic structure.' Idem, *Empire and Information*, 4. Bayly's ideas about the information order are elaborated in the next section.

14. In Indian history, the pathbreaking work was that of Cohn, *Forms of Knowledge*; Bayly, *Empire and Information*. The works on Punjab and Afghanistan are cited in the course of this chapter.

15. Stoler, *Along the Archival Grain*, here especially 44–51. Bayly, *Taming the Imperial Imagination*, 3, 179–211. Aside from other references within this chapter, see: Choudhury, 'Sinews of Panic'.

16. PAL–P, 9.2.1856, Nos 1–2.

17. Bayly, *Taming the Imperial Imagination*, 12. See, for a rich recent characterisation of the personalities, politics, and causes of the Anglo-Afghan War: Dalrymple, *Return of a King*. The causes of British policy have been much debated, see: Morrison, 'Twin Imperial Disasters', here, 268. Morrison seeks to interrogate the veracity of fears to explain away the Great Game, whereas this chapter tries to explore the relationship of emotions to policy.

18. NAI–F, Secret Committee, 21.11.1838, Nos 60–1.

19. Morrison, 'Twin Imperial Disasters'; idem, 'Camels and Colonial Armies'.

20. Dalrymple, *Return of a King*, 469.

21. Bayly, *Empire and Information*, 4. The remainder of this and the following paragraph draw on pp. 10–96.

22. Ibid., here, 5, and also 19.

23. On Hastings' penchant for statistical knowledge: Raj, *Relocating Modern Science*, 108–9.

24. Bayly, *Empire and Information*, 97–141.

25. For information (rather than intelligence) on the state of politics in northwest India reported to Bombay via the Thatta factory: MSA–SILB, 1760, No. 14, Letter Nos 31, 42, 207; MSA–SILB, 1767 No. 21, Letter No. 148; MSA–SILB, 1768, No. 22, Letter Nos 14, 105, 144, 168; MSA–SILB, 1769, No. 23, Letter No. 92. For competition between Bombay and Calcutta in the 1830s: Dalrymple, *Return of a King*, 49.

26. On commercial and political motives: Nightingale, *Trade and Empire*, 158–60.

27. Pottinger, *Travels*.

28. Heathcote, *Balochistan*, 27–9.

29. Bayly, *Empire and Information*, 48–9, and citation, 130.

30. Ibid., 128–41.

31. Hopkins, *Modern Afghanistan*.

32. Ibid., especially chapter 1.

33. Hopkins, *Modern Afghanistan*, especially chapter 1. For a list, albeit not exhaustive, of European travellers from 1783 to 1878 who left published accounts or some other documentary trace in Britain: Bayly, *Taming the Imperial Imagination*, 296–304.

34. Yapp, *Strategies of British India*, 200–32; Huttenback, *British Relations with Sind*, 20.

35. Ibid. See, also: Bayly, *Taming the Imperial Imagination*, 119–47, and 148–75 for the impact of the 1839 campaign on the further narrowing of differences.

36. Dalrymple, *Return of a King*, 100, 228, 230–1, 276–8. Here, Dalrymple follows other recent work emphasising the role of Afghan resistance, itself deep-rooted rather than springing suddenly in 1839–42, perhaps commencing as early as 1803 during the dynastic war and civil strife in Afghanistan: Bayly, *Taming the Imperial Imagination*, 187.

37. Dalrymple portrays a handsome and intellectually talented man who quickly grows out of lofty ambitions to show skill: *Return of a King*, 57, for his early adaptation.

38. Morrison, 'Twin Imperial Disasters', 292–3.

39. See, for instance: Bayly, *Empire and Information*, 55, 212–46.

40. See, for a rich characterisation from the eastern Mediterranean and beyond: Gürkan, 'Espionage', especially 97–130, 147–8. See, also: Ghobrial, *Whispers of Cities*, 19–21, 42–9. Such mutual interest between merchants and the establishment enabled the Company to weather its numerous moments of crisis: Wilson, *India Conquered*, here 28–29. On merchants as diplomats and the commercial objective of diplomatic missions, see, for example: Pinto, 'Diplomatic Agency of Art', especially 150, 154, 156–7.

41. Marshall, *Intelligence and Espionage*, here especially 3–5.

42. There were, of course, variations in the timing and extent of these changes. Whereas the English state only began institutionalising intelligence within the office of secretary of state over the later seventeenth century, the relocation of such functions in the chancellery and the incorporation of specialists in new intelligence technologies (e.g. cryptography, steganography) was earlier or more decisive elsewhere. Following the Venetians, the Habsburgs strove (albeit not entirely successfully) to bureaucratically centralise and institutionalise intelligence gathering in the sixteenth century, whereas their major rival in the Mediterranean world, the Ottoman Empire, retained such functions in individuals (not offices) in a manner more closely aligned with its English or Indian contemporaries; see: Gürkan, 'Espionage', especially pp. 80–8, 187–263, 345–431.

43. Ibid., 6–7, 32–3.

44. Laidlaw, *Colonial Connections*.

45. On the American impact: ibid., 6 and n. 17.

46. Hevia, *Imperial Security State*, 17–33. The extension of these technologies of the state to the modernising Ottoman Empire and Japan are discussed in the next chapter.

47. Ibid., 34.

48. Ibid., 36; Stokes, *English Utilitarians*.

49. Hevia, *Imperial Security State*, 8

50. Ibid., 66, for quotation of MacGregor. See, for the location of the new Intelligence Branch (established 1887) in the old Thugee and Dacoitee Department (founded in 1830) and the concern for co-ordinating intelligence *vis–à–vis* these threats: Condos, *Insecurity State*, 61.

51. Such changes were evidently in motion in the Bellew and Lumsden mission to Afghanistan in 1857–8: Bayly, *Taming the Imperial Imagination*, especially 224.

52. Hevia, *Imperial Security State*, 66–8. On the conduct of these practices, see: ibid., 73–106; Raj, *Relocating Modern Science*, 181–222.

53. Hevia, *Imperial Security State*, 72, although see the discussion on 157–8 relating Aylmer Cameron's critique of Charles MacGregor's selective and exaggerated reading of the intelligence archive in furtherance of his ambitions, described below.

54. Morrison, '"Natural" Frontier', citation from 169.

55. Gardner, 'Ready Materials for Another World', 72.

56. NAI–F, Secret F, March 1886, Nos 303–13. See, for further discussion of the development of British 'Russophobia' from the 1860s: Morrison, *Russian Rule in Samarkand*, 24, n. 37.

57. NAI–F, Secret F, March 1886, No. 303, 1.

58. Ibid., 3.

59. Ibid.

60. Bayly, *Indian Society*, 76–8.

61. The roll is reproduced in Appendix II. See, also: Hanifi, *Connecting Histories*, 155–6. In terms of the types of business organisation and networks that the roll reveals, it shows similarity to the 1747 Russian census of the Indian community at Astrakhan: Dale, *Indian Merchants*, 113–16. On the British Indian state's continued reliance on 'native newswriters' and the interpenetration (or leakiness) of their work with the surveillance structures and intelligence personnel of the Afghan (and Qajar) rulers: Crews, *Afghan Modern*, 103–13.

62. Although Indians responded to the transformations ushered in by the colonial state, stimulating the emergence of new epistemic communities as well as critique; Bayly, *Empire and Information*, chapters 5–6.

63. Ibid., 165.

64. Ibid., 143.

65. But the widening distance between coloniser or colonial state and Indian society meant that information panic could also originate in the latter: Yang, 'Conversation of Rumors', especially 493–5.

66. Bayly, *Taming the Imperial Imagination*, 179–291.

67. The customs system is discussed in the next chapter.

68. Singha, 'Punished by Surveillance', 265—the quotation is from R. N. Cust (1896).

69. Sauli, 'Circulation and Authority'.

70. Markovits, *et al.*, 'Circulation and Society under Colonial Rule', 8–9.

71. On the darkening of British representations of Afghans in the later nineteenth century: Bayly, *Taming the Imperial Imagination*, 228.

72. Bayly, *Birth of the Modern World*, 105–6; Bayly, *Taming the Imperial Imagination*, 248 and n. 89.

73. On the Indo-Afghan frontier, the fear of Wahhabism and 'Muhammadan fanatics' or 'Hindustani fanatics' was crystallised in the 'fanatical colony', at a place named Sitana, of armed Muslims supposedly of Wahabbist beliefs from Bengal who settled amongst the Yusufzai tribes. Established around 1824, the Sitana fanatics fought Sikh, then British, political authority. The fanatics were monitored, the British fearing their numbers were steadily swollen by fresh migrants from Patna and Kanpur; see: PAL–P, 24.2.1855, Nos 38–40; PAL–P, 24.3.1855, No. 74; PAL–P, 16.6.1855, No. 24. Finally, a punitive expedition was launched in 1863, lasting two months, the most protracted and violent of the pacification campaigns (or 'frontier wars') conducted along the frontier in the second half of the nineteenth century on account of a number of tribes joining the fray against what they perceived as a foreign and anti-Islamic belligerent power, and hardly a success in terms of outcome when balanced against expense and loss of life: Adye, *Sitana*, especially 16–18 for a summary of the origins of the Sitana colony, and 91–101 for an evaluation of the campaign and a statement of continued anxieties about frontier insecurity.

74. The Lahore archives are full of details of (attempted) assaults, assassinations, and outrages, fanatical uprisings, plunder raids, and blockades by Pashtun and other tribes into British territory or against British officers from 1849 onward that have been little examined by scholars, if at all. Adye counts twenty British campaigns in response, 1850–63: idem, *Sitana*, 94. Instead, much recent work has focussed on the formulation of a new legal discourse about the fanatic intimately tied to perceptions of the frontiersmen (and almost always men): Stephens, 'Phantom Wahabbi'; Kolsky, 'Colonial Rule of Law'; Condos, 'Fanaticism'. For a presentist analysis of the Sitana colony in the context of frontiersmen's resistance to authority: Hopkins and Marsden, *Fragments*, chapter 3.

75. Hevia, *Imperial Security State*, 212–13.

76. Leonard, 'Frontier Ethnography', 182–4. According to Nichols, the fantasy was rooted in the ways autochthonous participants—Afghan, Pashtun, Punjabi, Sikh—discussed the Durrani–Sikh or Pashtun frontier tribe–Sikh conflicts, not least as *jihad* (spiritual uprising), which was relayed to the British as early as the 1820s via the Company's presence at Ludhiana: Nichols, *Settling the Frontier*, 91–2.

77. Zaman, 'Revolutionary History'.

78. NAI–F, Foreign, 23.10.1847, Nos 44–5.

79. PAL–P, 8.7.1854, Nos 30–7; PAL–P, 12.8.1854, Nos 22–3; PAL–P, 18.8.1855, No. 36; PAL–P, 5.10.1856, Nos 11–12.

80. See, for example: NAI–F, Secret I, 1870, Nos 90–6, 8.

81. Speake, ed., *Travel and Exploration*, 503–4.

82. Levi, *Khoqand*, 133–4.

83. Bayly, *Taming the Imperial Imagination*, 65, on Masson.

84. Mallampalli, *Muslim Conspiracy*, here especially chapter 1, and *passim*, which describes such cases in greater detail, concentrating on the connection of Sayyid Ahmad's following to princely rulers in south India and their supposed concoction of a Wahhabi plot to overthrow British rule.

85. NAI–F, Secret Committee, 1.5.1839, No. 125.

86. Indians passing through central Asia to undertake Hajj were probably rare, although an Indian *hajji* is the protagonist of the Bukharan writer Fitrat Bukharayi's Persian-language story: *Bayanat-i Sayyah-i Hindi*.

87. Kane, *Russian Hajj*, 47–119; Slight, *British Empire and the Hajj*, 46–7.

88. NAI–F, Secret E., October 1882, No. 313, 4.

89. Slight, *British Empire and the Hajj*, especially 62–165.

90. See, for an example of the fear of Kabulis in the 1850s, and the resultant temporary restrictions on foreigners: *Press Lists of Old Records [...] Volume XVII*, 696.

91. For a longer discussion: Bhattacharya, 'Predicaments of Mobility', 194–5.

92. On information panic in central Asia: Morrison, 'Applied Orientalism', 645.

93. The causes and consequences have been amply studied. For a review: Wagner, 'The Marginal Mutiny'.

94. Cullen, *Statistical Movement*. This is not to privilege the metropolitan over the colonial. Rather, an interplay was evident, as in the formative phenomena of the British state's gathering of information regarding the health of armed forces in the colonies (45–52), for example, or the interplay of the Company and its servants, not with the British state directly, but with those metropolitan societies concurrently influencing, albeit lightly, the development of social statistics in Britain (77–90).

95. Falconer, 'Architecture and Ethnography', 69–85.

96. Metcalf, *Ideologies of the Raj*, 119.

97. Ryan, *Picturing Empire*, especially 156–8. See, also: Pinney, 'Classification and Fantasy'.

98. Metcalf, *Ideologies of the Raj*, 119, n. 2. Metcalf quotes correspondence from NAI. Towards the end of the decade, the Colonial Office in London issued a circular requesting similar sorts of photographs from across the British Empire: Ryan, *Picturing Empire*, 151.

99. Sonntag, trans., 'Foreword to the Turkestan Album'.

100. Brower, 'Islam and Ethnicity', 123.

101. Ibid., 123–32.

102. For, respectively, a historical and a historiographical survey: Schimmelpenninck van der Oye, *Russian Orientalism*; Brower and Lazzerini, eds, *Russia's Orient*, xi–xix.

103. Morrison, 'Applied Orientalism', 645–6. *Cf.* Brower, 'Islam and Ethnicity', 130.

104. Leonard, 'Colonial Ethnography'.
105. On Yusufzai recruitment: Adye, *Sitana*, 12; Nichols, *Settling the Frontier*, 277. On the sheer scale of military recruitment in Punjab, and the marked upturn from *c.* 1880: Yong, *Garrison State*; Mazumder, *Indian Army*.
106. Streets, *Martial Races*, 10.
107. For a critical approach to the subject: Rand and Wagner, 'Recruiting the "Martial Races"'.
108. Streets, *Martial Races*, 93; Hevia, *Imperial Security State*.
109. Kolff, *Naukar, Rajput and Sepoy*.
110. Hevia, *Imperial Security State*, 179.
111. Ballantyne, *Aryanism*, especially 33–4.
112. Ibid., 48–54; Metcalf, *Ideologies of the Raj*, chapter 3.
113. Leonard pinpoints a decisive shift from the 1870s, whereby such metropolitan organisations as the Anthropological Institute and the Folk-Lore Society established new methodological agendas for ethnographers in the colonial field, including on the Indo-Afghan frontier, with whom ethnographers were sometimes more involved (that is, in place of the colonial state): Leonard, 'Frontier Ethnography'. Note that Afghans had much earlier been interested in ethnogenesis, especially within the writing of genealogy (*nasab*) in the seventeenth and eighteenthcenturies by politically ambitious Pashtuns in the Indo-Afghan region and India proper, its role in Afghan historiography only adding charge to this branch of ethnographic inquiry in colonial India: Nichols, *Settling the Frontier*, 25–43; Gommans, *Indo-Afghan Empire*, 160–74.
114. Nichols, *Settling the Frontier*, 82–3.
115. Spiers, 'Highland Soldier'. See, also: Streets, *Martial Races*, chapter 2. The valorisation of the Afghan highlander was later contested and replaced with alternatives, including H. W. Bellew's depiction of 'a society under the thrall of corrupt priestly classes', its rulers dependent on looting and neglectful of the need for investment: Leonard, 'Frontier Ethnography', 182. Note, however, that Bellew's view recycled—almost verbatim—extant descriptions of Afghans; see: Adye, *Sitana*, 5–10.
116. Quoted in: Adye, *Sitana*, 4.
117. Note that the origins of genesis narratives, including the preoccupation with Biblical references and the 'lost tribes of Israel', are traceable to Elphinstone: Bayly, *Taming the Imperial Imagination*, 55–6, 66.
118. It was from their denigration in the Mughal context that Afghan patrons of the Mughal era onwards sought to 'retrieve' or construct Afghan origins and history as honourable: Green, 'Tribe, Diaspora, and Sainthood', 183–6.
119. Yong, *Garrison State*.
120. Vartavarian, 'Pacification and Patronage'.
121. On the Pashtuns' reluctance to forfeit their independence to the British, and their opportunistic (but unsuccessful) agitation during the 1857 Rebellion: *Gazetteer Peshawar District, 1897–98*, 87.

122. Condos, *Insecurity State*, 25–66, and the quotation on 36.

123. See for the early administration's anxiety over interpersonal violence in Peshawar District: Nicholas, *Settling the Frontier*, 121–5.

124. Condos, *Insecurity State*, *passim*, and quotation on 141.

125. Ibid., chapters 3–4.

126. The phrase is Morrison's: 'Imperial Citizenship', 334. On the legacy of military authoritarianism in Punjab to Pakistan, see: Jalal, *Democracy and Authoritarianism*, especially chapter 1.

127. Morrison, 'Imperial Citizenship', 350–1. *Cf.* Crews, *For Prophet and Tsar*, especially chapters 4–5.

128. Morrison, 'Applied Orientalism', 631 and n. 73.

129. Brower, 'Islam and Ethnicity', especially 119–22. On the phrase attributed to Lawrence: Bayly, *Taming the Imperial Imagination*, 242, n. 59.

130. Brower, 'Islam and Ethnicity', 130, citing official opinion from material in the Uzbekistan State Archives.

131. Morrison, 'Imperial Citizenship in the Russian Empire', 353.

132. Morrison, 'Sufism, Pan-Islamism and Information Panic'.

133. See, for details of Robert Sandeman's 'tribal service' system: Hevia, *Imperial Security State*, 113.

134. Condos, *Insecurity State*, 105–24; PAL–P, 17.5.1856, Nos 11–16; Dodwell, ed., *Indian Empire*, 92.

135. Condos, *Insecurity State*, 70–86.

136. Ibid., 86–94.

137. Note: the disappearance of jungle because of prior land clearance for arable and, perhaps, ecological change contributed to the arid expanse in the region that was now (re-)greened; Moosvi, *People, Taxation, and Trade*, 91–3.

138. Ali, *Panjab Under Imperialism*, 45.

139. Ibid., 59; Darling, *Punjab Peasant*, 115–16.

140. Ali, *Panjab Under Imperialism*.

141. Christensen, 'Tribesmen, Government and Political Economy', 177; Nichols, *Settling the Frontier*, especially 133–57, 196–7, 253–62. On irrigation in the Peshawar Cantonment area in 1849, the year following the annexation: PAL–P, 19.5.1849, Nos 1027–30.

142. Nichols, *Settling the Frontier*, 208–15.

143. Amrith, *Unruly Waters*, 124.

144. Morrison, 'Peasant Settlers', 389.

145. Ibid., 388. On the problem of the poor whites in other contexts, see, for instance: Fischer-Tiné, 'Britain's Other Civilising Mission'.

146. Morrison, 'Peasant Settlers', 393.

147. See, for example, an inquiry into breeding horses from Turki stock in the early 1860s: NAI–F, Military A, May 1863, Nos 16–19; NAI–F, Military B, February 1865, Nos 28–32. See, also, the report of the Napier Mission: NAI–F, Political A, February 1876, Nos 73–4.

148. See, for disappointment: NAI–F, Military B, February 1865, Nos 28–32, 3, 11; NAI–F, General B, March 1880, No. 153.

149. NAI–F, Frontier A, September 1888, No. 85, 1; NAI–F, Secret F, July 1889, No. 33. In 1896, when the Afghan amir was trying to enlarge the cavalry, the supply of remounts was so short that exports to India were prohibited. The restriction was not removed until Jandad Khan and other Kabuli horse dealers succeeded in petitioning the amir in 1898, although the prohibition on Turki and Afghan mares remained; see: NAI–F, Secret F, May 1896, No. 372, 2; NAI–F, Secret F, November 1898, No. 127, 1.

150. Bayly, *Indian Society*, 143–4.

151. The schemes discussed in this paragraph also aimed to replace existing decentralised breeding for cavalry on the precolonial *silladari* system; see: Ali, *Panjab Under Imperialism*, 130. On the modernity of these practices, and the Hissar stud, see: Caton, 'Imperial Ambition of Science'; idem, 'Scientific Breeding'.

152. Ali, *Panjab Under Imperialism*, 123–9.

153. Ibid., 130, 133–55.

154. Ibid., 156–7.

155. Feaver, ed., *Webbs in Asia*, 287–8.

156. Christensen, 'Tribesmen, Government and Political Economy', 179–80.

157. Ibid., 177–80.

158. Ibid., 178.

159. Nichols, *Settling the Frontier*, 42, 49.

160. In the formulation of the alliance, the amir reversed his former hostility to the British that had followed from their efforts to oust him from power during the 1839–42 invasion. On his armament: PAL–P, 18.10.1856, Nos 5–6 and 12–13. For the Company's permissiveness toward Shah Shuja's agents' purchases of arms and munitions in the Delhi bazaars in 1832, as an example of their promoting certain sorts of weaponisation in their own strategic interest, see: Dalrymple, *Return of a King*, 66.

161. Crews, 'Trafficking in Evil?', 127–9.

162. Crews, *Afghan Modern*, 95.

163. Ibid., 95–6.

164. Ibid., 96.

165. Note that munitions were also being smuggled by overland routes into Chinese territory: PAL–P, 17.7.1858, Nos 4–5; PAL–P, 16.10.1857, Nos 64–5.

166. For a discussion of the wider literary treatment of these themes: Bayly, *Taming the Imperial Imagination*, 7–8.

167. Napier deemed the disguise 'too transparent to deceive anybody' when considering how best to safely proceed incognito: NAI–F, Secret, October 1878, No. 4, 3.

168. PAL–P, 9.2.1856, Nos 1–2, 6.

169. Stoler, *Along the Archival Grain*, chapter 7.

170. PAL–P, 28.9.1850, Nos 71–3.

171. On efforts—which have been particularly concentrated upon the Indian context—to undo the silencing of women through colonial documentary practices: Ibid., 48, n. 99.

172. Hevia, *Imperial Security State*, 222; Drephal, '*Corps Diplomatique*', 971–2.

173. Bayly, *Empire and Information*, 91–4. In the context of early modern Europe, too, ladies-in-waiting and ambassadors' or diplomats' wives were important actors in espionage networks for female or male patrons, inside or beyond their immediate milieu. For details of such activities within the larger context of elite female households, see: Akkerman and Houben, *Politics of Female Households*.

174. *Cf.* de Vivo, *Information and Communication*, 112–17.

175. Wide, 'Astrakhan, Borqa', Chadari, Dreshi', 166. On Abdur Rahman's overhauling of the Afghan state's surveillance networks: Crews, *Afghan Modern*, 97.

176. Choudhury, 'Sinews of Panic', 988.

177. Dalrymple, *Return of a King*, 224–5.

178. These were not unique to the colonial context, however, and it is possible to think of emotions including anxiety and vulnerability as drivers of the patrimonial–bureaucratic politics and institutions of the Mughal Empire, of alliance-building and wars of succession, of the public execution or punishment of rebels and opponents as well as the dispensation and display of justice and mercy.

179. For instance: Bayly, *Taming the Imperial Imagination*; Dalrymple, *Return of a King*, Hopkins, *Modern Afghanistan*.

180. Bayly, *Taming the Imperial Imagination*, in spite of twice mentioning (127, 149) Stoler's provocation to read along and against the grain of the colonial archive to avoid overstating colonial power and reproducing its central problematics.

181. There is now a vast literature on plantations and labour in Assam and the north-eastern frontier, although the comparison, to the knowledge of the author of this book, remains to be analysed. See, for a recent introduction to these themes: Bennike, 'Governing Landscapes'.

182. Hopkins, *Ruling the Savage Periphery*.

183. Manjapra, 'Plantation Dispossessions'.

8. TECHNOLOGY

1. Yang, *Technology of Empire*, 8 and n. 24 for alternative conceptualisations of techno–imperialism.

2. Ibid., 18.

3. This connection ignores the tremendous role of domestic agents—in government and finance or in supplying technical expertise—in the early years of railway development in the Argentine before the 1880s, as well as their continuing to exert a powerful influence over the pace and direction of railway development during the 'railway mania' that lasted into the 1930s: Lewis, 'Rethinking the Role of Railway Companies'.

4. Cole, 'Precarious Empires'; Tagliacozzo, 'Lit Archipelago'. Unfortunately, Tagliacozzo does not bring the public goods dimension into his discussion, but this would offer a compelling avenue through which to more closely analyse inter–imperial co-operation (as opposed to rivalry).

5. NAI–F, Secret, September 1872, Nos 60–83, 29.

6. Kakar, *Government and Society*, 227.

7. PSA–F, April 1872, No. 4, 203.

8. Or, at least, the British thought it would alter the existing organisation of trade: Rose, *Tribes and Castes [...] Vol. III. L.–Z.*, 233. See, for indigenous responses to the introduction of these technologies elsewhere in India: Headrick, *Tentacles of Progress*, especially chapters. 2–4.

9. Cole, 'Precarious Empires'.

10. Ray, 'Asian Capital'. See also, indicatively: Iliffe, *Tanganyika*, 136–48; Arnold, *Everyday Technology*, especially chapter 2.

11. NAI–F, Frontier A, December 1885, Nos 3–8, frontmatter, 3.

12. NAI–F, Secret F, January 1885, No. 300, 1; NAI–F, Secret F, May 1888, No. 40, 8–9.

13. NAI–F, Frontier A, August 1887, Nos 31–7, frontmatter and 1.

14. NAI–F, Frontier A, May 1888, No. 295–300, 1–2.

15. Ibid., 2–3.

16. See, for example: NAI–F, Secret F, January 1895, No. 499; NAI–F, Frontier, May 1896 (Part B), Nos 1–16, 16.

17. NAI–F, Secret F, August 1891, Nos. 180–183, 1. See, also: NAI–F, Secret F, January 1891, Nos 141–2, 1.

18. See, also: NAI–F, Secret F, April 1889, No. 45, 1; NAI–F, Secret F, July 1889, No. 321, 3. *Cf.* Hanifi, *Connecting Histories*, 160–1.

19. Lydon, *Trans-Saharan Trails*, chapter 3.

20. Steinbach, *Punjaub*, 89–90; Lal, *Travels*, 141–2.

21. Hanifi, *Connecting Histories*, 114–20.

22. *Gazetteer Delhi District: 1883–4*, 132.

23. Parthasarathi, 'Historical Issues of Deindustrialisation', 426–34; Machado, 'Cloths of a New Fashion', 82–3.

24. On 'peasantisation', see: Washbrook, 'Economic Depression'. See, for recent scrutiny of the 'deindustrialisation' thesis: Roy, ed., *Cloth and Commerce*, especially 21–2; Roy, *Traditional Industry*. See, for a finessing and deepening of Roy's revisionist approach: Haynes, *Small Town Capitalism*, particularly 8–10.

25. Guha, 'Handloom Industry'. Beyond Punjab, Madras' weavers were also able to tap foreign markets to weather the storm of English imports: Specker, 'Madras Handlooms'. And weavers in western India experienced a brief resurgence in trade across the Indian Ocean: Haynes, *Small Town Capitalism*, 43, 65–6.

26. See references in the note, immediately above, and: Yanagisawa, 'Handloom Industry'; Roy, *Traditional Industry*, especially 1–98.

27. Upward adaptation in Punjab included the production of: (1) Tinsel-embellished cotton cloths: *Gazetteer Jalandhar District: 1883–4*, 48; *Gazetteer Ludhiana District: 1888–9*, 158; *Gazetteer Shahpur District: 1897*, 186; *Gazetteer Amritsar District: 1883–4*, 45; *Gazetteer Multan District: 1901–2*, 248. (2) Block–printing floral and other motifs in gold and silver: *Gazetteer Hoshiarpur District: 1883–4*, 111. See, for an existing example: block-printed cotton (nineteenth-century, Punjab), V&A, Accession No. IS 6171B. (3) Embellishing imported English cloth: *Bahawalpur State, with Maps: 1904*, 267; *Gazetteer Lahore District: 1883–4*, 97. See, for an existing example: muslin with roghan work (c. 1880, Multan), V&A, Accession No. IS 411–1883. (4) Imitation of English patterns, including checks: *Gazetteer Lahore District: 1893–4*, 186; *Gazetteer Gujrat District: 1892–3*, 128; *Gazetteer Ludhiana District: 1888–9*, 158.

28. *Gazetteer Hoshiarpur District: 1883–4*, 111; Roy, *Traditional Industry*, 62–3.

29. Mathur, *India by Design*, 30–3. See, also: McGowan, *Crafting the Nation*, chapter 3, which discusses Kipling's career.

30. Haynes, *Small Town Capitalism*, especially 2, 45–52.

31. See, for the developing definition of what was, or was not, an artisanal, traditional craft: McGowan, *Crafting the Nation*, chapter 1.

32. V&A, Samples of Cotton Fabrics Worn by the Agricultural Population of the Punjab Showing the Patterns Peculiar to Different Races, Accession No. IS. 7916.

33. Dowleans, *Catalogue of the Contributions from India*, Section III, 6.

34. Seldom is much made of the two as parallel projects by scholars interested in the latter, for example: Falconer, 'Pure Labor of Love'.

35. *Gazetteer Lahore District: 1883–4*, 97. See, also: Kessinger, *Vilyatpur*, 58–9.

36. *Gazetteer Jalandhar District. 1883–4*, 46; *Gazetteer Ferozepore District: 1888–9* 106; *Ferozepore District, Statistical Tables: 1904*, 75; *Gazetteer Lahore District: 1883–4*, 97, 186.

37. *Gazetteer Shahpur District: 1897*, 186; *Gazetteer Jhang District: 1883–4*, 130; *Gazetteer Kohat District: 1883–4*, 110–11; Ibbetson, *Panjab Castes*, 302–3.

38. See, for the cotton boom: Harnetty, 'Cotton Exports', 426–7. On the role of middlemen: Sharma, *Artisans of the Punjab*, 70–3. On commercialisation: Roy, *Traditional Industry*. For the wider context to the weavers' agglomeration and the growth of towns: Haynes, *Small Town Capitalism*, chapter 2.

39. For details of ten types of coarse cloth woven in Gujrat in western Punjab: *Gazetteer Gujrat District: 1892–3*, 128.

40. *Gazetteer Lahore District: 1893–4*, 186. See, also: *Bahawalpur State, with Maps: 1904*, 267.

41. *Gazetteer Lahore District: 1883–4*, 97.

42. *Gazetteer Dera Ismail Khan District: 1883–4*, 142; *Bahawalpur State, with Maps: 1904*, 267. There are samples of such cloths in the V&A's Samples of Cotton Fabrics.

43. *Gazetteer Jalandhar District: 1883–4*, 46; *Gazetteer Jhang District: 1883–4*, 130; *Jhang District, with Maps: 1908*, 114.

44. Roy, *Cloth and Commerce*, 21–2.

45. See, for a detailed description of the organisation and operation of the inter-regional cloth trade from the files of the Punjab Police and Home departments: Bhattacharya, 'Predicaments of Mobility', 172–3.

46. Birdwood, *Industrial Arts*, vol. II, 78–80.

47. *Gazetteer Lahore District: 1883–4*, 97; *Gazetteer Mooltan District: 1883–4*, 108–9.

48. *Gazetteer Mooltan District: 1883–4*, 108–9. On the survival of chintz printing into the twentieth century: Trevaskis, *Punjab*, vol. II, 206.

49. The Punjabi chintz fragments are uncatalogued and have not been photographed, but can otherwise be viewed in the archives of the Victoria and Albert Museum, London: *Samples of Cotton Fabrics*, IS. 7916. The European chintzes found in Peshawar can be viewed on the museum's online repository, for example: the swatch with accession number IS. 1739—http://collections.vam.ac.uk/item/O476167/textile-sample-unknown/ [accessed: 27 August 2020]; or IS. 1734—http://collections.vam.ac.uk/item/O476171/textile-sample-unknown/ [accessed: 27 August 2020].

50. See, the discrepancies between: India Museum, *Inventory*, 44–6; V&A, [India Museum] Slip Book No. 11501 to 11750 and [India Museum] Slip Book No. 11589–11601. The V&A's Shaw Collection was inherited from the former museum of the East India Company, the remainder of the objects sent to the Ashmolean Museum in Oxford, with the V&A's inventory including a long list of items under the separate heading 'Samples of Textiles from Central Asia, collected at the fair held at Peshawar, December 1869. Nos. 1708 to 1764. Found in packing case no. 2, and replaced in it'.

51. See, below, for discussion of relative price differentials. See, also, the purchase prices in Peshawar: V&A, [India Museum] Slip Book Nos 11501 to 11750, Nos 11589–601. Unfortunately, no comparable set of prices exists for domestically produced chintz.

52. Meller, *Russian Textiles*, 196–7, for reproductions from her private collection of chintzes from *c.* 1860 to 1960, which complements the samples from *c.* 1750–60 reproduced in Arseneva, *Ivanovskie Sittsy*, discussed in chapter 6.

53. For the differential between handloom and mill–made cloth, and the ambiguity surrounding the survival of the former: Haynes, *Small Town Capitalism*, 94.

54. See, for Shikarpur's imports and its re-exports to overland markets in the late 1840s: NAI–F, Foreign, 18.7.1851, Nos 15–25, 181.

55. Calcutta was the main source of English cotton-textile imports in the 1870s, as evinced in the Punjab Trade Reports: IOR/V/24/4166. See, for redistribution: *Hoshiarpur District, with Maps*, 133, 152; *Gazetteer Ambala District: 1883–4*, 53; *Gazetteer Gujrat District: 1892–3*, 128; *Gazetteer Muzaffargarh District*, 106; *Jullundur District and Kapurthala State, with Maps: 1904*, 223. On re-exports: NAI–F, General A, March 1870, Nos 2–3, 7–8.

56. Appendix III.

57. *Gazetteer Jhang District: 1883–4*, 130.

58. IOR/V/24/4166, ETP (1873–4), 8.

59. See, for a map of the frontier posts: IOR/V/24/4166, ETP (1874–5).

60. Appendix III.

61. *Gazetteer Hoshiarpur District: 1883–4*, 111.

62. Latifi, *Industrial Punjab*, 4–5.

63. Ibid., 97–8; *Gazetteer Multan District: 1901–2*, 248; Watt, *Indian Art at Delhi*, 244–6; Birdwood, *Industrial Arts*, vol. II, 78–80. On the survival of the village dyer and printer: Rose, *Tribes and Castes [...] Vol. II. A.–K.*, 166; Crooke, *Natives of Northern India*, 137.

64. Badenoch, *Punjab Industries*, 1–2; Latifi, *Industrial Punjab*, 6.

65. Darling, *Rusticus Loquitur*, 51; Trevaskis, *Punjab*, vol. I, 221, vol. II, 205; Badenoch, *Punjab Industries*, 2–4; Latifi, *Industrial Punjab*, 7. For the long unwinding of village weaving: Kessinger, *Vilyatpur*, 157–61.

66. NAI–F, Secret I, 1870, Nos 90–6, 8; IOR/V/24/4167, ETP (1887–8), 1–2.

67. The second issue was put explicitly by the Punjab Government: NAI–F, Frontier A, August 1887, Nos 31–7, frontmatter, 2.

68. IOR/V/24/4166, ETP (1874–5), Table I.

69. IOR/V/24/4168, ETP (1895–6), frontmatter, 1; Curzon, *Russia in Central Asia*. Sauer, *Gateways to India*, was a popular pamphlet warning of the effects of the Russian railway system's extension.

70. IOR/V/24/4167, ETP (1890–1), frontmatter, 2. According to Alfred Leix, caravan transportation in fact improved: *Turkestan and its Textile Crafts*, 11.

71. See, for the anxiety of the Punjab and British Indian governments in relation to reliance on Peshawari traders: NAI–F, Frontier A, December 1885, Nos 3–8, frontmatter, 3; NAI–F, Frontier A, August 1887, Nos 31–7, frontmatter, 2. The Afghan amir also relied on Peshawari traders for trade-related information; see: NAI–F, Frontier A, August 1887, No. 32, 1.

72. NAI–F, Secret F, June 1892, Nos 11–69, 4.

73. NAI–F, Secret F, July 1896, No. 119, 2. According to H. A. Rose, Superintendent of the 1901 Punjab census and Punjab ethnography, the term Kuchi is synonymous with Powinda: Rose, *Tribes and Castes [...] Vol. II. A.–K.*, 552.

74. Although the amir's taxation was set at the standard rate of one-fortieth of the value of a camel-load (i.e. 2.5 per cent *ad valorem*) in accordance with the Sharia, additional arbitrary exactions at various points vexed the traders; see: IOR/V/24/4167, ETP (1887–8), 1–2.

75. IOR/V/24/4168, ETP (1895–6), 3; BL, IOR/V/24/4168, ETP (1897–8), frontmatter, 2.

76. NAI–F, Secret, September 1872, Nos. 193–4, 26. See, also: IOR/V/24/4167, ETP (1881–2), 9–11. This weakness was in spite of the tremendous efforts at centralisation under Abdur Rahman: Noelle, *State and Tribe*, 219, for discussion of extent of the centre's control over outlying territory under Dost Mohammad Khan. During his reign, Kabulis migrated to Balkh and Bukhara to escape the 'exorbitant territorial taxes' levied by the amir: ibid., 63–4.

77. See, for evidence of diversion via Quetta: IOR/V/24/4168, ETP (1896–7), 3. See, for the state's control of trade: Hanifi, *Connecting Histories*, 158–9.

78. NAI–F, Frontier A, August 1887, Nos 31–7, frontmatter, 1.

79. Geyer, *Russian Imperialism*, chapters 6–7.

80. Amongst the Asian informants were Shikarpuri financiers and 'Rahman Kul, an Akshal (Elder) of Shibarghan in Balkh–Turkistan', for example: NAI–F, Secret I, June 1869, Nos 49–57, 1. See, also: NAI–F, Secret I, 1870, Nos 90–6, 3–4; NAI–F, Secret, September 1872, Nos 193–4, 24.

81. NAI–F, Secret I, 1870, Nos 90–6, 5; NAI–F, Secret E, October 1882, Nos 186–201, 20.

82. NAI–F, Secret M, 1870, No. 47, 1–2; NAI–F, Secret I, 1870, Nos 90–6, 7–8. See, also: NAI–F, Secret, January 1882, Nos 671–2; NAI–F, Secret E, June 1883, Nos 309–10.

83. NAI–F, Secret I, 1870, Nos 90–6, 7. The rates were reported in the *Turkestan Gazette* in January 1882: NAI–F, Secret E, October 1882, Nos 186–201, 20. See, for weight equivalences: NAI–F, Frontier, May 1896 (Part B), Nos 1–16, 9.

84. NAI–F, Secret F, May 1888, No. 40, 6. See, also: NAI–F, Secret I, 1870, Nos 90–6, 6–7; NAI–F, Secret, September 1872, Nos 193–4, 24.

85. IOR/V/24/4167, ETP (1887–8), 1–2.

86. NAI–F, Secret F, May 1888, No. 40, 9.

87. See, for example: Anon., *Reports in Relation to Trade*, 35–7.

88. Fitzpatrick, *Great Russian Fair*, 63–4.

89. NAI–F, Secret F, May 1888, No. 40, 9; NAI–F, Secret, September 1872, Nos 193–4, 24. For examples of Russian chintzes with thick floral designs: Meller, *Russian Textiles*, 74–9, 82–9, 93–9, 104–7

90. Carlano, 'Russian Printed Cottons', 86.

91. Such examples are evident in the samples collected by Meller and reproduced in: Meller, ed., *Russian Textiles*, 64, 46, 174, and 175 (respectively). See, for a striking chintz fabric with calligraphy manufactured by Praskovya Vitova and Sons in Ivanovo in 1896: Arseneva, *Ivanovskie Sittsy*, plate 111.

92. Carlano, 'In Celebration', 32, 35; Carlano, 'Russian Printed Cottons', 88.

93. For examples of Manchester chintzes found in central Asia: Meller, ed., *Russian Textiles*, 172–3. On the restrictions: NAI–F, Secret F, June 1895, No. 500, 1.

94. See, for the British–Russian split in sphere of influence: Kakar, *Government and Society*, 214–15. See, also, for trade and trade policy under Abdur Rahman's successor, Habibullah: Gregorian, *Emergence of Modern Afghanistan*, 195–8. McChesney, *Waqf*, highlights the long-standing integration of northern Afghanistan into central Asia.

95. Metcalf, *Imperial Connections*, chapters 3–4. Recently, historians have consulted the testimony written by Indian soldiers—including Punjabis, although their voices are perhaps disproportionately quiet—relating to their service in global conflicts to resurrect subaltern perspectives: Singh, *Testimonies of Indian*; Yang, 'China and India Are One'.

96. Lally, 'Economic Development in Colonial Punjab', especially 1–2.

97. This paragraph draws on arguments made more fully in: Lally, 'Economic Development in Colonial Punjab'.

98. NAI–F, Foreign, 12.9.1845, Nos 58–60, 7.

99. See, for example: *Gazetteer Mooltan District: 1883–4*, 140–41; *Gazetteer Dera Ghazi Khan District: 1883–4*, 3.

100. *Gazetteer Mooltan District: 1883–4*, 140.

101. Roseberry, *Imperial Rule in Punjab*, 144, 154. R. H. Davies stated the trade declined from Rs 1,000,000 to Rs 100,000 over the 1850s: *Report*, 38.

102. IOR/E/4/804, 843.

103. Khilnani, *British Power in the Punjab*, 100–1, 113–14.

104. Ibid., 109; Roseberry, *Imperial Rule in Punjab*, 144. For details of the disastrous First and Second Summary Settlements: *Gazetteer Mooltan District: 1883–4*, 125–8.

105. *Gazetteer Mooltan District: 1883–4*, 129. For detailed discussion of the post-Mutiny settlement as it affected the state's relations with the agriculturalists and landowners: Roseberry, *Imperial Rule in Punjab*, chapters 9–10.

106. PAL–R, 8.9.1860, Nos 55–8, 3–4; PAL–R, 1.12.1860, No. 23, 5–7. Note: the Second Regular Settlement of 1873 attempted to raise revenue demands in Punjab, although its contribution to the declining cultivation of indigo is unclear, and certainly antedated the decline; see: *Gazetteer Mooltan District: 1883–4*, 131–6. See, for detailed discussion of the post-Mutiny settlement as it affected the state's relations with the agriculturalists and landowners: Roseberry, *Imperial Rule in Punjab*, chs. 9–10.

107. Hunter, *Indian Empire*, 596–97; *c.f.* Ilahi and Seth, *Economic Survey*, 50.

108. The calculations are made on the basis of the statistics pertaining to the acreage under crops, which were published in the *Punjab District Gazetteers*. Generally, these were published for each district in 1883–4, 1898, 1888–9,

1892–3 and 1904, and provide comparable statistics from 1873–4 to 1901–2. Because of the differences in data-range between the volumes, there are no statistics for all but seven districts (Dera Ghazi Khan, Firozpur, Gujrat, Gurdaspur, Lahore, Montgomery and Sialkot) for eight years from 1882–93 to 1889–90 (inclusive) and, thus, these years are omitted. Although indigo acreage is tabulated alongside other crops for most of the districts, including those where only a few acres were sown with indigo, there are some districts for which indigo acreage is omitted as a category. In Shahpur, for example, zero acres under indigo were recorded in the volume from 1883–4, and so subsequent volumes drop indigo altogether. It must be inferred, therefore, that there was no indigo cultivation at all in districts where indigo acreage is excluded as a category.

109. *Cf.* Aitchison, *Catalogue*, 41. Note that the district commissioners suspected that revenue and village officers under- rather than over-estimated the extent of cultivation: PAL–R, 8.9.1860, Nos 55–8, 4.

110. NAI–F, Foreign, 17.9.1858, Nos 206–9, 1–3.

111. Kessinger, *Vilyatpur*, 87.

112. Hunter, *Indian Empire*, 596–7; *cf.* Ilahi and Seth, *Economic Survey*, 50.

113. PAL–R, 1.12.1860, No. 23, 7; NAI–F, Foreign, 12.9.1845, Nos 58–60, 7–8; Baden-Powell, *Hand-Book of the Economic Products*, 440.

114. NAI–F, Foreign, 17.9.1858, Nos 206–9, Table No. 1. See, also: Andrew, *Indus and its Provinces*, 64–5.

115. PAL–R, 1.12.1860, No. 23, 7–8; PAL–R, 18.1.1862, Nos 40–1, 1; PAL–R, 29.3.1862, Nos 31–2, 1.

116. PAL–R, 21.3.1863, Nos 29–30, 3–4.

117. See, for quality: Morris, 'Appendix A.', 164; Baden-Powell, *Hand-Book of the Economic Products*, 440. For output: *Multan District, Statistical Tables: 1904*.

118. IOR/E/4/848, 778–9; Morris, *Report*, Appendix F.

119. On the former, see: Lally, 'Economic Development in Colonial Punjab'.

120. Bayly, *Rulers, Townsmen and Bazaars*, 264. See, for a survey of the changing nature and profitability of the Bengal indigo economy after *c.* 1830: Ray, 'Indigo Dye Industry', 218–24.

121. For a detailed history of the Society, and a comparable effort to establish sericulture in Punjab, see: Lally, 'Economic Development in Colonial Punjab'.

122. PAL–R, 5.3.1864, Nos 38–40.

123. PAL–R, 23.4.1864, No. 11, 2.

124. Ibid., 2.

125. *Gazetteer Mooltan District: 1883–4*, 97.

126. See, for the ongoing technological developments in the Bengal indigo industry in the second half of the nineteenth century: Kumar, *Indigo Plantations and Science*, chapter 3.

127. PAL–R, 1.12.1860, No. 23, 7–8; *Gazetteer Muzaffargarh District*, 91.

128. See, for the efforts of Hakim Singh and Ganda Mal of Sialkot, deemed inadequate at the 1864 Exhibition: Baden-Powell, *Hand-Book of the Economic Products*, 440, 460–1.
129. NAI–F, General A, February 1873, Nos 50 and 53. The five firms were: Schoene, Kilburn and Company; Borradaile, Schiller and Company; Wattenbach, Heilgers and Company; Ernsthausen and Oesterley; Schroder, Smidt and Company. See, for indigo shipments from British India to Russia (Asiatic and European) in the mid 1890s, when the annual volume of trade had risen to over 3000 cwt.: NAI–F, Frontier, May 1896 (Part B), Nos 1–16, 9, 13.
130. For examples of bright-blue cloths manufactured in Ivanovo in the early and mid nineteenth century, as well as a sample dated to 1863: Arseneva, *Ivanovskie Sittsy*, plates 58, 83, 139, respectively.
131. NAI–F, Secret E, October 1882, Nos 186–201, 25; *Gazetteer Hazara District: 1883–4*, 144; *Gazetteer Kohat District: 1883–4*, 110–11, 114–15. NAI–F, Secret M, 1870, No. 47, 1–2; NAI–F, Secret, September 1872, Nos 193–4, 23; NAI–F, Secret F, April 1895, Nos 81–94, 4. For indigo imports into Bukhara: Kaushik, 'Economic Relations', 62–4.
132. NAI–F, Secret F, June 1887, No. 183, 1. The substitution of fancy printed fabrics for indigo-dyed dark coarse cloths was also under way amongst the increasingly prosperous poppy-cultivating peasantry in Persia: NAI–F, Secret F, February 1885, No. 22, 4.
133. NAI–F, Frontier A, December 1888, No. 103, 8.
134. Indigo cultivation in Afghanistan was restricted to the south and taken to market in Kandahar: Khan, *Afghanistan and its Inhabitants*, 151; NAI–F, Secret F, February 1890, Nos 161–89, 6.
135. NAI–F, Secret I, June 1869, Nos 49–57, 6. See, also: NAI–F, Secret F, April 1895, Nos 81–94, 4.
136. NAI–F, Secret I, 1869, No. 181, 10; NAI–F, Secret I, June 1869, Nos 49–57, 1; NAI–F, Secret E, October 1882, Nos 186–201, 20; NAI–F, Frontier, May 1896 (Part B), Nos 1–16, 9. Of course, correspondents sometimes confused restrictions on British Indian trade with tales of private extortion by profiteering customs officials on British Indian traders, mistaking the second as stories of state-sponsored abuse of merchants, thus stoking British Russophobia; see, for example: NAI–F, Secret A, August 1882, Nos 349–59.
137. NAI–F, Secret E, October 1882, Nos 186–201, 20.
138. NAI–F, Secret E, June 1883, No. 313, 24.
139. The data for are compiled from the annual external trade reports for Punjab (1869-70 to 1909-10) and the North-West Frontier Province (1901–02 to 1909–10): IOR/V/24/4166, IOR/V/24/4167, IOR/V/24/4168, IOR/V/24/4269.
140. IOR/V/24/4167: ETP (1879–80—reprint with corrections), 29. See, also: NAI, Foreign, Secret E, October 1882, Nos 186–201, 28–9.

141. Prices ranged from Rs 73 to Rs 80 per maund in the later 1880s, around Rs 20 more than in the 1860s or 1840s: IOR/V/24/4167: ETP (1885–6), 15.

142. NAI–F, Frontier, May 1896 (Part B), Nos 1–16, 9.

143. See, for a history of anilines: Balfour-Paul, *Indigo*, 81–4.

144. NAI–F, Political, 14.12.1835, Nos 64–5, 8; PAL–P, 8.9.1860, Nos 55–8, 6.

145. See, for prohibition in Persia for the protection of the carpet industry: NAI–F, Secret E, August 1885, Nos 114–18. See, for promotion of indigo paste: Armstrong, 'Indigo Situation in India', 410–12.

146. Banerjee, *Agrarian Society of the Punjab*, 51–2.

147. Ibid., 49; Kessinger, *Vilyatpur*, 107.

148. Ali, *Panjab Under Imperialism*, 45, 92, 158; Darling, *Punjab Peasant*, 115–16.

149. PAL–R, 8.9.1860, Nos 55–8, 5.

150. There is no mention of indigo cultivation in the new Chenab Colony, for example: *Gazetteer Chenab Colony: 1904*.

151. Banerjee, *Agrarian Society of the Punjab*, 58–67.

152. Morrison, *Russian Rule in Samarkand*, 239.

153. Banerjee, *Agrarian Society of the Punjab*, 12, 52. Kabul, for example, drew in wheat supplies from the Indus and Oxus valleys: Harlan, *Central Asia*, 40, 51–52.

154. Hailey, *Monograph*, 21.

155. Lally, 'Crafting Colonial Anxieties'.

156. Latifi, *Industrial Punjab*, 38–9; *Gazetteer Multan District: 1901–2*, 248; *Gazetteer Lahore District: 1893–4*, 185.

157. Federico, *Silk Industry*, 43–6.

158. Kessinger, *Vilyatpur*, 147–8.

159. Sharma, *Artisans of the Punjab*, 107–18. In the twentieth century, the lower castes took to collective action—such as the Ad-Dharm movement of the Chamars in the 1920s—to counter upper-caste oppression: ibid., 107–18.

160. Ibid., 71.

161. See, for incomes: Mazumder, *Indian Army*, 24–30. See, for the change in clothing: Darling, *Rusticus Loquitur*, 3–4. See, also: Dewey, 'Military Expenditure in British India', 102.

162. Such as Attock and Muzaffargarh: Darling, *Rusticus Loquitur*, 280–1, 313.

163. Malhotra, *Gender, Caste, and Religious Identities*, 36. The activities of the various missionary societies were almost entirely town centred; see: Webster, 'Mission Sources'.

164. Malhotra, *Gender, Caste, and Religious Identities*, 36.

165. Ibid., 38–42.

166. IOR V/24/4166, ETP (1871–2 and 1872–3), 5; Curzon, *Russia in Central Asia*, 254–6, 408.

167. NAI–F, Political A, May 1864, No. 10, 2–3; Simmonds, 'On Silk', 358; Davies, *Report*, 40.

168. Davies, *Report*, 74.

169. Wardle, *Descriptive Catalogue*, 24.

170. Maxwell-Lefroy and Ansorge, *Report*, vol. II, 60, for statistics quoted from Geoghegan's earlier work; Davies, *Report*, 72.

171. Meakin, *Russian Turkestan*, 36; Federico, *Silk Industry*, 37–8.

172. Eugene Schuyler names the Italians as 'Barbieri, Adamoli and others': *Turkistan*, vol. I, 200; NAI–F, General A, May 1863, Nos 63–71, 83. Despite the Russian imperial decree forbidding the trade in eggs, Barbieri apparently purchased and transported 892 lbs. of silkworms out of Turkestan: NAI–F, Secret H, 1870, No. 15.

173. See, for claims of large harvests: IOR/V/24/4166: ETP (1871–2 and 1872–3), 5. The data are compiled from the annual external trade reports for Punjab (1869–70 to 1909–10) and the North-West Frontier Province (1901–02 to 1909-10): IOR/V/24/4166, IOR/V/24/4167, IOR/V/24/4168, IOR/V/24/4269. Note: the 'Karakoram' series includes aggregates the trade from Ladakh and Yarkand with that from Kashmir, not least because there often no reasonable way to distinguish the former from the latter in the returns, since the trade was routed through Kashmir.

174. Rizvi, *Ladakh*, 107.

175. See, for the scheme: Federico, *Silk Industry*, 178–9.

176. Ibid., 100–1.

177. While Italy led the way, China and Japan were swift in adopting new technologies such as steam-reeling; see: Federico, *Silk Industry*, chapter 7.

178. Landsell, *Russian Central Asia*, vol. I, 455.

179. Schuyler, *Turkistan*, vol. I, 90, 199.

180. Ibid., vol. I, 199.

181. NAI–F, General A, February 1873, No. 53, 3–4; Matthee, *Politics of Trade in Safavid Iran*, especially 204–18; Khodarkovsky, 'Russia in the North Caucasus', 425–7.

182. See, for Tsarist underdevelopment: Weinerman, 'Polemics', 466. See, also: Meakin, *Russian Turkestan*, 36–8.

183. Cookson, *Monograph*, 5.

184. BCP, IOR/P/419/81 [1841–2] to IOR/P/419/91 [1849–50].

185. Note: some Persian silk shipped directly from 'Mekran and Muscat' supplemented the larger re-export trade from Bombay. See, for sources from Karachi and Vikkur, 1845–7: Note: the 1845 figures are for the final quarter only and the 1847 figures are for the first three quarters only. NAI–F, Secret, 25.7.1846, Nos 96–102; NAI–F, Secret, 31.10.1846, Nos 83–95; NAI–F, Secret, 26.12.1846, Nos 88–112; NAI–F, Secret, 29.5.1847, Nos 71–86; NAI–F, Secret, 31.7.1847, Nos 75–88; NAI–F, Secret, 28.8.1847, Nos 106–17; NAI–F, Secret, 28.1.1848, Nos 9–11.

186. Karachi was the source of only one-fifth of Punjab's imports, relative to

four-fifths via Delhi and Amritsar in the mid 1860s: NAI–F, Political A, May 1864, No. 10, 3. Bombay's silk re-exports were already entirely routed through the railway network in 1873–4, from which year returns from the SPDR Company are first available: IOR/V/24/4166: ETP (1873–4), Table IV.A. See, also: Hurd, 'Railways', 753–4, 757.

187. Federico, *Silk Industry*, 35–6, 39.

188. Hailey, *Monograph*, 13.

189. See, for statistical evidence of the China via Bombay imports: IOR/V/24/4166—trade-related reports for years from 1869–70 until 1874–5, whereafter Punjab's trade returns are for its foreign trade only, thus excluding trade with Bombay or Calcutta. See, for the Punjabi traders' agents operating in Bombay: Maxwell-Lefroy and Ansorge, *Report*, vol. II, 66; Edwardes, *Silk Fabrics of the Bombay Presidency*, 4.

190. Maxwell-Lefroy and Ansorge, *Report*, vol. II, 58–9. See, also: IOR/V/24/4167, ETP (1883–4), 2.

191. See: Appendix I.

192. Federico, *Silk Industry*, 125–6.

193. Ibid., 67, 100, 125; Hailey, *Monograph*, 14.

194. Cookson, *Monograph*, 2. Yet, size was also added after cleaning to make the thread stronger and easier to weave, as well as heavier; see: Edwardes, *Silk Fabrics of the Bombay Presidency*, 17.

195. *Gazetteer Peshawar District: 1897–8*, 224; Edwardes, *Silk Fabrics of the Bombay Presidency*, 17.

196. NAI–F, Foreign, 17.11.1854, Nos 273–7, 13–14. In British India, one *tola* was the equivalent of 11.3 grams.

197. Hailey, *Monograph*, 14.

198. Maxwell-Lefroy and Ansorge, *Report*, vol. II, 64. See, also: *Gazetteer Amritsar District, 1892–3*, 112.

199. Rawlley, *Silk Industry and Trade*, 26–7; Hailey, *Monograph*, 14.

200. Meakin, *Russian Turkestan*, 39–40.

201. Latifi, *Industrial Punjab*, 39.

202. *Gazetteer Amritsar District, 1892–3*, 112.

203. Maxwell-Lefroy and Ansorge, *Report*, vol. II, 72.

204. Ibid., vol. I, 168, and vol. II, 64–5.

205. Badenoch, *Punjab Industries*, 12.

206. Gauba, 'Amritsar', 354.

207. Headrick, *Tools of Empire*. See, also: Headrick, *Power over Peoples*.

208. See, for instance: Rogan, *Incorporating the Periphery*.

209. Huber, *Channelling Mobilities*, 15–16.

210. Minawi, *Ottoman Scramble for Africa*.

211. See, also, for the role of Sino-Japanese inter-imperial rivalry in driving Japan's investment in telecommunications technologies in mainland east Asia: Yang, *Technology of Empire*.

212. Adas, *Machines*, especially chapters 4–5.

213. Huber, *Channelling Mobilities*, 16–20, Adas, *Machines*, chapter 4.

214. Makdisi, 'Ottoman Orientalism', 779.

215. O'Sullivan, 'Ottoman Technocrats in Kabul', 1848.

216. See, for instance: Kakar, *Government and Society*.

217. This was also true of productive technology, at least in colonial India's textile sector, where older forms of (often high-labour and low-capital intensive) technologies and techniques remained in use in mills and factories well into the postcolonial period, for example. See: Chandavarkar, *Origins of Industrial Capitalism*.

218. Huber, *Channelling Mobilities*, especially 141–71.

219. Minawi, *Ottoman Scramble*, chapters 1 and 4; Cole, 'Precarious Empires'.

220. On the vulnerability of the Indus steamboat schemes to local ecology: Dewey, *Steamboats on the Indus*.

221. See, also, for the 'malfunction' of modern technologies and the countertempos thus produced: Barak, *On Time*, *passim*.

222. Carrère d'Encausse, *Islam and the Russian Empire*, 39–40.

223. Tuna, *Imperial Russia's Muslims*, 6–7, 103–24.

224. *Cf.* Cole, 'Precarious Empires'.

225. On the railways overlaying eighteenth-century routes, and thus connecting existing—rather than new—enterprise in Argentina, see: Lewis, 'Rethinking the Role of Railway Companies', 119.

226. Morris, *Report*, 2.

227. Ali, *Panjab Under Imperialism*, 61.

228. Grewal, *Colonialism and Urbanisation*, 151. See, for the dominance of the Khatris, Aroras, and Banias of Multan and other parts of Punjab in the grain trade, and their shift into trade and production in general: Grewal, 'Business Communities of Punjab', especially 214–21.

229. Under imperial rule, Japan's colonies experienced some transformation in the agrarian sector while remaining primarily oriented around agriculture and serving a provisioning role in the fulfilment of metropolitan needs. Yet, the stellar postwar economic performance of Japan's former colonies—namely Korea and Taiwan—has led a number of scholars to find the roots of this trajectory in Japanese colonialism itself, drawing attention to the introduction of higher-yield crop varieties, the construction of transport infrastructure, the investment in industry (especially by the Japanese conglomerates, or *zaibatsu*), and the state's emphasis on education. In turn, this has supported the notion of Japanese 'colonial exceptionalism'; that Japanese rule was more conducive to economic development than that of Western imperial powers. But Booth and Deng have recently and convincingly drawn attention to the dubiousness of such arguments by rigorously comparing the variety of Japanese policies in a number of different overseas territories with

American, British, and Dutch policies in east and south-east Asia: Booth and Deng, 'Japanese Colonialism in Comparative Perspective'.

230. Crews, *Afghan Modern*, 93–4.

CONCLUSION

1. I have argued elsewhere, furthermore, that the early history of colonial Punjab (i.e. in the 1840s–60s) has been especially neglected because it is thought to fit poorly or be marginal to analysis of the larger themes of Indian and Punjabi history under mature colonialism: Lally, 'Economic Development in Colonial Punjab'.

2. On the impact of lorries in the early twentieth century, including the gradual displacement of their Indian owner-operators from free movement through Afghanistan to Iran: Crews, *Afghan Modern*, 147–9 and 140–52.

3. For a global history of Afghanistan during his reign and in subsequent decades: ibid., 125–52.

4. Chaudhury, 'INSTC'.

5. Marsden, *Trading Worlds*.

6. Ahmed, *Taliban*.

7. Marsden, *Trading Worlds*, 51–2.

8. Marsden notes but does not discuss whether the relations Muslim Afghans form with Hindus and Sikhs are characterised primarily by '*mudaraba* partnership […] in which "one party brings capital, and the other personal effort"' or the *mufawada* version, where "each partner delegates mutual responsibility for buying and selling"': ibid., 63.

9. Ibid., 173–6.

10. On Pashtun tribes and warlords in the modern period: Colás and Mabee, *Mercenaries, Pirates*, 133–58.

11. Marsden, *Trading Worlds*, 67–70.

12. Ibid., 78.

13. O'Connor, 'Longue Durée of Knowledge Production'.

14. *Cf.* Levi, *Khoqand*, especially 210, 220–2.

15. Lydon, *Trans-Saharan Trails*, 49.

16. This is discussed especially in chapter 1, including n. 146.

17 Curtin, *Cross Cultural Trade*.

APPENDIX I: VARIETIES AND PRICES OF SILK

1. Bombay Commercial Proceedings: BL, IOR/P/419/39 [1801–2] to IOR/P/419/90 [1848–9].

2. See, for Bengal's silk centres: Bhattacharya, 'Regional Economy—Eastern India', 282.

3. NAI (F), Political, 9.5.1836, No. 42, paragraph 12; NAI (F), Political, 25.9.1837, Nos 87–96, 18–22, 53–4, 68; NAI (F), Secret, 27.9.1841, Nos 127–30, 41, 43–5; NAI (F), Political, 4.9.1847, Nos 26–30.

4. BL, IOR/V/24/4166: 'Note on the Trade Statistics of the Punjab for the Years 1871–72 and 1872–73', 6; Hailey, *Monograph on the Silk Industry*, 14–16; *Gazetteer of the Peshawar District: 1897–8*, 224.

APPENDIX II: BRITISH SUBJECTS TRADING IN CENTRAL ASIA

1. NAI (F), Secret F, March 1886, No. 305.

APPENDIX III: VOLUME AND VALUE OF COTTON CLOTH EXPORTS FROM PUNJAB, 1869–70 TO 1909–10

1. The data are compiled from the annual external trade reports for Punjab (1869–70 to 1909–10) and the North-West Frontier Province (1901–2 to 1909–10): BL, IOR/V/24/4166, IOR/V/24/4167, IOR/V/24/4168, IOR/V/24/4269.

BIBLIOGRAPHY

Adas, Michael, *Machines as the Measure of Men. Science, Technology, and Ideologies of Western Dominance* (Ithaca: Cornell University Press, 1989).

Adelman, Jeremy, 'Mimesis and Rivalry: European Empires and Global Regimes', *JGH*, vol. 10, no. 1 (2015), 77–98.

Adshead, S. A. M., *Central Asia in World History* (Basingstoke: Macmillan, 1993).

Adye, John, *Sitana: A Mountain Campaign on the Borders of Afghanistan in 1863* (London: Richard Bentley, 1867).

Ahmad, Aziz, 'The British Museum Mīrzānāma and the Seventeenth Century Mīrzā in India', *Iran*, vol. 13, no. 1 (1975), 99–110.

Ahmed, Rashid, *Taliban. The Story of Afghan Warlords* (London: Pan, 2001).

Aitchison, James Edward Tierney, *A Catalogue of the Plants of the Punjab and Sindh* (London: Taylor and Francis, 1869).

Akkerman, Nadine, and Birgit Houben, *The Politics of Female Households. Ladies-in-Waiting Across Early Modern Europe* (Leiden: Brill, 2013).

Alam, Muzaffar, *The Crisis of Empire in Mughal North India. Awadh and the Punjab, 1707–1748* (New Delhi: Oxford University Press, 1991).

———, *The Languages of Political Islam. India 1200–1800* (Chicago: University of Chicago Press, 2004).

———, 'Trade, State Policy and Regional Change: Aspects of Mughal–Uzbek Commercial Relations, c.1550–1750', *JESOH*, vol. 37, no. 3 (1994), 202–27.

Alam, Muzaffar, and Sanjay Subrahmanyam, *Indo-Persian Travels in the Age of Discoveries, 1400–1800* (Cambridge: Cambridge University Press, 2007).

Alavi, Rafi Ahmad, 'New Light on Mughal Cavalry', in *Medieval India—A Miscellany. Volume II*, ed. S. Nurul Hasan, *et al.* (London: Asia Publishing House, 1972).

Alder, Garry, *Beyond Bokhara. The Life of William Moorcroft, Asian Explorer and Pioneer Veterinary Surgeon, 1767–1825* (London: Century, 1985).

Ali, Imran, *The Panjab Under Imperialism, 1885–1947* (Princeton: Princeton University Press, 1988).

Ali, M. Athar, 'Organisation of the Nobility: Mansab, Pay, Conditions of Service', in *Warfare and Weaponry in South Asia 1000–1800*, ed. Jos J. L. Gommans and Dirk H. A. Kolff (New Delhi: Oxford University Press, 2001).

Ali, Shahamet, ed., *The History of Bahawalpur, with Notices of the Adjacent Countries of Sindh, Afghanistan, Multan, and the West of India* (London: James Madden, 1848).

Ambala District and Kalsia State, Statistical Tables: 1904 (Lahore: Civil and Military Gazette Press, 1909).

Ames, Frank, *Woven Masterpieces of Sikh Heritage. The Stylistic Development of the Kashmir Shawl under Maharaja Ranjit Singh 1780–1839* (Woodbridge: Antique Collectors' Club, 2010).

Amrith, Sunil, *Unruly Waters. How Mountain Rivers and Monsoons Have Shaped South Asia's History* (London: Penguin, 2018).

Amritsar District, Statistical Tables: 1904 (Lahore: Civil and Military Gazette Press, 1904).

Anand, M. R., *Maharaja Ranjit Singh as Patron of the Arts* (New Delhi, 1981).

Andrew, W. P., *India and Her Neighbours* (London: William H. Allen and Company, 1878).

————, *The Indus and its Provinces, their Political and Commercial Importance Considered in Connexion with Improved Means of Communication* (London: William Allen and Company, 1859).

Anon., 'A Character of the Sieks. From the Observations of Colonel Pollier and Mr. George Forster', in *The Asiatic Annual Register, or, A View of the History of Hindustan, and of the Politics, Commerce and Literature of Asia, for the Year 1802* (London: J. Debrett, 1803).

————, 'Report on Indigo', in *Reports and Documents Connected with the Proceedings of the East-India Company in Regard to the Culture and Manufacture of Cotton-Wool, Raw Silk, and Indigo, in India* (London: J. L. Cox and Sons, 1836).

————, 'Report on Raw-Silk', in *Reports and Documents Connected with the Proceedings of the East-India Company in Regard to the Culture and Manufacture of Cotton-Wool, Raw Silk, and Indigo, in India* (London: J. L. Cox and Sons, 1836).

————, *Reports by Her Majesty's Secretaries of Embassy and Legation, on the Manufactures and Commerce of the Countries in Which They Reside* (London: Harrison and Sons, 1858).

————, *Reports in Relation to Trade with Turkey in Asia, Persia, and Central Asia* (London: Foreign and Commonwealth Office, 1878).

————, *Salihotra* (Agra: Latafat Press, 1871).

————, *Sublime Indigo* (Marseille: Musées de Marseille, 1987).

————, 'Tour to Lahore', in *The Asiatic Annual Register, Vol. XI for the Year 1809* (London: T. Cadell and W. Davies, 1811).

————, 'Trade Beyond the Indus and Sutlej' [Part I], *The Calcutta Monthly Journal*, new series, vol. v (May–August 1834), 541–55.

Appadurai, Arjun, *The Social Life of Things. Commodities in Cultural Perspective* (Cambridge: Cambridge University Press, 1986).

Armitage, David, and Sanjay Subrahmanyam, eds, *The Age of Revolutions in Global Context, c.1760–1840* (Basingstoke: Palgrave Macmillan, 2010).

Arnold, David, *Everyday Technology. Machines and the Making of India's Modernity* (London: University of Chicago Press, 2015).

————, *The Tropics and the Traveling Gaze. India, Landscape, and Science 1800–1856* (New Delhi: Permanent Black, 2005).

Arseneva, E. V., *Ivanovskie Sittsy XVIII–Nachala XX Veka* (Ivanovo Printed Textiles 18th to Early 20th Centuries) (Leningrad: Khudozhnik RSFSR, 1983).

Asad, Talal, 'Ethnographic Representation, Statistics and Modern Power', *Social Research*, vol. 61, no. 1 (1994), 55–88.

Asher, Catherine B., 'A Ray from the Sun: Mughal Ideology and the Visual Construction of the Divine', in *The Presence of Light: Divine Radiance and Religious Experience*, ed. Matthew T. Kapstein (London: University of Chicago Press, 2004).

————, and Cynthia Talbot, *India Before Europe* (Cambridge: Cambridge University Press, 2006).

Askari, Nasreen, and Rosemary Crill, *Colours of the Indus. Costume and Textiles of Pakistan* (London: Merrell Holberton/V&A, 1997).

Aslanian, Sebouh, *From the Indian Ocean to the Mediterranean. The Global Trade Networks of Armenian Merchants from New Julfa* (Berkeley: University of California Press, 2011).

————, 'Trade Diaspora versus Colonial State: Armenian Merchants, the English East India Company, and the High Court of Admiralty in London, 1748–1752', *Diaspora: A Journal of Transnational Studies*, vol. 13, no. 1 (2004), 37–100.

Babur, *The Baburnama. Memoirs of Babur, Prince and Emperor*, ed. Wheeler Thackston (New York: Oxford University Press, 1996).

Badenoch, A.C., *Punjab Industries, 1911–1917* (Lahore: Superintendent, Government Printing, 1917).

Baden-Powell, B. H., *Hand-Book of the Economic Products of the Punjab, with a Combined Index and Glossary of Technical Vernacular Words. Vol. I. Economic Raw Produce* (Roorkee: Thomason Civil Engineering College, 1868).

————, *Hand-Book of the Manufactures and Arts of the Punjab. Forming Vol. II to the 'Hand-book of the Economic Products of the Punjab'. Prepared Under the Orders of Government* (Lahore: Punjab Printing Company, 1872).

BIBLIOGRAPHY

Bag, Sailendra Kumar, *The Changing Fortunes of the Bengal Silk Industry 1757–1783* (Calcutta: Manasi Press, 1989).

Bahawalpur State, Statistical Tables: 1904 (Lahore: Civil and Military Gazette Press, 1908).

Bahawalpur State, with Maps: 1904 (Lahore: Civil and Military Gazette Press, 1908).

Baillie, Alexander F., 'Sind', in *The British Empire Series, Vol. I*, ed. William Sheowring (London: Kegan Paul, Trench, Trübner and Company, 1899).

Baker, Patricia L., *Islamic Textiles* (London: British Museum Press, 1995).

Bal, S. S., 'Amritsar in the Eighteenth Century', in *The City of Amritsar. A Study of Historical, Cultural, Social and Economic Aspects*, ed. Fauja Singh (New Delhi: Oriental Publishers, 1978).

Balfour-Paul, Jenny, *Indigo* (London: The British Museum Press, 2011).

Ballantyne, Tony, *Orientalism and Race. Aryanism in the British Empire* (Basingstoke: Palgrave Macmillan, 2002).

Banerjee, Himadri, *Agrarian Society of the Punjab (1849–1901)* (New Delhi: Manohar, 1982).

Bang, Peter Fibiger, and Dariusz Kolodziejczyk, eds, *Universal Empire. A Comparative Approach to Imperial Culture and Representation in Eurasian History* (Cambridge: Cambridge University Press, 2012).

Banga, Indu, *Agrarian System of the Sikhs: Late Eighteenth and Early Nineteenth Century* (New Delhi: Manohar, 1978).

Barak, On, *On Time. Technology and Temporality in Modern Egypt* (Berkeley: University of California Press, 2013).

Barkawi, Tarak, 'States and Armed Force in International Context', in *Mercenaries, Pirates, Bandits and Empires. Private Violence in Historical Context*, ed. Alejandro Colás and Bryan Mabee (London: C. Hurst and Co., 2010).

Barkey, Karen, *Bandits and Bureaucrats. The Ottoman Route to State Centralization* (Ithaca, N.Y.: Cornell University Press, 1997).

Bauer, Arnold J., *Goods, Power, History. Latin America's Material Culture* (Cambridge: Cambridge University Press, 2001).

Bayly, C. A., '"Archaic" and "Modern" Globalisation in the Eurasian and African Arena, c.1750–1850', in *Globalization in World History*, ed. A. G. Hopkins (London: Pimlico, 2002).

————, *Empire and Information. Intelligence Gathering and Social Communication in India, 1780–1870* (New Delhi: Cambridge University Press, 1999).

————, *Indian Society and the Making of the British Empire* (Cambridge: Cambridge University Press, 1990).

————, *Rulers, Townsmen and Bazaars. North Indian Society in the Age of British Expansion 1770–1870* (Oxford: Oxford University Press, 1983).

————, 'The Age of Hiatus: The North Indian Economy and Society, 1830–50', in *Indian Society and the Beginnings of Modernisation c.1830–1850*, ed.

C.H. Philips and Mary Doreen Wainwright (London: School of Oriental and African Studies, 1976).

—————, *The Birth of the Modern World. Global Connections and Comparisons, 1780–1914* (Oxford: Blackwell, 2004).

—————, 'The First Age of Global Imperialism, *c*.1760–1830', *The Journal of Imperial and Commonwealth History*, vol. 26, no. 2 (1998), 28–47.

—————, 'The Origins of *Swadeshi* (Home Industry): Cloth and Indian Society, 1700–1930' in *The Social Life of Things. Commodities in Cultural Perspective*, ed. Arjun Appadurai (Cambridge: Cambridge University Press, 1986).

—————, 'The Pre-History of "Communalism"? Religious Conflict in India, 1700–1860', *MAS*, vol. 19, no. 2 (1985), 177–203.

—————, 'Town Building in North India, 1790–1830', *MAS*, vol. 9, no. 4 (1975), 483–504.

Bayly, Christopher, and Susan Bayly, 'Eighteenth-Century State Forms and the Economy', in *Arrested Development in India. The Historical Dimension*, ed. Clive Dewey (New Delhi: Manohar, 1988).

Bayly, Martin J., *Taming the Imperial Imagination. Colonial Knowledge, International Relations, and the Anglo-Afghan Encounter, 1808–1878* (Cambridge: Cambridge University Press, 2016).

Bayly, Susan, *Caste, Society and Politics in India from the Eighteenth Century to the Modern Age* (Cambridge: Cambridge University Press, 1999).

Beckert, Sven, 'American Danger: United States Empire, Eurafrica, and the Territorialisation of Industrial Capitalism, 1870–1950', *The American Historical Review*, vol. 122, no. 4 (2017), 1137–70.

Beckwith, Christopher I., *Empires of the Silk Road. A History of Central Eurasia from the Bronze Age to the Present* (Oxford: Princeton University Press, 2009).

Bennike, Rune, 'Governing Landscapes: Territorialisation and Exchange at South Asia's Himalayan Frontier', *South Asia: Journal of South Asian Studies*, vol. 40, no. 2 (2017), 217–21.

Benton, Lauren, and Adam Clulow, 'Empires and Protection: Making Interpolity Law in the Early Modern World', *JGH*, vol. 12, no. 1 (2017), 74–92.

Berg, Maxine, and Elizabeth Eger, eds, *Luxury in the Eighteenth Century. Debates, Desires and Delectable Goods* (Basingstoke: Palgrave, 2003).

Berg, Maxine, Felicia Gottmann, Hanna Hodacs, and Chris Nierstrasz, eds, *Goods from the East, 1600–1800. Trading Eurasia* (Basingstoke: Palgrave Macmillan, 2015).

Bernier, François, *Travels in the Mogul Empire, A.D. 1656–1668*, trans. I. Brock (London: Archibald Constable, 1891).

Berridge, P. S. A., *Couplings to the Khyber. The Story of the North Western Railway* (Newton Abbott: David and Charles Publishers, 1969).

Berry, Christopher, *The Concept of Luxury. A Conceptual and Historical Investigation* (Cambridge: Cambridge University Press, 1994).

Bhattacharya, Bhaswati, 'Armenian European Relationship in India, 1500–1800: No Armenian Foundation for European Empire?', *JESOH*, vol. 48, no. 2 (2005), 277–322.

————, 'Predicaments of Mobility: Peddlers and Itinerants in Nineteenth-Century Northwestern India', in *Society and Circulation. Mobile People and Itinerant Cultures in South Asia, 1750–1950*, ed. Claude Markovits, Jacques Pouchepadass, and Sanjay Subrahmanyam (London: Anthem Press, 2006).

Bhattacharya, S., 'Regional Economy—Eastern India', in *The Cambridge Economic History of India. Volume 2: c.1757–c.1970*, ed. Dharma Kumar and Meghnad Desai (Cambridge: Cambridge University Press, 1983).

Biddulph, J., *Tribes of the Hindoo Koosh* (Calcutta: Office of Superintendent of Government Printing, 1880).

Birdwood, George C. M., *The Industrial Arts of India*, 2 vols (London: Chapman and Hall, 1880).

Blackwell, William L., *The Industrialization of Russia. An Historical Perspective* (New York: Thomas Y. Crowell, 1970).

Blake, Stephen P., *Shahjahanabad. The Sovereign City in Mughal India, 1639–1739* (Cambridge: Cambridge University Press, 2002).

————, 'The Patrimonial–Bureaucratic Empire of the Mughals', *JAS*, vol. 39, no. 1 (1979), 77–94.

Blanchard, Ian, *Russia's 'Age of Silver'. Precious-Metal Production and Economic Growth in the Eighteenth Century* (London: Routledge, 1989).

Blok, Anton, 'The Peasant and the Brigand: Social Banditry Reconsidered', *CSSH*, vol. 14, no. 4 (1972), 494–503.

Bloom, Jonathan M., *Paper before Print: The History and Impact of Paper in the Islamic World* (New Haven and London: Yale University Press, 2001).

Bloom, Jonathan, and Sheila Blair, eds, *And Diverse Are Their Hues* (New Haven: Yale University Press, 2011).

Booth, Anne, and Kent Deng, 'Japanese Colonialism in Comparative Perspective', *Journal of World History*, vol. 28, no. 1 (2017), 61–98.

Bose, Sugata, *A Hundred Horizons. The Indian Ocean in the Age of Global Empire* (Cambridge, Mass.: Harvard University Press, 2006).

Bourne, John, *Indian River Navigation* (London: William H. Allen and Company, 1849).

Bowen, Huw, 'Bullion for Trade, War, and Debt-Relief: British Movements of Silver to, around, and from Asia, 1760–1833', *MAS*, vol. 44, no. 3 (2010), 445–75.

Bradsher, Keith, 'Hauling New Treasure Along the Silk Road', *The New York Times* (accessed 22 February 2018): https://www.nytimes.com/2013/07/21/business/global/hauling-new-treasure-along-the-silk-road.html?pagewanted=1&_r=1&adxnnl=1&adxnnlx=1397383363-CcBkx%ADAWjK%20klUp98HdPT4A

Braudel, Fernand, *The Mediterranean and the Mediterranean World in the Age of Philip II* (London: Collins, 1972).

Broadberry, Stephen, and Steve Hindle, 'Editor's Introduction', *EHR*, vol. 64, Special Issue: Asia in the Great Divergence (2011), 1–7.

Brower, Daniel, 'Islam and Ethnicity: Russian Colonial Policy in Turkestan', in *Russia's Orient. Imperial Borderlands and Peoples, 1700–1917*, ed. Daniel R. Brower and Edward J. Lazzerini (Bloomington: Indiana University Press, 1997).

Brower, Daniel R., and Edward J. Lazzerini, eds, *Russia's Orient. Imperial Borderlands and Peoples, 1700–1917* (Bloomington: Indiana University Press, 1997).

Bukharayi, Fitrat, *Bayanat–i Sayyah–i Hindi* (Istanbul, 1912).

Burke, Peter, *The Fortunes of the Courtier. The European Reception of Castiglione's Cortegiano* (Cambridge: Polity Press, 1995).

———, 'The Meaning of Things in the Early Modern World', in *Treasured Possessions from the Renaissance to the Enlightenment*, ed. Victoria Avery, Melissa Calaresu, and Mary Laven (London: Philip Wilson Publishing, 2015).

Burnes, Alexander, *Travels into Bokhara: Together with A Narrative of a Voyage on the Indus*, 2 vols (Karachi: Oxford University Press, 1973).

Burton, Audrey, 'Bukharan Trade 1558–1718', *Papers on Inner Asia*, no. 23 (Bloomington: Indiana, 1993).

———, *The Bukharans: A Dynastic, Diplomatic and Commercial History 1550–1702* (Richmond: Curzon, 1997).

Burton, Richard F., *Sind Revisited: With Notices of The Anglo-Indian Army; Railroads; Past, Present, and Future, Etc.* (London: Richard Bentley and Son, 1877).

Bushkovitch, Paul, *The Merchants of Moscow 1580–1650* (Cambridge: Cambridge University Press, 1980).

Calaresu, Melissa, 'Making and Eating Ice Cream in Naples: Rethinking Consumption and Sociability in the Eighteenth Century', *Past and Present*, vol. 220, no. 1 (2013), 35–78.

Campbell, Gwyn, 'Servitude and the Changing Face of the Demand for Labour in the Indian Ocean World, *c.* 1800–1900', in *Indian Ocean Slavery in the Age of Abolition*, ed. Robert Harms, Bernard Freamon, and David Bight (New Haven: Yale University Press, 2013).

Canby, Sheila, 'Persian Horse Portraits and their Cousins', in David Alexander, ed., *Furusiyya: The Horse in the Art of the Near East* (Riyadh: The King Abdulaziz Public Library, 1996).

Carlano, Annie, 'In Celebration of a Uniquely Russian Sense of Surface

Design', in *Russian Textiles. Printed Cloth for the Bazaars of Central Asia*, ed. Susan Meller (New York: Abrams, 2007).

———, 'The Inside Story. Russian Printed Cottons for the Central Asian Market, 1850–1950', *HALI. The International Magazine of Antique Carpet and Textile Art*, no. 107 (November/December 1997), 86–9.

Carless, T. G., 'Memoir on the Bay, Harbour, and Trade, of Kurachee', in *Selections from the Records of the Bombay Government. No. XVII. New Series*, ed. R. Hughes Thomas (Bombay: Bombay Education Society's Press, 1855).

Carrère d'Encausse, Hélène, *Islam and the Russian Empire. Reform and Revolution in Central Asia*, trans. Quintin Hoare (London: I. B. Tauris and Company, 1988).

Carroll, Patrick, *Science, Culture and Modern State Formation* (Berkeley: University of California Press, 2006).

Carroll, Stuart, *Blood and Violence in Early Modern France* (Oxford: Oxford University Press, 2006).

———, 'Thinking with Violence', *History and Theory*, Theme Issue 55 (2017), 23–43.

———, ed., *Cultures of Violence. Interpersonal Violence in Historical Perspective* (Basingstoke: Palgrave Macmillan, 2007).

Casale, Giancarlo, *The Ottoman Age of Exploration* (Oxford: Oxford University Press, 2010).

Caton, Brian, 'Social Categories and Colonisation in Panjab, 1849–1920', *IESHR*, vol. 41, no. 1 (2004), 33–50.

———, 'The Colonial Birth of Scientific Breeding and Veterinary Medicine in Punjab', in *Proceedings of the XXXVIII International Congress of the World Association for the History of Veterinary Medicine*, ed. Max Becker (Zürich: Swiss Association of the History of Veterinary Medicine, 2008).

———, 'The Imperial Ambition of Science and its Discontents: Animal Breeding in Nineteenth–Century Punjab', in *Shifting Ground: People, Animals and Mobility in India's Environmental History*, ed. Mahesh Rangarajan and K. Sivaramakrishnan (New Delhi: Oxford University Press, 2014).

Chakravarty-Kaul, Minoti, *Common Lands and Customary Law. Institutional Change in North India over the Past Two Centuries* (Delhi: Oxford University Press, 1996).

Chandavarkar, Rajnarayan, *The Origins of Industrial Capitalism in India: Business Strategies and the Working Classes in Bombay, 1900–40* (Cambridge: Cambridge University Press, 1994).

Chatterjee, Kumkum, 'Collaboration and Conflict: Bankers and Early Colonial Rule in India: 1757–1813', *IESHR*, vol. 30, no. 3 (1993), 283–310.

Chaudhuri, K. N., 'India's Foreign Trade and the Cessation of the East India

Company's Trading Activities, 1828–40', *EHR*, new series, vol. 19, no. 2 (1966), 345–63.

———, 'The East India Company and the Export of Treasure in the Early Seventeenth Century', *EHR*, new series, vol. 16, no. 1 (1963), 23–38.

———, 'The Structure of Indian Textile Industry in the Seventeenth and Eighteenth Centuries', *IESHR*, vol. 11, nos 2–3 (1974), 127–82.

———, *The Trading World of Asia and the English East India Company 1660–1760* (Cambridge: Cambridge University Press, 1978).

———, *Trade and Civilisation in the Indian Ocean: An Economic History from the Rise of Islam to 1750* (Cambridge: Cambridge University Press, 1985).

Chaudhury, Dipanjan Roy, 'INSTC to be Operationalised Mid-Jan 2018', *The Economic Times* (accessed 25 August 2020): https://economictimes.india-times.com/news/economy/foreign-trade/instc-to-be-operationalised-mid-jan-2018-game-changer-for-indias-eurasia-policy/article-show/61926321.cms

Chaudhury, Sushil, *From Prosperity to Decline. Eighteenth Century Bengal* (New Delhi: Manohar, 1995).

———, 'International Trade in Bengal Silk and the Comparative Role of Asians and Europeans, circa. 1700–1757', *MAS*, vol. 29, no. 2 (1995), 373–86.

Choudhury, D. K. Lahiri, 'Sinews of Panic and the Nerves of Empire: The Imagined State's Entanglement with Information Panic, India *c.* 1880–1912', *MAS*, vol. 38, no. 4 (2004), 965–1002.

Chowdhury, B., *Growth of Commercial Agriculture in Bengal (1757–1900)* (Calcutta: R. K. Maitra, 1964).

Christensen, R.O., 'Tribesmen, Government and Political Economy on the North-West Frontier', in *Arrested Development in India. The Historical Dimension*, ed. Clive Dewey (New Delhi: Manohar, 1988).

Clarence-Smith, William Gervase, *Islam and the Abolition of Slavery* (London: Hurst & Company, 2006).

Cohn, B. S., *Colonialism and its Forms of Knowledge* (Princeton: Princeton University Press, 1996).

Cohn, Samuel, 'Renaissance Attachment to Things: Material Culture in Last Wills and Testaments', *EHR*, vol. 65, no. 3 (2012), 984–1004.

Colás, Alejandro, and Bryan Mabee, *Mercenaries, Pirates, Bandits and Empires. Private Violence in Historical Context* (London: C. Hurst and Co., 2010).

Cole, Camille Lyans, 'Precarious Empires: A Social and Environmental History of Steam Navigation on the Tigris', *Journal of Social History*, vol. 50, no. 1 (2016), 74–101.

Condos, Mark, '"Fanaticism" and the Politics of Resistance along the North-West Frontier of British India', *CSSH*, vol. 58, no. 3 (2016), 717–45.

———, *The Insecurity State. Punjab and the Making of Colonial Power in British India* (Cambridge: Cambridge University Press, 2017).

Cookson, H. C., *Monograph on the Silk Industry of the Punjab, 1886–87* (Lahore: Punjab Government Press).

Cooper, Alanna E., *Bukharan Jews and the Dynamics of Global Judaism* (Bloomington: Indiana University Press, 2012).

Coote, C. H., and E. Delmar Morgan, eds, *Early Voyages and Travels to Russia and Persia by Anthony Jenkinson and Other Englishmen*, 2 vols (London: Hakluyt Society, 1886).

Crews, Robert, 'Trafficking in Evil? The Global Arms Trade and the Politics of Disorder', in *Global Muslims in the Age of Steam and Print, 1850–1930*, ed. James L. Gelvin and Nile Green (Berkeley: University of California Press, 2014).

Crews, Robert D., *Afghan Modern. The History of a Global Nation* (Cambridge, Mass.: The Belknap Press of Harvard University Press, 2015).

———, *For Prophet and Tsar. Islam and Empire in Russia and Central Asia* (Cambridge, Mass.: Harvard University Press, 2006).

Crill, Rosemary, *Marwar Painting. A History of the Jodhpur Style* (Mumbai: India Book House Pvt Ltd, 2009).

———, 'Textiles in the Punjab', in *The Arts of the Sikh Kingdoms*, ed. Susan Stronge (London: V&A Publications, 1999).

Crill, Rosemary, and Kapil Jariwala, eds, *The Indian Portrait 1560–1860*, (London: National Portrait Gallery, 2010).

Crooke, W., *Natives of Northern India* (London: Archibald Constable and Company, 1907).

Crosby, Jr., Alfred W., *The Columbian Exchange. Biological and Cultural Consequences of 1492* (Westport: Greenword, 1972).

Cullen, Michael J., *The Statistical Movement in Early Victorian Britain: The Foundations of Empirical Social Research* (New York: Barnes and Noble, 1975).

Cummins, Stephen, 'Enmity and Peace-Making in the Kingdom of Naples, *c*.1600–1700' (unpublished doctoral dissertation, University of Cambridge, 2015), 169.

———, *Governing Hatred: Enmity and Peace-Making in Early Modern Naples* (forthcoming).

Curry-Machado, Jonathan, ed., *Global Histories, Imperial Commodities, Local Interactions* (Basingstoke: Palgrave Macmillan, 2013).

Curtin, Philip, *Cross-Cultural Trade in World History* (Cambridge: Cambridge University Press, 1984).

Curzon, G. N., *Russia in Central Asia in 1889 and the Anglo-Russian Question* (London: Cass, 1967).

Dale, Stephen F., 'Empires and Emporia: Palace, Mosque, Market, and Tomb in Istanbul, Isfahan, Agra, and Delhi', *JESOH*, vol. 53, no. 1/2 (2010), 212–29.

BIBLIOGRAPHY

Dale, Stephen, *Indian Merchants and Eurasian Trade, 1600–1750* (Cambridge: Cambridge University Press, 1994).

Dale, Stephen Frederic, 'Indo-Russian Trade in the Eighteenth Century', in *South Asia and World Capitalism*, ed. Sugata Bose (New Delhi: Oxford University Press, 1990).

Dale, Stephen, 'Silk Road, Cotton Road or Indo-Chinese Trade in Pre-European Times', *MAS*, vol. 43, no. 1 (2009), 79–88.

———, 'The Legacy of the Timurids', in *India and Central Asia. Commerce and Culture, 1500–1800*, ed. Scott C. Levi (Delhi: Oxford University Press, 2007).

Dale, Stephen F., and Alam Payind, 'The Ahrari Waqf in Kabul in the Year 1546 and the Mughul Naqshbandiyyah', in *India and Central Asia. Commerce and Culture, 1500–1800*, ed. Scott C. Levi (Delhi: Oxford University Press, 2007).

Dalmia, Vasudha, and Munis D. Faruqui, eds, *Religious Interactions in Mughal India* (Delhi: Oxford University Press, 2014).

Dalrymple, William, *Return of a King. Shah Shuja and the First Battle for Afghanistan, 1839–42* (London: Bloomsbury 2012).

Danker, Uwe, 'Bandits and the State: Robbers and the Authorities in the Holy Roman Empire in the Late Seventeenth and Early Eighteenth Centuries', in *The German Underworld. Deviants and Outcasts in German History*, ed. Richard J. Evans (London: Routledge, 1988).

Darling, Malcolm Lyall, *Rusticus Loquitur, or the Old Light and the New in the Punjabi Village* (London: Humphrey Milford, 1930).

Darling, Malcolm, *The Punjab Peasant in Prosperity and Debt* (London: Geoffrey Cumberlege/Oxford University Press, 1947, 4th edn).

Darwin, John, *After Tamerlane. The Global History of Empire* (London: Penguin, 2008).

Davies, R. H., *Report on the Trade and Resources of the Countries on the North-Western Boundary of British India* (Lahore: Government Press, 1862).

Davies, R. H., and W. Blyth, eds, *Report on the Revised Settlement of the Umritsur, Sowrian, and Turun Tarun Purgunnahs of the Umritsur District in the Umritsur Division* (Lahore: Hope Press, 1860).

Davini, Roberto, 'Bengali Raw Silk, the East India Company and the European Global Market, 1770–1833', *JGH*, vol. 4, no. 1 (2009), 57–79.

de Vivo, Filippo, *Information and Communication in Venice. Rethinking Early Modern Politics* (Oxford: Oxford University Press, 2007).

Delhi District, Statistical Tables: 1904 (Lahore: Civil and Military Gazette Press, 1904).

Deloche, Jean, *Transport and Communication in India Prior to Steam Locomotion. Volume I: Land Transport*, trans. James Walker (New Delhi: Oxford University Press, 1993).

Dera Ghazi Ismail District, Statistical Tables: 1904 (Lahore: Civil and Military Gazette Press, 1904).

Desai, Vishakha, 'Timeless Symbols: Royal Portraits from Rajasthan 17th–19th Centuries', in *The Idea of Rajasthan. Explorations in Regional Identity. Vol. I: 'Constructions'*, ed. K. Schomer, J. Erdman, D. Lodrick, and L. Rudolph (New Delhi: Manohar, 1994).

Dewey, Clive, 'Some Consequences of Military Expenditure in British India. The Case of the Upper Sind Sagar Doab, 1849–1947', in *Arrested Development in India. The Historical Dimension*, ed. Clive Dewey (New Delhi: Manohar, 1988).

———, *Steamboats on the Indus. The Limits of Western Technological Superiority in South Asia* (New Delhi: Oxford University Press, 2014).

Dhamija, Jasleen, and Jyotindra Jain, *Handwoven Fabrics of India* (Ahmedabad: Mapin Publishing, 1983).

Dhavan, Purnima, *When Sparrows Became Hawks. The Making of the Sikh Warrior Tradition, 1699–1799* (Oxford: Oxford University Press, 2011).

di Cosmo, Nicola, 'Kirghiz Nomads on the Qing Frontier: Tribute, Trade, or Gift Exchange?', in *Political Frontiers, Ethnic Boundaries, and Human Geographies in Chinese History*, ed. Nicola di Cosmo and Don J. Wyatt (London: Routledge Curzon, 2003).

Digby, Simon, *War-Horse and Elephant in the Delhi Sultanate. A Study of Military Supplies* (Karachi: Oxford Orient Monographs, 1971).

Dimitriyev, G. L., 'From the History of Indian Colony in Central Asia (Second Half of the XIX Century–Beginning of the XX Century)', in *India and Central Asia. Cultural, Economic and Political Links*, ed. Surendra Gopal (New Delhi: Shipra Publications, 2001).

Dirks, Nicholas B., *Castes of Mind. Colonialism and the Making of Modern India* (Princeton: Princeton University Press, 2001).

Diverkar, V.D., 'Regional Economy—Western India', in *The Cambridge Economic History of India. Volume 2: c.1757–c.1970*, ed. Dharma Kumar and Meghnad Desai (Cambridge: Cambridge University Press, 1983).

Dobbin, Christine, *Asian Entrepreneurial Minorities. Conjoint Communities in the Making of the World Economy 1570–1940* (London: Routledge, 1996).

Dodwell, H. H., ed., *The Cambridge History of the British Empire. Volume V. The Indian Empire 1858–1918* (Cambridge: Cambridge University Press, 1932).

Dowleans, A. M., *Official, Classified, and Descriptive Catalogue of the Contributions from India to the London Exhibition of 1862* (Calcutta: Savielle and Cranenburgh, 1862).

Drayton, Richard, and David Motadel, 'Discussion: The Futures of Global History', *JGH*, vol. 13, no. 1 (2018), 1–21.

Drephal, Maximilian, '*Corps Diplomatique*: The Body, British Diplomacy, and Independent Afghanistan, 1922–47', *MAS*, vol. 51, no. 4 (2017), 956–90.

Durrani, Ashiq, *History of Multan (From the Early Period to 1849 AD)* (Lahore: Vanguard Books, 1991).

Dwyer, Philip, 'Violence and its Histories: Meanings, Methods, Problems', *History and Theory*, Theme Issue 55 (2017), 7–22.

Earles, Joseph, *A Treatise on Horses* (Calcutta, 1788).

Eaton, Natasha, 'Nomadism of Colour: Painting, Technology and Waste in the Chromo–Zones of Colonial India *c.* 1765–*c*.1860', *Journal of Material Culture*, vol. 17, no. 1 (2012), 61–81.

Eaton, Richard M., *A Social History of the Deccan, 1300–1761. Eight Indian Lives* (Cambridge: Cambridge University Press, 2005).

———, 'Temple Desecration and Indo-Muslim States', in *Beyond Turk and Hindu. Rethinking Religious Identities in Islamicate South Asia*, ed. David Gilmartin and Bruce B. Lawrence (Gainesville: University of Florida Press, 2000).

Eden, Emily, *Up the Country. Letters from India* (London: Virago, 1997).

Eden, Jeff, 'Beyond the Bazaars: Geographies of the Slave Trade in Central Asia', *MAS*, vol. 51, no. 4 (2017), 919–55.

Edwardes, S. M., *A Monograph on the Silk Fabrics of the Bombay Presidency* (Bombay, 1900).

Elias, Norbert, *The Civilizing Process. The History of Manners and State Formation and Civilisation* (Oxford: Blackwell, 1994).

Elphinstone, Mountstuart, *An Account of the Kingdom of Caubul, and its Dependencies in Persia, Tartary, and India* (London: Longman, Hurst, Rees, Orme, and Brown, 1815).

Ernst, Carl W., and Bruce B. Lawrence, *Sufi Martyrs of Love. The Chishti Order in South Asia and Beyond* (Basingstoke: Palgrave Macmillan).

Ewald, Janet J., 'Crossers of the Sea: Slaves, Freedmen, and Other Migrants in the Northwestern Indian Ocean, *c.* 1750–1914', *The American Historical Review*, vol. 105, no. 1 (2000), 69–91.

Ewart, William, *Settlement in India and Trade with Central Asia. Speech of W. Ewart, Esq., M.P., in the House of Commons, March 23, 1858* (London: James Ridgway, 1858).

Falconer, John, 'A Passion for Documentation: Architecture and Ethnography', in *India Through the Lens. Photography 1840–1911*, ed. Vidya Dehejia (Washington DC: Freer Gallery of Art and Arthur M. Sackler Gallery, 2000).

———, '"A Pure Labor of Love": A Publishing History of *The People of India*', in *Colonialist Photography. Imag(in)ing Race and Place*, ed. Eleanor M. Hight and Gary D. Sampson (London: Routledge, 2002).

———, ed., *Afghanistan Observed 1830–1920* (London: The British Library, 2010).

Farooqui, Mahmood, *Besieged. Voices from Delhi 1857* (Viking: Delhi, 2010).

Faroqhi, Suraiya, *A Cultural History of the Ottomans. The Imperial Elite and its Artefacts* (London: I. B. Tauris, 2016).

Faruqui, Munis D., 'At Empire's End: The Nizam, Hyderabad and Eighteenth-Century India', *MAS*, vol. 43, no. 1 (2009), 5–43.

———, *The Princes of the Mughal Empire, 1504–1719* (Cambridge: Cambridge University Press, 2012).

Fazl, Abu'l, *Ain-i Akbari*, ed. H. Blochmann, 3 vols (Calcutta: Asiatic Society of Bengal, 1873).

Feaver, George, ed., *The Webbs in Asia. The 1911–12 Travel Diary* (London: Macmillan, 1992).

Federico, Giovanni, *An Economic History of the Silk Industry, 1830–1930* (Cambridge: Cambridge University Press, 2009).

Fenech, Louis E., *The Darbar of the Sikh Gurus. The Court of God in the World of Men* (New Delhi: Oxford University Press, 2008).

———, *The Sikh Zafar-Namah of Guru Gobind Singh. A Discursive Blade in the Heart of the Mughal Empire* (New York: Oxford University Press, 2013).

Ferozepore District, Statistical Tables: 1904 (Lahore: Civil and Military Gazette Press, 1908).

Ferrier, J. P., *Caravan Journeys and Wanderings in Persia, Afghanistan, Turkistan and Beloochistan, with Historical Notices of the Countries Lying Between Russia and India*, ed. W. Jesse and H. D. Seymour (London: J. Murray, 1856).

———, *History of the Afghans*, trans. William Jesse (London: John Murray, 1858).

Findlen, Paula, ed., *Early Modern Things. Objects and their Histories, 1500–1800* (London: Routledge, 2013).

Findly, Ellison B., 'The Capture of Maryam-uz-Zamānī's Ship: Mughal Women and European Traders', *Journal of the American Oriental Society*, vol. 108, no. 2 (1988), 227–38.

Fischer-Tiné, Harald, 'Britain's Other Civilising Mission: Class Prejudice, European 'Loaferism' and the Workhouse-System in Colonial India', *IESHR*, vol. 42, no. 3 (2005), 295–338.

Fitzpatrick, Anne, *The Great Russian Fair. Nizhnii Novgorod, 1840–90* (Basingstoke: Macmillan, 1990).

Floor, Willem, *The Dutch East India Company (VOC) and Diewel–Sind (Pakistan) in the 17th and 18th Centuries (Based on Original Dutch Sources)* (Islamabad: Institute of Central and West Asian Studies, 1993/4).

Foltz, Richard, 'Cultural Contacts between Central Asia and Mughal India', in *India and Central Asia. Commerce and Culture, 1500–1800*, ed. Scott C. Levi (Delhi: Oxford University Press, 2007).

———, *Mughal India and Central Asia* (Karachi: Oxford University Press, 1998).

Forbes Watson, John, *The Textile Manufactures and Costumes of the People of India* (London: William H. Allen and Company, 1867).

Foster, W., ed., *Early Travels in India, 1583–1619* (Oxford: Oxford University Press, 1921).

———, *The English Factories in India 1634–1636* (Oxford: Clarendon Press, 1911).

———, *The English Factories in India 1637–1641* (Oxford: Clarendon Press, 1912).

———, ed. *The English Factories in India 1642–1645* (Oxford: Clarendon Press, 1913).

———, ed. *The English Factories in India 1646–1650* (Oxford: Clarendon Press, 1914).

Francklin, William, *The History of the Reign of Shah-Aulum, the Present Emperor of Hindostaun* (London: Cooper and Graham, 1798).

Fraser, D., *The Marches of Hindustan, the Record of a Journey in Thibet, Trans-Himalaya India, Chinese Turkestan, Russian Turkestan, and Persia* (Edinburgh/London: William Blackwood & Sons, 1907).

Frechtling, Louis E., 'Anglo-Russian Rivalry in Eastern Turkistan, 1863–1881', *Journal of The Royal Central Asian Society*, vol. 26, no. 3 (1939), 471–89.

Gaastra, Femme S., 'The Textile Trade of the VOC the Dutch Response to the English Challenge', *South Asia: Journal of South Asian Studies*, vol. 19, Special Issue (1996), 85–95.

Gamsa, Mark, 'Refractions of China in Russia, and of Russia in China: Ideas and Things', *JESOH*, vol. 60, no. 5 (2017), 549–84.

Gänger, Stefanie, 'Circulation: Reflections on Circularity, Entity, and Liquidity in the Language of Global History', *JGH*, vol. 12, no. 3 (2017), 303–18.

Gardner, Alexander, *Memoirs of Alexander Gardner*, ed. H. Pearse (Edinburgh, 1898).

Gardner, Kyle, 'The Ready Materials for Another World: Frontier, Security, and the Hindustan–Tibet Road in the 19th Century Northwestern Himalaya', *Himalaya. The Journal of the Association for Nepal and Himalaya Studies*, vol. 33, no. 1 (2013), 71–84.

Gardner, Kyle James, 'Border Making, Geography, and the Limits of Empire in the Northwestern Himalaya, 1846–1962' (unpublished doctoral dissertation, University of Chicago, 2018).

Garrett, H. L. O., trans. and ed., *The Punjab a Hundred Years Ago, as Described by V. Jacquemont (1831) and A. Soltykoff (1842)* (Lahore: Superintendent Government Printing, 1935).

Gauba, Anand, *Amritsar. A Study in Urban History (1840–1947)* (Jalandhar: ABS Publications, 1988).

BIBLIOGRAPHY

Gauba, Anand, 'Amritsar: A Centre of Trade and Industry', in *The City of Amritsar. A Study of Historical, Cultural, Social and Economic Aspects*, ed. Fauja Singh (New Delhi: Oriental Publishers, 1978).

Gazetteer of the Ambala District: 1883–4 (Lahore: Punjab Government Press, 1884).

Gazetteer of the Amritsar District: 1883–4 (Calcutta: Calcutta Central Press Co., 1884).

Gazetteer of the Amritsar District: 1892–3 (Lahore: Punjab Government Press, 1893).

Gazetteer of the Chenab Colony: 1904 (Lahore: Civil and Military Gazette Press, 1905).

Gazetteer of the Delhi District: 1883–4 (Calcutta: Calcutta Central Press Co., 1884).

Gazetteer of the Dera Ghazi Khan District: 1883–4 (Calcutta: Calcutta Central Press Co., 1884).

Gazetteer of the Dera Ghazi Khan District: 1897–8 (Lahore: Civil and Military Gazette Press, 1898).

Gazetteer of the Dera Ismail Khan District: 1883–4 (Lahore: Arya Press, 1884).

Gazetteer of the Ferozepore District: 1883–4 (Lahore: Civil and Military Gazette Press, 1884).

Gazetteer of the Ferozepore District: 1888–9 (Lahore: Civil and Military Gazette Press, 1898).

Gazetteer of the Gujranwala District: 1883–4 (Lahore: Sang-e-Meel Publications, 1989).

Gazetteer of the Gujranwala District: 1893–4 (Lahore: Civil and Military Gazette Press, 1895).

Gazetteer of the Gujrat District: 1883–4 (Lahore: Arya Press, 1884).

Gazetteer of the Gujrat District: 1892–3 (Publisher unknown: 1893. Retrieved from https://ia801603.us.archive.org/25/items/in.ernet. dli.2015.35649/2015.35649.Gujrat-District-Gazetteer.pdf [accessed 25 August 2020]).

Gazetteer of the Gurdaspur District: 1883–4 (Lahore: Arya Press, 1884).

Gazetteer of the Gurdaspur District: 1891–2 (Lahore: Civil and Military Gazette Press, 1892).

Gazetteer of the Hazara District 1907 (London: Chatto & Windus, 1908).

Gazetteer of the Hazara District: 1883–4 (Lahore: Civil and Military Gazette Press, 1884).

Gazetteer of the Hoshiarpur District: 1883–4 (Lahore: Civil and Military Gazette Press, 1884).

Gazetteer of the Jalandhar District: 1883–4 (Lahore: Arya Press, 1884).

Gazetteer of the Jhang District: 1883–4 (Lahore: Arya Press, 1884).

Gazetteer of the Jhelum District: 1883–4 (Calcutta: Calcutta Central Press Co., 1884).

Gazetteer of the Kangra District, Parts II to IV—Kulu, Lahaul, and Spiti: 1897 (Lahore: Civil and Military Gazette Press, 1899).

Gazetteer of the Kangra District,Vol. I, Kangra Proper: 1883–4 (Calcutta: Calcutta Central Press Co., 1884).

Gazetteer of the Kohat District: 1883–4 (Calcutta: Calcutta Central Press Co., 1884).

Gazetteer of the Lahore District: 1883–4 (Calcutta: Calcutta Central Press Co., 1884).

Gazetteer of the Lahore District: 1893–4 (Lahore: Civil and Military Gazette Press, 1894).

Gazetteer of the Ludhiana District: 1883 (Lahore: Arya Press, 1883).

Gazetteer of the Ludhiana District: 1888–9 (Calcutta: Calcutta Central Press Co., 1889).

Gazetteer of the Montgomery District: 1883–4 (Lahore: Arya Press, 1884).

Gazetteer of the Montgomery District: 1898–9 (Lahore: Civil and Military Gazette Press, 1900).

Gazetteer of the Mooltan District: 1883–4 (Lahore: Arya Press, 1884).

Gazetteer of the Multan District: 1901–2 (Lahore: Civil and Military Gazette Press, 1902).

Gazetteer of the Muzaffargarh District: 1883–4 (Lahore: Arya Press, 1884).

Gazetteer of the Peshawar District: 1883–4 (Calcutta: Calcutta Central Press Company, 1884).

Gazetteer of the Peshawar District: 1897–8 (Lahore: Sang-e-Meel Publications, 1989).

Gazetteer of the Rawalpindi District: 1883–4 (Lahore: Civil and Military Gazette Press, 1884).

Gazetteer of the Rawalpindi District: 1894–5 (Lahore: Civil and Military Gazette Press, 1895).

Gazetteer of the Shahpur District: 1883–4 (Calcutta: Calcutta Central Press Co., 1884).

Gazetteer of the Shahpur District: 1897 (Lahore: Civil and Military Gazette Press, 1897).

Gazetteer of the Sialkot District: 1883–4 (Lahore: Civil and Military Gazette Press, 1884).

Geoghegan, J., *Silk in India* (Calcutta: Office of the Superintendent of Government Printing, 1872).

Gerritsen, Anne, and Giorgio Riello, 'Spaces of Global Interactions. The Material Landscapes of Global History', in *Writing Material Culture History*, ed. Anne Gerritsen and Giorgio Riello (London: Bloomsbury, 2015).

————, eds, *The Global Lives of Things. The Material Culture of Connections in the Early Modern World* (London: Routledge, 2015).

Geyer, Dietrich, *Russian Imperialism. The Interaction of Domestic and Foreign Policy 1860–1914*, trans. Bruce Little (Leamington Spa: Berg Publishers, 1987).

Ghobrial, John-Paul, *The Whispers of Cities. Information Flows in Istanbul, London, and Paris in the Age of William Trumbull* (Oxford: Oxford University Press, 2013).

Gidwani, Vinay, and K. Sivaramakrishnan, 'Circular Migration and Rural Cosmopolitanism in India', *Contributions to Indian Sociology*, vol. 37, nos 1–2 (2003), 339–67.

Gill, Bir Good, 'The Venture of the Central Asian Trading Company in Eastern Turkistan, 1874–5', *Asian Affairs*, vol. 87, no. 3 (2000), 181–8.

————, 'Trade of the Punjab with Eastern Turkistan: Its Ramifications 1865–1877', in *Punjab History Conference, Nineteenth Session, March 22–24, 1985. Proceedings* (Patiala: Publication Bureau, Punjab University, 1987).

Godfrey, S. H., 'The Trade of Ladakh with China and Thibet', in *A Summer in High Asia*, ed. F. E. S. Adair (London: W. Thacker and Company, 1899).

Golden, Peter B., *An Introduction to the History of the Turkic People. Ethnogenesis and State Formation in Medieval and Modern Eurasia and the Middle East* (Wiesbaden: Otto Harrassowitz, 1992).

————, *Central Asia in World History* (Oxford: Oxford University Press, 2011).

Goldstone, Jack A., *Revolution and Rebellion in the Early Modern World* (Berkeley: University of California Press, 1991).

Golombek, Lisa, 'The Draped Universe of Islam', in *Content and Context of Visual Arts in the Islamic World*, ed. Priscilla P. Soucek (London: Pennsylvania University Press, 1988).

Gommans, Jos J. L., 'Afghāns in India', in *Encyclopaedia of Islam, Three*, ed. Gudrun Krämer, Denis Matringe, John Nawas, and Everett Rowson (Brill Online, 2013)—http://referenceworks.brillonline.com/entries/encyclo-paedia–of–islam–3/afghans–in–india–COM_0013 (Accessed: 29 July 2013).

————, 'Indian Warfare and Afghan Innovation', in *Warfare and Weaponry in South Asia 1000–1800*, ed. Jos J. L. Gommans and Dirk H. A. Kolff (New Delhi: Oxford University Press, 2001).

————, 'Mughal India and Central Asia in the Eighteenth Century: An Introduction to a Wider Perspective', in *India and Central Asia: Commerce and Culture, 1500–1800*, ed. Scott. C. Levi (New Delhi: Oxford University Press, 2007).

————, *Mughal Warfare. Indian Frontiers and High Roads to Empire, 1500–1700* (London: Routledge, 2002).

————, 'The Embarrassment of Political Violence in Europe and South Asia, *c.* 1100–1800' in *Violence Denies.Violence, Non–Violence and the Rationalisation of Violence in South Asian Cultural History*, ed. Jan E. M. Houben and Karel R. Van Kooij (Leiden: Brill, 1999).

————, *The Indian Frontier. Horse and Warband in the Making of Empires* (Delhi: Manohar, 2018).

————, *The Rise of the Indo-Afghan Empire, c.1710–1780* (New Delhi: Oxford University Press, 1999).

Good, Peter, 'In the Service of the Shah? The East India Company in the Persian Gulf 1600–1750' (unpublished doctoral dissertation, University of Essex, 2018).

Gopal, Surendra, ed., *India and Central Asia. Cultural, Economic and Political Links* (New Delhi: Shipra Publications, 2001).

————, ed., *Indians in Russia in the 17th and 18th Centuries* (Calcutta: Naya Prokash, 1988).

Gordon, Stewart N., 'Symbolic and Structural Constraints on the Adoption of European-style Military Technologies in the Eighteenth Century', in *Rethinking Early Modern India*, ed. Richard B. Barnett (New Delhi: Manohar, 2002).

Green, Nile, 'Blessed Men and Tribal Politics: Notes on Political Culture in the Indo-Afghan World', *JESOH*, vol. 49, no. 3 (2006), 344–60.

————, *Bombay Islam. The Religious Economy of the West Indian Ocean, 1840–1915* (Cambridge: Cambridge University Press, 2011).

————, 'From the Silk Road to the Railroad (and Back): The Means and Meanings of the Iranian Encounter with China', *Iranian Studies*, vol. 48, no. 2 (2013), 165–92.

————, *Making Space. Sufis and Settlers in Early Modern India* (Delhi: Oxford University Press, 2012).

————, 'Persian Print and the Stanhope Revolution: Industrialization, Evangelicalism, and the Birth of Printing in Early Qajar Iran', *CSSAAME*, vol. 30 (2010), 473–90.

————, 'Tribe, Diaspora, and Sainthood in Afghan History', *JAS*, vol. 67, no. 1 (2008), 171–211.

Green, Toby, 'Africa and the Price Revolution: Currency Imports and Socioeconomic Change in West and West-Central Africa during the Seventeenth Century', *Journal of African History*, vol. 57, no. 1 (2016), 1–24.

Greenblatt, Stephen, *Renaissance Self-Fashioning. From More to Shakespeare* (Chicago: University of Chicago Press, 2005, first edn. 1980).

Greenshields, Malcolm, *An Economy of Violence in Early Modern France. Crime and Justice in the Haute Auvergne, 1587–1664* (University Park: Pennsylvania University Press, 1994).

Gregorian, Vartan, *The Emergence of Modern Afghanistan. Politics of Reform and Modernisation, 1880–1946* (Stanford: Stanford University Press, 1969).

Grehan, James, *Everyday Life and Consumer Culture in Eighteenth-Century Damascus* (Seattle: University of Washington Press, 2007).

————, 'Smoking and "Early Modern" Sociability: The Great Tobacco Debate in the Ottoman Middle East (Seventeenth to Eighteenth Centuries)', *The American Historical Review*, vol. 111 no. 5 (2006), 1352–77.

Greif, Avner, *Institutions and the Path to the Modern Economy: Lessons from Medieval Trade* (Cambridge: Cambridge University Press, 2006).

Grewal, J. S., 'Business Communities of Punjab', in *Business Communities of India. A Historical Perspective*, ed. Dwijendra Tripathi (New Delhi: Manohar, 1984).

————, *The Sikhs of the Punjab* (Cambridge: Cambridge University Press, 1998).

Grewal, J. S., and Indu Banga, eds, *Early Nineteenth-Century Panjab from Ganesh Das's* Chār Bāgh-i-Panjāb *[1849]* (Amritsar: Guru Nanak University, 1975).

Grewal, J. S., and Irfan Habib, eds, *Sikh History from Persian Sources. Translations of Major Texts* (New Delhi: Tulika, 2001).

Grewal, J. S., and Veena Sachdeva, 'Urbanisation in the Mughal Province of Lahore (c. 1550–1850)', in *Five Thousand Years of Urbanisation: The Punjab Region*, ed. Reeta Grewal (New Delhi: Manohar, 2005).

Grewal, Reeta, *Colonialism and Urbanisation in India. The Punjab Region* (New Delhi: Manohar, 2009).

Grewe, Bernd-Stefan, and Karin Hofmeester, eds, *Luxury in Global Perspective: Objects and Practices, 1600–2000* (New York: Cambridge University Press, 2016).

Griffiths, John, 'A Memorandum on the Panjab and Kandahar', in *Early European Accounts of the Sikhs*, ed. Ganda Singh (Calcutta: Indian Studies Past and Present, 1962).

Gross, Jo-Ann, 'The Naqshbandiya Connection. From Central Asia to India and Back (16th–19th Centuries)', in *India and Central Asia. Commerce and Culture, 1500–1800*, ed. Scott C. Levi (Delhi: Oxford University Press, 2007).

Grover, B. R., 'An Integrated Pattern of Commercial Life in the Rural Society of North India during the Seventeenth and Eighteenth Centuries', in *Money and the Market in India 1100–1700*, ed. Sanjay Subrahmanyam (New Delhi: Oxford University Press, 1994).

Guha, Sumit, 'The Handloom Industry of Central India: 1825–1950', in *Cloth and Commerce. Textiles in Colonial India*, ed. Tirthankar Roy (New Delhi: Sage, 1996).

Gujranwala District, Statistical Tables: 1904 (Lahore: Civil and Military Gazette Press, 1907).

Gujrat District, Statistical Tables: 1904 (Lahore: Civil and Military Gazette Press, 1908).

Gupta, Satya Prakash, *The Agrarian System of Eastern Rajasthan (c.1650–c.1750)* (New Delhi: Manohar, 1986).

Gurdaspur District, Statistical Tables: 1904 (Lahore: Civil and Military Gazette Press, 1908).

Gürkan, Emrah Safa, 'Espionage in the Sixteenth-Century Mediterranean: Secret Diplomacy, Mediterranean Go-Betweens and the Ottoman Habsburg Rivalry' (unpublished doctoral dissertation, Georgetown University, 2012).

Habib, Irfan, *An Atlas of the Mughal Empire* (Aligarh: Aligarh Muslim University, 1982).

————, *The Agrarian System of Mughal India, 1556–1707* (Delhi: Oxford University Press, revised edn., 2009).

Haider, Najaf, 'The Network of Monetary Exchange', in *Cross Currents and Community Networks: The History of the Indian Ocean World*, ed. Himanshu Prabha Ray and Edward Alpers (New Delhi: Oxford University Press, 2007).

Hailey, William Malcom, *Monograph on the Silk Industry of the Punjab, 1899* (Lahore: Civil and Military Gazette Press, 1899).

Hale, J.R., *Renaissance Europe. Individual and Society, 1480–1520* (Berkeley: University of California Press, 1971).

Hamid, Usman, and Pasha M. Khan, 'Introduction. Moving Across the Persian Cosmopolis', *CSSAAME*, vol. 37, no. 3 (2017), 491–3.

Hamilton, Alexander, *A New Account of the East Indies*, 2 vols (London, 1744).

Hanifi, Shah Mahmoud, *Connecting Histories in Afghanistan. Market Relations and State Formation on a Colonial Frontier* (Stanford: Stanford University Press, 2011).

Hanway, Jonas, *An Historical Account of the British Trade Over the Caspian Sea: With a Journal of Travels from London Through Russia into Persia; and Back Through Russia, Germany and Holland*, 2 vols (London: T. Osborne and Company, 1753).

Harlan, Josiah, *Central Asia. Personal Narrative of General Josiah Harlan, 1823–1841*, ed. Frank E. Ross (London: Luzac and Company, 1939).

Harms, Robert, 'Introduction', in *Indian Ocean Slavery in the Age of Abolition*, ed. Robert Harms, Bernard Freamon, and David Bight (New Haven: Yale University Press, 2013).

Harnetty, Peter, 'Cotton Exports and Indian Agriculture, 1861–1870', *EHR*, new series, vol. 24 (1971), 426–7.

Hart, S.V.W., 'Report on the Town and Port of Kurachee', in *Selections from the Records of the Bombay Government. No. XVII. New Series*, ed. R. Hughes Thomas (Bombay: Bombay Education Society's Press, 1855).

Hasan, Farhat, *State and Locality in Mughal India: Power Relations in Western India, c.1572–1730* (Cambridge: Cambridge University Press, 2004).

Hashimi, Zain, *The Faras-nama of Hashimi*, ed. D. C. Phillott (Calcutta: Asiatic Society, 1910).

Haynes, Douglas E., *Small Town Capitalism in Western India. Artisans, Merchants and the Making of the Informal Economy, 1870–1960* (Cambridge: Cambridge University Press, 2012).

Haynes, Douglas E., Abigail McGowan, Tirthankar Roy, and Haruka Yanagisawa, eds, *Towards a History of Consumption in South Asia* (New Delhi: Oxford University Press, 2010).

Hayward, G. S. W., 'Route from Jellalabad to Yarkand Through Chitral, Badakhshan, and Pamir Steppe, Given by Mahomed Amin of Yarkand, with Remarks by G. S. W. Hayward', *Proceedings of the Royal Geographical Society of London*, vol. 13 (1868–9), 122–30.

Hazarah, Fayz Muhammad Katib, *The History of Afghanistan. Fayz Muhammad Katib Hazarah's Siraj al-tawarikh. Volume 1. The Saduzai Era 1747–1843*, trans. R. D. McChesney and M. M. Khorrami (Leiden: Brill, 2013).

Headrick, Daniel, *Power over Peoples. Technology, Environments, and Western Imperialism, 1400 to the Present* (Princeton: Princeton University Press, 2010).

———, *The Tentacles of Progress. Technology Transfer in the Age of Imperialism, 1850–1940* (Oxford: Oxford University Press, 1988).

———, *The Tools of Empire. Technology and European Imperialism in the Nineteenth Century* (Oxford: Oxford University Press, 1981).

Heathcote, T. A., *Balochistan, the British and the Great Game. The Struggle for the Bolan Pass, Gateway to India* (London: Hurst and Company, 2015).

Hellmich, Christina, 'Cosmopolitan Relationships in the Crossroads of the Pacific Ocean', in *Writing Material Culture History*, ed. Anne Gerritsen and Giorgio Riello (London: Bloomsbury, 2015).

Hemneter, Ernest, 'The Castes of Indian Dyers', *CIBA Review No. 2* (Basle, October 1937).

Hevia, James, *The Imperial Security State. British Colonial Knowledge and Empire-Building in Asia* (Cambridge: Cambridge University Press, 2012).

Hobsbawm, E. J., *Bandits* (London: Weidenfeld and Nicolson, 1969).

———, *Primitive Rebels. Studies in Archaic Forms of Social Movement in the 19th and 20th Centuries* (Manchester: Manchester University Press, 1959).

Hofmeester, Karin, 'Diamonds as Global Luxury Commodity', in *Luxury in Global Perspective: Objects and Practices, 1600–2000*, ed. Bernd-Stefan Grewe and Karin Hofmeester (New York: Cambridge University Press, 2016).

Holdich, Thomas, *The Gates of India, Being An Historical Narrative* (London: Macmillan and Company, 1910).

Hopkins, B. D., 'Race, Sex and Slavery: "Forced Labour" in Central Asia and

Afghanistan in the Early 19th Century', *MAS*, vol. 42, no. 4 (2008), 629–71.

————, *The Making of Modern Afghanistan* (Basingstoke: Palgrave Macmillan, 2012).

Hopkins, Benjamin D., *Ruling the Savage Periphery. Frontier Governance and the Making of the Modern State* (Cambridge, Mass.: Harvard University Press, 2020).

Hopkins, Benjamin, and Magnus Marsden, *Fragments of the Afghan Frontier* (London: C. Hurst & Co., 2011).

Hoshiarpur District, Statistical Tables: 1904 (Lahore: Civil and Military Gazette Press, 1904).

Hoshiarpur District, with Maps: 1904 (Lahore: Civil and Military Gazette Press, 1905).

House of Commons, *Report from the Select Committee on the Affairs of the East India Company; with Minutes of Evidence in Six Parts, and an Appendix and Index to Each. Part II. Finance and Accounts—Trade* (London, 1832).

HP, '22 July 2013, Modern–Day Silk Road Optimizes HP's Supply Chain' (accessed 13 April 2014): http://www8.hp.com/hpnext/posts/modern–day–silk–road–optimizes–hp–s–supply–chain#.U0qT1vldVYX.

Huang, Xuelei, 'Deodorizing China: Odour, Ordure, and Colonial (Dis)Order in Shanghai, 1840s–1940s', *MAS*, vol. 50, no. 3 (2016), 1092–1122.

Huber, Valeska, *Channelling Mobilities. Migration and Globalisation in the Suez Canal Region and Beyond, 1869–1914* (Cambridge: Cambridge University Press, 2013).

Hughes, A. W., *A Gazetteer of the Province of Sindh* (London: George Bell and Sons, 1874).

Hunt, Margaret, 'The 1689 Mughal Siege of East India Company Bombay: Crisis and Historical Erasure', *History Workshop Journal*, no. 84 (2017), 149–69.

Hunter, W. W., *The Indian Empire: Its Peoples, History, and Products* (London: W. H. Allen and Company, 1893).

Hurd, John M., 'Railways', in *The Cambridge Economic History of India. Volume 2: c.1757–c.1970*, ed. Dharma Kumar and Meghnad Desai (Cambridge: Cambridge University Press, 1983).

Hussain, Iqbal, 'Jagirdari in the Eighteenth Century: A Case Study of Two Afghan Families of Western Awadh', in *Rethinking Early Modern India*, ed. Richard B. Barnett (New Delhi: Manohar, 2002).

Huttenback, Robert A., *British Relations with Sind 1799–1843. An Anatomy of Imperialism* (Oxford: Oxford University Press, 2007).

————, *Kashmir and the British Raj 1847–1947* (Oxford: Oxford University Press, 2004).

BIBLIOGRAPHY

Hutton, James, *Central Asia: From the Aryan to the Cossack* (London: Tinsley Brothers, 1875).

Hyam, Ronald, 'British Imperial Expansion in the Late Eighteenth Century', *The Historical Journal*, vol. 10, no. 1 (1967), 113–24.

Ibbetson, Denzil, *Panjab Castes: Being a Reprint of the Chapter on "The Races, Castes and Tribes of the People" in the Report on the Census of the Panjab Published in 1883 by the Late Sir Denzil Ibbetson, K.C.S.I.* (Lahore: Government Printing, 1916).

Ilahi, Faiz, and R. K. Seth, *An Economic Survey of Durrana Langana, a Village in the Multan District of the Punjab. Inquiries (Punjab Village Surveys. 11)* (Punjab: Board of Economic Inquiry, 1938).

Iliffe, John, *A Modern History of Tanganyika* (Cambridge: Cambridge University Press, 1979).

India Museum, *Inventory of the Collection of Examples of Indian Art and Manufactures Transferred to the South Kensington Museum* (London: George Edward Eyre and William Spottiswoode, 1880).

Irvine, William, 'Ahmad Shah, Abdali, and the Indian Wazir, 'Imad-ul-Mulk (1756–7)', *The Indian Antiquary, a Journal of Oriental Research*, xxxvi (1907).

——, *The Army of the Indian Moghuls: Its Organization and Administration* (London: Luzac and Company, 1903).

Izzatullah Khan, Mir, *Travels in Central Asia by Meer Izzut-Oollah in the Years 1812–13*, ed. P. Henderson (Calcutta: Foreign Department Press, 1872).

Jacquemont, Victor, *Letters from India; Describing a Journey in the British Dominions of India, Tibet, Lahore, and Cashmeer. During the Years 1828, 1829, 1830, 1831. Undertaken by Order of the French Government*, 2 vols (London: Edward Churton, 1835).

Jain, Kajri, *Gods in the Bazaar. The Economies of Indian Calendar Art* (Durham, N.C.: Duke University Press, 2007).

Jalal, Ayesha, *Democracy and Authoritarianism in South Asia* (Cambridge: Cambridge University Press, 1995).

Jhang District, Statistical Tables: 1904 (Lahore: Civil and Military Gazette Press, 1908).

Jhang District, with Maps: 1908 (Lahore: Civil and Military Gazette Press, 1910).

Jhelum District, Statistical Tables: 1904 (Lahore: Civil and Military Gazette Press, 1905).

Joshi, Chitra, 'Dak Roads, Dak Runners, and the Reordering of Communication Networks', *International Review of Social History*, vol. 57, no. 3 (2012), 169–89.

Jullundur District and Kapurthala State, Statistical Tables: 1904 (Lahore: Civil and Military Gazette Press, 1908).

BIBLIOGRAPHY

Jullundur District and Kapurthala State, with Maps: 1904 (Lahore: Civil and Military Gazette Press, 1908).

Kafadar, Cemal, *Between Two Worlds. The Construction of the Ottoman State* (Berkeley: University of California Press, 1995).

Kakar, Hasan Kawun, *Government and Society in Afghanistan. The Reign of Amir Abd al-Rahman Khan* (Austin: University of Texas Press, 1979).

Kakar, M. Hassan, *A Political and Diplomatic History of Afghanistan 1863–1901* (Leiden: Brill, 2006).

Kane, Eileen, *Russian Hajj. Empire and the Pilgrimage to Mecca* (Ithaca: Cornell University Press, 2015).

Kang, Kanwarjit, 'Murals of Amritsar', in *The City of Amritsar. A Study of Historical, Cultural, Social and Economic Aspects*, ed. Fauja Singh (New Delhi: Oriental Publishers, 1978).

Kangra District, Statistical Tables: 1904 (Lahore: Civil and Military Gazette Press, 1908).

Kapila, Shruti, 'Race Matters: Orientalism and Religion, India and Beyond *c*. 1770–1880', *MAS*, vol. 41, no. 3 (2007), 471–513.

Kaushik, Devendra, 'The Economic Relations between India and Central Asia', in *India and Central Asia. Cultural, Economic and Political Links*, ed. Surendra Gopal (New Delhi: Shipra Publications, 2001).

Kaye, J. W., ed., *Yarkand (Forsyth's Mission). Return to an Address of the Honourable The House of Commons, dated 24 February 1871* (London: India Office, 1871).

Kessinger, Tom G., 'Regional Economy—North India', in *The Cambridge Economic History of India. Volume 2: c.1757–c.1970*, ed. Dharma Kumar and Meghnad Desai (Cambridge: Cambridge University Press, 1983).

————, *Vilyatpur 1848–1968. Social and Economic Change in a North Indian Village* (Berkeley: University of California Press, 1974).

Khan, Iqbal Ghani, 'The Awadh Scientific Renaissance and the Role of the French: *c*.1750–1820', *Indian Journal of History of Science*, vol. 38, no. 3 (2003), 273–301.

Khan, Muhammad Hayat, *Afghanistan and its Inhabitants. Translated from the Hayat-i-Afghani of Muhammad Hayat Khan*, ed. Henry Priestly (Lahore: Indian Public Opinion Press, 1874).

Khan, Sa'adat Yan, *Faras Nama e Rangin*, trans. D. C. Phillott (London: Bernard Quartich, 1911).

Khanikoff, N., *Bokhara: Its Amir and Its People*, trans. Clement A. de Bode (London: James Madden, 1845).

Khazanov, Anatoly M., *Nomads and the Outside World* (Madison: University of Wisconsin Press, 1994).

Khazeni, Arash, *Sky Blue Stone. The Turquoise Trade in World History* (Berkeley: University of California Press, 2014).

————, 'The City of Balkh and the Central Eurasian Caravan Trade in the Early Nineteenth Century', *CSSAAME*, vol. 30, no. 3 (2010), 463–72.

————, 'Through an Ocean of Sand: Pastoralism and the Equestrian Culture of the Eurasian Steppe', in *Water on Sand. Environmental Histories of the Middle East and North Africa*, ed. Alain Mikhail (Oxford: Oxford University Press, 2013).

Khilnani, N. M., *British Power in the Punjab 1839–1858* (Bombay: Asia Publishing House, 1972).

Khodarkovsky, Michael, 'Of Christianity, Enlightenment, and Colonialism: Russia in the North Caucasus, 1550–1800', *The Journal of Modern History*, vol. 71, no. 2 (1999), 394–430.

————, *Where Two Worlds Met. The Russian State and the Kalmyk Nomads, 1600–1771* (London: Cornell University Press, 1992).

Khoury, Dina Rizk, 'The Ottoman Centre versus Provincial Power-Holders: An Analysis of the Historiography', in *Cambridge History of Turkey: Volume 3: The Later Ottoman Empire, 1603–1839*, ed. Suraiya N. Faroqhi (Cambridge: Cambridge University Press, 2006).

Kim, Kwangmin, *Borderland Capitalism. Turkestan Priduce, Qing Silver, and the Birth of an Eastern Market* (Stanford: Stanford University Press, 2016).

————, 'Profit and Protection: Emin Khwaja and the Qing Conquest of Central Asia, 1759–1777', *JAS*, vol. 71, no. 3 (2012), 603–26.

King, B. B., *The Blue Mutiny. The Indigo Disturbances in Bengal 1859–1862* (Bombay: Oxford University Press, 1966).

Kipling, Rudyard, *Kim* (London: Macmillan, 1901).

Kirpal Singh, 'Amritsar During Maharaja Ranjit Singh's Time', in *The City of Amritsar. A Study of Historical, Cultural, Social and Economic Aspects*, ed. Fauja Singh (New Delhi: Oriental Publishers, 1978).

Kolff, Dirk H. A., *Naukar, Rajput and Sepoy. The Ethnohistory of the Military Labour Market in Hindustan* (Cambridge: Cambridge University Press, 1990).

Kolsky, Elizabeth, 'The Colonial Rule of Law and the Legal Regime of Exception: Frontier "Fanaticism" and State Violence in British India', *American Historical Review*, vol. 120, no. 4 (2015), 1218–46.

Kruijtzer, Gijs, *Xenophobia in Seventeenth-Century India* (Amsterdam: Leiden University Press, 2009).

Kumar, Prakash, *Indigo Plantations and Science in Colonial India* (Cambridge: Cambridge University Press, 2012).

Lafont, Jean-Marie, *Indika. Essays in Indo-French Relations 1630–1976* (New Delhi: Manohar, 2000).

Lahore District, Statistical Tables: 1904 (Lahore: Civil and Military Gazette Press, 1905).

Laidlaw, Zoë, *Colonial Connections, 1815–45. Patronage, the Information*

Revolution and Colonial Government (Manchester: Manchester University Press, 2005).

Lal, Busawan, *Memoirs of the Puthan Soldier of Fortune the Nuwab Ameer-ood-Doulah Mohummud Ameer Khan, Chief of Seronj, Tonk, Rampoora, Neemahera, and Other Places in Hindoostan. Compiled in Persian by Busawan Lal, Naeeb-Moonshee to the Nuwab*, trans. H. T. Prinsep (Calcutta: G. H. Huttmann, Military Orphan Press, 1832).

Lal, Mohan, *Travels in the Panjab, Afghanistan, and Turkistan, to Balk, Bokhara, and Heart; and a Visit to Great Britain and Germany* (Jullundhar: Modest Printers, 1971).

Lally, Jagjeet, '"Beyond Tribal Breakout": Afghans, Empire, and the Economy, *c.* 1747–1818', *Journal of World History*, vol. 30, no. 1 (2019), 369–97.

————, 'Colour as Commodity: Colonialism and the Sensory Worlds of South Asia', *Third Text: A Journal of Contemporary Arts and Culture*, Special Issue/Forum—Decolonising Colour (2017–18).

————, 'Crafting Colonial Anxieties: Silk and the Salvation Army in British India, *circa* 1900–20', *MAS*, vol. 50, no. 3 (2016), 765–807.

————, 'Empires and Equines: The Horse in Art and Exchange in South Asia, *c.*1600–1850', *CSSAAME*, vol. 35, no. 1 (2015), 96–116.

————, 'H is for Horse', in *Animalia: An Anti-Imperial Bestiary for Our Times*, ed. Antoinette Burton and Renisa Mawani (Durham, N.C.: Duke University Press, 2020).

————, 'Introduction to the Third Edition. Afghans and their History between South Asia and the World', in *The Rise of the Indo-Afghan Empire, c. 1710–1780* by Jos J. L. Gommans (Delhi: Manohar, 2018).

————, 'Trial, Error and Economic Development in Colonial Punjab: The Agri-Horticultural Society, the State and Sericulture Experiments, *c.* 1840–70', *IESHR*, vol. 52, no. 1 (2015), 1–27.

Landsell, Henry, *Russian Central Asia; including Kuldja, Bokhara, Khiva and Merv*, 2 vols (London: Sampson Low, Marston, Searle, and Rivington, 1885).

Lane, Kris, *Colour of Paradise. The Emerald in the Age of Gunpowder Empires* (New Haven: Yale University Press, 2010).

Langley, Edward Archer, *Narrative of a Residence at the Court of Meer Ali Moorad; with Wild Sports in the Valley of the Indus*, 2 vols (London: Hurst and Blackett, 1860).

Latifi, A., *The Industrial Punjab: A Survey of Facts, Conditions and Possibilities* (Bombay, Calcutta, London, New York: Longmans, Green and Company, 1911).

Laven, Peter, 'Banditry and Lawlessness on the Venetian *Terraferma* in the Later Cinquecento', in *Crime, Society and the Law in Renaissance Italy*, ed. Trevor Dean and K. J. P. Lowe (Cambridge: Cambridge University Press, 1994).

BIBLIOGRAPHY

Lawrence, Bruce B., *Shattering the Myth. Islam beyond Violence* (Princeton: Princeton University Press, 1998).

Lee, Jonathan L., *The 'Ancient Supremacy'. Bukhara, Afghanistan and the Battle for Balkh, 1731–1901* (Leiden: Brill, 1996).

Lefèvre, Corinne, 'In the Name of the Fathers: Mughal Genealogical Strategies from Babur to Shah Jahan', *Religions of South Asia*, vol. 5, nos 1–2 (2011), 409–42.

Leix, Alfred, *Turkestan and its Textile Crafts* (Hampshire: Crosby Press, 1974).

Lemire, Beverly, *Dress, Culture and Commerce. The English Clothing Trade Before the Factory, 1660–1800* (Basingstoke: Macmillan, 1997).

———, *Fashion's Favourite: The Cotton Trade and the Consumer in Britain, 1660–1800* (Oxford: Oxford University Press, 1991).

Leonard, Karen, 'The "Great Firm" Theory of the Decline of the Mughal Empire', *CSSH*, vol. 21, no. 2 (1979), 151–67.

Leonard, Zak, 'Colonial Ethnography on India's North-West Frontier, 1850–1910', *The Historical Journal*, vol. 59, no. 1 (2016), 175–96.

Levi, Scott C., 'Early Modern Central Asia in World History', *History Compass*, vol. 10/11 (2012), 866–78.

———, 'Hindus Beyond the Hindu Kush: Indians in the Central Asian Slave Trade', *Journal of the Royal Asiatic Society*, third series, vol. 12, no. 3 (2002), 277–88.

———, 'India, Russia and the Eighteenth-Century Transformation of the Central Asian Caravan Trade', *JESOH*, vol. 42, no. 4, (1999), 519–48.

———, 'Multanis and Shikarpuris: Indian Diasporas in Historical Perspective', in *Global Indian Diasporas. Exploring Trajectories of Migration and Theory*, ed. Gijsbert Oonk (IIAS/Amsterdam University Press, 2007).

———, 'The Fergana Valley at the Crossroads of World History: The Rise of Khoqand, 1709–1822', *JGH*, vol. 2, no. 2 (2007), 213–32.

———, *The Indian Diaspora in Central Asia and its Trade, 1550–1900* (Leiden: Brill, 2002).

———, *The Rise and Fall of Khoqand, 1709–1806. Central Asia in the Global Age* (Pittsburgh: University of Pittsburgh Press, 2017).

———, ed., *India and Central Asia: Commerce and Culture, 1500–1800* (New Delhi: Oxford University Press, 2007).

Lewis, Colin M., 'Britain, the Argentine and Informal Empire: Rethinking the Role of Railway Companies', in *Informal Empire in Latin America: Culture, Commerce, and Capital*, ed. Matthew Brown (Oxford: Blackwell, 2008).

Liu, Xinru, *Silk and Religion. An Exploration of Material Life and the Thought of People AD 600–1200* (New Delhi: Oxford University Press, 1998).

Lockyer, Charles, *An Account of the Trade in India* (London: Samuel Crouch, 1711).

Logofet, D. N., *The Land of Wrong. The Khanate of Bokhara and its Present Condition* (Simla: Government Monotype Press, 1910).

Ludhiana District, Statistical Tables: 1904 (Lahore: Civil and Military Gazette Press, 1905).

Luis, Francisco José, 'Guru Nanak Shah Faqir. Sufi and Shi'a Elements in the Representation of Guru Nanak', in *Mazaar, Bazaar. Design and Visual Culture in Pakistan*, ed. Saima Zaidi (Karachi: Oxford University Press, 2009).

Lydon, Ghislaine, *On Trans-Saharan Trails. Islamic Law, Trade Networks, and Cross-Cultural Exchange in Nineteenth-Century Western Africa* (Cambridge: Cambridge University Press, 2009).

Machado, Pedro, 'Cloths of a New Fashion: Indian Ocean Networks of Exchange and Cloth Zones of Contact in Africa and India in the Eighteenth and Nineteenth Centuries', in *How India Clothed the World. The World of South Asian Textiles, 1500–1850*, ed. Giorgio Riello and Tirthankar Roy (Leiden: Brill, 2009).

————, *Ocean of Trade. South Asian Merchants, Africa and the Indian Ocean, c. 1750–1850* (Cambridge: Cambridge University Press, 2015).

Mackenzie, Helen, *Six Years in India. Delhi: The City of the Great Mogul. With an Account of The Various Tribes in Hindostan; Hindoos, Sikhs, Affghans, Etc. A New Edition of 'The Mission, The Camp, and The Zenana'* (London: Richard Bentley, 1857).

Madra, Amandeep Singh, and Parmjit Singh, *The Golden Temple of Amritsar. Reflections of the Past (1808–1959)* (London: Kashi House, 2011).

Mahmoud, Samir, 'Colour and the Mystics. Light, Beauty, and the Spiritual Quest', in Jonathan Bloom and Sheila Blair, eds, *And Diverse Are Their Hues* (New Haven: Yale University Press, 2011).

Makdisi, Ussama, 'Ottoman Orientalism', *The American Historical Review*, vol. 107, no. 3 (2002), 768–96.

Malcolm, John, *Sketch of the Sikhs* (London: John Murray, 1812).

Malhotra, Anshu, *Gender, Caste, and Religious Identities. Restructuring Class in Colonial Punjab* (New Delhi: Oxford University Press, 2002).

Malhotra, Karamjit K., *The Eighteenth Century in Sikh History. Political Resurgence, Religious and Social Life, and Cultural Articulation* (New Delhi: Oxford University Press, 2016).

Mallampalli, Chandra, *A Muslim Conspiracy in British India? Politics and Paranoia in the Early Nineteenth-Century Deccan* (Cambridge: Cambridge University Press, 2017).

Mancini-Lander, Derek J., 'Tales Bent Backward: Early Modern Local History in Persianate Transregional Contributions', *Journal of the Royal Asiatic Society*, third series, vol. 28, no. 1 (2018), 23–54.

Manjapra, Kris, 'Plantation Dispossessions: The Global Travel of Agricultural Racial Capitalism', in *American Capitalism. New Histories*, ed. Sven Beckert and Christine Desan (New York: Columbia University Press, 2018).

Marino, John A., 'Wheat and Wool in the Dogana of Foggia. An Equilibrium Model for Early Modern European Economic History', *Mélanges de l'Ecole Française de Rome. Moyen-Age, Temps Modernes*, vol. 100, no. 2 (1988), 871–92.

Markovits, Claude, *Merchants, Traders, Entrepreneurs. Indian Business in the Colonial Era* (Basingstoke: Palgrave Macmillan, 2008).

————, *The Global World of Indian Merchants, 1750–1947. Traders of Sind from Bukhara to Panama* (Cambridge: Cambridge University Press, 2000).

————, Jacques Pouchepadass, and Sanjay Subrahmanyam, 'Introduction: Circulation and Society under Colonial Rule', in *Society and Circulation. Mobile People and Itinerant Cultures in South Asia, 1750–1950*, ed. Claude Markovits, Jacques Pouchepadass, and Sanjay Subrahmanyam (London: Anthem Press, 2006).

Marsden, Magnus, *Trading Worlds. Afghan Merchants Across Modern Frontiers* (London: Hurst and Company, 2016).

Marshall, Alan, *Intelligence and Espionage in the Reign of Charles II, 1660–1685* (Cambridge: Cambridge University Press, 1994).

Marshall, P. J., *The Making and Unmaking of Empires. Britain, India and America*, c. *1750–1783* (Oxford: Oxford University Press, 2005).

————, ed., *The Eighteenth Century in Indian History. Evolution or Revolution?* (New Delhi: Oxford University Press, 2003).

Martin, Marina, 'An Economic History of Hundi, 1858–1978' (unpublished doctoral dissertation, London School of Economics, 2012).

Maskiel, Michelle, and Adrienne Mayor, 'Early Modern Legens of Poison Khil'ats in India', in *Robes of Honour. Khil'at in Pre-Colonial and Colonial India*, ed. Stewart Gordon (New Delhi: Oxford University Press, 2003).

Masson, Charles, *Narrative of Various Journeys in Balochistan, Afghanistan and the Panjab* (London: Richard Bentley, 1842).

Mathur, Saloni, *India by Design. Colonial History and Cultural Display* (Berkeley: University of California Press, 2007).

Matthee, Rudi, *The Pursuit of Pleasure. Drugs and Stimulants in Iranian History, 1500–1900* (Princeton: Princeton University Press, 2005).

Matthee, Rudi, Willem Floor, and Patrick Clawson, *The Monetary History of Iran. From the Safavids to the Qajars* (London: I. B. Tauris, 2013).

Matthee, Rudolph P., *The Politics of Trade in Safavid Iran. Silk for Silver, 1600–1730* (Cambridge: Cambridge University Press, 1999).

Maxwell-Lefroy, H., and E. C. Ansorge, *Report on an Inquiry into the Silk Industry in India*, 2 vols (Calcutta: Government Press, 1917).

Mazlish, Bruce, 'Comparing Global History to World History', *Journal of Interdisciplinary History*, vol. 28, no. 3 (1998), 385–95.

Mazumder, Rajit K., *The Indian Army and the Making of Punjab* (New Delhi: Permanent Black, 2003).

McAleer, John, 'Displaying its Wares: Material Culture, the East India

Company and British Encounters with India in the Long Eighteenth Century', in *India and Europe in the Global Eighteenth Century*, ed. Simon Davies, Daniel Sanjiv Roberts, and Gabriel Sanchez Espinosa (Oxford: Oxford University Press, 2014).

McCabe, Ina Baghdiantz, *The Shah's Silk for Europe's Silver. The Eurasian Trade of the Julfa Armenians in Safavid Iran and India (1530–1750)* (Atlanta: Scholars Press/University of Pennsylvania, 1999).

McChesney, R. D., *Waqf in Central Asia. Four Hundred Years in the History of a Muslim Shrine, 1480–1889* (Princeton: Princeton University Press, 1991).

McDow, Thomas, 'Deeds of Freed Slaves: Manumission and Economic and Social Mobility in Pre-Abolition Zanzibar', in *Indian Ocean Slavery in the Age of Abolition*, ed. Robert Harms, Bernard Freamon, and David Bight (New Haven: Yale University Press, 2013).

McGowan, Abigail, *Crafting the Nation in Colonial India* (Basingstoke: Palgrave Macmillan, 2009).

McLeod, W. H., *Guru Nanak and the Sikh Religion* (Delhi: Oxford University Press, 1996).

McNeill, J. R., 'The Eccentricity of the Middle East and North Africa's Environmental History', in *Water on Sand. Environmental Histories of the Middle East and North Africa*, ed. Alain Mikhail (Oxford: Oxford University Press, 2013).

McNeill, John, *Progress and Present Position of Russia in the East* (London: J. Murray, 1836).

Meadows, Monica, 'The Horse: Conspicuous Consumption of Embodied Masculinity in South Asia, 1600–1850' (unpublished doctoral dissertation, University of Washington, 2013).

Meakin, Annette M. B., *In Russian Turkestan. A Garden of Asia and its People* (London: George Allen, 1903).

Meisami, Julie Scott, '"I Guess That's Why They Call it the Blues": Depictions of Majnun in Persian Illustrated Manuscripts', in *And Diverse Are Their Hues*, ed. Jonathan Bloom and Sheila Blair (New Haven: Yale University Press, 2011).

Melikian-Chirvani, A. S., 'Ranjit Singh and the Image of the Past', in *The Arts of the Sikh Kingdoms*, ed. Susan Stronge (London: V&A Publications, 1999).

Meller, Susan, ed., *Russian Textiles. Printed Cloth for the Bazaars of Central Asia* (New York: Abrams, 2007).

Metcalf, Thomas R., *Ideologies of the Raj* (New Delhi: Cambridge University Press, 2010).

———, *Imperial Connections. India in the Indian Ocean Arena, 1860–1920* (Berkeley, London: University of California Press, 2007).

Mianwali District, Statistical Tables: 1904 (Lahore: Civil and Military Gazette Press, 1905).

Mignolo, Walter D., 'The Many Faces of Cosmo-Polis: Border Thinking and Critical Cosmopolitanism', *Public Culture*, vol. 12, no. 3 (2000), 721–48.

Mikhail, Alain, *Nature and Empire in Ottoman Egypt: An Environmental History* (Cambridge: Cambridge University Press, 2011).

Millward, James A., *Beyond the Pass. Economy, Ethnicity, and Empire in Qing Central Asia, 1759–1864* (Stanford: Stanford University Press, 1998).

———, *Eurasian Crossroads. A History of Xinjiang* (London: Hurst and Company, 2007).

———, *The Silk Road. A Very Short Introduction* (Oxford: Oxford University Press, 2013).

Minawi, Mostafa, *The Ottoman Scramble for Africa. Empire and Diplomacy in the Sahara and the Hijaz* (Stanford: Stanford University Press, 2016).

Mir, Farina, *The Social Space of Language. Vernacular Culture in British Colonial Punjab* (Berkeley: University of California Press, 2010).

Miran, Jonathan, 'The Red Sea', in *Oceanic Histories*, ed. David Armitage, Alison Bashford, and Sujit Sivasundaram (Cambridge: Cambridge University Press, 2017).

Moin, A. Azfar, *The Millennial Sovereign. Sacred Kingship and Sainthood in Islam* (Cambridge: Cambridge University Press, 2012).

Monahan, Erika, 'A Siberian Trader. Urasko Kaibulin', in *Portraits of Old Russia. Imagined Lives of Ordinary People, 1300–1725*, ed. Donald Ostrowsku and Marshall T. Poe (London: M. E. Sharpe, 2011).

———, *The Merchants of Siberia. Trade in Early Modern Eurasia* (Ithaca: Cornell University Press, 2016).

Montgomerie, T. G., 'Report of the Mirza's Exploration of the Route from Caubul to Kashgar', *Proceedings of the Royal Geographical Society of London*, vol. 15 (1870–1), 181–204.

Moorcroft, William, *Travels in the Himalayan Provinces of Hindustan and the Panjab; in Ladakh and Kashmir; in Peshawar, Kabul, Kunduz, and Bokhara; by Mr. William Moorcroft and Mr. George Trebeck, from 1819 to 1825*, ed. Horace Hayman Wilson, 2 vols (London: John Murray, 1841).

Moosvi, Shireen, 'Economic Profile of the Punjab (Sixteenth–Seventeenth Centuries)', in *Precolonial and Colonial Punjab*, ed. R. Grewal and S. Pall (New Delhi: Manohar, 2005).

———, *People, Taxation, and Trade in Mughal India* (New Delhi: Oxford University Press, 2012).

———, *The Economy of the Mughal Empire, c.1595. A Statistical Study* (New Delhi: Oxford University Press, 1987).

Morris, 'Appendix A. Memo. on the Cultivation and Manufacture of Indigo in the Mooltan District Written at the Time of the 1st Regular Settlement by Mr. Morris, Settlement Officer', in *Gazetteer of the Mooltan District: 1883–4* (Lahore: Arya Press, 1884).

———, 'Appendix B. The Inundation Canals of the Mooltan District (by

Mr. Morris, A.D. 1860)', in *Gazetteer of the Mooltan District: 1883–4* (Lahore: Arya Press, 1884).

Morris, J. H., *Report on the Revised Settlement of the Mooltan District, in the Mooltan Division* (Lahore: Punjabee Press, 1860).

Morrison, A. S., *Russian Rule in Samarkand 1868–1910. A Comparison with British India* (Oxford: Oxford University Press, 2008).

Morrison, Alexander, '"Applied Orientalism" in British India and Tsarist Turkestan', *CSSH*, vol. 51, no. 3 (2009), 619–47.

———, 'Camels and Colonial Armies: The Logistics of Warfare in Central Asia in the Early 19th Century', *JESOH*, vol. 57, no. 4 (2014), 443–85.

———, 'Introduction: Killing the Cotton Canard and Getting Rid of the Great Game: Rewriting the Russian Conquest of Central Asia, 1814–1895', *CAS*, vol. 33, no. 2 (2014), 131–42.

———, 'Metropole, Colony, and Imperial Citizenship in the Russian Empire', *Kritika: Explorations in Russian and Eurasian History*, vol. 13, no. 2 (2012), 327–64.

———, '"*Nechto Eroticheskoe*", "*courir après l'ombre*"?—Logistical Imperatives and the Fall of Tashkent, 1859–1865', *CAS*, vol. 33, no. 2 (2014), 153–69.

———, 'Peasant Settlers and the "Civilising Mission" in Russian Turkestan, 1865–1917', *The Journal of Imperial and Commonwealth History*, vol. 43, no. 3 (2015), 387–417.

———, 'Russian, Khoqand, and the Search for a "Natural" Frontier, 1863–1865', *Ab Imperio*, vol. 2014, no. 2 (2014), 166–92.

———, 'Sufism, Pan-Islamism and Information Panic: Nil Sergeevich Lykosin and the Aftermath of the Andijan Uprising', *Past and Present*, no. 214 (2012), 255–304.

———, 'Twin Imperial Disasters. The Invasions of Khiva and Afghanistan in the Russian and British Official Mind, 1839–1842', *MAS*, vol. 48, no. 1 (2014), 253–300.

Moss, David, 'Bandits and Boundaries in Sardinia', *Man*, new series, vol. 14, no. 3 (1979), 477–96.

Mousavi, Sayed Askar, *The Hazaras of Afghanistan. An Historical, Cultural, Economic and Political Study* (Richmond: Curzon Press, 1998).

Mukherjee, Rila, *Merchants and Companies in Bengal: Kasimbazar and Judgia in the Eighteenth Century* (New Delhi: Pragati Publications, 2006).

Multan District, Statistical Tables: 1904 (Lahore: Civil and Military Gazette Press, 1908).

Munshee, Munphool Meer, 'On Gilgit and Chitral', *Proceedings of the Royal Geographical Society of London*, vol. 13, no. 2 (1868–9), 130–3.

Murphy, Anne, *The Materiality of the Past. History and Representation in Sikh Tradition* (Oxford: Oxford University Press, 2012).

Murphy, Veronica, *Origins of the Mughal Flowering Plant Motif* (London: Indar Pasricha Fine Arts, 1996).

Muzaffargarh District, Statistical Tables: 1904 (Lahore: Civil and Military Gazette Press, 1908).

Muzaffargarh District, with Maps: 1904 (Lahore: Civil and Military Gazette Press, 1908).

N. W. Frontier Province District Gazetteers, vol. IIIB. Kohat District, Statistical Tables, 1904 (Lahore: Civil and Military Gazette Press, 1909).

Nadri, Ghulam A., *Eighteenth-Century Gujarat. The Dynamics of Its Political Economy, 1750–1800* (Leiden: Brill, 2009).

———, *The Political Economy of Indigo in India, 1580–1930* (Leiden: Brill, 2016).

Nalivkin, Vladimir, and Maria Nalivkina, *Muslim Women of the Fergana Valley*, ed. Marianne Kemp, trans. Mariana Markova (Bloomington: Indiana University Press, 2016).

Naqvi, Hameeda Khatoon, *Mughal Hindustan: Cities and Industries 1556–1803* (Karachi: National Book Foundation, 1974).

Nejatie, Sajjad, 'Iranian Migrations in the Durrani Empire', *CSSAAME*, vol. 37, no. 3 (2017), 494–504.

Neumann, B., A. T. Vafeidis, J. Zimmermann, and R. J. Nicholls, 'Future Coastal Population Growth and Exposure to Sea-Level Rise and Coastal Flooding—A Global Assessment', *PLoS ONE*, vol. 10, no. 3 (2015), 1–34.

Newby, L. J., 'Bondage on Qing China's Northwestern Frontier', *MAS*, vol. 47, no. 3 (2013), 968–94.

———, *The Empire and the Khanate. A Political History of Qing Relations with Khoqand c.1760–1860* (London: Brill, 2005).

Newman, Andrew J., *Safavid Iran. Rebirth of a Persian Empire* (London: I. B. Tauris, 2006).

Nichols, Robert, 'Afghan Historiography: Classic Study, Conventional Narrative, National Polemic', *History Compass*, vol. 3, no. 1 (2005), 1–16.

———, *A History of Pashtun Migration, 1775–2006* (Karachi: Oxford University Press, 2008).

———, *Settling the Frontier. Land, Law, and Society in the Peshawar Valley, 1500–1900* (Karachi: Oxford University Press, 2001).

Nightingale, Pamela, *Trade and Empire in Western India 1784–1806* (Cambridge: Cambridge University Press, 1970).

Noelle-Karimi, Christine, 'Afghan Polities and the Indo-Persian Literary Realm. The Durrani Rulers and their Portrayal in Eighteenth-Century Historiography', in *Afghan History Through Afghan Eyes*, ed. Nile Green (London: C. Hurst & Co., 2015).

———, 'Maps and Spaces', *International Journal of Middle East Studies*, vol. 45, no. 1 (2013), 142–5.

———, 'The Abdali Afghans between Multan, Qandahar and Herat in the

Sixteenth and Seventeenth Centuries', in *Beyond Swat. History, Society and Economy along the Afghanistan–Pakistan Frontier*, ed. Benjamin D. Hopkins and Magnus Marsden (London: C. Hurst & Co., 2013).

Noelle, Christine, *State and Tribe in Nineteenth-Century Afghanistan. The Reign of Amir Dost Muhammad Khan (1826–1863)* (Richmond: Curzon Press, 1997).

North-West Frontier Province District Gazetteers: Peshawar District, Part B (Lahore: Civil and Military Gazette Press, 1908).

North, Douglas, *Understanding the Process of Economic Change* (Princeton: Princeton University Press, 2005).

O'Connor, Aeron, 'Intertextuality and Other Syntheses of Knowledge in and around Tajikistan: Narratives of a Longue Durée of Knowledge Production' (unpublished doctoral dissertation, University College London, 2018).

O'Hanlon, Rosalind, 'Cultural Pluralism, Empire and the State in Early Modern South Asia—A Review Essay', *IESHR*, vol. 44, no. 3 (2007), 363–81.

———, 'Kingdom, Household and Body History. Gender and Imperial Service under Akbar', *MAS*, vol. 41, no. 5 (2007), 889–923.

———, 'Manliness and Imperial Service in Mughal North India', *JESOH*, vol. 42, no. 1 (1999), 47–93.

O'Rourke, Kevin, and Jeffrey Williamson, 'When did Globalisation Begin?', *European Review of Economic History*, vol. 6, no. 1 (2002), 23–50.

O'Sullivan, Michael B., '"The Little Brother of the Ottoman State": Ottoman Technocrats in Kabul and Afghanistan's Development in the Ottoman Imagination, 1908–23', *MAS*, vol. 50, no. 6 (2016), 1846–87.

Oberoi, Harjot, *The Construction of Religious Boundaries. Culture, Identity and Diversity in the Sikh Tradition* (Delhi: Oxford University Press, 1994).

Omrani, Bijan, 'Making Money in Afghanistan—The First Western Entrepreneurs 1880–1919', *Asian Affairs*, vol. 43 (2012), 374–92.

Pahlen, K. K., *Mission to Turkestan. Being the Memoirs of Count K. K. Pahlen 1908–1909*, ed. Richard A. Pierce, trans. N. J. Couriss (London: Oxford University Press, 1964).

Palat, Ravi Arvind, 'Maritime Trade, Political Relations and Residential Diplomacy in the World of the Indian Ocean', in Abdul Sheriff and Engseng Ho, eds, *The Indian Ocean. Oceanic Connections and the Creation of New Societies* (London: C. Hurst and Co, 2014).

Pallas, Peter Simon, *Travels through the Southern Provinces of the Russian Empire, in the Years 1793 and 1794. Translated from the German of P. S. Pallas, Counsellor of State to his Imperial Majesty of all the Russias, Knight, &c.*, 2 vols (London: A. Strahan, 1802).

Parker, Charles H., 'The Reformation in Global Perspective', *History Compass*, vol. 12, no. 12 (2014), 924–34.

Parker, Geoffrey, *Global Crisis: War, Climate Change and Catastrophe in the Seventeenth Century* (New Haven: Yale University Press, 2014).

Parthasarathi, Prasannan, 'Historical Issues of Deindustrialisation in Nineteenth-Century South India', in *How India Clothed the World. The World of South Asian Textiles, 1500–1850*, ed. Giorgio Riello and Tirthankar Roy (Leiden: Brill, 2009).

———, *Why Europe Grew Rich and Asia Did Not. Global Economic Divergence, 1600–1850* (Cambridge: Cambridge University Press, 2011).

Parthasarathi, Prasannan, and Giorgio Riello, 'The Indian Ocean in the Long Eighteenth Century', *Eighteenth-Century Studies*, vol. 48, no. 1 (2014), 1–19.

Peck, Linda Levy, *Consuming Splendor: Society and Culture in Seventeenth-Century England* (Cambridge: Cambridge University Press, 2005).

Pelsaert, Francisco, *Jahangir's India, the Remonstrantie of Francisco Pelsaert*, trans. W. H. Moreland and P. Geyl (Cambridge: W. Heffer and Sons, 1925).

Pinney, Christopher, 'Classification and Fantasy in the Photographic Construction of Caste and Tribe', *Visual Anthropology*, vol. 3 (1990), 259–88.

Pinto, Carla Alferes, 'The Diplomatic Agency of Art between Goa and Persia', in *Global Gifts. The Material Culture of Diplomacy in Early Modern Eurasia*, ed. Zoltán Biedermann, Anne Gerritsen, and Giorgio Riello (Cambridge: Cambridge University Press, 2017).

Porter, Yves, *Painters, Painting and Books: An Essay on Indo-Persian Technical Literature, 12–19th Centuries*, trans. S. Butani (New Delhi: Manohar, 1994).

Postans, T., 'Memorandum Relative to the Trade in Indigo', in *Selections from the Records of the Bombay Government. No. XVII. New Series*, ed. R. Hughes Thomas (Bombay: Bombay Education Society's Press, 1855).

Pottinger, Henry, *Travels in Beloochistan and Sinde; Accompanied by a Geographical and Historical Account of those Countries, With a Map* (London: Longman, Hurst, Rees, Orme, and Brown, 1816).

Poujol, Catherine, 'Approaches to the History of Bukharan Jews' Settlement in the Fergana Valley, 1867–1917', *CAS*, vol. 12, no. 4 (1993), 549–56.

Prakash, Om, *European Commercial Enterprise in Pre-Colonial India* (Cambridge: Cambridge University Press, 1998).

———, *The Dutch East India Company and the Economy of Bengal, 1630–1720* (Princeton: Princeton University Press, 1985).

———, 'The Indian Maritime Merchant, 1500–1800', *JESOH*, vol. 47, no. 3 (2004), 435–57.

Prange, Sebastian R., '"Trust in God, but Tie Your Camel First." The Economic Organisation of the Trans-Saharan Slave Trade Between the Fourteenth and Nineteenth Centuries', *JGH*, vol. 1, no. 2 (2006), 219–39.

Press Lists of Old Records in the Punjab Secretariat. Volume I. Delhi Residency and Agency, 1806–1857 (Lahore: Government Printing, 1915).

BIBLIOGRAPHY

Press Lists of Old Records in the Punjab Secretariat. Volume II. Delhi Residency and Karnal Agencies, 1804–1816 (Lahore: Government Printing, 1915).

Press Lists of Old Records in the Punjab Secretariat. Volume III. Ludhiana, Karnal and Ambala Agency, 1809–1840 (Lahore: Government Printing, 1915).

Press Lists of Old Records in the Punjab Secretariat. Volume IV. Ludhiana, Karnal and Ambala Agencies, Issues from 1810–1840 (Lahore: Government Printing, 1915).

Press Lists of Old Records in the Punjab Secretariat. Volume VI. Ludhiana Agency. Correspondence with Government, 1831–1840 (Lahore: Government Printing, 1915).

Press Lists of Old Records in the Punjab Secretariat. Volume VII. North-West Frontier Agency, Correspondence with Government, 1840–1845 (Lahore: Government Printing, 1915).

Press Lists of Old Records in the Punjab Secretariat. Volume XVII. From 1859 to 1868. Judicial Department (Lahore: Government Printing, 1925).

Purchas, Samuel, *Hakluytus Posthumus or Purchas His Pilgrimes. Contayning a History of the World in Sea Voyages and Lande Travells by Englishmen and Others*, vol. IV (Glasgow: James MacLehose and Sons, 1905).

Rahman, M. Raisur, *Locale, Everyday Islam, and Modernity. Qasbah Towns and Muslim Life in Colonial India* (New Delhi: Oxford University Press, 2015).

Radkau, Joachim, *Nature and Power. A Global History of the Environment*, trans. Thomas Dunlap (Cambridge: Cambridge University Press, 2008).

Raj, Kapil, *Relocating Modern Science. Circulation and the Construction of Knowledge in South Asia and Europe, 1650–1900* (Basingstoke: Palgrave Macmillan, 2007).

Ramaswamy, Sumathi, *The Goddess and the Nation. Mapping Mother India* (Durham, N.C.: Duke University Press 2010).

Rand, Gavin, and Kim Wagner, 'Recruiting the "Martial Races": Identities and Military Service in Colonial India', *Patterns of Prejudice*, vol. 46, nos 3–4 (2012), 232–54.

Rattray, James, *The Costumes of the Various Tribes, Portraits of Ladies of Rank, Celebrated Princes and Chiefs, Views of the Principal Fortresses and Cities, and Interior of the Cities and Temples of Afghaunistan, from Original Drawings* (London: Herring & Remington, 1848).

Rawalpindi District, Statistical Tables: 1907 (Lahore: Civil and Military Gazette Press, 1909).

Rawalpindi District, with Maps: 1907 (Lahore: Civil and Military Gazette Press, 1909).

Rawlinson, H. C., 'On Trade Routes between Turkestan and India', *Proceedings of the Royal Geographical Society of London*, vol. 13, no. 1 (1868–9), 10–25.

Rawlley, Ratan C., *The Silk Industry and Trade. A Study in the Economic Organisation of the Export Trade of Kashmir and Indian Silks, with Special Reference to their Utilization in the British and French Markets* (London: P. S. King & Son, 1919).

Ray, Indrajit, 'The Indigo Dye Industry in Colonial Bengal: A Re-Examination', *IESHR*, vol. 41 (2004), 218–24.

———, 'The Silk Industry in Bengal during Colonial Rule: The "De–Industrialisation" Thesis Revisited', *IESHR*, vol. 42 (2005) pp. 339–75.

Ray, Rajat K., 'Asian Capital in the Age of European Expansion: The Rise of the Bazaar, 1800–1914', *MAS*, vol. 29, no. 3 (1995), 449–554.

Reid, Anthony, and Radin Fernando, 'Shipping on Melaka and Singapore as an Index of Growth, 1760–1840', *South Asia: Journal of South Asian Studies*, vol. 19, Special Issue (1996), 59–84.

Reindl-Kiel, Hedda, 'No Horses for the Enemy: Ottoman Trade Regulations and Horse Gifting', in *Pferde in Asien: Geschichte, Handel und Kultur. Horses in Asia: History, Trade and Culture*, ed. Bert G. Fragner, Ralph Kauz, Roderich Ptak, and Angela Schottenhammer (Wien: Österreichische Akademie der Wissenschaften, 2009).

Rezakhani, Khodadad, 'The Road That Never Was: The Silk Road and Trans-Eurasian Exchange' *CSSAAME*, vol. 30, no. 3 (2010), 420–33.

Richards, J. F., 'The Imperial Crisis in the Deccan', *JAS*, vol. 35, no. 2 (1976), 237–56.

———, 'Mughal State Finance and the Premodern World Economy', *CSSH*, vol. 23, no. 2 (1981), 285–308.

———, 'The Formulation of Imperial Authority under Akbar and Jahangir', in *Kingship and Authority in South Asia*, ed. John F. Richards (Madison, 1981).

———, *The Mughal Empire* (Cambridge: Cambridge University Press, 1993).

Richards, J. F., and V. N. Rao, 'Banditry in Mughal India: Historical and Folk Perceptions', *IESHR*, vol. 17, no. 1 (1990), 95–120.

Riello, Giorgio, *Cotton. The Fabric that Made the Modern World* (Cambridge: Cambridge University Press, 2013).

Riello, Giorgio, and Prasannan Parthasarathi, *The Spinning World. A Global History of Cotton Textiles, 1200–1850* (Oxford: Oxford University Press, Pasold Studies in Textile History, 2009).

Riello, Giorgio, and Tirthankar Roy, eds, *How India Clothed the World. The World of South Asian Textiles, 1500–1850* (Leiden: Brill, 2009).

Rizvi, Janet, *Ladakh. Crossroads of High Asia* (New Delhi: Oxford University Press, 1996).

———, *Trans-Himalayan Caravans. Merchant Princes and Peasant Traders in Ladakh* (New Delhi: Oxford University Press, 1999).

Rizvi, Kishwar, *Affect, Emotion, and Subjectivity in Early Modern Muslim Empires: New Studies in Ottoman, Safavid, and Mughal Art and Culture* (Leiden: Brill, 2017).

Robinson, David, *Bandits, Eunuchs, and the Son of Heaven. Rebellion and the*

Economy of Violence in Mid-Ming China (Honolulu: University of Hawai'i Press, 2001).

Robinson, Francis, 'Ottomans–Safavids–Mughals: Shared Knowledge and Connective Systems', *Journal of Islamic Studies*, vol. 8, no. 2 (1997), 151–84.

Roche, Daniel, *Humeurs Vagabondes. De la Circulation des Hommes et de l'Utilité des Voyages* (Paris: Fayard, 2003).

Rogan, Eugene, *Incorporating the Periphery. The Ottoman Extension of Direct Rule over Southeastern Syria (Transjordan), 1867–1914* (Cambridge: Cambridge University Press, 1999).

Romaniello, Matthew P., 'True Rhubarb? Trading Eurasian Botanical and Medical Knowledge in the Eighteenth Century', *JGH*, vol. 11, no. 1 (2016), 3–23.

Rose, H. A., ed., *A Glossary of the Tribes and Castes of the Punjab and North-West Frontier Province. Vol. I* (Lahore: Superintendent Government Printing, 1919).

———, ed., *A Glossary of the Tribes and Castes of the Punjab and North-West Frontier Province. Vol. II. A.–K.* (Lahore: Civil and Military Gazette Press, 1911).

———, ed., *A Glossary of the Tribes and Castes of the Punjab and North-West Frontier Province. Vol. III. L.–Z. With Appendices A.–L.* (Lahore: Civil and Military Gazette Press, 1914).

Roseberry, J. R., *Imperial Rule in Punjab: The Conquest and Administration of Multan, 1818–1881* (New Delhi: Manohar, 1987).

Rota, Giorgio, 'The Horses of the Shah: Some Remarks on the Organisation of the Safavid Royal Stables, Mainly Based on Three Persian Handbooks of Administrative Practice', in *Pferde in Asien: Geschichte, Handel und Kultur. Horses in Asia: History, Trade and Culture*, ed. Bert G. Fragner, Ralph Kauz, Roderich Ptak, and Angela Schottenhammer (Wien: Österreichische Akademie der Wissenschaften, 2009).

Roy, Tirthankar, *A Business History of India. Enterprise and the Emergence of Capitlaism from 1700* (Cambridge: Cambridge University Press, 2018).

———, *India in the World Economy. From Antiquity to the Present* (Cambridge: Cambridge University Press, 2012).

———, ed., *Cloth and Commerce. Textiles in Colonial India* (New Delhi: Sage, 1996).

Rublack, Ulinka, 'Material Invention from the Reanissance to the Enlightenment', in *Treasured Possessions from the Renaissance to the Enlightenment*, ed. Victoria Avery, Melissa Calaresu, and Mary Laven (London: Philip Wilson Publishing, 2015).

Ruff, Julius R., *Violence in Early Modern Europe* (Cambridge: Cambridge University Press, 2001).

Ryan, James R., *Picturing Empire. Photography and the Visualisation of the British Empire* (London: Reaktion Books, 1997).

Sachdeva, Veena, *Polity and Economy of the Punjab during the Late Eighteenth Century* (New Delhi: Manohar, 1993).

Sajdi, Dana, ed., *Ottoman Tulips, Ottoman Coffee. Leisure and Lifestyle in the Eighteenth Century* (London: I. B. Tauris, 2007).

Sani, Muhammad, *Advice on the Art of Governance. Mau'izah-i Jahangiri of Muhammad Baqir Najm-i Sani*, ed. Sajida Sultana Alvi (Albany: State University of New York Press, 1989).

Sarkar, Jadunath, *The India of Aurangzib (Topography, Statistics, and Roads), Compared with the India of Akbar, with Extracts from the* Khulasatu-t-tawarikh *and the* Chahar Gulshan (Calcutta: Bose Brothers, 1901).

Sauer, George, *The Gateways to India, or, Russian Commerce in Central Asia* (London: Edward Stanford, 1877).

Sauli, Arnaud, 'Circulation and Authority. Police, Public Space and Territorial Control in Punjab, 1861–1920', in *Society and Circulation. Mobile People and Itinerant Cultures in South Asia, 1750–1950*, ed. Claude Markovits, Jacques Pouchepadass, and Sanjay Subrahmanyam (London: Anthem Press, 2006).

Savory, R. M., 'The Safavid Administrative System', in *The Cambridge History of Iran. Volume 6. The Timurid and Safavid Periods*, ed. Peter Jackson and Laurence Lockhart (Cambridge: Cambridge University Press, 1986).

Schimmelpenninck van der Oye, David, *Russian Orientalism. Asia in the Russian Mind from Peter the Great to the Emigration* (New Haven: Yale University Press, 2010).

Schofield, Katherine Butler, 'Did Aurangzeb Ban Music? Questions for the Historiography of His Reign', *MAS*, vol. 41, no. 1 (2007), 77–121.

Schuyler, Eugene, *Turkistan. Notes of a Journey in Russian Turkistan, Khokand, Bukhara and Kuldja* (London: Sampson, Low, Marston, Searle, and Rivington, 1876).

Sen, Sudipta, *Empire of Free Trade. The East India Company and the Making of the Colonial Marketplace* (Philadelphia: University of Pennsylvania Press, 1998).

Sergeev, Evgeny, *The Great Game 1856–1907: Russo-British Relations in Central and East Asia* (Washington DC: Johns Hopkins University Press, 2013).

Sethia, Madhu Tandon, *Rajput Polity. Warriors, Peasants and Merchants* (Jaipur: Rawat Publications, 2003).

Shahpur District, Statistical Tables: 1904 (Lahore: Civil and Military Gazette Press, 1907).

Sharma, G. D., 'Ports of Gujarat in the Nineteenth Century: Trading Networks and Commercial Practices', in *Ports and Their Hinterlands in India (1700–1950)*, ed. Indu Banga (New Delhi: Manohar, 1992).

Sharma, Harish C., *Artisans of the Punjab. A Study of Social Change in Historical Perspective (1849–1947)* (New Delhi: Manohar, 1996).

BIBLIOGRAPHY

Shastitko, Peter M., 'Preface', in *Russo-Indian Relations in the Nineteenth Century. A Selection of Documents. English Translation*, ed. Purabi Roy (Calcutta: Asiatic Society, 1999).

Shaw, Robert, *Visits to High Tartary, Yarkand, and Kashgar (Formerly Chinese Tartary), and Return Journey Over the Karakoram Pass* (London: John Murray, 1871).

Shortt, J., *An Essay on the Culture and Manufacture of Indigo*, *to which was Awarded the Prize of Eight Hundred Rupees by the Madras Government, 1860* (Madras: H. Smith, 1860).

Shukla, P. K., *Indigo and the Raj. Peasant Protests in Bihar, 1780–1917* (New Delhi: Pragati Publications, 1993).

Sialkot District, Statistical Tables: 1904 (Lahore: Civil and Military Gazette Press, 1908).

Simakoff, N., *Les Arts Decoratifs de L'Asie Centrale Receuil de 50 Planches en Chromolithographie avec Texte Explicatif par N. Simakoff* (St Petersbourg: A. Devrient pour La Societe Imperiale D'Encouragement Aux Beaux–Arts, 1879).

Simmonds, P. L., 'On Silk Cultivation and Supply in India', *Journal of the Society of Arts*, vol. 17 (1869),.

Singh, Ashok B. Rajshirke, 'The Merchant Communities in Surat: Trade, Trade Practices and Institutions in the Late Eighteenth Century', in *Ports and Their Hinterlands in India (1700–1950)*, ed. Indu Banga (New Delhi: Manohar, 1992).

Singh, Balwant, *The Army of Maharaja Ranjit Singh* (Lahore: Lahore Book Shop, 1932).

Singh, Chetan, *Region and Empire. Panjab in the Seventeenth Century* (New Delhi: Oxford University Press, 1991).

Singh, Dilbagh, *The State, Landlords and Peasants. Rajasthan in the 18th Century* (New Delhi: Manohar, 1990).

Singh, Fauja, *Military System of the Sikhs During the Period 1799–1849* (New Delhi: Motilal Banarsidass, 1964).

Singh, Gajendra, *The Testimonies of Indian Soldiers and the Two World Wars. Between Self and Sepoy* (London: Bloomsbury, 2015).

Singh, Ganda, *Ahmad Shah Durrani. Father of Modern Afghanistan* (London: Asia Publishing House, 1959).

———, ed., *Early European Accounts of the Sikhs* (Calcutta: Indian Studies Past and Present, 1962), 82.

Singha, Radhika, 'Punished by Surveillance: Policing "Dangerousness" in Colonial India, 1872–1918', *MAS*, vol. 49, no. 2 (2015), 249–69.

Sivasundaram, Sujit, '"A Christian Benares": Orientalism, Science and the Serampore Mission of Bengal', *IESHR*, vol. 44, (2007), 111–45.

———, 'Cosmopolitanism and Indigeneity in Four Violent Years: The Fall of the Kingdom of Kandy and the Great Rebellion Revisited', in *Sri Lanka at the Crossroads of History*, ed. Zoltan Biedermann and Alan Strathern (London: UCL Press, 2017).

———, *Islanded. Britain, Sri Lanka, and the Bounds of an Indian Ocean Colony* (Chicago: The University of Chicago Press, 2013).

———, 'The Indian Ocean', in *Oceanic Histories*, ed. David Armitage, Alison Bashford, and Sujit Sivasundaram (Cambridge: Cambridge University Press, 2017).

———, 'Towards a Critical History of Connection: The Port of Colombo, the Geographical "Circuit," and the Visual Politics of New Imperialism, *ca.* 1880–1914', *CSSH*, vol. 59, no. 2 (2017), 346–84.

———, 'Trading Knowledge: The East India Company's Elephants in India and Britain', *The Historical Journal*, vol. 48, no. 1 (2005), 27–63.

Sladen, E. B., *Official Narrative of the Expedition to Explore the Trade Routes to China via Bhamo* (Calcutta: Government Printing, 1870).

Slaughter, Mihill, *Railway Intelligence, January 1861. Under the Sanction of the Committee of the Stock Exchange* (London, 1861).

Slight, John, *The British Empire and the Hajj, 1865–1956* (Cambridge, Mass.: Harvard University Press, 2015).

Smith, Alison K., 'A Microhistory of the Global Empire of Cotton: Ivanovo, the "Russian Manchester"', *Past & Present*, vol. 244, no. 1 (2019), 163–93.

Sneath, David, *The Headless State. Aristocratic Orders, Kinship Society, and Misrepresentations of Nomadic Inner Asia* (New York: Columbia University Press, 2007).

Sonntag, Heather S., trans., 'Foreword to the Turkestan Album' <http://www.loc.gov/rr/print/coll/TurkAlbForeword.pdf> (Library of Congress, 2006–7) [accessed: 26 January 2013].

Sood, Gagan D. S., *India and the Islamic Heartlands. An Eighteenth-Century World of Circulation and Exchange* (Oxford: Oxford University Press, 2016).

Speake, Jennifer, ed., *Literature of Travel and Exploration. An Encyclopedia. Volume Two. G to P.* (New York: Fitzroy Dearborn, 2003).

Specker, Konrad, 'Madras Handlooms in the Nineteenth Century', in *Cloth and Commerce. Textiles in Colonial India*, ed. Tirthankar Roy (New Delhi: Sage, 1996).

Spiers, Edward M., 'Highland Soldier: Imperial Impact and Image', *Northern Scotland*, vol. 1 (new series), no. 1 (2010), 76–87.

Sprenger, Aloys, *A Catalogue of the Arabic, Persian and Hindustany Manuscripts, of the Libraries of the King of Oudh* (Calcutta: Baptist Mission Press, 1854).

Steensgaard, Niels, *The Asian Trade Revolution of the Seventeenth Century. The East India Companies and the Decline of the Caravan Trade* (Chicago: University of Chicago Press, 1974).

Steinbach, Henry, *The Punjaub; Being a Brief Account of the Country of the Sikhs;*

its Extent, History, Commerce, Productions, Government, Manufactures, Laws, Religion, Etc. (London: Smith, Elder and Co., 1846).

Stephens, Julia, 'The Phantom Wahabbi? Liberalism and the Muslim Fanatic in Mid–Victorian India', *MAS*, vol. 47, no. 1 (2013), 22–52.

Stern, Philip J., *The Company-State. Corporate Sovereignty and the Early Modern Foundations of the British Empire in India* (Oxford: Oxford University Press, 2011).

Stirling, Edward, *The Journals of Edward Stirling in Persia and Afghanistan 1828–1829 from Manuscripts in the Archives of the Royal Geographic Society*, ed. Jonathan L. Lee (Naples: Istituto Universitario Orientale, 1991).

Stokes, Eric, *The English Utilitarians and India* (Oxford: Clarendon Press, 1959).

———, *The Peasant Armed: The Indian Rebellion of 1857* (Oxford: Oxford University Press, 1986).

Stoler, Ann Laura, *Along the Archival Grain. Epistemic Anxieties and Colonial Common Sense* (Princeton: Princeton University Press, 2010).

Streets, Heather, *Martial Races: The Military, Race, and Masculinity in British Imperial Culture, 1857–1914* (Manchester: Manchester University Press, 2004).

Stronge, Susan, 'The Arts at the Court of Maharaja Ranjit Singh', in *The Arts of the Sikh Kingdoms*, ed. Susan Stronge (London: V&A Publications, 1999).

———, ed., *The Arts of the Sikh Kingdoms* (London: V&A Publications, 1999).

Struve, Lynn, ed., *The Qing Formation in World-Historical Time* (Cambridge: Harvard East Asian Monographs, 2004).

———, ed. and trans., *Voices from the Ming-Qing Cataclysm. China in Tigers' Jaws* (New Haven: Yale University Press, 1993).

Struve, Peter, 'English Tissue-Printing in Russia: An Episode in Russian Economic History', *The Slavonic and East European Review*, vol. 19 (1939–40), 303–10.

Studer, Roman, 'India and the Great Divergence: Assessing the Efficiency of Grain Markets in Eighteenth- and Nineteenth-Century India', *Journal of Economic History*, vol. 68, no. 2 (2008), 393–437.

Subrahmanyam, Sanjay, and C.A. Bayly, 'Portfolio Capitalists and the Political Economy of Early Modern India', *IESHR*, vol. 25, no. 4 (1988), 401–24.

Subrahmanyam, Sanjay, *Courtly Encounters. Translating Courtliness and Violence in Early Modern Eurasia* (Cambridge, Mass.: Harvard University Press, 2012).

———, ed., *Merchant Networks in the Early Modern World* (Aldershot: Ashgate, 1996).

Sumner, Christina, 'Flowers of the Hearth: Textiles', in *Bright Flowers. Textiles and Ceramics of Central Asia*, ed. Christina Sumner and Guy Petherbridge (Sydney: Powerhouse Publishing, 2004).

Tagliacozzo, Eric, 'The Lit Archipelago: Coast Lighting and the Imperial

Optic in Insular Southeast Asia, 1860–1910', *Technology and Culture*, vol. 46, no. 2 (2005), 306–28.

―――, 'Trade, Production, and Incorporation: The Indian Ocean in Flux, 1600–1900', *Itinerario: European Journal of Overseas History*, vol. 26, no. 1 (2002), 75–106.

―――, 'Violent Undertowns: Smuggling as Dissent in Nineteenth-Century Southeast Asia', in *Mercenaries, Pirates, Bandits and Empires. Private Violence in Historical Context*, ed. Alejandro Colás and Bryan Mabee (London: C. Hurst and Co., 2010).

Tagore, Rabindranath, *Selected Short Stories*, trans. William Radice (London: Penguin, 2005).

Talbot, Ian, *Punjab and the Raj 1849–1947* (New Delhi: Manohar, 1988).

Tapper, Richard, 'Introduction', in *The Conflict of Tribe and State in Iran and Afghanistan*, ed. Richard Tapper (London: Croom Helm, 1983).

Tavernier, Jean-Baptiste, *Tavernier's Travels in India*, ed. V. Ball, 2 vols (London: Macmillan and Company, 1889).

Tezcan, Baki, *The Second Ottoman Empire. Political and Social Transformation in the Early Modern World* (Cambridge: Cambridge University Press, 2010).

Thapar, Romila, *Somnatha. Many Voices of History* (New Delhi: Viking, 2004).

Thomas, George, *Military Memoirs of Mr. George Thomas*, ed. William Francklin (London: John Stockdale, 1805).

Thomas, R. Hughes, ed., *Selections from the Records of the Bombay Government. No. XVII.—New Series* (Bombay: Bombay Education Society's Press, 1855).

Thompstone, Stuart, 'Ludwig Knop, "The Arkwright of Russia"', *Textile History*, vol. 15 (1984), 45–73.

Thomson, Janice E., *Mercenaries, Pirates, and Sovereigns. State-Building and Extraterritorial Violence in Early Modern Europe* (Princeton: Princeton University Press, 1994).

Trevaskis, Hugh Kennedy, *The Punjab of To-Day. An Economic Survey of the Punjab in Recent Years (1890–1925)*, 2 vols (Lahore: Civil and Military Gazette Press, 1932).

Trevor-Roper, Hugh, 'The Invention of Tradition: The Highland Tradition of Scotland', in Eric Hobsbawm and Terence Ranger, eds, *The Invention of Tradition* (Cambridge: Cambridge University Press, 1983).

Trivedi, K. K., 'The Share of Mansabdars in State Revenue Resources: A Study of the Maintenance of Animals', *IESHR*, vol. 24, no. 4 (1987), 411–21.

Truschke, Audrey, *Aurangzeb. The Life and Legacy of India's Most Controversial King* (Stanford, California: Stanford University Press, 2017).

―――, *Culture of Encounters. Sanskrit at the Mughal Court* (New York: Columbia University Press, 2016).

————, 'Setting the Record Wrong: A Sanskrit Vision of Mughal Conquests', *South Asian History and Culture*, vol. 3, no. 3 (2012), 373–96.

Tuna, Mustafa, *Imperial Russia's Muslims. Islam, Empire, and European Modernity, 1788–1914* (Cambridge: Cambridge University Press, 2015).

Uchastinka, Z. V., *A History of Russian Hand Paper-Mills and their Watermarks* (Hilvershum: The Water Publications Society, 1962).

Vambery, Arminius, *Travels in Central Asia* (London: John Murray, 1864).

Vartavarian, Mesrob, 'Pacification and Patronage in the Maratha Deccan, 1803–1818', *MAS*, vol. 50, no. 6 (2016), 1749–91.

Verma, Tripta, *Karkhanas Under the Mughals from Akbar to Aurangzeb. A Study in Economic Development* (New Delhi: Pragati Publications, 1994).

Vigne, Godfrey Thomas, *A Personal Narrative of a Visit to Ghuzni, Kabul, and Afghanistan, and of a Residence at the Court of Dost Mohamed* (London: Whittaker and Company, 1840).

Vink, Markus P. M., 'Indian Ocean Studies and the "New Thalassology"', *JGH*, vol. 2, no. 1 (2007), 41–62.

Wagner, Kim, 'The Marginal Mutiny: The New Historiography of the Indian Uprising of 1857', *History Compass*, vol. 9/10 (2011), 760–6.

————, *Thuggee. Banditry and the British in Early Nineteenth-Century India* (Basingstoke: Palgrave, 2007).

Wakeman Jr., Frederick, *The Great Enterprise. The Manchu Reconstruction of Imperial Order in Seventeenth-Century China* (Berkeley: University of California Press, 1985).

Waley, Muhammad Isa, 'Notes on an Illustrated Persian Manuscript on Horses, *Faras–Nama*, in the Royal Library Windsor Castle', in *Furusiyya: The Horse in the Art of the Near East*, ed. David Alexander (Riyadh: The King Abdulaziz Public Library, 1996).

Wallerstein, Immanuel, *The Modern World-system. Capitalist Agriculture and the Origins of the European World-economy in the Sixteenth Century* (London: Academic Press 1974).

Wardle, Thomas, *On the History and Growing Utilisations of Tussur Silks* (London: Trounce, 1891).

————, *Royal Commission and Government of India Silk Culture Court: Descriptive Catalogue* (London: William Clowes & Sons, 1886).

Washbrook, David, 'Economic Depression and the Making of "Traditional Society" in Colonial India 1820–1855', *Transactions of the Royal Historical Society*, sixth series, vol. 3 (1993), 237–63.

————, 'From Comparative Sociology to Global History: Britain and India in the Pre-History of Modernity', *JESOH*, vol. 40, no. 4 (1997), 410–43.

Watt, George, *Indian Art at Delhi, 1903. Being the Official Catalogue of the Delhi Exhibition, 1902–1903* (Calcutta: Superintendent of Government Printing, 1903).

————, *Pamphlet on Indigo* (Calcutta, 1890).

Webb, James L. A., 'The Horse and Slave Trade Between the Western Sahara and Senegambia', *The Journal of African History*, vol. 34, no. 2 (1993), 22146.

Webster, John C. B., 'Mission Sources of Nineteenth-Century Punjab History', in *Sources on Punjab History*, ed. W. Eric Gustafson and Kenneth W. Jones (New Delhi: Manohar, 1975).

Weinerman, Eli, 'The Polemics between Moscow and Central Asians on the Decline of Central Asia and Tsarist Russia's Role in the History of the Region', *The Slavonic and East European Review*, vol. 71, no. 3 (1993), 428–81.

Werbner, Pnina, *Pilgrims of Love. The Anthropology of a Global Sufi Cult* (London: Hurst, 2003).

Wide, Thomas, 'Astrakhan, Borqa', Chadari, Dreshi. The Economy of Dress in Early-Twentieth-Century Afghanistan', in *Anti-Veiling Campaigns in the Muslim World. Gender, Modernism and the Politics of Dress*, ed. Stephanie Cronin (London: Routledge, 2014).

Willis Jr., E., 'European Consumption and Asian Production in the Seventeenth and Eighteenth Centuries', in *Consumption and the World of Goods*, ed. J. Brewwer and R. Porter (Abingdon, Oxfordshire: Routledge, 1993).

Wilson, Jon, *India Conquered. Britain's Raj and the Chaos of Empire* (London: Simon and Schuster, 2016).

Wink, André, *Al-Hind. The Making of the Indo-Islamic World. Volume III. Indo-Islamic Society 14th–15th Centuries* (Leiden: Brill, 2004).

Wong, J. Y., 'British Annexation of Sind in 1843: An Economic Perspective', *MAS*, vol. 31 (1997), 225–44.

Wood, John, *A Journey to the Source of the River Oxus* (London: John Murray, 1872).

Yago, Kazuhiko, 'The Russo-Chinese Bank (1896–1910): An International Bank in Russia and Asia', in *The Origins of International Banking in Asia. The Nineteenth and Twentieth Centuries*, ed. Shizuya Nishimura, Toshio Suzuki, and Ranald Michie (Oxford: Oxford University Press, 2012).

Yanagisawa, Haruka, 'The Handloom Industry and its Market Structure: The Case of the Madras Presidency in the First Half of the Twentieth Century', in *Cloth and Commerce. Textiles in Colonial India*, ed. Tirthankar Roy (New Delhi: Sage, 1996).

Yang, Anand, 'A Conversation of Rumors: The Language of Popular "Mentalitès" in Late Nineteenth-Century Colonial India', *Journal of Social History*, vol. 20, no. 3 (1987), 485–505.

————, *Bazaar India. Markets, Society, and the Colonial State in Gangetic Bihar* (Berkeley: University of California Press, 1998).

————, 'China and India Are One: A Subaltern's Vision of "Hindu China" during the Boxer Expedition of 1900–1901', in *Asia Inside Out: Changing Times*, ed. Eric Tagliacozzo, Helen F. Siu, and Peter Perdue (London: Harvard University Press, 2015).

Yang, Daqing, *Technology of Empire. Telecommunications and Japanese Imperialism 1930–1945* (Cambridge, Mass.: Harvard University Press, 2010).

Yapp, Malcolm, *Strategies of British India. Britain, Iran, Afghanistan 1798–1850* (Oxford: Oxford University Press, 1980).

————, 'The Legend of the Great Game', *Proceedings of the British Academy*, vol. 111 (2001), 179–98.

Yarwood, A. T., *Walers: Australian Horses Abroad* (Victoria, Australia: Melbourne University Press, 1989).

Yaycioglu, Ali, *Partners of the Empire: The Crisis of the Ottoman Order in the Age of Revolutions* (Stanford: Stanford University Press, 2016).

————, *Power, Wealth and Death: The Moral Economy of State-Society in the Ottoman Empire* (forthcoming).

Yong, Tan-Tai, *The Garrison State: The Military, Government, and Society in Colonial Punjab, 1849–1947* (New Delhi: Sage, 2005).

Zaidi, Saima, ed., *Mazaar, Bazaar. Design and Visual Culture in Pakistan* (Karachi: Oxford University Press, 2009).

Zaman, Faridah, 'Revolutionary History and the Postcolonial Muslim: Re-Writing the "Silk Letter Conspiracy" of 1916', *South Asia: Journal of South Asian Studies*, vol. 39, no. 3 (2016), 626–43.

Ziad, Waleed, 'Transporting Knowledge in the Durrani Empire. Two Manuals of Naqshbandi–Mujaddidi Sufi Practice', in *Afghan History Through Afghan Eyes*, ed. Nile Green (London: C. Hurst & Co., 2015).

Ziegler, Norman P., 'Evolution of the Rathor State of Marvar: Horses, Structural Change and Warfare', in *The Idea of Rajasthan. Explorations in Regional Identity. Vol. II: 'Institutions'*, ed. K. Schomer, J. Erdman, D. Lodrick, and L. Rudolph (New Delhi: Manohar, 1994)

INDEX

Note: Page numbers followed by "*n*" refer to notes, "*f*" refer to figures.